THE ART & LIFE OF

MICHAEL BIRCH

II

III

IV

V

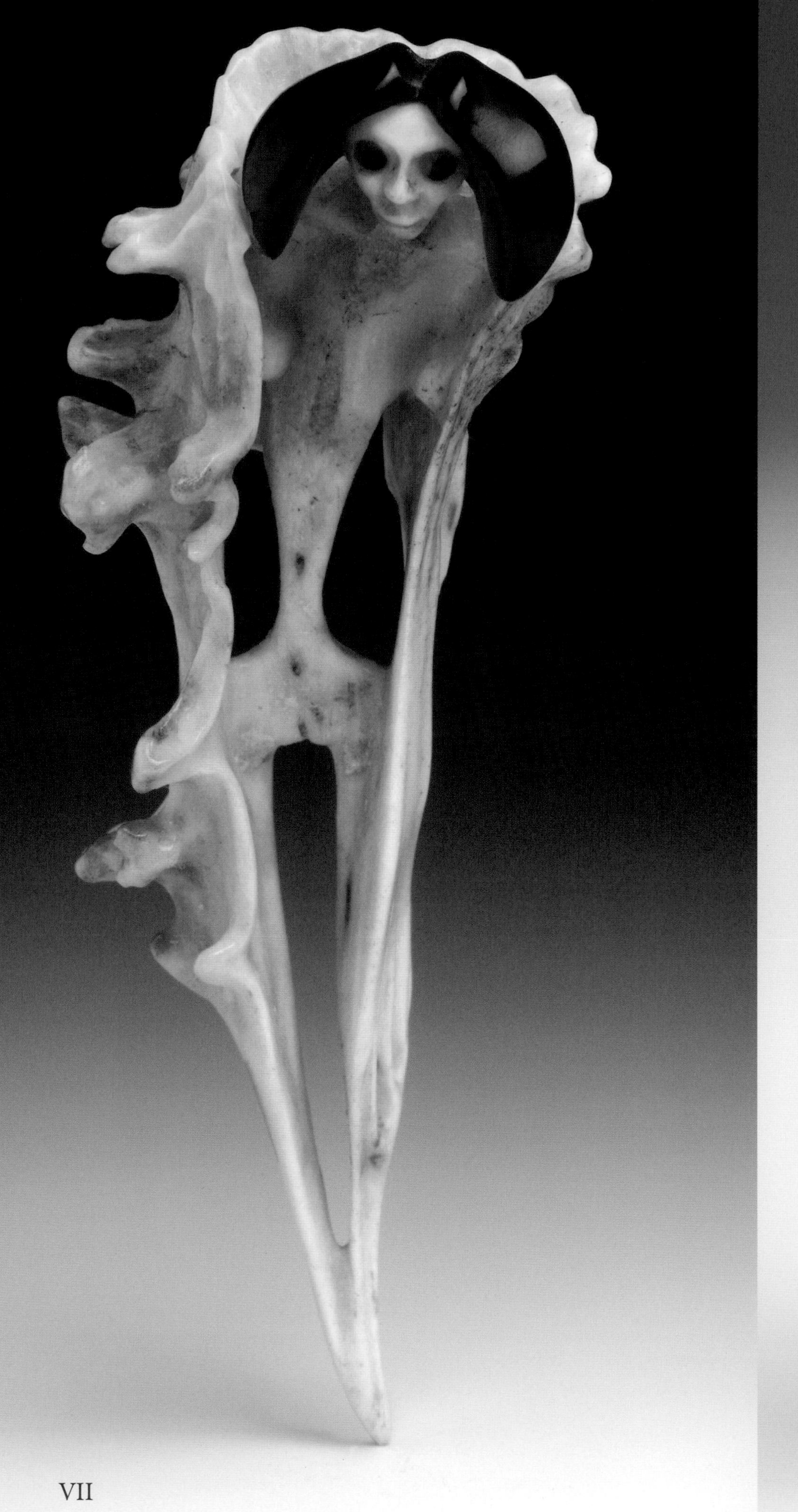

VII

VIII

IX

X

XII

XIII

XIV

XV

XVI

XVII

XVIII

XIX

XX

XXI

XXII

XXIII

XXIV

XXV

XXVI

XXVII

XXVIII

The Gallery

I The Samurai
Siberian mammoth ivory.
Height 3.7cm 1994.

II Lao Tsze
Body in mastodon ivory.
Head in rare Lebanese gold amber (Ching Peh).
Height 7cm 1999.

III Portrait of My Father
Hippopotamus incisor on wooden base.
Height 9.2cm 1994.

IV Small fish in shark tooth
Narwhal ivory and shark tooth.
Length 9.8cm c.1980

V The Magic Whirlpool with Yin/Yang symbol
Hippopotamus incisor.
Length 8.5cm. 2000.

VI Oscar Wilde as an epigram emerging from a double Möbius
Siberian mammoth ivory.
Height 6.5cm 1997.

VII Disappearing Ghost
Roebuck antler. Hair in buffalo horn.
Height 9.3 cm 1978.

VIII Coral diver
Nigerian ebony, pink coral and buffalo horn.
Height 9.7cm 1977.

IX Extraterrestrial Tengu
Hippopotamus incisor.
Height 7.7cm 1995.

X Mermaid
Ebony. Hair in ivory.
Height 9.5cm 1977.

XI The Two Faces of Daruma
Hippopotamus incisor.
Height: 6.7cm. 1997.

XII Dosojin
Elephant Ivory and rhinoceros horn.
Height 6cm 1976.

XIII Doctor Möbius in Symbiosis with his own Discovery
Siberian mammoth ivory
Height 7.7cm 1997.

XIV Young Centaur Paying Respectful Attention to Advice from his Elders
Siberian mammoth ivory, stained.
Height 7.4cm 1994.

XV Tengu Princeling
Alaskan umimatsu.
Height 9.4cm 2002.

XVI The Millennium Phoenix Hatchling
Lacquered Pink Ivory wood. Eyes in ebony.
Height 6cm 1996.

XVII A Dutchman with Attitude
Roebuck antler. Buttons in jade cabochons.
Hat in Molokai Taxis deer antler.
Height: 7.6cm. 1999.

XVIII Bean pod
Hippopotamus incisor.
Length: 9.6cm 2002

IXX Yin/Yang Bean Pod representing the female form
Elephant ivory and ebony.
Dewdrops in oyster pearls.
Height 9.6cm 1977.

XX Baku
Seal netsuke. Rhinoceros Horn.
Height 7.9cm 1977.

XXI The Beckoner
Siberian mammoth ivory.
Height 8.7cm 1996.

XXII Mermaid
Elephant ivory. Hair in rhinoceros horn.
Height 7.9cm 1978.

XXIII A Standing Racoon-faced Dog
Hippopotamus incisor.
Height 8cm 1996.

XXIV The Dancing Vixen
Mastodon. Definitions in wood,
abalone and inlaid lacquer.
Height 8.3cm 1996.

XXV The Venus Torso
Pacific umimatsu and amber. Eyes set in gold.
Height 7.5cm 1998.

XXVI The Lovelorn Ghost
Sashi form. Elephant ivory.
Hair in rhinoceros horn.
Height 15.8cm 1978.

XXVII Fukurokuju, God of Longevity
Boar's tooth. Nigerian ebony face.
Height 10cm 1998.

XXVIII Baku
Elephant ivory.
Height 9cm 1983.

THE ART & LIFE OF

MICHAEL BIRCH

The Product of an Active Mind

EDITED BY
JKL Birch

DESIGNED BY
Grant Bradford

For Michael, A Promise Fulfilled,
with the help of so many friends

FIRST EDITION
PUBLISHED 2013 BY
ARBONLAMBERT
PUBLISHING

TEXT & EDITORIAL
Janet Birch

DESIGNED & PRODUCED BY
Grant Bradford
TUNBRIDGE WELLS, KENT

PHOTOSHOP &
DIGITAL MASTERING
Steve Kashdan

TYPESETTING &
PAGE PLANNING
Tony Sambrook

STUDIO PHOTOGRAPHY
Derek Askem

PRINT & PRODUCTION
CONSULTANT
Roger Multon

SCANNING
MODERN AGE
REPRO HOUSE

PRINTING & BINDING
TOPPAN LEEFUNG PRINTERS

ArbonLambert Publishing, 59 St John's Road, Tunbridge Wells, Kent TN4 9TT

A CIP catalogue record for this book is available from the British Library

ISBN 1 872900 25 9

Foreword

Michael Birch was a consummate artist, and one who excelled in very many fields. He had an instinctive eye for design and, even before he reached his teens, was drawing and carving with a skill which belied his tender years. Although he was perhaps most well known, particularly in his later years, for the innovative netsuke which he carved with great skill, he was also a gifted sculptor, a pictorial artist, both in watercolours and as a graphic illustrator, a poet, a writer, a humourist and a raconteur. I have to admit that I am at a loss to say which of his qualities I most admired, although I think that humour is his facet that I remember most fondly. This character trait is also exhibited in his art, be it sculptures in large or miniature form, caricaturing the 17th century Dutch settlers in Japan or his paintings of badgers in human attire.

I first met Michael when I was working as a cataloguer and auctioneer at Sotheby's in London. I was immediately impressed with his knowledge of antique netsuke, his finely honed taste and his eye for quality. He built a relatively small but extremely fine collection of netsuke. I was not aware of it at the time, but during this period, Michael was sharpening his skills as a netsuke carver, making some miniature versions of his larger sculptures, as well as many original designs.

It is, indeed, for his netsuke that he will probably be remembered by most connoisseurs and in this field he was an outstanding leader. His work was admired by collectors around the world but, perhaps as importantly, he and his work were held in high esteem by other contemporary artists in Japan and elsewhere. To me, his work stood out for its ingenuity — treating well known and oft repeated subjects in a completely fresh manner that encouraged the viewer to not only admire the workmanship but also to think about the conception and its meaning.

Having worked with and studied netsuke for many years, I have been privileged to have seen and handled numerous private collections around the world. The majority of these have been of antique netsuke, with comparatively few contemporary examples. It has been noticeable therefore that much of Michael's work has been proudly acquired by collectors who hitherto have only been interested in the traditional examples of the genre.

Michael is missed by many but, like other great artists who have gone before, we are grateful for the legacy, in the form of his work, which remains for all to see, to hold and to admire for generations to come.
It is fitting that Janet Birch has worked diligently to write and produce this wonderful book in which collectors and a wider audience will find a well rounded picture of the man, his life and work.

Neil Davey

NEIL DAVEY

JAPANESE ART CONSULTANT
FORMERLY SENIOR DIRECTOR
SOTHEBY'S, LONDON

*One of my most treasured objects is not a netsuke at all,
but the auctioneer's gavel that Michael made for me in 1984*

Contents

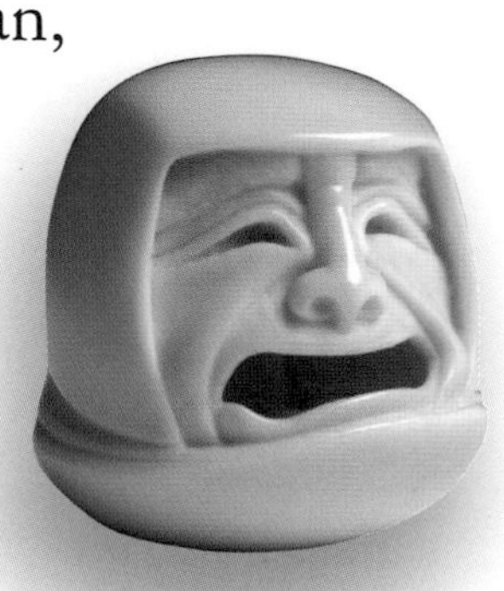

Introduction

Michael Birch's cosmopolitan upbringing in an Anglo-French family in Egypt left him feeling a little out of place, never wholly English in England or wholly French in France, while his social mores owed much to the Bedouins with whom he spent some of his childhood years. After overhearing an aunt commenting: Mickey is a nice boy, but he'll never amount to anything, he spent a lifetime trying to live down that lack of confidence in him. He always strived to be the best at whatever challenge he took on. He wanted to play the piano like Oscar Petersen, to sing like Frank Sinatra, to dance like Fred Astaire; and although he was not able to achieve those particular ambitions, he ensured that he achieved as much as was possible in whatever field he chose. But the driving force throughout his life was his need to express his artistic talents.

At various times he excelled in the fields of sculpture, painting and pottery; although destined to be an artist, he spent fifteen years building a multi-million pound international business from an initial investment of just fifteen pounds; he won industrial design awards; he wrote, filmed and photographed; and when he was finally able to fulfil his dream to return to an artistic life expressing his creativity, he was as successful as he had hoped.

Art, in all its aspects, was always at the forefront of his thoughts. He wrote about its importance as a means of self expression:

Art is the most reliable archival record of a civilization; indeed, the true history of humankind is to be found in its sublime creations. It is what separates us from all other species on this planet. Art is a product of human personality that is inherent in all humans. It is a continuous and intensely personal way for all human beings, without exception, to express their responses to the world as they see it. The fact is that no two persons express in exactly the same way that ineffable quality called art. It is an intrinsic part of what we are. It is like a fingerprint of the spirit – mysterious and unique to each individual. . .

Finally, after twenty years, two promises are fulfilled; one to myself, and one to my late husband, Michael. In 1992, while trying to find some storage space, I opened a sizable cupboard which I found full of photographic equipment and thousands of photographs, slides, transparencies and negatives. Curiosity caught hold and I sat on the floor dipping into packets and trays. I discovered a treasure trove of a family's life and of an artist's talents. Nothing was in any order, but that afternoon, I promised myself that one day I would sort out all those pictures.

Three years later, when Michael was carving again after a long lapse, he got out his camera to record his latest work. At a loose end, I began the task of trying to sort the pictures into some semblance of order. I had no idea of the size of the task I had set myself. Over time, when I occasionally learned of the material used, or some other fact about a particular piece, I recorded it on a slowly developing list. One day, when discussing the list, it was suggested that it might be interesting to produce a small booklet of the information I had gathered. Michael agreed but was very clear that I was to put everything away and that nothing should be done until after his death.

I did as he asked, but over the years I continued to make notes of anything I thought might be useful. Then in the autumn of 2006, he asked me if I had made any preparatory plans for the book about his work. At that point I had made none; so I quickly prepared three or four pages showing an illustration of the piece, the title, the materials used, and any other information I had found. He looked at it briefly, said that he thought it was good, and told me to put the project away 'until later'.

I have enjoyed collecting the information regarding Michael's works of art which were created over a seventy year period. His netsuke make the largest contribution to the book, but also included are some of his paintings in oils and inks; his larger sculptures; his pottery; his designs for book illustrations and covers; and his spectacle frames. I have included quotations from Michael's letters and articles regarding specific pieces and, with their permission, comments from other artists and from collectors and dealers.

In the Biography I have given the factual details of his life. Michael was one of those individuals to whom things happen and his inherent restlessness prompted him to take risks. He was not only willing to take advantage of every opportunity which presented itself, but for most of his adult life he was in the fortunate position to be able to do so. I have made little attempt to analyse his character; I am far too close to the subject and not qualified to do so. Any comment on his motives or behaviour have been extracted from his own writings; from conversations which, inevitably over a twenty year period, were occasionally repeated; or from personal insights which were shared by many of those who knew him for far longer than I.

As sought-after works of art, Michael's pieces are distributed in collections around the world. In many instances, I have had to rely on the archival photographs to show the diverse range of his ideas and designs for his work, but I have been fortunate to be able to arrange for over one hundred and fifty of his pieces to be specially photographed and these form the core of the illustrations in the book.

Michael had an artistic talent to surpass most, yet was practical enough to design machinery and tools; he was demanding in his expectations of himself and of others, and genuine in his praise, which had to be earned; he was willing to try any foodstuffs, however unusual, yet was afraid of heights; he was generous to family and friends, and to eager collectors; he had a wonderful sense of humour and of irony, yet was prone to great rages. I would not have missed our life together for any wealth in the world.

Compiling this book has taken much longer than I ever imagined and, while I have received a great deal of help from many others, any factual errors are all my own. I am so pleased that I am able to finally fulfil the promise I made to him. I hope he would approve.

Janet Birch

JANET BIRCH
TUNBRIDGE WELLS

The Gods

Fukurokuju is the Japanese God of Longevity and of Good Luck, and is always depicted with a full beard and a tall forehead, often longer than his body. His high forehead contains all the wisdom gained from his long life, although how much luck contributed to his long life and how much was due to the wisdom gained throughout his extended years is unclear.

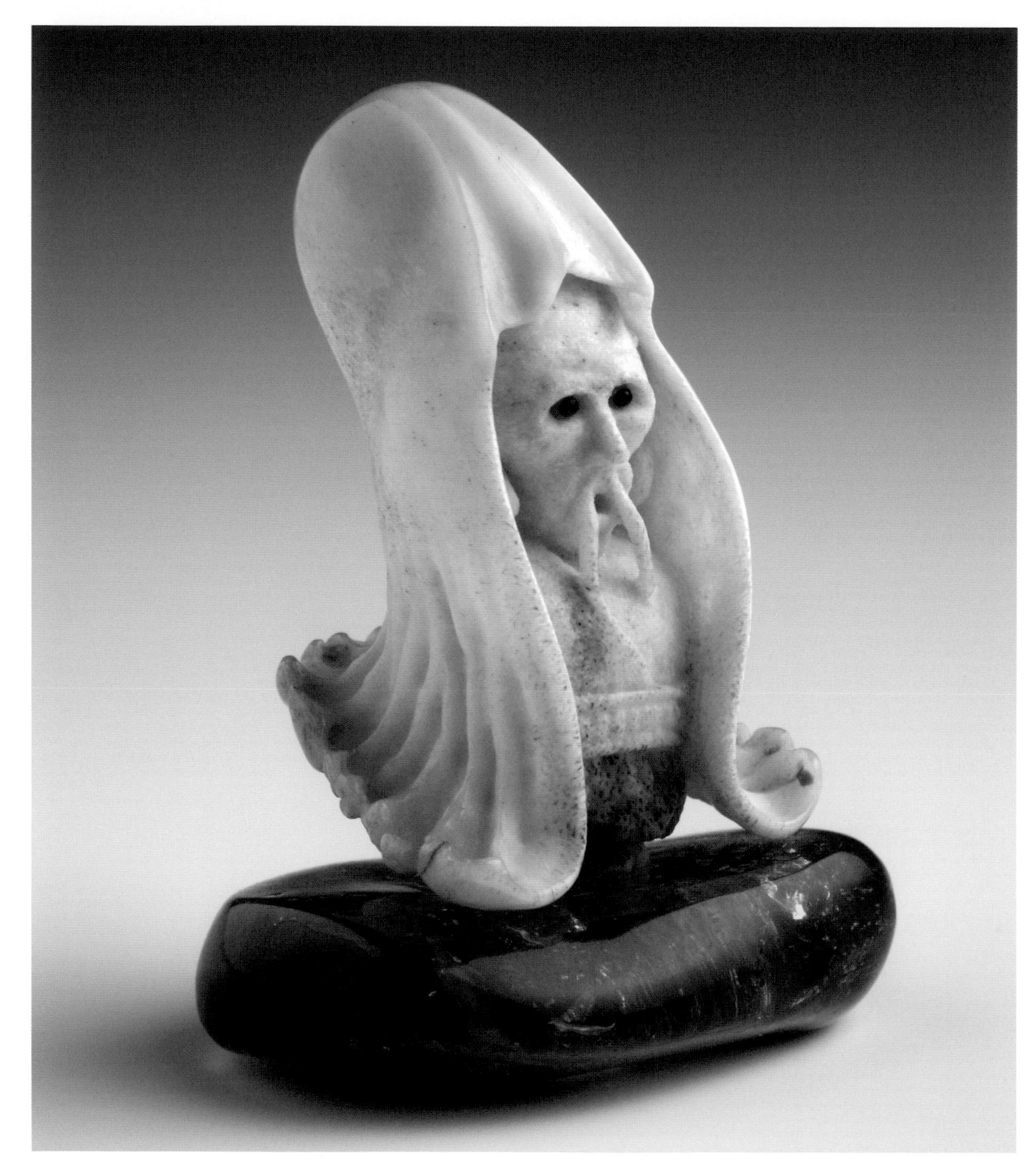

Fukurokuju standing on an amber boulder

Stag antler.
Double inlaid eyes in drawn crystal rod.
Boulder in amber.
Height 5.0cm. 1995.

Exhibited The Carvings of Michael Henry Birch N.K.C. New York 1995.

Illustrated I.N.S.J. Vol. 16 No. 2 1996.

Exhibited & Illustrated The Carvings of Michael Henry Birch I.N.S.C. Honolulu 1997.

Exhibited Michael Henry Birch Sculptures 11th Vienna Netsuke Symposium Galerie Zacke Vienna Austria. 1997.

Exhibited Michael Birch Netsuke Carver and Sculptor National College of Art & Design Dublin 1997.

Exhibited & Illustrated Tactiles by Michael Henry Birch I.N.S.C. Boston 2001.

Exhibited & Illustrated Netsuke Sculptures by Michael Henry Birch I.N.S.C. Honolulu 2004.

The coronets of antlers have a naturally uneven edge and this depiction of Fukurokuju and those following show the variety of forms of antler that Michael used to represent the folds and edges of the cloak. (See also the use of antler in representations of Dutchmen and Tanuki.)

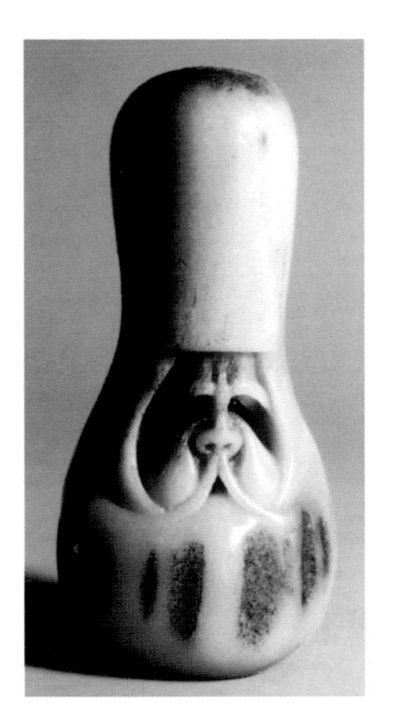

Fukurokuju

Stag antler.
Height: 6.1cm. C.1980.

Exhibited Netsuke by Birch London Netsuke Convention 1980.

Illustrated Living Masters of Netsuke by Miriam Kinsey, 1983.

Exhibited Contemporary Netsuke, Miniature Sculpture from Japan and Beyond,
The Bowers Museum of Cultural Art Santa Ana California 1997.

In her book, Miriam Kinsey wrote:

Stag antler which is over 150 years old and translucent with age. In designing a netsuke of amber and gold of this happy god Fukurokuju, Michael first did this simple working model from stag antler. It appealed to us and we were happy to add it to our Michael Birch collection.

Fukurokuju takes shape on a Möbius surface

Stag antler. Double inlaid eyes in drawn crystal rod.
Height 5.0cm. 1994.

Exhibited The Carvings of Michael Henry Birch N.K.C. New York 1995.

Exhibited & Illustrated Tactiles by Michael Henry Birch I.N.S.C. Boston 2001.

Fukurokuju, God of Longevity

Boar's tooth. Nigerian ebony face.
Height 10.0cm. 1998.

Exhibited & Illustrated Tactiles by Michael Henry Birch I.N.S.C. Boston 2001.

Dosojin

Bull elephant ivory and blue cow horn.
Height 4.0cm. 1975.

Illustrated I.N.C.S.J. Vol. 4 No. 1 1976.

Exhibited & Illustrated Michael Birch Netsuke and Sculpture Eskenazi Oriental Art London 1976.

Exhibited Sotheby's Bond St. London. 1994.

Illustrated I.N.S.J. Vol. 16 No. 2 1996.

Exhibited Michael Birch Netsuke Carver and Sculptor National College of Art & Design Dublin 1997.

This netsuke joins two materials, one light and one dark and fuses them into an abstract anthropomorphic form.

His expression is priceless, as are his contours and connotations.

ROBERT O. KINSEY

Rocking Fukurokuju

Oosik. Face in stag antler. Double inlaid eyes in drawn crystal rod.
Height 4.3cm. 1994.

Exhibited & Illustrated The Japanese Art of Miniature Carving Minneapolis Institute of Arts Minnesota 1999.

Exhibited & Illustrated The Japanese Art of Miniature Carving Herbert F. Johnson Museum of Art Cornell University Ithaca New York 1999.

Oosik is a term used by the North American Inuit people for the baculum or penis bone of walruses, seals, sea lions and polar bears. The bone exists in most mammals including primates but not in humans.

Michael carved this piece so that the base is uneven. When placed on a flat surface he rocks gently when put down and comes to a halt with a shudder.

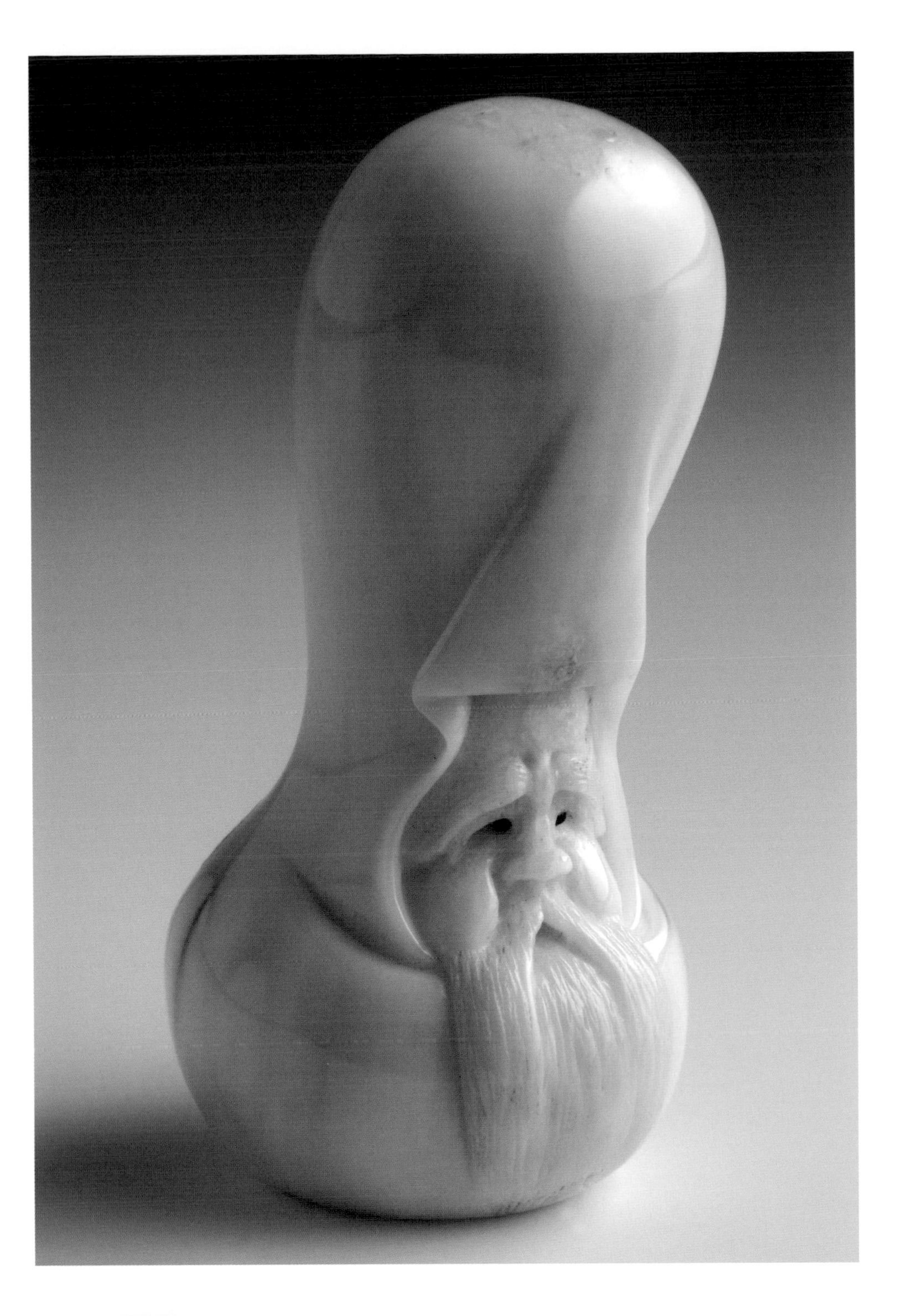

Fukurokuju, the symbol of Long Life

Kagamibuta netsuke.
Umimatsu & Gold.
Height 4.9cm. C.1995.

Exhibited The Carvings of Michael Henry Birch N.K.C. New York 1995.

Exhibited Michael Birch Netsuke Carver and Sculptor National College of Art & Design Dublin 1997.

Exhibited & Illustrated Tactiles by Michael Henry Birch I.N.S.C. Boston 2001.

Exhibited & Illustrated Netsuke Sculptures by Michael Henry Birch I.N.S.C. Honolulu 2004.

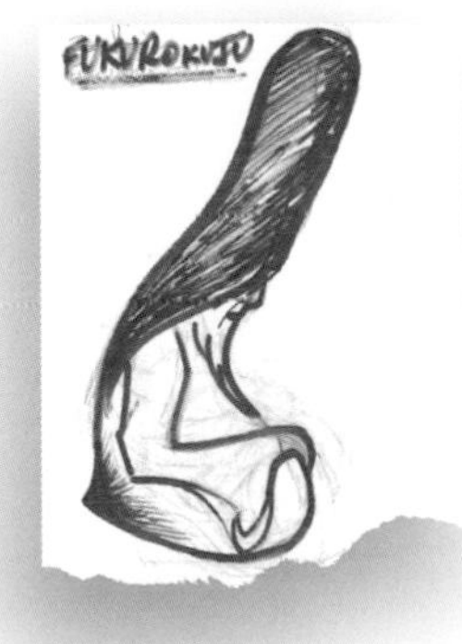

Fukurokuju

Shunga netsuke.
Walrus Ivory. Eyes in drawn crystal rod.
Height: 7.0cm. 1979.

Exhibited Netsuke by Birch London Netsuke Convention 1980.

Carved from the middle section of a large and very old tusk, the material has the rich colour and markings of old age.

Bishamon-Ten, one of the seven Gods of Luck, is the God of Wealth and Riches, and is the defender of the Buddhist faith.
He is depicted here with Benten, the only one of the seven to be female. She represents the attributes of Learning, Literature, Music and Art.

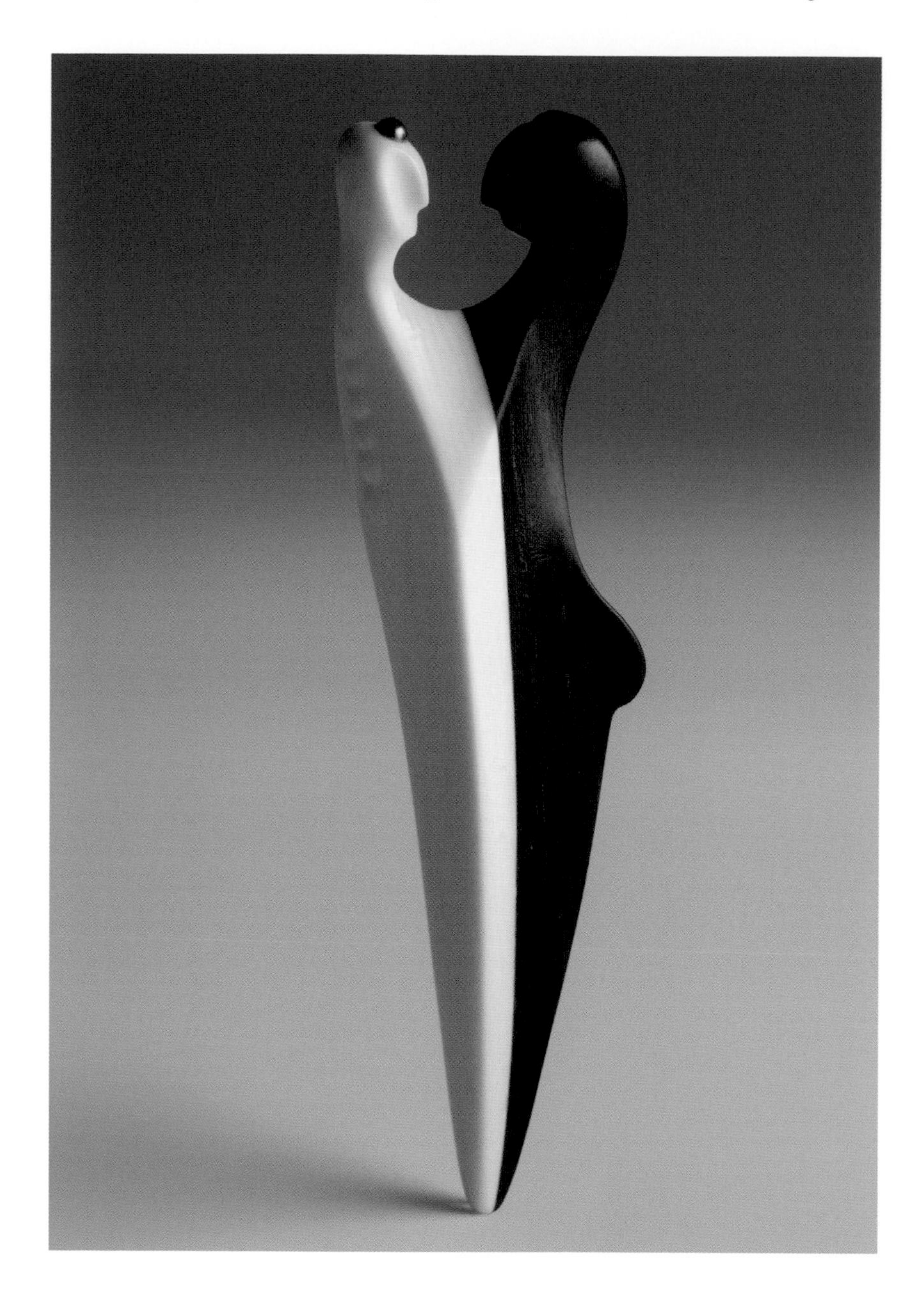

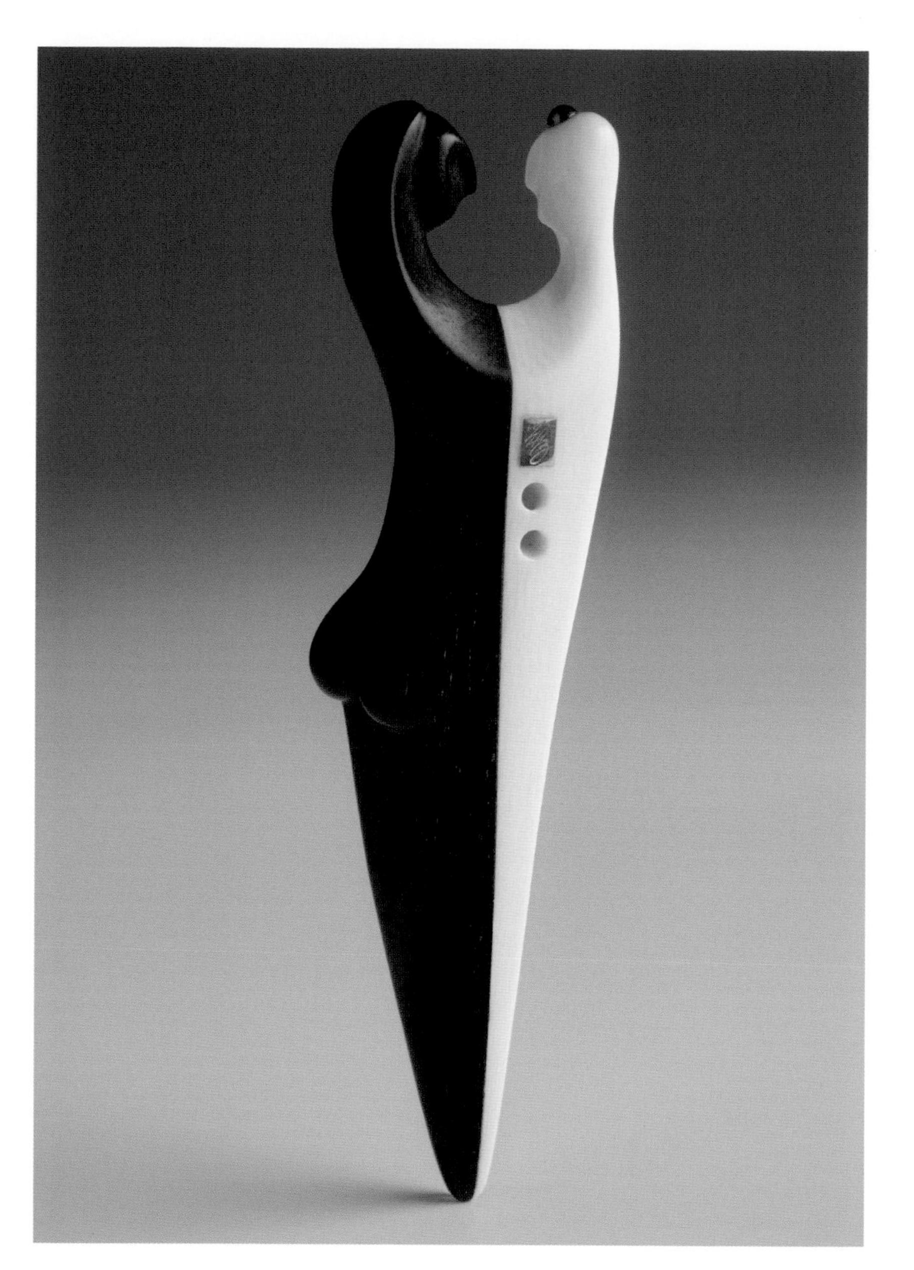

Bishamon-Ten and Benten

Sashi netsuke.
Elephant ivory and Nigerian ebony. Mussel pearl inlay.
Height: 12.0cm. C.1981.

Exhibited Michael Birch Netsuke Carver and Sculptor
National College of Art & Design Dublin 1997.

Abstract Dosojin based on a seed shape

Elephant ivory carved from a billiard ball.
Height 3.8cm. 1948.

Illustrated I.N.C.S.J. Vol. 4 No. 1 1976.

Dosojin is one of the most important fundamental elements in primordial Japanese folk religion, itself the foundation for Shinto. As the phallic deity supreme, Dosojin helps to ensure fecundity and abundance in agriculture, and protects against sickness and evil spirits.

It symbolises sexual equality and the safeguarding against death through sexual activity. It is also called the 'road ancestor deity', for it serves as guardian spirit of roads and travellers. This unique male/female deity is represented in a variety of images: sometimes merged into one form; as a husband/wife loving couple; or in some places as a triad of separate divinities.

It can be found depicted in several different ways including: the rudimentary simplicity of natural phallus-shaped stones; two trees planted side by side, often at crossroads; straw effigies created for village festivals; and by sophisticatedly carved stone sculptures of embracing couples.

I have attempted in this carving to express the universality of the concept of Dosojin by combining several of the principal elements: the loving couple, phallicism, yin/yang, male/female, with a number of less obvious images – ambiguously merged – which I leave to the observer to interpret in his/her own way.

MHB 1976

I have seen a version lying on its side, and once described as a bird, not quite what Michael had in mind when he carved the piece and wrote the above.

Dosojin

Elephant ivory and rhinoceros horn.
Height 6.0cm. 1976.

Illustrated Handbook to London Netsuke Fair and Convention 1990.

Illustrated Graphics World October 1993.

Illustrated I.N.S.J. Vol. 16 No2 1996.

Exhibited Sotheby's Bond Street London 1994.

Exhibited Michael Henry birch Sculptures 11th Vienna Netsuke Symposium Galerie Zacke Vienna Austria 1997.

Exhibited Michael Bbirch Netsuke Carver and Sculptor National College of Art & Design Dublin 1997.

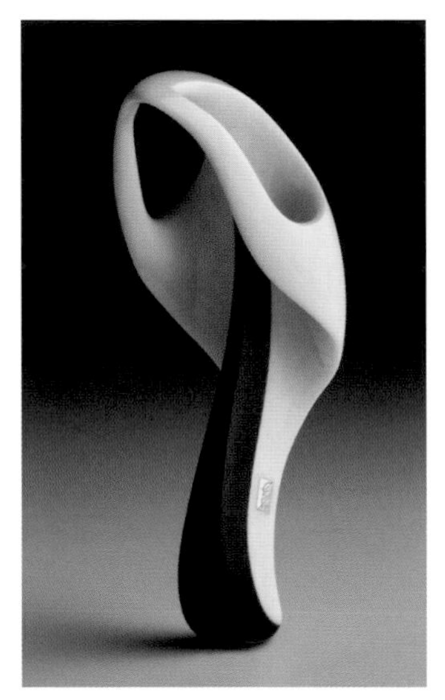

ACTUAL SIZE

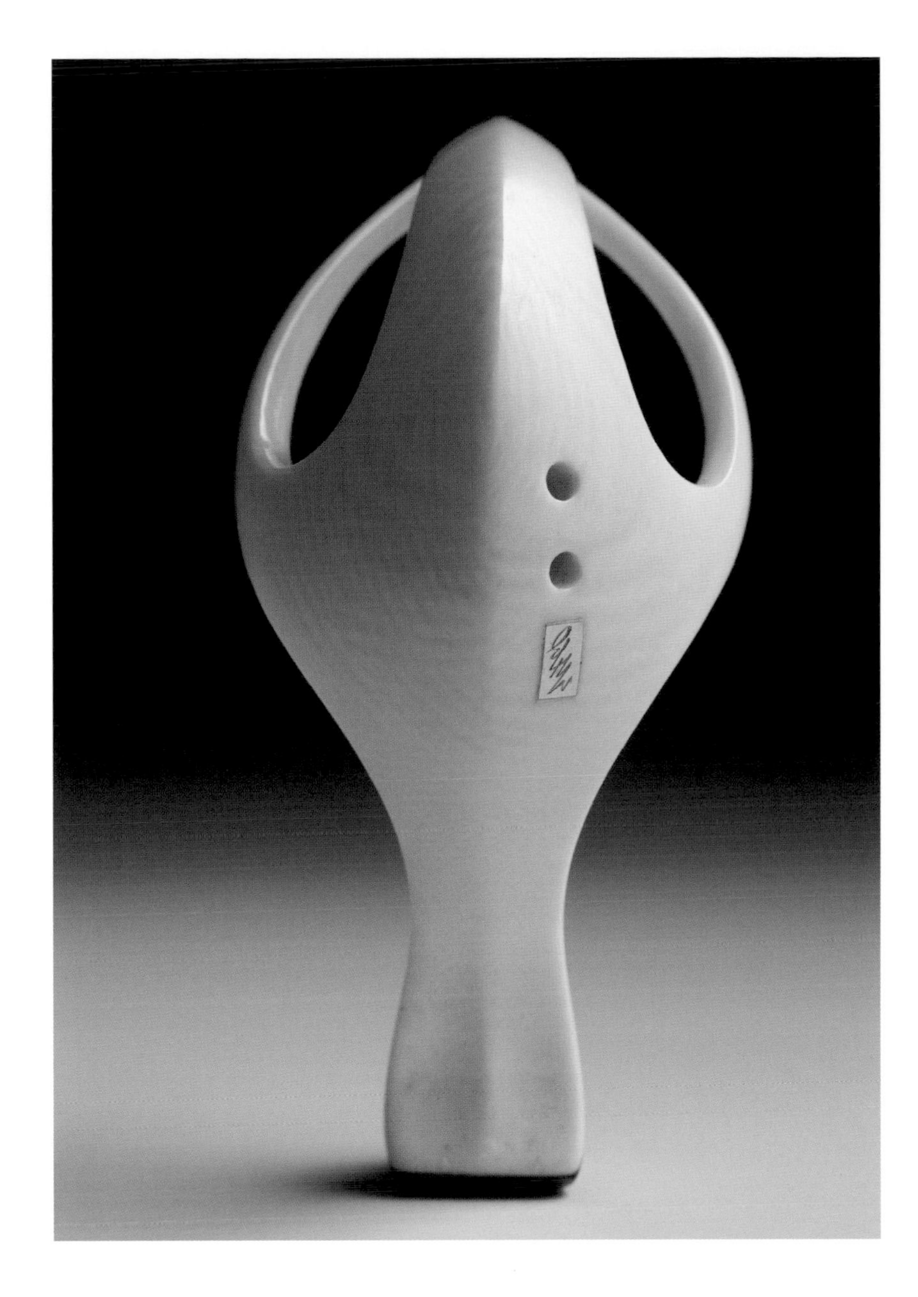

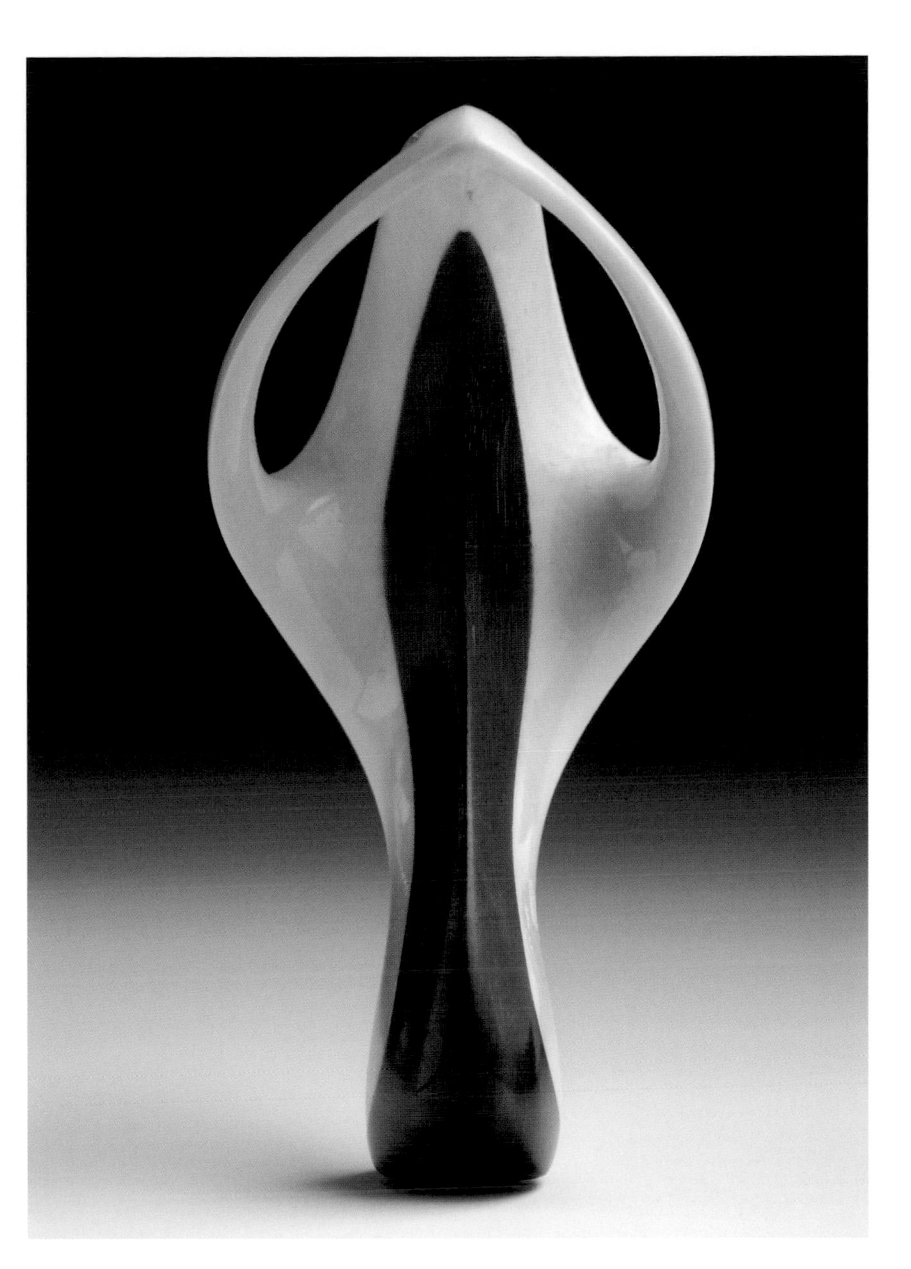

Dosojin

Elephant ivory and rhinoceros horn.
Height 7.5cm. 1977.

Illustrated Contrasting Styles by Robert G Sawyers.

Exhibited The Carvings of Michael Henry Birch I.N.C.S.C. Honolulu 1977.

Exhibited N.K.C. Kansas City 1977.

Illustrated Living Masters of Netsuke by Miriam Kinsey 1983.

Illustrated Christies New York auction catalogue 1985.

Illustrated Butterfield & Butterfield San Francisco auction catalogue 1998.

Illustrated Michael Birch (Part Duex) and others by Nicholas Westover Euronetsuke 2009.

Believed to have been born more than three thousand years ago, or to be a legendary figure, the venerable Lao Tsze is considered the founder of the Taoist system of philosophy.
This teaches the three ways to reach harmony: by dwelling on the beauty of nature – by being self-sufficient – and by desiring nothing. The two ancient materials, mastodon tusk that could be up to twenty-three million years old, and Lebanese amber, the oldest examples of which are 125-135 million years old, are a symbolic analogue of the great age of this antiquated deity.

MHB 1999

Lao Tsze

Body in mastodon ivory, head in rare Lebanese gold amber (Ching Peh). Eyes in drawn crystal rod.
Height 7cm 1999.

Exhibited & Illustrated: Tactiles by Michael Henry Birch, INSC Chicago 1999.

Exhibited & Illustrated: Tactiles by Michael Henry Birch, INSC Boston 2001.

Exhibited & Illustrated: Netsuke Sculptures by Michael Henry Birch, INSC Honolulu 2004.

ACTUAL SIZE

The piece of amber was purchased in Lyme Regis on Dorset's Jurassic coast during a visit to the carver Guy Shaw. It was not only the exceptional colour of the specimen that attracted Michael's eye. During its formation small bubbles of air became trapped in the hardening resin. At some time in its history, probably during a forest fire, the amber became hot and these air bubbles expanded causing small fractures in the amber. It was these fractures, or spangles, that he had been looking for to represent the sparks or synapses in the brain of this God of Wisdom.

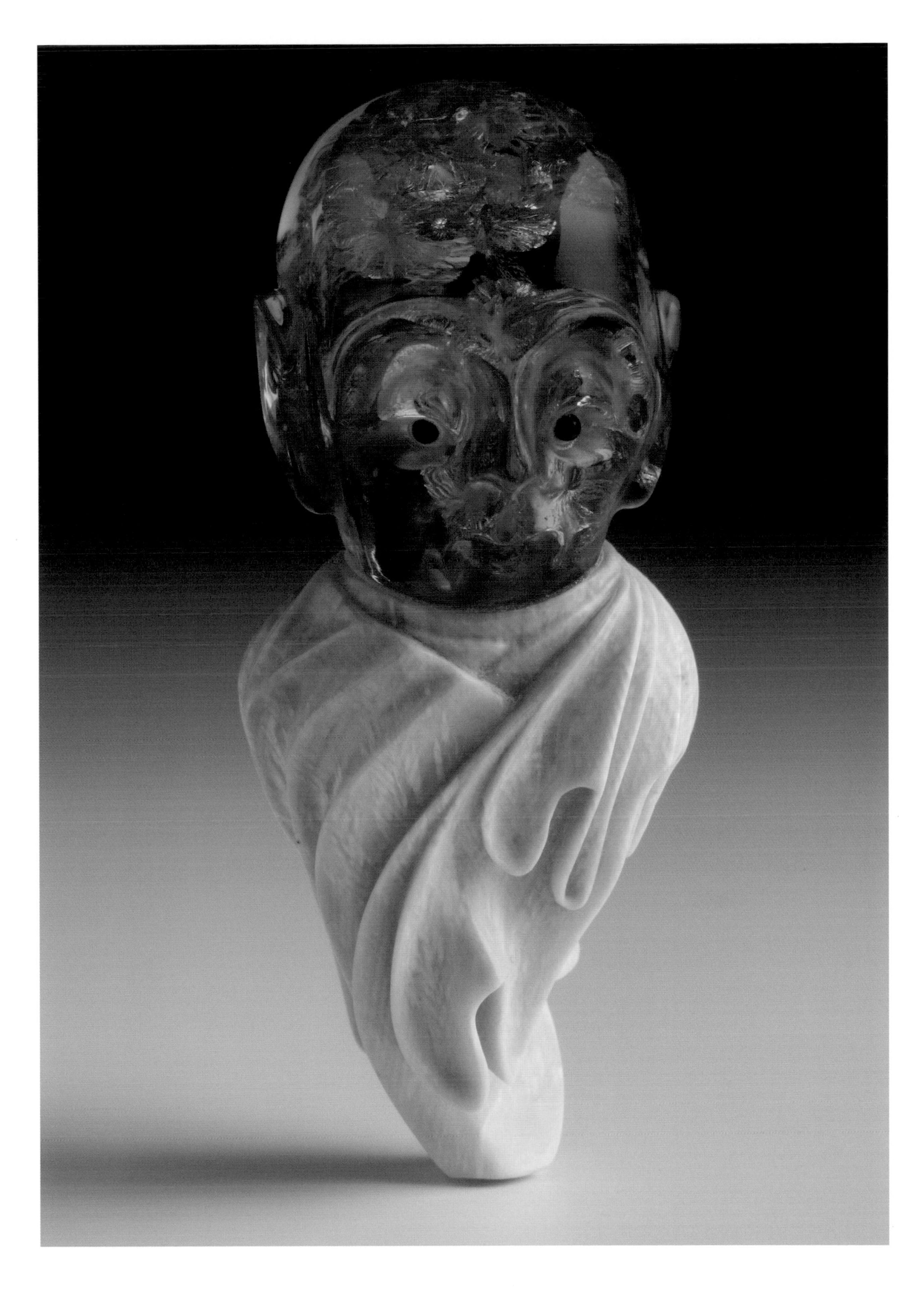

The three dome-headed gods – Lao Tsze, Fukurokuju and Jurojin – travel endlessly on opposing planes of the same surface. They converge momentarily into a single identity in this netsuke. This is the first of several carvings using a three-dimensional conceptual shape which has a single surface and a single edge and which is not found in nature although, in this carving, the Möbius shape is composed of forms borrowed from nature.

The Three Gods of Long Life

Hippopotamus incisor.
Height: 5.2cm. 1995.

Exhibited The Carvings of Michael Henry Birch N.K.C. New York, 1995.

Illustrated I.N.S.J. Vol. 16, No. 2 1996.

Exhibited & Illustrated The Carvings of Michael Henry Birch I.N.S.C. Honolulu 1997.

Illustrated Contemporary Netsuke, Miniature Sculpture from Japan and Beyond, The Bowers Museum of Cultural Art Santa Ana California 1997.

Exhibited & Illustated Michael Henry Birch Sculptures, 11th Vienna Netsuke Symposium, Galerie Zacke Vienna Austria 1997.

Exhibited Michael Birch Netsuke Carver and Sculptor, National College of Art & Design Dublin 1997.

The Spirit World

There are hundreds of ghosts, spectres and goblins in Japanese mythology. Michael found them a rich source of subject matter.

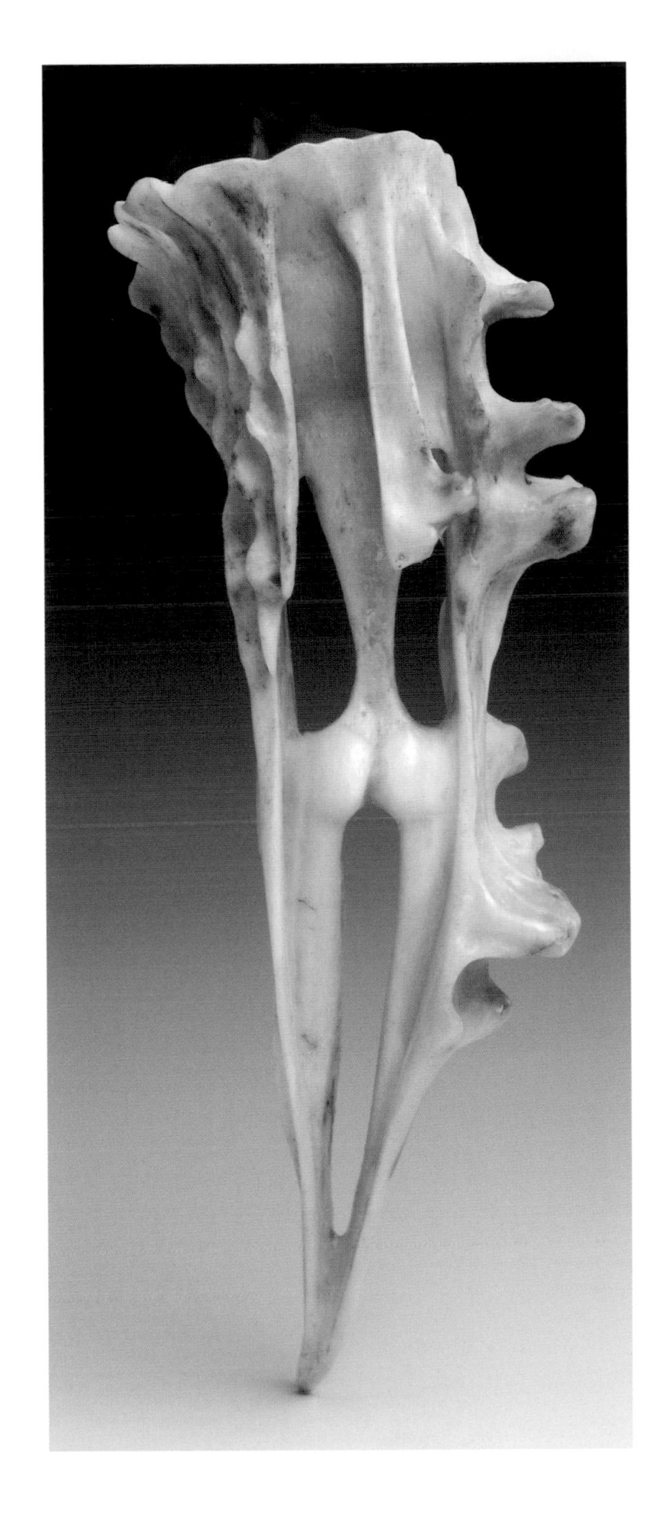

Disappearing Ghost

Roebuck antler, hair in buffalo horn.
Eyes double inlaid in drawn crystal rod.
Height 9.3 cm. 1978.

Exhibited & Illustrated Netsuke Sculptures by Michael Henry Birch I.N.S.C. Honolulu 2004.

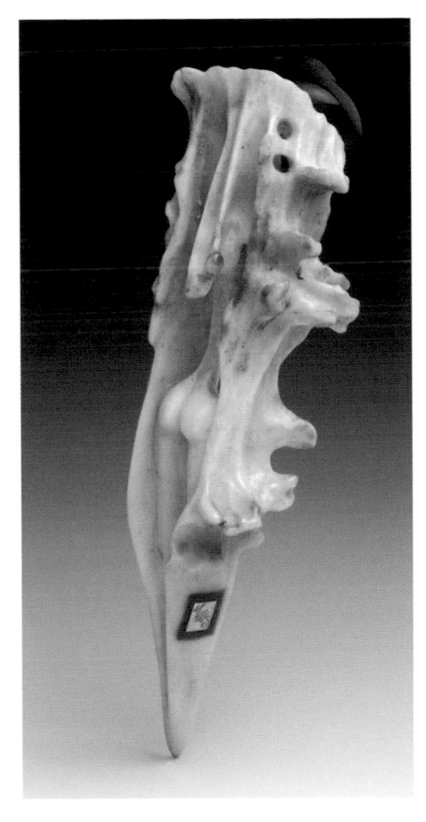

ACTUAL SIZE

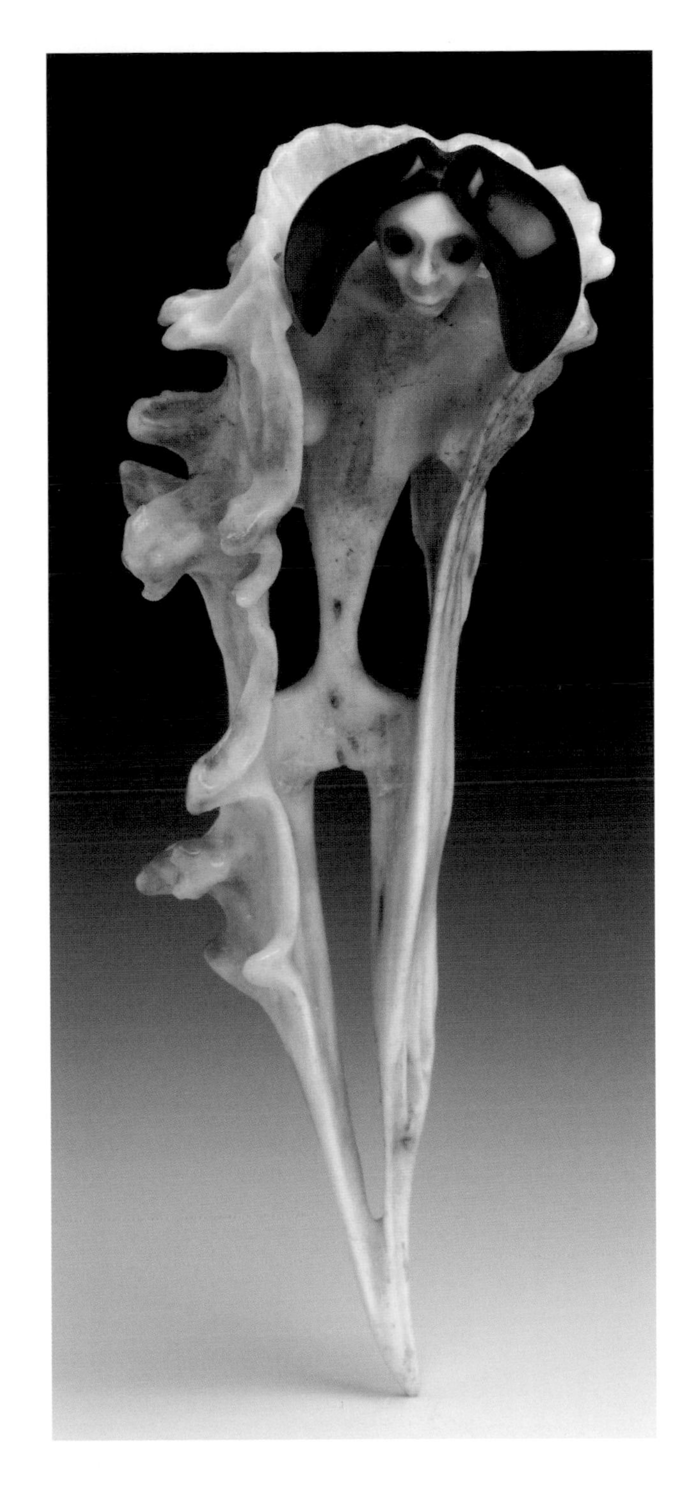

ACTUAL SIZE

The Pregnant Ghost

Body in Chinese stag antler. Hair in Baltic amber. Eyes in drawn crystal rod.
Height 6.3cm. 1998.

Exhibited & Illustrated Tactiles by Michael Henry Birch I.N.S.C. Chicago 1999.

Exhibited & Illustrated Tactiles by Michael Henry Birch I.N.S.C. Boston 2001.

This ghost is in a state of transition midway between life and death, and is illustrated by the contrasting conditions of her hands. The right is fleshed while the left is skeletal and her eyes, the right is large and brown while the left is small and blue.

MHB

ACTUAL SIZE

Metamorphosis of a Phantom

Body in Siberian mammoth ivory.
Hair in black methyl-methacrilate resin.
Right eye double inlaid amber and drawn crystal rod. Left eye double inlaid drawn crystal rod.

Height 5.7cm. 1998.

Exhibited & Illustrated Tactiles by Michael Henry Birch I.N.S.C. Chicago 1999.

Exhibited & Illustrated Tactiles by Michael Henry Birch I.N.S.C. Boston 2001.

Exhibited & Illustrated Netsuke Sculptures by Michael Henry Birch I.N.S.C. Honolulu 2004.

Ghost

Roebuck antler hair in rhinoceros horn. Eyes in drawn crystal rod.
Height 10.5cm. 1979.

Exhibited Netsuke by Birch London Netsuke Convention 1980.

Exhibited I.N.C.S.C. Honolulu 1981.

Illustrated Sotheby's Floyd Segal Collection Auction Catalogue 1999.

Illustrated I.N.S.J. Vol. 19 No. 4 1999.

Ghost

Boxwood. Hair in ebony. Eyes in drawn crystal rod.
1977.

Exhibited N.K.C. Kansas City 1977.

Illustrated I.N.C.S.J. Vol. 6 No. 3 1978.

Ghost with Flowing Hair

Elephant ivory. Hair in blonde rhinoceros horn. Eyes in drawn crystal rod.
Height 9.5cm. 1977.

Exhibited & Illustrated Eighteenth to Twentieth Century Netsuke Eskenazi Oriental Art London 1978.

Illustrated I.N.C.S.J. Vol. 6 No. 2 1978.

Illustrated I.N.S.J. Vol. 16 No. 2 1996.

Exhibited & Illustrated Contemporary Netsuke The Kinsey Collection Accompanied by H.I.H. Prince Takamado Collection by Robert O. Kinsey Chiba City Museum of Art Japan. 2001.

Illustrated Contemporary Netsuke The H.I.H. Prince Takamado Collection The Tobacco & Salt Museum Tokyo Japan. 2003.

Exhibited & Illustrated Netsuke The Prince Takamado Collection Tokyo National Museum Japan 2011.

Some twenty years ago, I met several of the master netsuke carvers in Tokyo and took the opportunity to ask each one to carve a ghost for me on commission. I made it a condition that each should carve his piece with the total freedom to depict the subject as he wished and not as would be expected by his dealer. In other words these were to be carver's carvings.

Some months later the carvings arrived in England and the results were fascinating and rather surprising — none was in the usual style of the carver's pieces for general sale. I still have them in my possession.

I was, however, reminded by master carver Ryushi at the New York Convention in 1995, that I had also undertaken to carve a ghost and to abide by the same conditions. Jogged by Ryushi's kindly reminder, I decided last fall to carve an entirely different ghost; a truly ghostly ghost, tightly coiled and compact, at one with the dark flames from which she was about to spring up and startle her treacherous lover. In other words I was going to attempt a carver's carving and depict the subject strikingly but with the greatest economy of means.

I carved the Ghost from a flawless section of ivory cut from an exceptionally rare piece of mastodon tusk given to me by master carver Masatoshi about sixteen years ago. This fossil ivory is over a million years of age. I then exhibited her in Honolulu where Ryushi held her in his hand for quite a while, turning her over several times, and examining her very carefully. Finally he looked at me with a smile and said: 'I see you have carved a fine ghost at last.' Carvers, you will note, have long memories.

MHB 1997

The Ghostly Ghost

North American mastodon tusk, deeply stained. 1996.

Exhibited & Illustrated The Carvings of Michael Henry Birch I.N.S.C. Honolulu 1997.

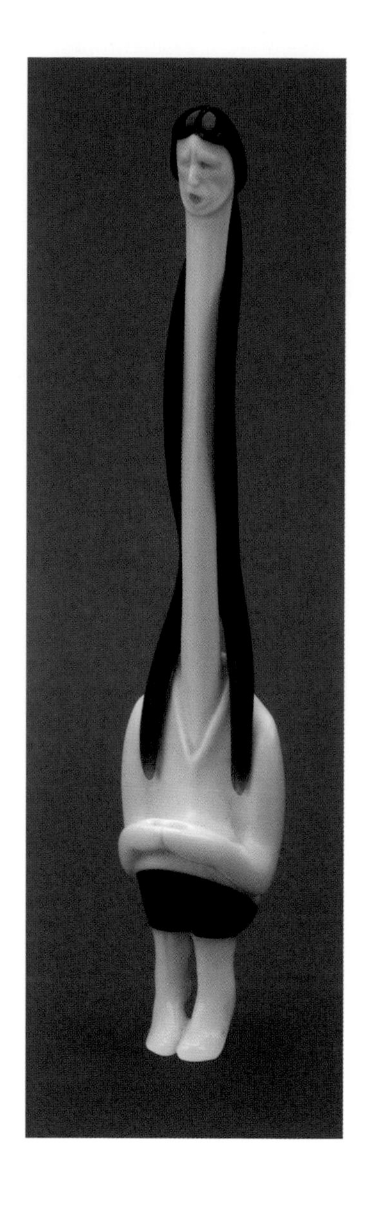

Rokurokubi - The Long-necked Goblin

Elephant ivory and rhinoceros horn.
Height 11.5cm. 1976.

Exhibited N.K.C., Kansas City 1977.

Illustrated Christie's, New York, Auction Catalogue 1985.

According to legend, a red line appeared around the long neck of these Chinese goblins on the day before their head was able to wander freely at night. Belief in the existence of these goblins was still found in China up to the end of the nineteenth century.

Ghost

Elephant ivory & rhinoceros horn
1977.

Exhibited N.K.C., Kansas City 1977.

The Lovelorn Ghost

Sashi form.
Elephant ivory, Hair in rhinoceros horn.
Height 15.8cm. 1978.

The Volcanic Marine Ghost

Alaskan umimatsu with skeletal marine organism inclusions. Inlaid lacquer flames.
Eyes double inlaid amber and drawn crystal rod.
Height 9.5cm. 1999.

Exhibited & Illustrated Tactiles by Michael Henry Birch I.N.S.C. Chicago 1999.

Illustrated Contemporary Netsuke The H.I.H. Prince Takamado Collection The Tobacco & Salt Museum Tokyo Japan. 2003.

Exhibited & Illustrated Netsuke The Prince Takamado Collection Tokyo National Museum Japan 2011.

The subtle shade changes of the inlaid polychrome lacquer flame pattern represent the ghost's emergence from a deep-sea volcanic eruption.

Jo and Uba

Elephant ivory.
Width 5.8cm. 1978.

Exhibited The Carvings of Michael Henry Birch I.N.S.C. Honolulu 1979.

According to legend, a maiden spirit living in a pine tree in Takasago in Banshu, was seen just once by a young man who immediately fell in love with her.
They married and had a long and happy life together. They died within minutes of each other and their spirits remained in the pine forest. Michael portrayed these lovers in the form of the bifurcated trunk that was their home.
Sharen Chappell believes that in this netsuke, the faces of Jo and Uba have been replaced with those of Okame and Fukurokuju, both associated with shunga, and also occasionally depicted together as an elderly couple.

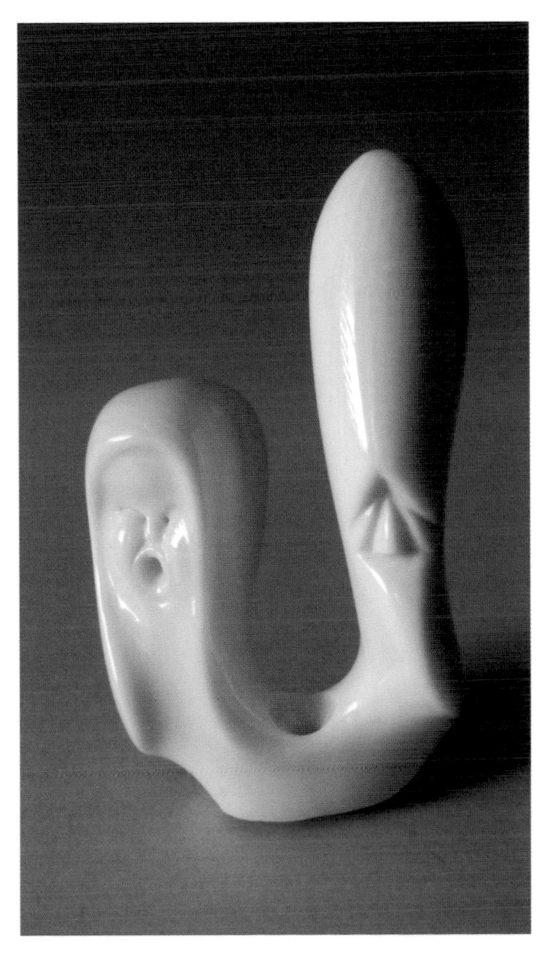

The Impolite Sprite

The unspeakably rude goblin whose real name cannot be mentioned in polite company.
Stag antler. Eyes in drawn crystal rod.
Height 4.8cm. 1999.

Exhibited briefly at Tactiles by Michael Henry Birch I.N.S.C. Chicago 1999.

Following the rejection of a commissioned piece, Michael retaliated by carving a small imp with an extended proboscis in the form that illustrates a rude expression.
At the following I.N.S. Convention and following a good sushi lunch with plenty of saké Michael placed the carving in his display showcase and invited the person concerned to view it. The gentleman took one look, turned on his heel and, without comment, walked away.
The piece, which has never been offered for sale, remained a carving which always made Michael smile.

Wise Men

Both real and legendary figures appear in this group, most notable Daruma in his various forms, but also three depictions of what Michael believed to be an interesting example of unconscious body language.

Daruma, according to legend, was Dharma the son of a sixth century Indian king. He travelled to China where he settled in a temple to contemplate the doctrine of Zen. After spending nine years crouched in motionless meditation – during which time he was exposed to temptations by demons of both sexes, had his ears and other sensitive parts bitten by rats, and his legs became atrophied – he arrived at the profound conclusion that 'nothing has ever really existed'. He is said to have crossed the sea on a reed and arrived in Japan in 813 AD.

MHB

ACTUAL SIZE

Daruma

Elephant ivory.

Height 3.7cm. 1974.

Exhibited and Illustrated Michael Birch, Netsuke and Sculpture Eskenazi Oriental Art London 1976.

Illustrated I.N.C.S.J. Vol.4 No.1 1976.

Exhibited Sotheby's Bond St. London. 1994.

Illustrated I.N.S.J. Vol.16 No.2 1996.

Michael carved this netsuke from a billiard ball for his father in return for a childhood gift of a netsuke of the same subject.

Daruma is frequently portrayed as a limbless cloaked figure emerging from his trance-like state with a jaw-breaking yawn. He is also a popular subject for children's toys where he is depicted in various irreverent guises. Daruma is sometimes portrayed in ironic vein as a woman based on the ungallant notion held by some Japanese artists that a woman could be temperamentally incapable of remaining meditatively silent for nine years.

MHB

Daruma Head

Elephant ivory.
4.1cm. 1978.

Illustrated I.N.C.S.J. Vol. 6 No. 3 1978.

Exhibited The Carvings of Michael Henry Birch I.N.S.C. Honolulu 1979.

Illustrated Living Masters of Netsuke by Miriam Kinsey 1983.

MIRIAM KINSEY WROTE:
Reminiscent of a netsuke Michael Birch's father gave to him when he was eight years old this is a highly tactile and amusing netsuke. The squinting eyes and stifled yawn create a wry expression. The very old ivory is beautifully polished and gives pleasure to the hand.

Daruma

Elephant ivory.
Height 3.5cm. 1977.

THE COLLECTOR WROTE:
I can't begin to tell you how very pleased I am with the netsuke. It is superb! and I shall treasure it... Be rest assured it will always be in my collection.

Yawning Daruma

He is seated in meditation, wearing a monk's robe.
Stag antler.
Height: 4.4cm. 1980.

Exhibited I.N.C.S.C. Honolulu 1981.

Illustrated Sotheby's Floyd Segal Collection Auction Catalogue 1999.

Illustrated I.N.S.J. Vol. 19 No.4 1999.

ACTUAL SIZE

The Two Faces of Daruma

Double Mobius.
Hippopotamus incisor. Eyes in drawn crystal rod.
Height 6.7cm. 1997.

Exhibited & Illustrated Tactiles by Michael Henry Birch I.N.S.C., Chicago, 1999.

Exhibited & Illustrated Tactiles by Michael Henry Birch I.N.S.C. Boston 2001.

Exhibited & Illustrated Netsuke Sculptures by Michael Henry Birch I.N.S.C. Honolulu 2004.

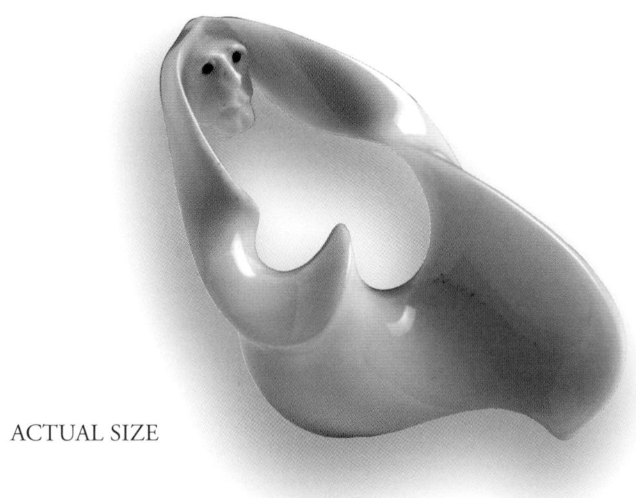

ACTUAL SIZE

Composed of forms borrowed from nature and melded into the double Möbius shape, the two faces are linked on the same spiritual plane by their determination to worship a god. While never leaving the same surface, either of the monks may find himself on another plane if he loses that resolve.

MHB

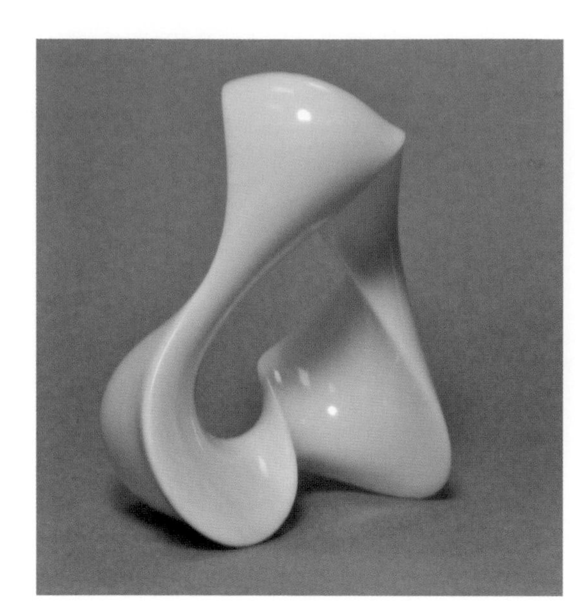

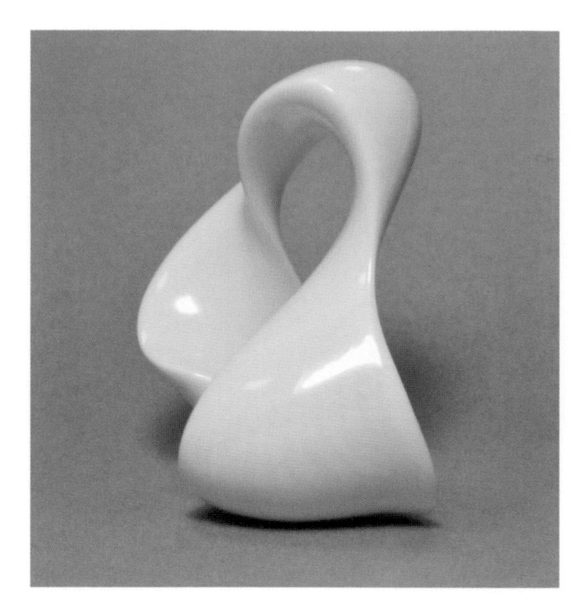

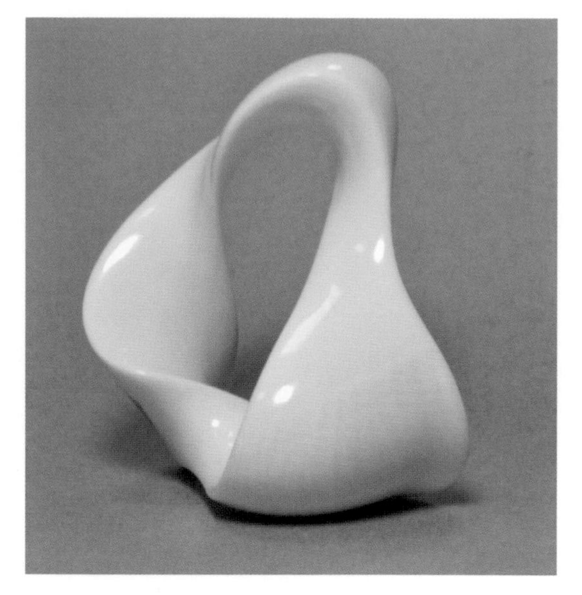

Double Möbius Daruma

Elephant ivory.
Height 5.3cm. 1979.

Exhibited Netsuke by Birch London Netsuke Convention 1980.

Exhibited Sotheby's Bond St. London. 1994.

Illustrated The Eye Within the Eye in The Appreciation of Ancient Arts and Crafts Japan 1994.

Exhibited The Tobacco and Salt Museum Tokyo 1995.

Illustrated Netsuke Takumi & Share Japan 1995.

Illustrated Netsuke Japan 1995.

Illustrated I.N.S.J. Vol. 16 No. 2 1996.

Exhibited Contemporary Netsuke Miniature Sculpture from Japan and Beyond The Bowers Museum of Cultural Art Santa Ana California 1997.

Exhibited & Illustrated Contemporary Netsuke The Kinsey Collection Accompanied by H.I.H. Prince Takamado Collection by Robert O. Kinsey Chiba City Museum of Art Japan 2001.

Illustrated Contemporary Netsuke The H.I.H. Prince Takamado Collection The Tobacco & Salt Museum Tokyo Japan 2003.

Illustrated I.N.C.S.J. Vol. 24 No. 3 2004.

Illustrated Michael Birch 1926-2008 Euronetsuke 2009.

IN RELATION TO THIS PIECE, ROBERT O. KINSEY WROTE ABOUT WHAT HE CALLED THE TRIUMPHS AND TRAGEDIES OF ART COLLECTOR ADDICTS:

Collecting art objects is often an addiction. Motives for collecting are various and basically of no concern to anyone but the collector himself or herself.

Functionally the 'World of Netsuke' is tripartite, comprised of the artists who create, of the dealers who sell, and of the collectors who buy. Sometimes there are cross-current variations. An artist may create and also sell and perhaps may also collect. My wife and I were solely collectors. Michael Birch was a most creative artist and also a major collector, sometimes selling his art works himself and sometimes selling through professional art dealers.

The triumphs of collectors are when they occasionally succeed in acquiring a much prized treasure despite formidable competition from other collectors and dealers.

The tragedies of a collector are when an exceptionally prized treasure is lost to another collector. I once had such an experience from which I shall never recover.

It involved a magnificent netsuke created by Michael Birch. I had glanced at it hurriedly but did not have a chance to examine it carefully.

Some months later I was invited to a private dinner party in Tokyo with His Imperial Highness Prince Norihito Takamado at the home of Mrs. Bunran 'Wendy' Makino, who is my main art dealer in Japan. There were just the three of us, His Highness, Mrs. Makino, and myself. His Highness and I were long time friends. We often gave joint exhibitions of our netsuke collections at museums in Japan and the United States. As usual His Highness brought with him a dozen or so of his new netsuke acquisitions to show me. I examined them carefully while we were having cocktails in Mrs. Makino's drawing room. Among them was the Michael Birch netsuke that I had hurriedly overlooked. It was a spectacular Möbius strip carving, in ivory, of Daruma, the first Zen patriarch of Buddhism. I examined it carefully and couldn't believe that I could have let such a treasure get away from me.

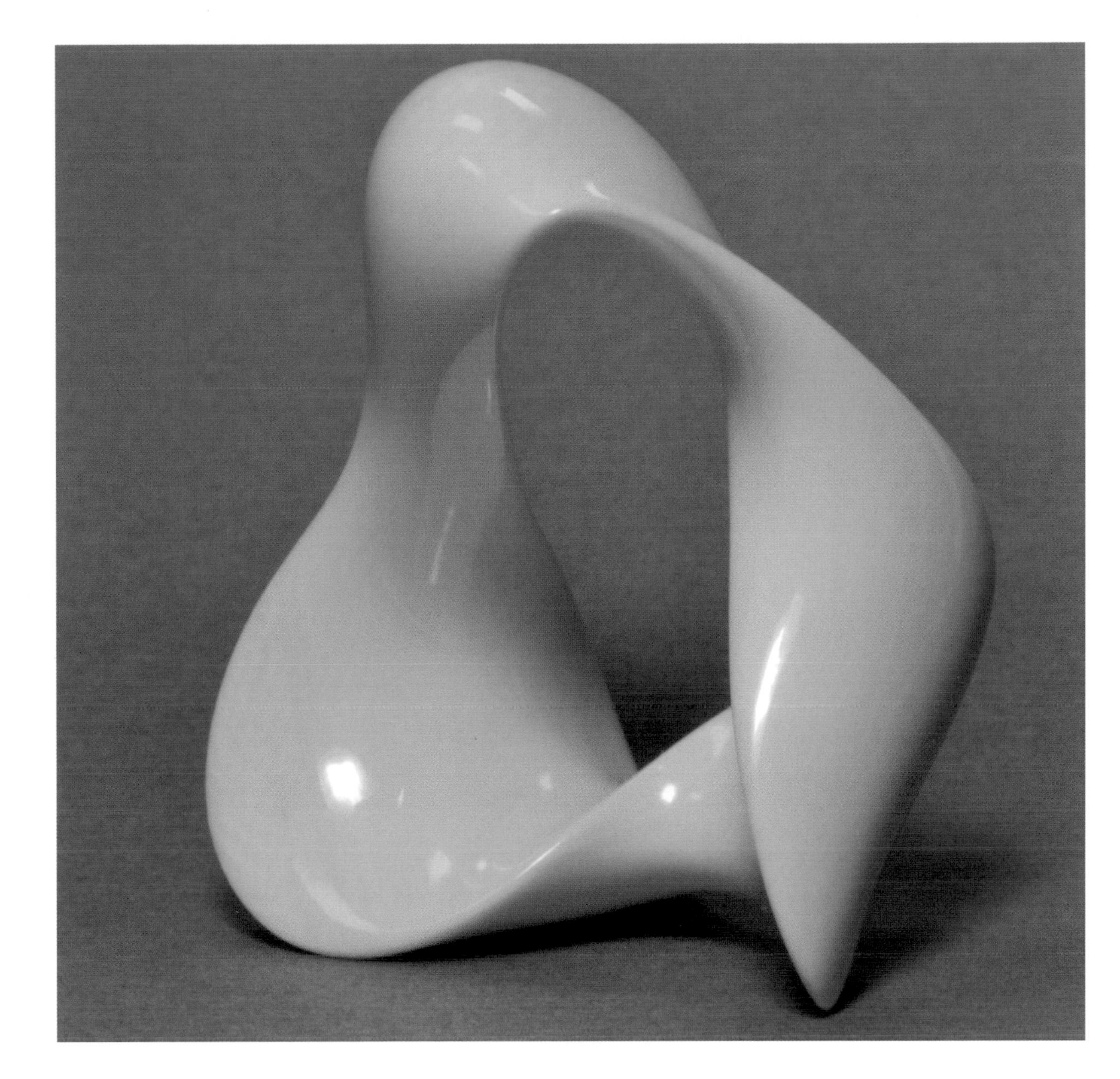

**Michael considered this netsuke to be one of his finest carvings and he was not alone.
The deceptively simple elegance of this carving was achieved by the finest attention to detail.
This is a carving where one-tenth of a millimetre too much or too little would have given an entirely different result.**

When we arrived back at my hotel, the parking attendants immediately recognized the imperial insignia on the Prince's limo and rushed over to be of service.
When I got out of the car, the Prince also left the car, together with his two servants. I thought he might merely want to shake my hand. Instead, he and his driver grabbed me in a tight hold while his security agent searched me thoroughly. The hotel attendants watched in open mouth astonishment. I asked what the hell was going on, and his Highness amiably replied that he merely wanted to make sure I hadn't stolen his Birch netsuke of Daruma. Then he got back into his limo, laughing his head off and waving a jovial goodbye. The parking attendants continued to stare at me aghast as I entered the hotel.
To make me feel even worse about 'the one that got away', His Highness then featured his Michael Birch netsuke treasure as the frontispiece of his book titled *Contemporary Netsuke – The H.I.H. Prince Takamado Collection.*

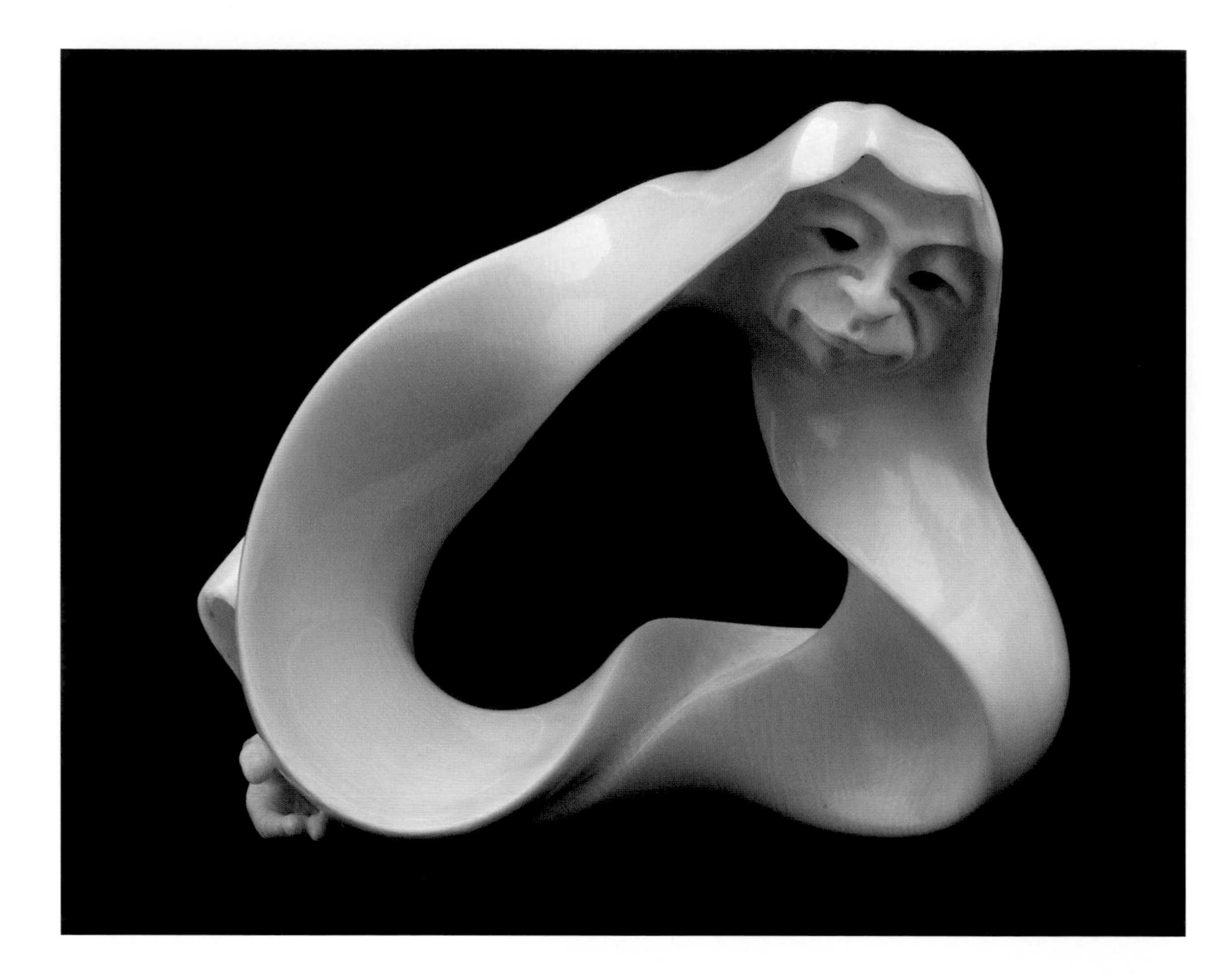

Apart from his face only Daruma's hand, extended from his kimono sleeve is portrayed.

TO THE COLLECTOR MICHAEL WROTE

It is the trickiest face I have ever achieved and well I'm rather proud of that slightly enigmatic expression he's wearing.

MHB

The Foxy Daruma

Double Möbius.
Hippopotamus incisor.
Eyes in drawn crystal rod.
Height 5.0cm Width 6.0cm. 1996.

Exhibited & Illustrated The Carvings of Michael Henry Birch I.N.S.C. Honolulu 1997.

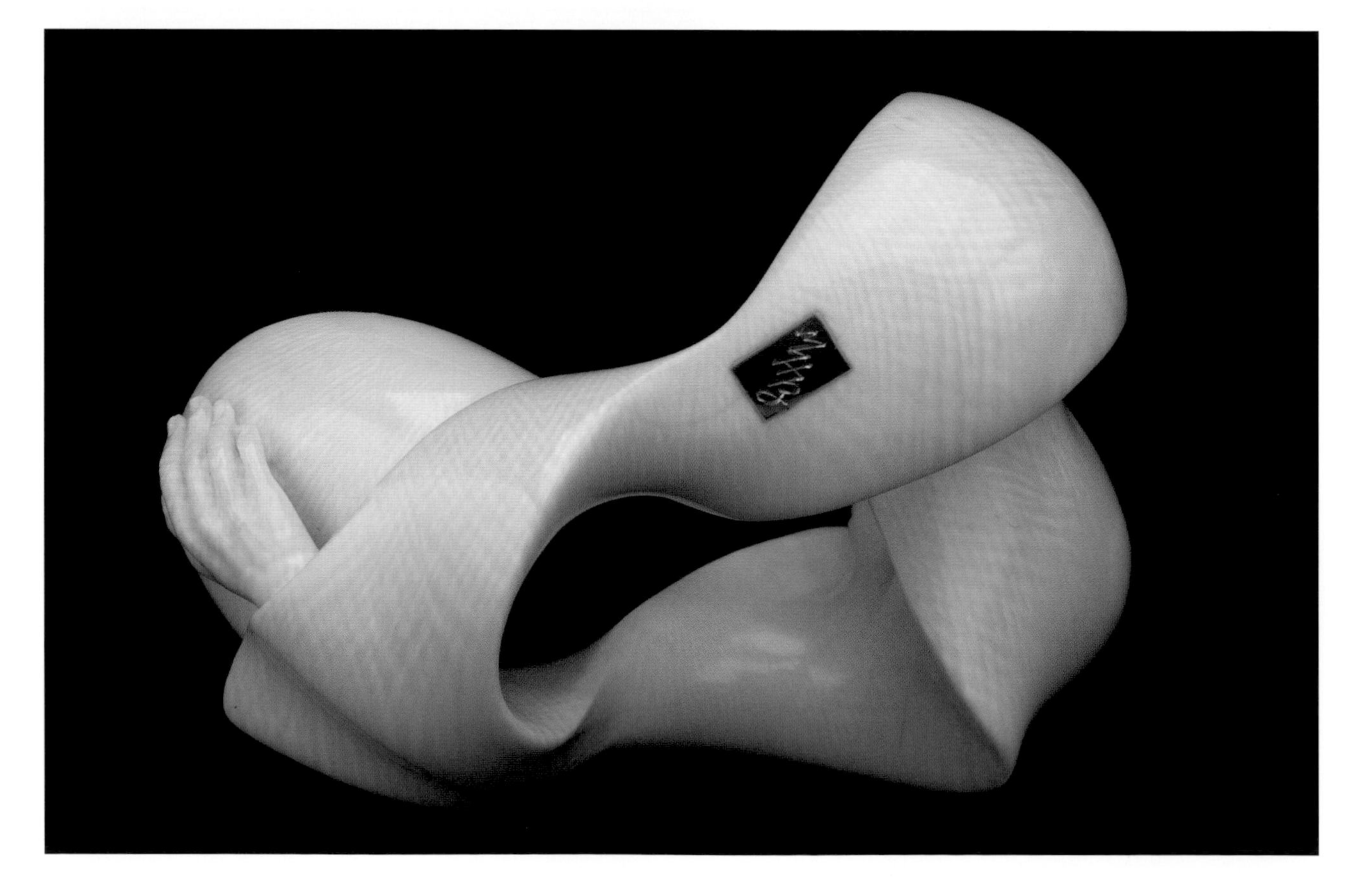

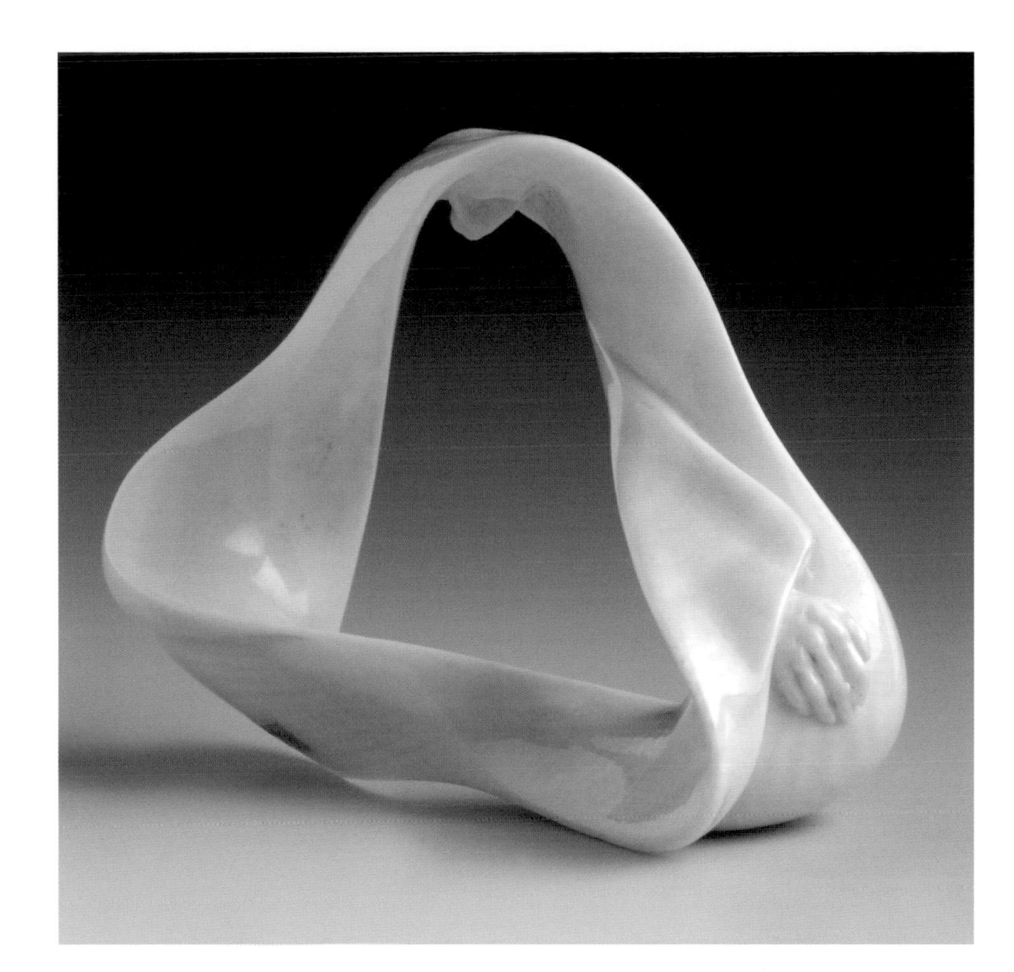

Vestiges of Daruma

Double Möbius.
Siberian Mammoth ivory.
Height 4.0cm Width 5.5cm. 1995.

Illustrated Michael Birch (Part Duex) and Others by Nicolas Westover Euronetsuke 2009.

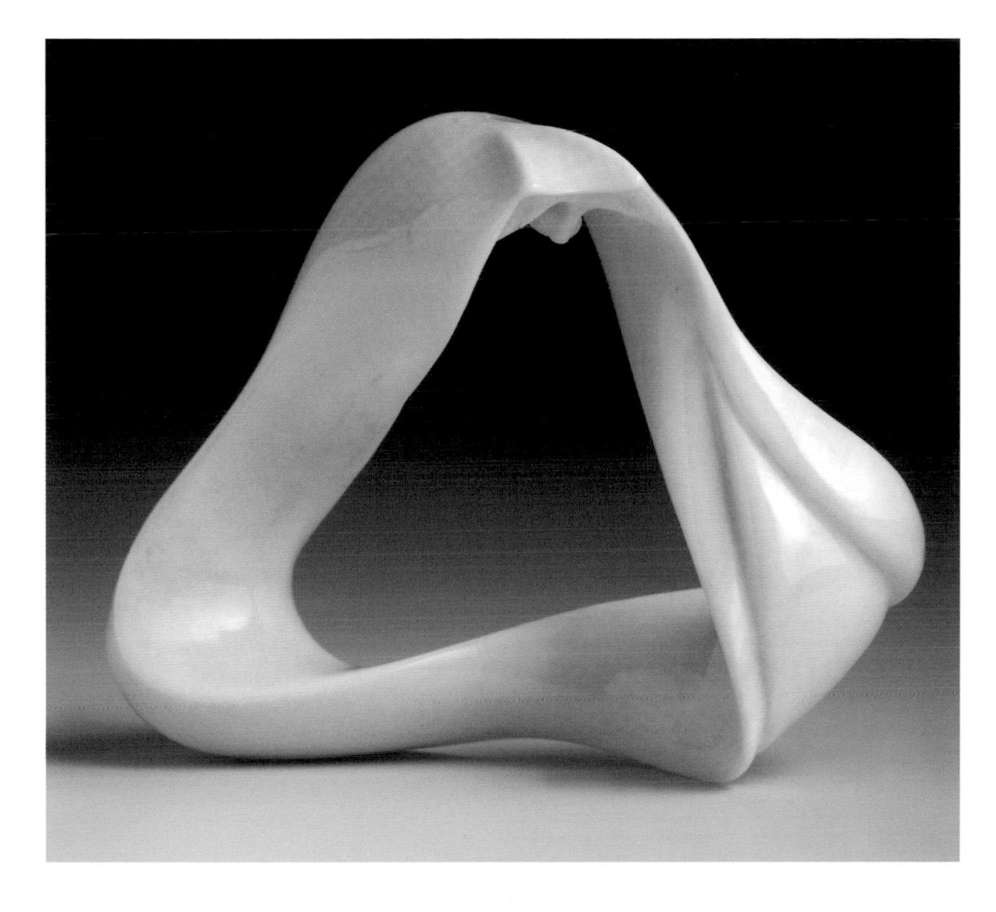

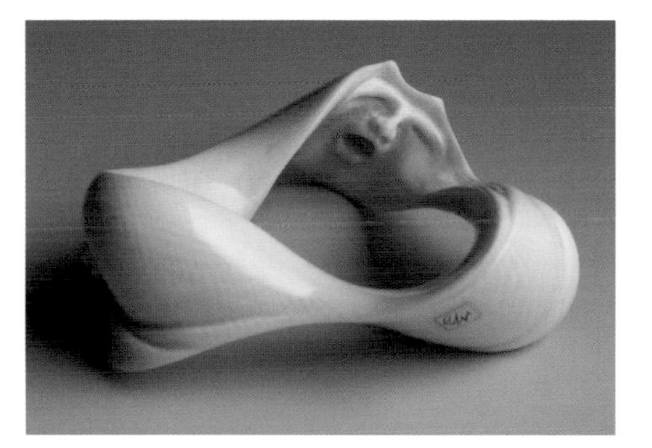

ACTUAL SIZE

Carved from an ancient fish-net sinker Michael found in 1975 on the Honolulu seabed at a depth of 50 feet, it took years to dry out.

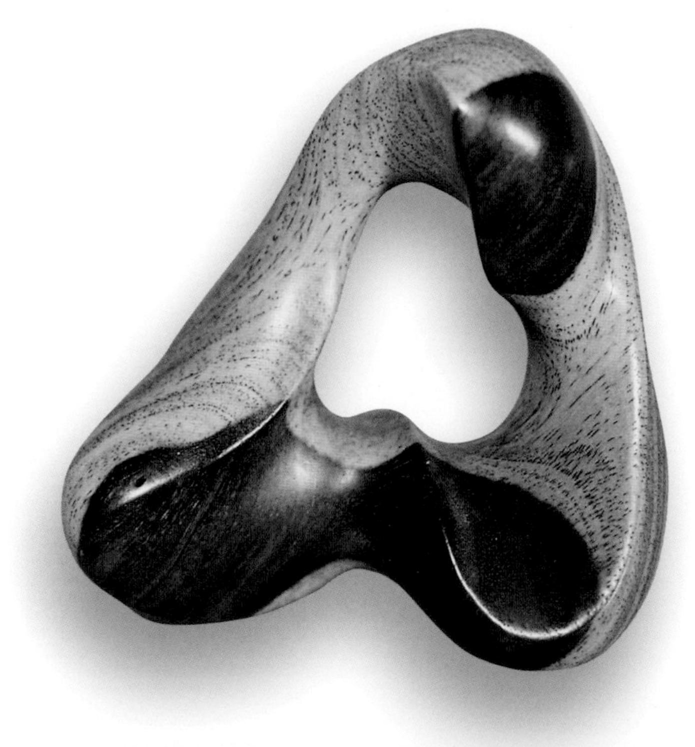

The Six Faces of Daruma

Single Mobius.
Lignum Vitae.
Height 6.4cm. 1996.

Exhibited & Illustrated The Carvings of Michael Henry Birch I.N.S.C. Honolulu 1997.

Exhibited & Illustrated Contemporary Netsuke The Kinsey Collection Accompanied by H.I.H. Prince Takamado Collection by Robert O. Kinsey Chiba City Museum of Art Japan. 2001.

Daruma Meditating

Single Möbius.
Pink ivory wood.
Height 5.4cm Width 5.4cm. 2003.

Exhibited & Illustrated Netsuke Sculptures by Michael Henry Birch I.N.S.C. Honolulu 2004.

Echoes in Daruma's Heart

Lacquered pink ivory wood.
Height 4.3cm. 1996.

Exhibited & Illustrated The Carvings of Michael Henry Birch I.N.S.C. Honolulu 1997.

Exhibited & Illustrated Tactiles by Michael Henry Birch, I.N.S.C. Boston 2001.

Exhibited & Illustrated Netsuke Sculptures by Michael Henry Birch I.N.S.C. Honolulu 2004.

Snowman Daruma

Botswana cow-elephant ivory. Eyes in jet.
Height 5cm. C.1983.

IN HIS LETTER TO THE COLLECTOR MICHAEL WROTE:
This netsuke is carved from African elephant ivory and this is evidenced by the 'engine-turned decussating appearance' as T. K. Perriman of the Pitt Rivers Museum in Oxford describes it. The tusk came from Botswana and was recorded as a 'cow-elephant incisor tusk'.
I used a section from the upper half of the tusk to carve your netsuke. The decussive pattern is bilaterally symmetrical on the netsuke, and is quite pronounced. I have also deliberately left a trace of the central nerve, so it is easy to get an impression of the diameter of the section of the tusk I have used from the markings I have described.
These markings, or configuration, emphasise the 'ivoriness' of the piece, which is important in a carving whose surface has not been engraved with hair-work or other simulated texture. As for the subject matter:
This netsuke is rather more in the nature of a 'carver's piece' than a 'dealer's piece'. This is not very easy to explain except to say that it is the very kind of netsuke I would expect to swap with another carver for an anecdotal piece carved by him (or her). . . it is a combination of quotations, one might say: It represents, basically a snowman Daruma, which is a popular subject with children in Japan. It is also, in a sense, an objet trouvé, a pebble, which has superficially been converted into a subject-matter netsuke by carving a hand-print and adding a pair of eyes — a fortuitous 'found object' in other words. It is also a predominantly tactile piece — a fingertip fits snugly into the yawning mouth concavity, the pearl eyes provide a meniscus pair for the fingertips to stroke and the whole piece itself is a large contemplative hand-bead.

MHB

For these four carvings, Michael greatly simplified the subject to represent Toy Daruma for children

Snowman Daruma

Elephant ivory. Eyes in pearls.
1983.

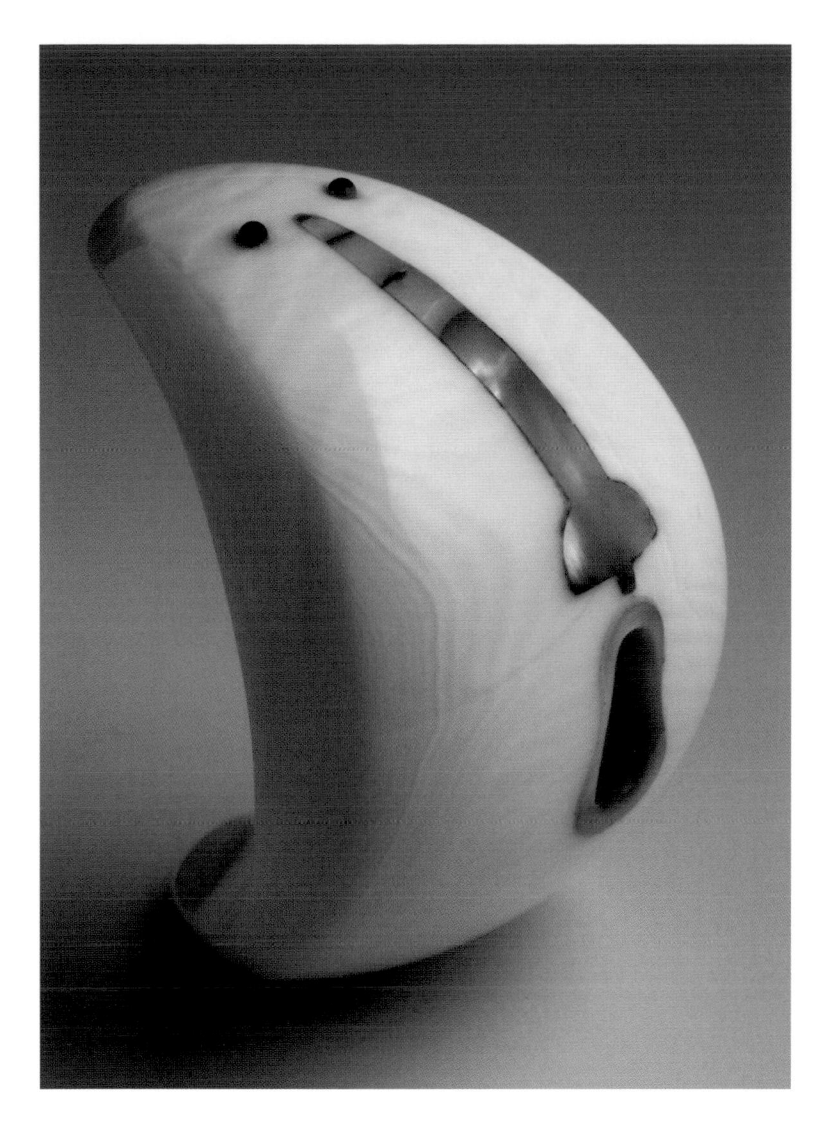

Daruma seen yawning

Elephant ivory, mother-of-pearl and abalone. Eyes in drawn crystal rod.
Height 3.5cm.

Illustrated Michael Birch (Part Duex) and Others
Nicholas Westover Euronetsuke 2009.

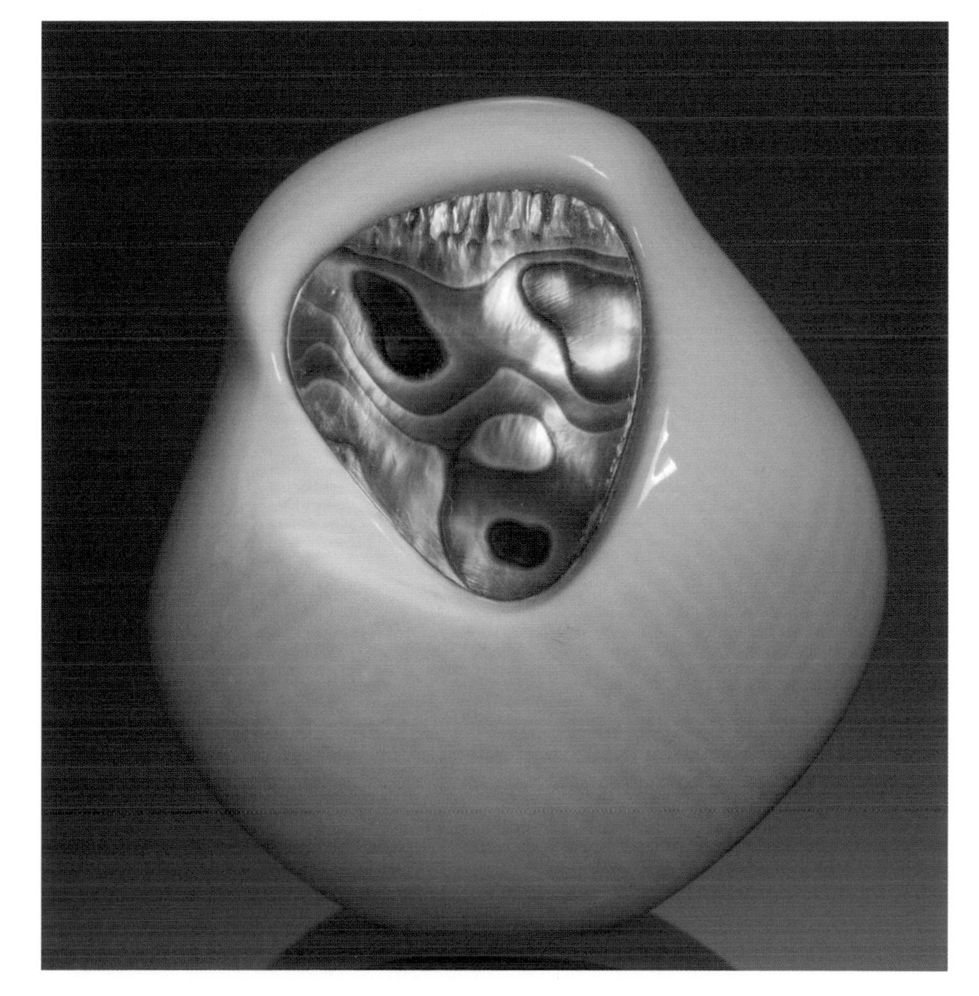

Daruma

Elephant ivory and abalone.
Height 4.9cm. C.1983.

It was the natural markings on the abalone shell that suggested the yawning face of Daruma.

Shaman

Eland horn and olive wood. Eyes in drawn crystal rod.

Height 7.8cm. 1998.

Exhibited & Illustrated Tactiles by Michael Henry Birch I.N.S.C. Chicago 1999.

Exhibited & Illustrated Tactiles by Michael Henry Birch I.N.S.C. Boston 2001.

The shaman is at one with his esoteric spirit of medicine.

MHB

The Wizard

Stag antler. Greater kudu horn tip. Eyes in drawn crystal rod.
Height c.9.5cm. 1993.

Exhibited & Illustrated The Carvings of Michael Henry Birch I.N.S.C. Honolulu 1997.

Exhibited & Illustrated Tactiles by Michael Henry Birch I.N.S.C. Boston 2001.

Exhibited & Illustrated Netsuke Sculptures by Michael Henry Birch I.N.S.C. Honolulu 2004.

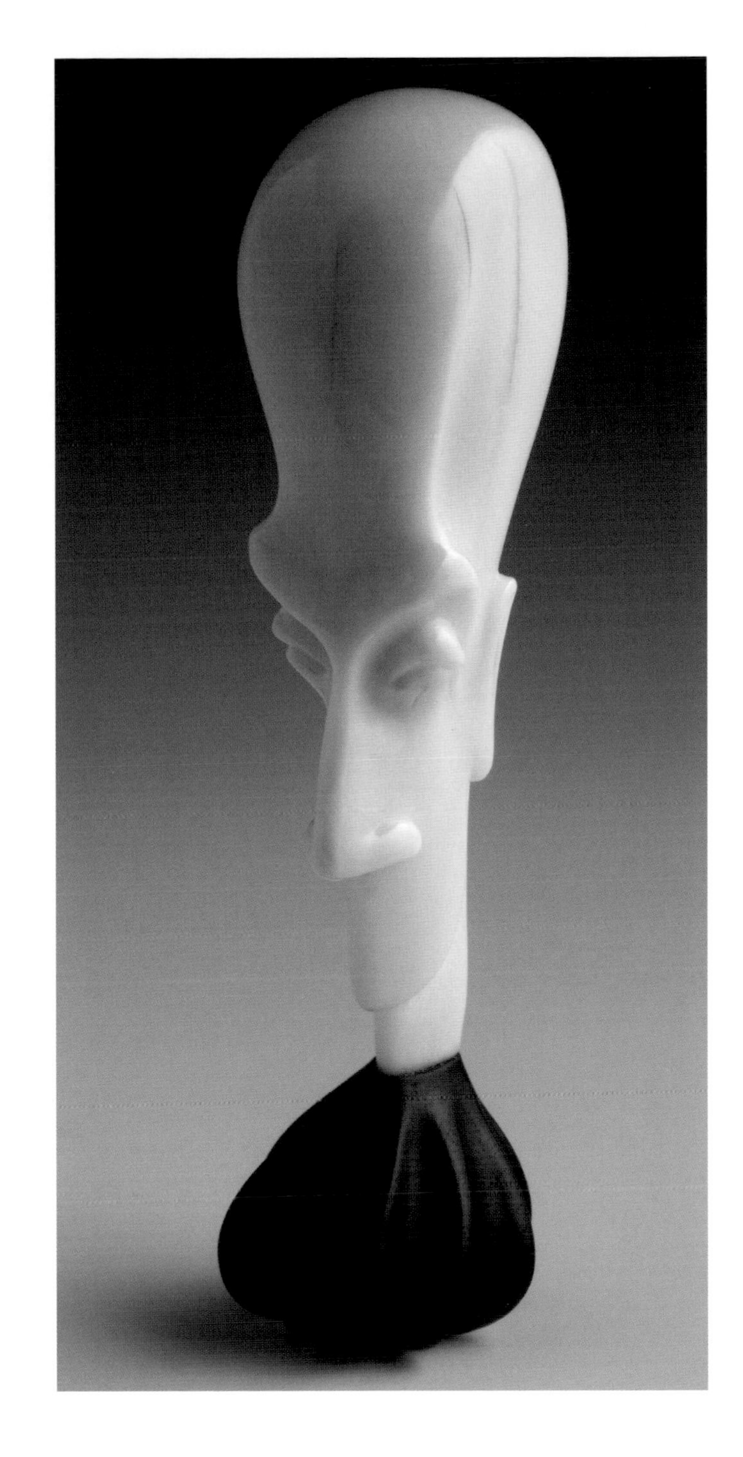

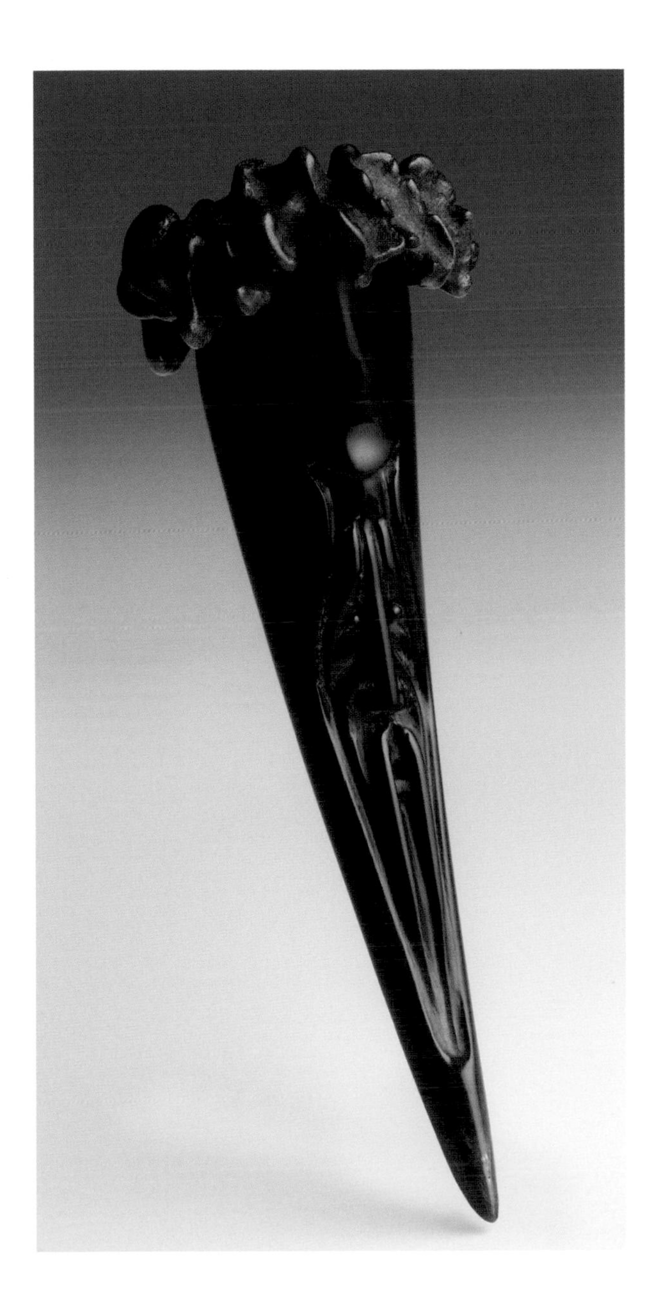

Portrait of an Ancestor

Tip of kudu horn. Headgear is a stag antler coronet. Eyes in drawn crystal rod. When reversed, the netsuke depicts Fukurokuju.
Height 10.0cm. 1996.

Exhibited & Illustrated Tactiles by Michael Henry Birch I.N.S.C. Boston 2001.

Portrait of My Father

Hippopotamus incisor on wooden stand.
Height 9.2cm. 1994.

Exhibited The Carvings of Michael Henry Birch N.K.C. New York 1995.

Exhibited Michael Birch Netsuke Carver and Sculptor National College of Art & Design Dublin 1997.

Exhibited & Illustrated Tactiles by Michael Henry Birch I.N.S.C. Boston 2001.

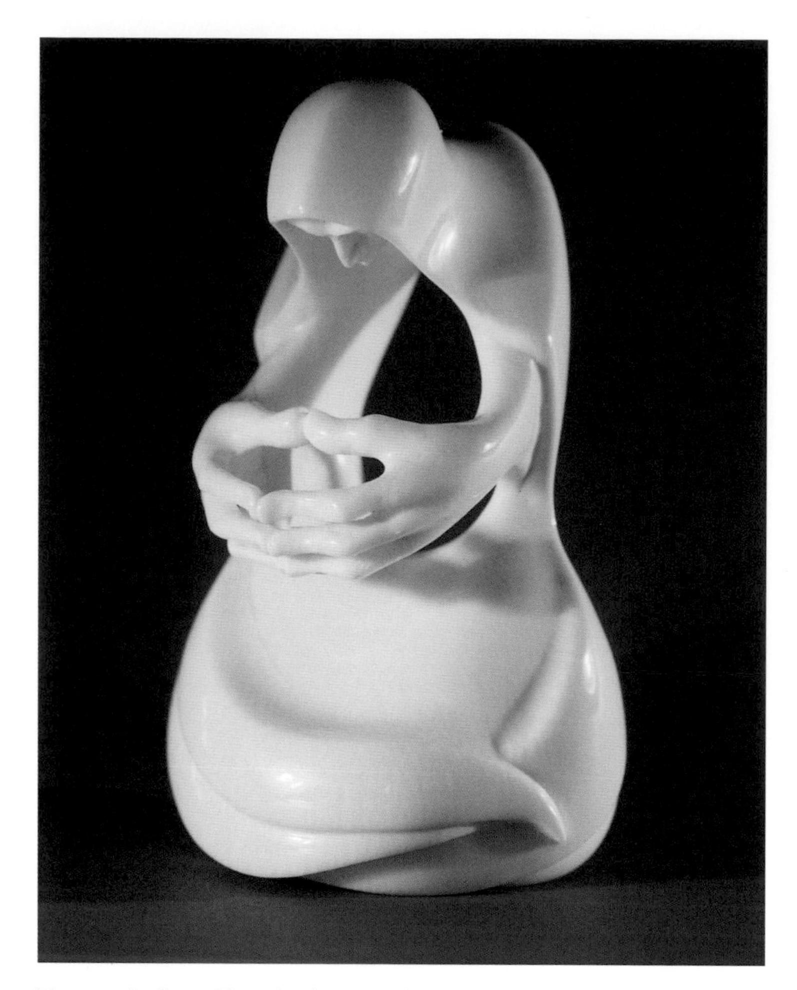

This was the first of four that he created.

Examples of a wide-spread unconscious body language, a gesture frequently displayed by persons instinctively desiring to appear sincere, trustworthy, knowledgeable, relaxed, self-assured, unemotional and, among other things, at ease with the world. Alternatively, it can be a useful means of parking one's hands in neutral for a brief period, until they can be put to better use as an animated accompaniment to speech.

MHB

Trust Me

Hippopotamus incisor.
Height 7.2cm. 1997.

Illustrated International Netsuke Society European Chapter Lecture Sotheby's London 1997.

Exhibited & Illustrated Tactiles by Michael Henry Birch I.N.S.C. Chicago 1999.

Exhibited & Illustrated Tactiles by Michael Henry Birch I.N.S.C. Boston 2001.

Trust Me

Siberian mammoth ivory. Eyes in drawn crystal rod.
Height 4.6cm. 1999.

Exhibited & Illustrated Tactiles by Michael Henry Birch I.N.S.C. Chicago 1999.

Illustrated Contemporary Netsuke The H.I.H. Prince Takamado Collection The Tobacco & Salt Museum Tokyo Japan. 2003.

ABOUT THESE 'TRUST ME' PIECES, CHARLES KINSEY HAS WRITTEN:

Approximately 45 years ago I got a formal education in the behavioural sciences and Industrial Design / Architecture. I studied under the late R. Buckminster Fuller, Bucky was noted for giving lectures that would go on for hours. He often would give these lectures while standing up with his eyes closed and just go on for hours about World Design Science and "Planet Earth". One of his favorite subjects was "Thinking out Loud" which later became the title of one of his books. He was hard to take your eyes off of while he was talking. He would hold his hands up in front of himself with his fingers together without touching often for hours. While working in his office one day I asked him what the hand thing was all about. He said that he felt that it helped him keep focused on his subject matter and expressed how confident he was with his thought process. He was continually thinking and developing thoughts. This hand positioning left a large impression on me and I have noticed many very successful people hold their hands in this manner when expressing ideas. It could be a sign of arrogance, confidence, assertiveness, but is a trait that is very strong.

Michael Birch netsuke pieces of "Trust Me" are a strong statement of the deep thinking of the artist. Many netsuke artists display their skill of carving and talent as true artist in the work that they produce. Michael does much more, he expresses his sense of humor as well as his deep thought into the science of body language.

The pieces that he created reflect his study of the behavioral science which he observed over time. Michael expresses his complexity of thought that went into the creation of each piece. I had many discussions with him as to what was the genesis behind these pieces and he expressed that he had indeed made a strong statement of the thought process behind this human behavior. The Michael Birch Netsuke pieces "Trust Me" make you stop and think.

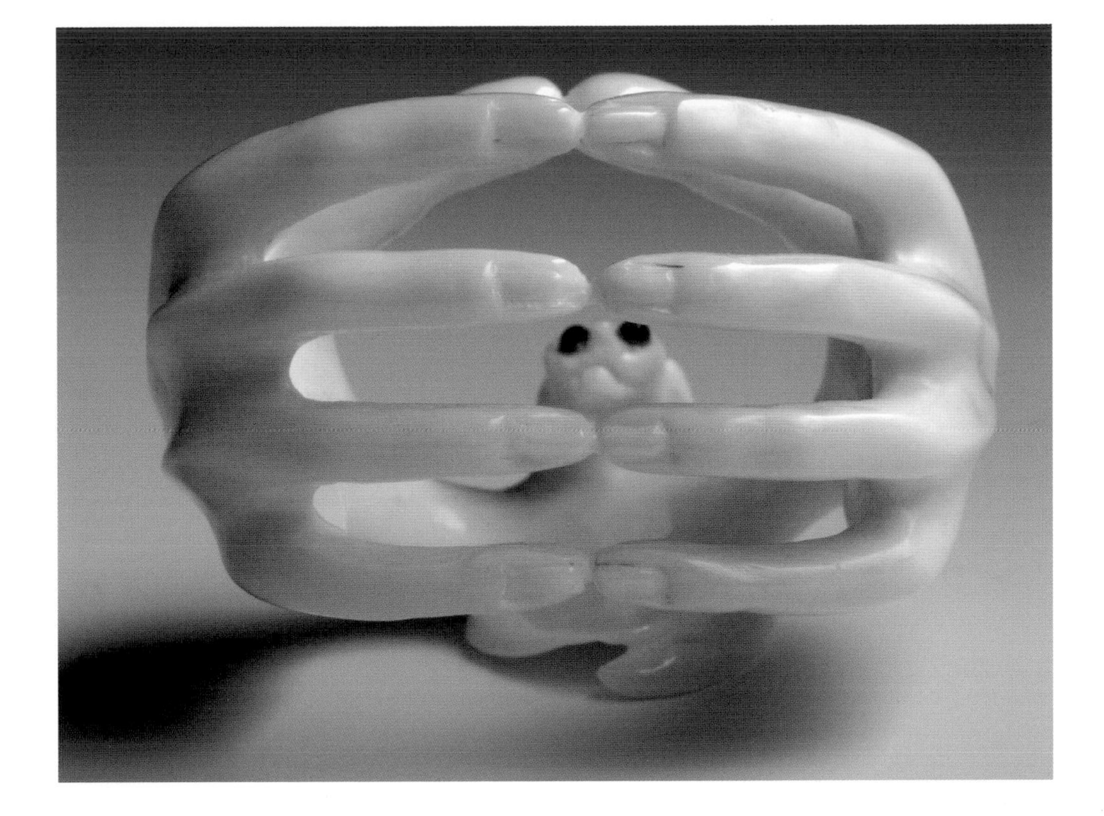

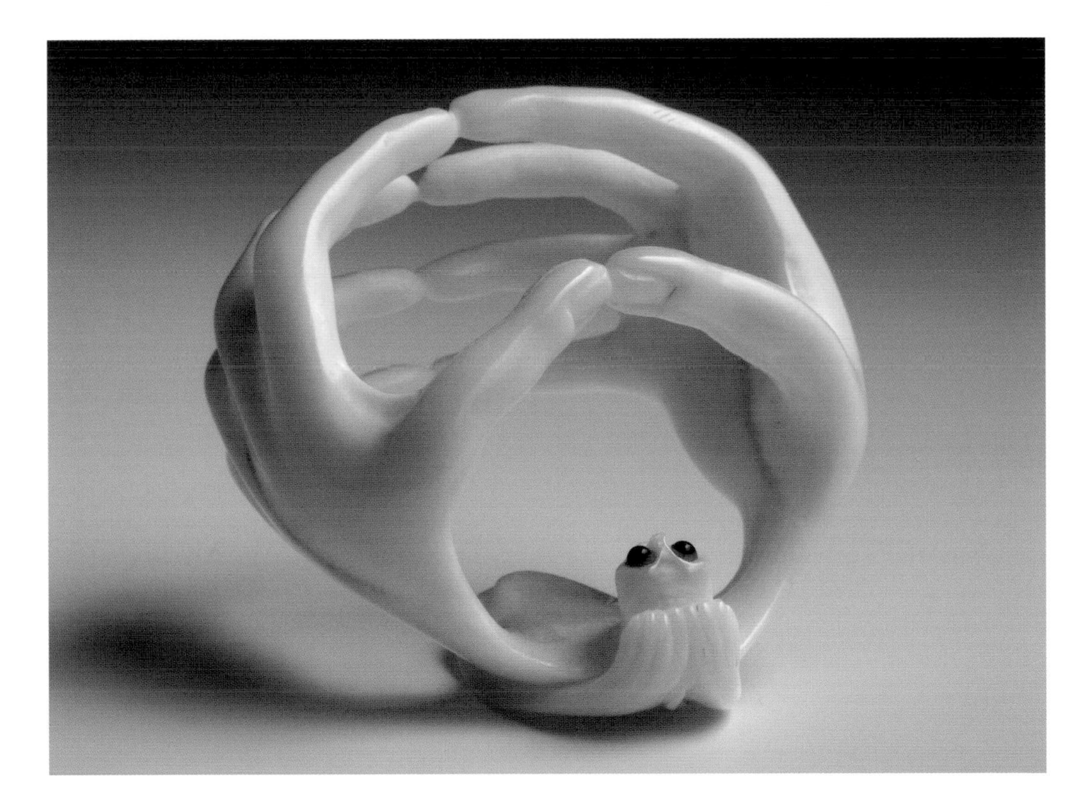

Even motivated ghosts do it

Hippopotamus incisor. Eyes double inlaid in drawn crystal rod.
Height 3.0cm Width 4.3cm. 2000.

Exhibited & Illustrated Tactiles by Michael Henry Birch I.N.S.C. Boston 2001

Myths & Legends

Mythology of China and Japan is a rich source of inspiration for many netsuke carvers and Michael was no different. Included in this group are Ashinaga and Tenaga the model of mutual self-help, Baku the nightmare-snatching elephant-like animal, the shape-shifting fox that transforms in a human figure, Kappa the amphibious monster with a penchant for young girls, the Chinese Kirin, Mermaids, Karashishi the Chinese the lion-dogs, Shojo the cheerful drunk, Tanuki the mischievous badger-like creature and the bird-like Tengu. Michael also created the two Greek legendary figures of a Centaur and a Satyr.

The Baku is a mythical Chinese animal that uses its elephant-like trunk to snatch bad dreams and nightmares from the air. Images and depictions are given to wish the recipient 'sweet dreams'.

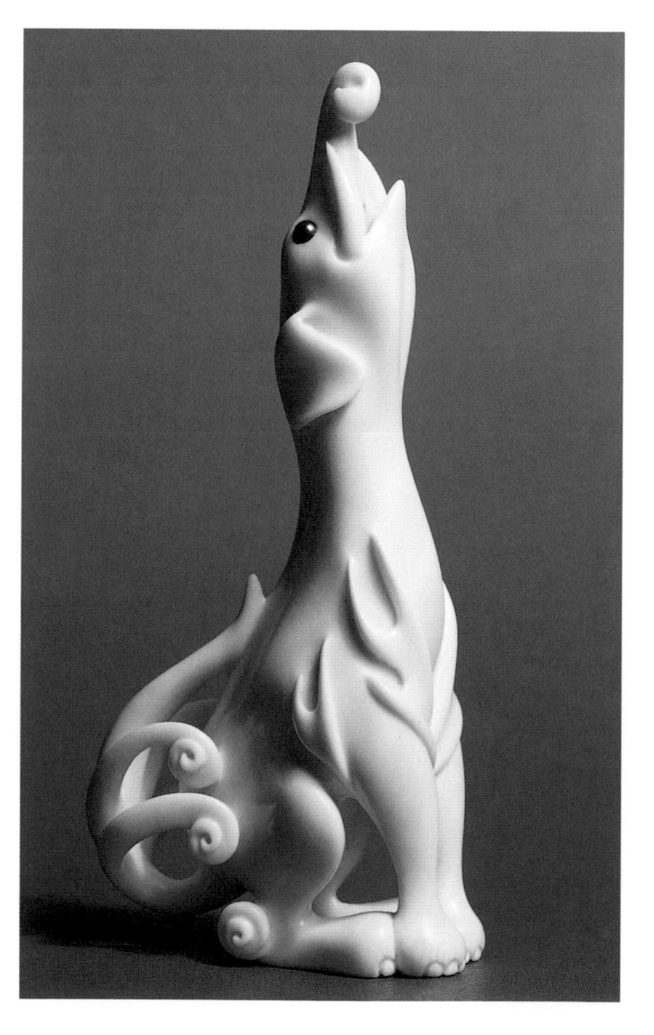

Baku

Elephant ivory. Eyes in mussel pearls.
Height 10.3cm. 1978.

Illustrated I.N.C.S.J. Vol. 6 No. 3 1978.

Exhibited N.K.C. Minneapolis 1979.

Illustrated lecture Notion to Netsuke Minneapolis 1979.

Exhibited N.K.C. Honolulu 1983.

Illustrated Graphics World October 1993.

ACTUAL SIZE

Baku

Seal netsuke.
Rhinoceros horn.
Eyes in drawn glass rod.
Height 7.9cm. 1977.

Exhibited N.K.C. Kansas City 1977.

Exhibited Sotheby's Bond St. London. 1994.

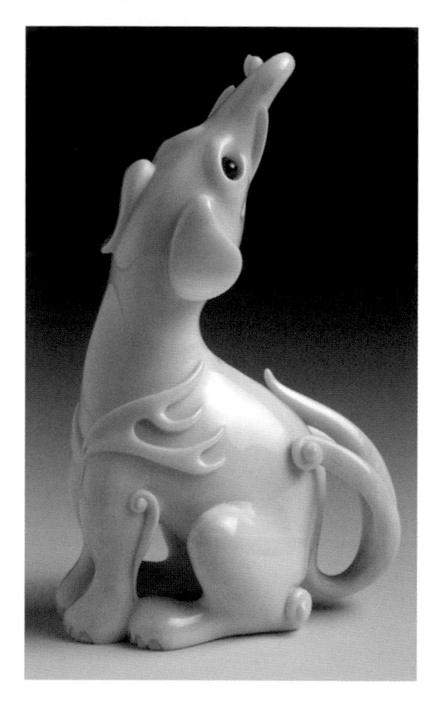

ACTUAL SIZE

Baku

Elephant ivory. Black mussel pearl eyes.
Height 9.0cm. 1983.

Illustrated Ivory an International History and Illustrated Survey Published by Harry N. Abrams Inc. New York 1987.

Exhibited & Illustrated London Netsuke Fair and Convention 1990.

Exhibited Sotheby's Bond St. London. 1994.

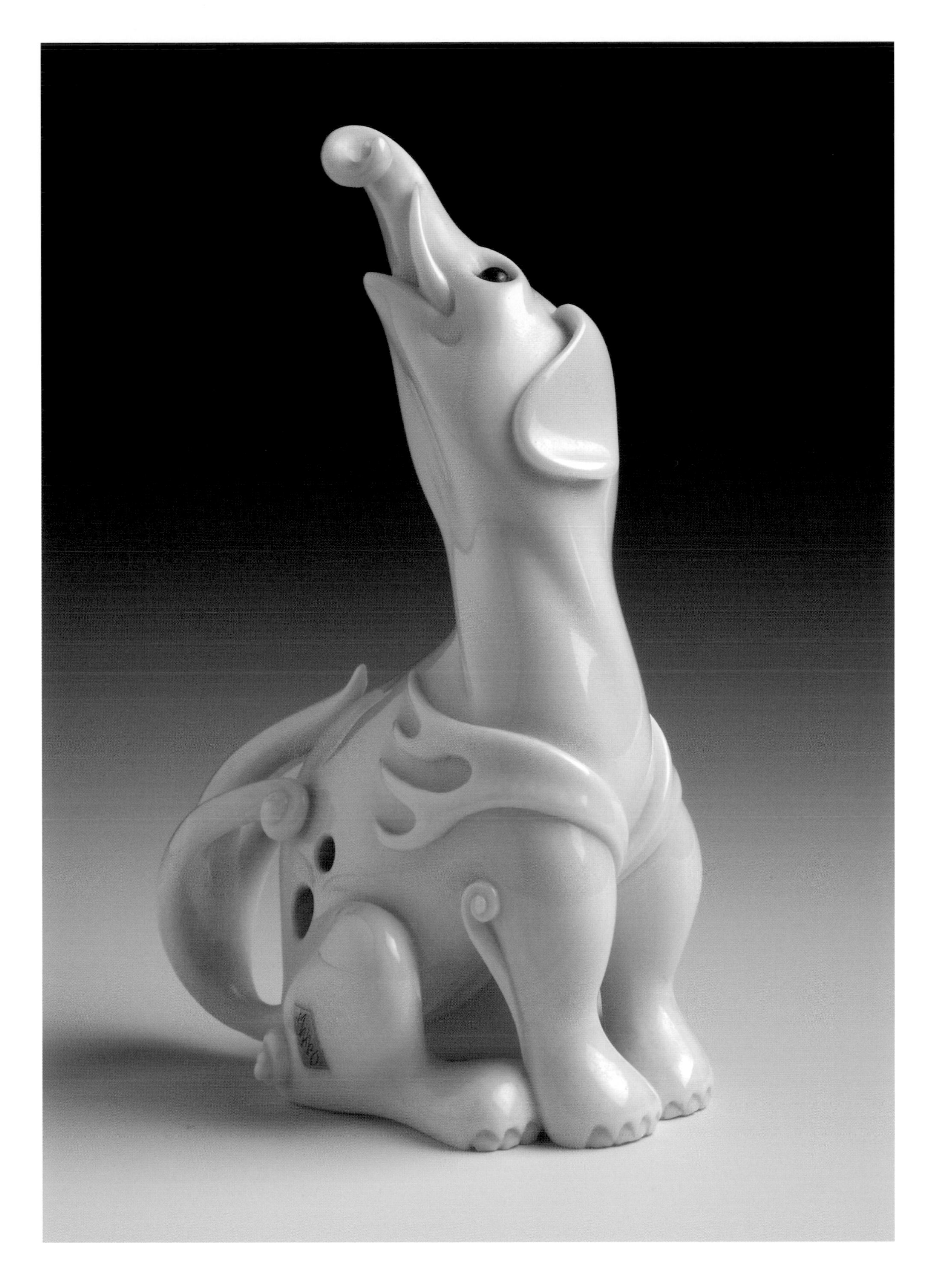

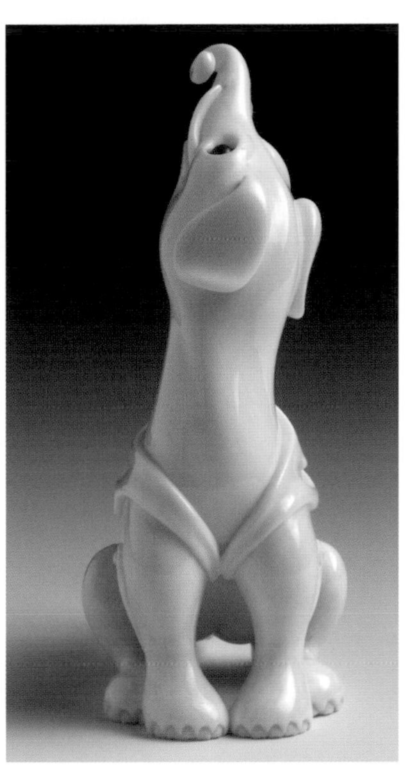

ACTUAL SIZE

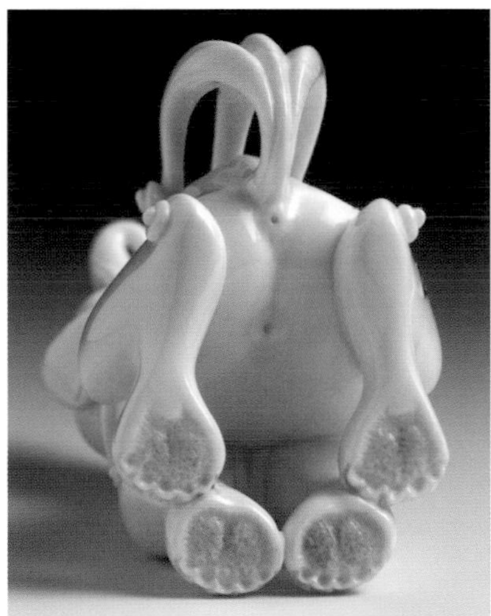

Netsuke are always carved in the round and the underneath of the carving, normally unseen in sculptures, is just as important as the rest.

Baku

Stained boxwood. Mussel pearl eyes.
1979.

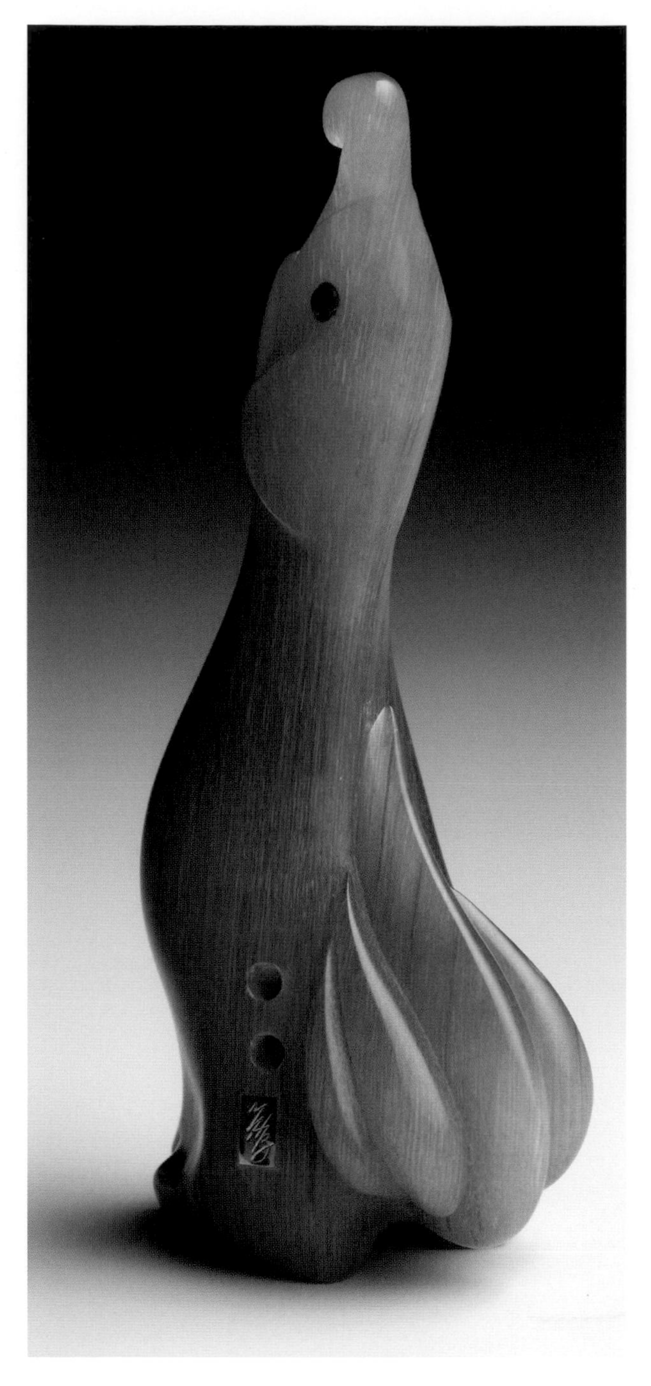

Baku

Rhinoceros horn. Eyes in ruby cabochon.
Height 9.5cm. 1980.

Exhibited Netsuke by Birch London Netsuke Convention 1980.

Exhibited Michael Birch Netsuke Carver and Sculptor National College of Art & Design Dublin 1997.

An eager, but ailing, collector supplied a boar's tusk necklace and left the subject of the carving to Michael.

I did agonise for quite a while over the best subject to select for this important piece. The stereotype crab, snail or centipede Iwami style obviously would not do. It came to me a few days later, when it struck me that one of the nicest things that a husband could wish for his wife is to have happy dreams – and what better companion than a friendly baku?

MHB

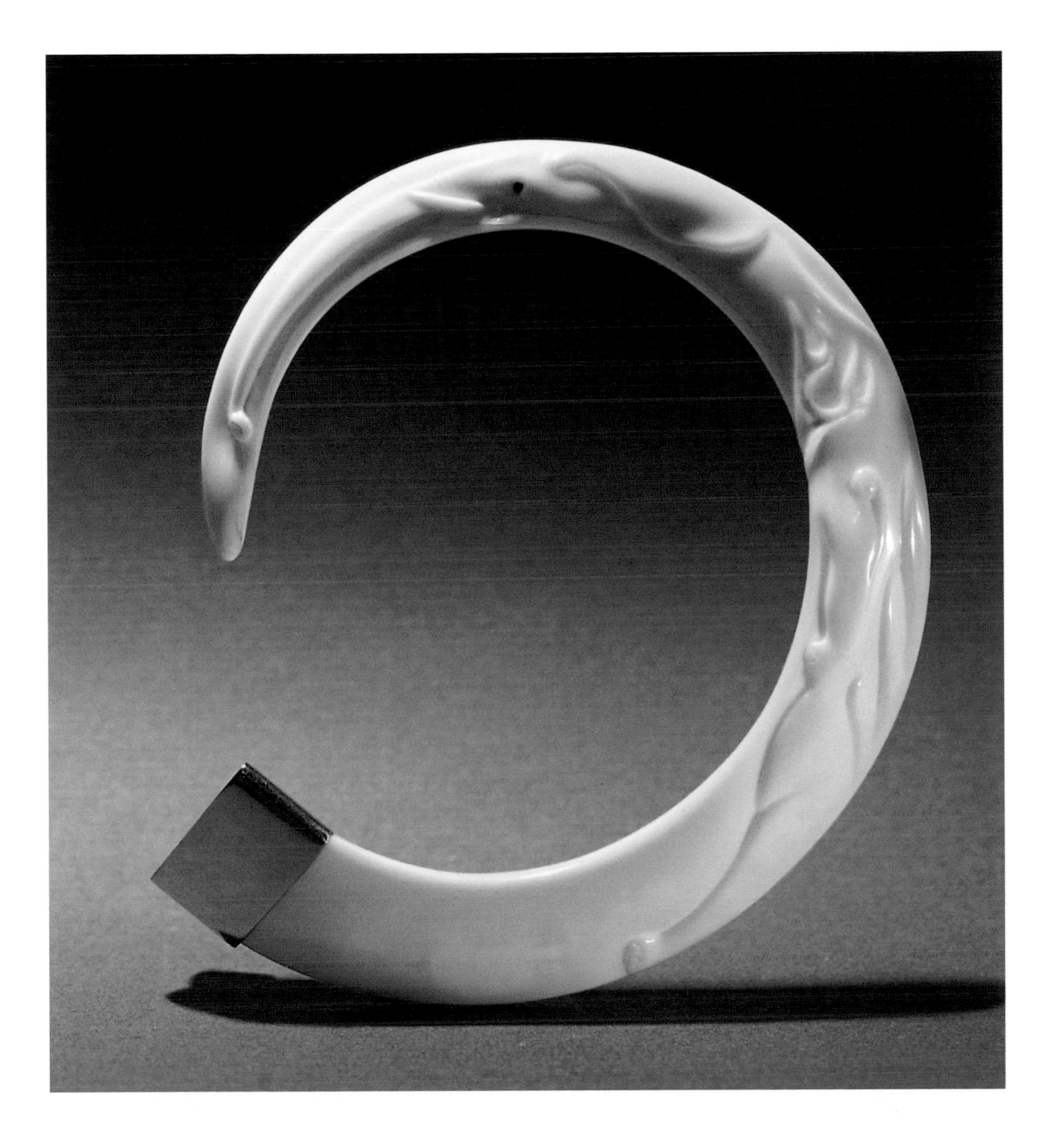

Michael's design decision was confirmed as the correct one when he received a letter from the collector's wife:

Your letter gave [him] a spark of energy. He couldn't wait to see the carving. Michael, your subject could not have been any better. . . This baku has become one of the most important things in my life now.
I had not worn the boar's tooth more than a few times a year, I now wear it almost daily and always keep pointing it at [my husband]. . . and. . . telling the Baku that he is hungry and must eat all the bad dreams.

Baku

Boar's tusk with mussel pearl eye.
1998.

Yet another myth prevalent in many cultures is that of the shape-shifting fox that turns into a human at dusk, reverting to a fox at dawn.

Michael portrayed this subject both as male and female figures in mid-transformation.

Shape-shifting Fox

Mastodon. Definitions of body, limbs, tail and hat in wood and inlaid lacquer. Eyes in mother-of-pearl and inlaid lacquer.

Height 8.3cm. 1996.

Exhibited Michael Henry Birch Sculptures 11th Vienna Netsuke Symposium Galerie Zacke Vienna Austria. 1997.

Exhibited & Illustrated Netsuke Sculptures by Michael Henry Birch I.N.S.C. Honolulu 2004.

ACTUAL SIZE

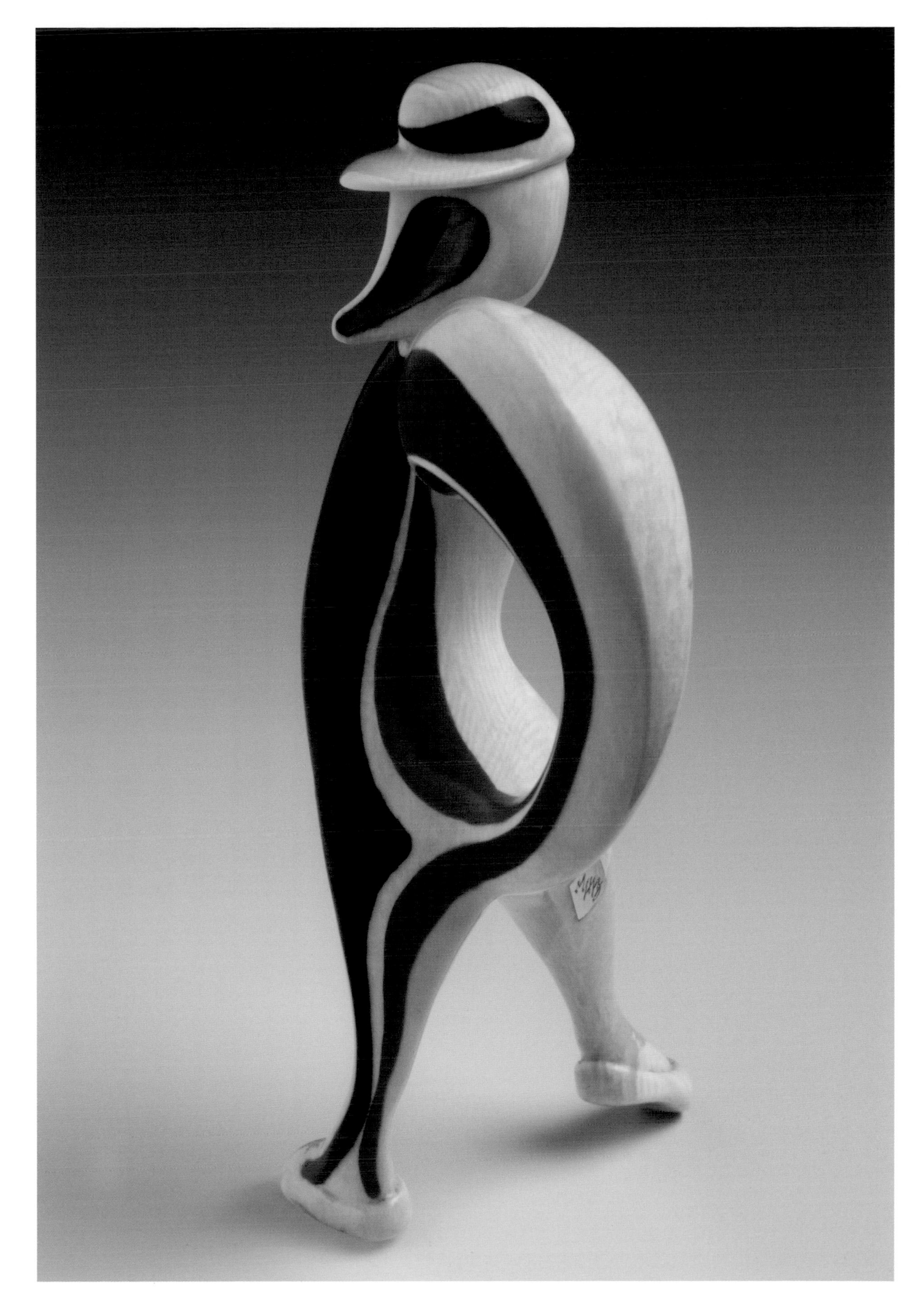

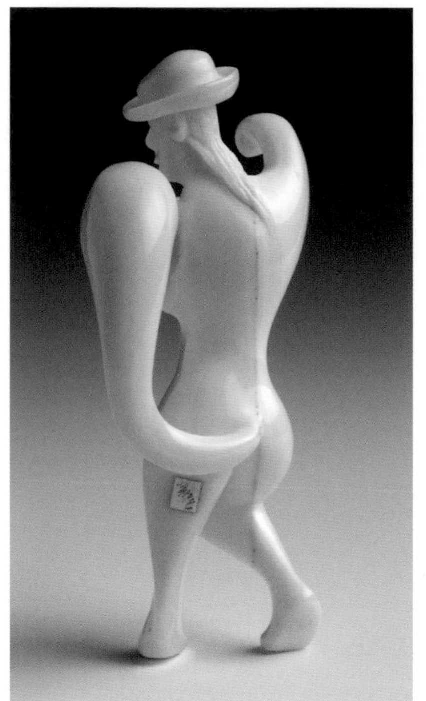

ACTUAL SIZE

Dancing Girl Fox

Hippopotamus incisor. Inlaid black lacquer eyes.

Height 8.0cm. 1999.

Exhibited & Illustrated Tactiles by Michael Henry Birch I.N.S.C. Boston 2001.

Exhibited & Illustrated Netsuke Sculptures by Michael Henry Birch I.N.S.C. Honolulu 2004.

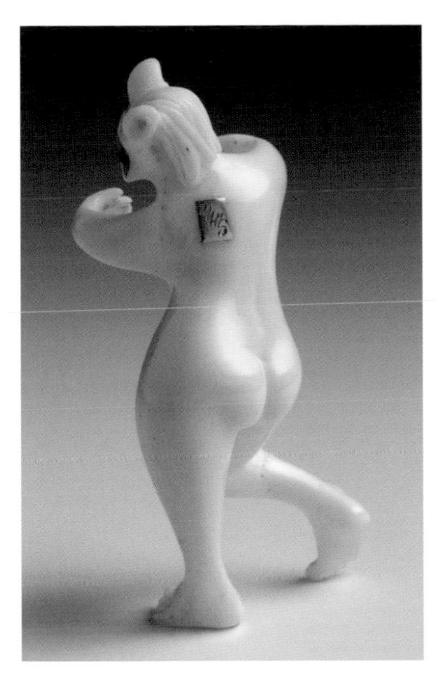

ACTUAL SIZE

Dancing Woman Fox

Hippopotamus incisor. Facial markings in inlaid black lacquer. Eyes in drawn crystal rod.

Height 7.2cm. 2003.

Exhibited & Illustrated Netsuke Sculptures by Michael Henry Birch I.N.S.C. Honolulu 2004.

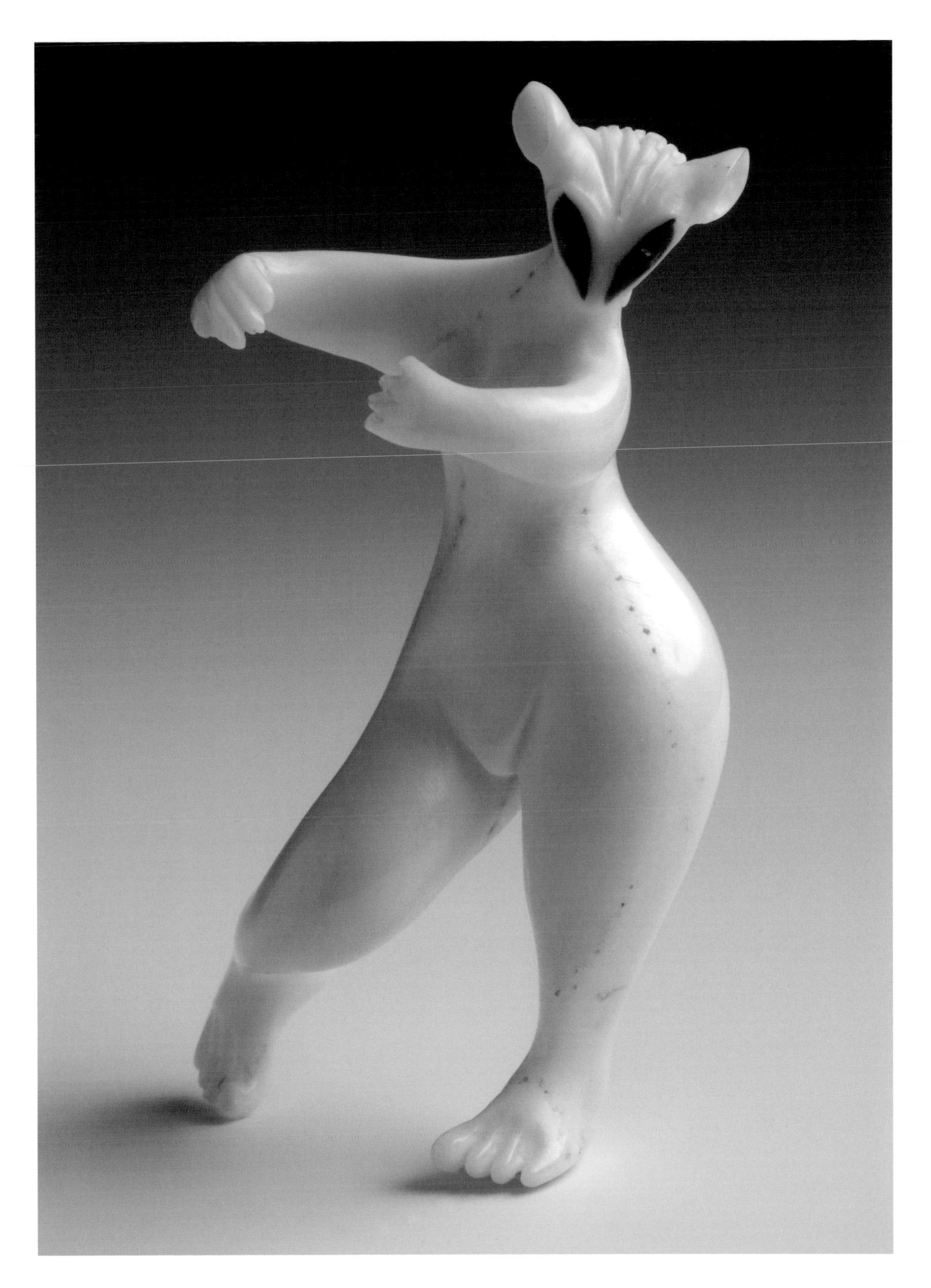

I Saw This Fox

Siberian mammoth ivory.
Facial markings in inlaid black lacquer.
Eyes in drawn crystal rod.
Height 8.0cm. 1998.

Exhibited & Illustrated Tactiles by Michael Henry Birch I.N.S.C. Chicago 1999.

Illustrated The Poetry of Netsuke by Robert O. Kinsey 2004.

Michael wrote the following poem to accompany the netsuke

It was midnight in the forest
When I saw this fox
Dancing.
His footwork was light
And the music came
From the wind whistling
Through the quavering aspen leaves.

It was midnight in the forest
When I saw this fox
Glancing.
At the moonbeams
Flickering in cadence
Through the canopy
As he turned into . . . something else.

The Fox Maiden

Macassar ebony. Facial markings in inlaid black lacquer. Eyes in drawn crystal rod.
Height 7.6cm. 1995.

Exhibited & Illustrated The Carvings of Michael Henry Birch I.N.S.C. Honolulu 1997.

The Kappa is a mythical amphibious monster in Japanese legend. It entices children into the water – finding young girls especially delectable – and there it devours them. In districts supposedly inhabited by Kappa the villagers throw cucumbers [his favourite vegetable] into the water at harvest time in order to appease the creatures.

MHB

Kappa

Sashi netsuke.
Stag antler coronet un-carved. Eyes in mussel pearls and drawn crystal rod. Body stained to simulate cucumber skin.
Height 15.2.cm. 1978 & 1994.

Exhibited N.K.C. Minneapolis 1979.

Illustrated lecture Notion to Netsuke Minneapolis 1979.

Exhibited Netsuke by Birch London Netsuke Convention 1980.

Exhibited The Carvings of Michael Henry Birch N.K.C. New York 1995.

Illustrated I.N.S.J. Vol. 16 No. 2 1996.

Illustrated Butterfield & Butterfield Fine Asian Works of Art Auction catalogue 1998.

This is one of the few pieces that Michael re-visited. He first completed the carving in 1978 and exhibited it in 1979 and 1980. Then in 1994 he re-carved the face and stained the body to simulate both the turtle carapace and the skin of a cucumber of which the Kappa is fond.

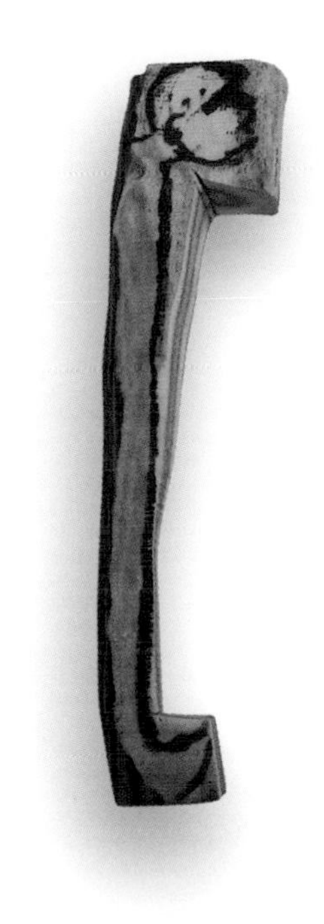

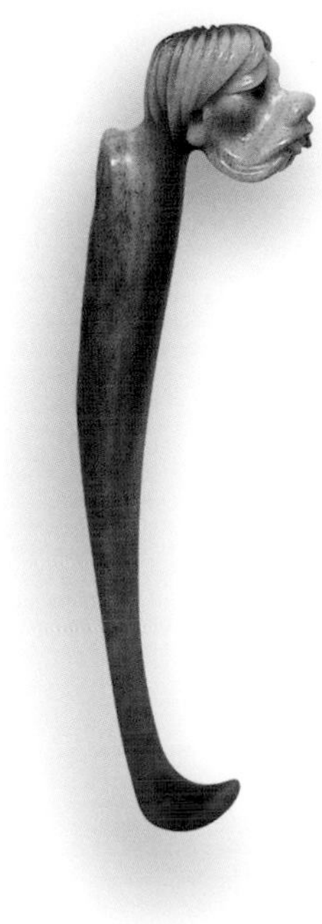

Kappa

Obi netsuke.
Stag antler. Eyes in mussel pearls.
1978.

Illustrated lecture Notion to Netsuke Minneapolis 1979.

Exhibited Netsuke by Birch London Netsuke Convention 1980.

Illustrated London International Convention Handbook London 1984.

Exhibited & Illustrated Michael Henry Birch Sculptures 11th Vienna Netsuke Symposium Galerie Zacke Vienna Austria. 1997.

Kappa

Obi netsuke.
Stag antler. Eyes in amber.
Height 13.5cm. C.1980.

The Kirin is an ancient mythical creature of Chinese origin. Its name is derived from the Chinese words k'i (male animal) and lin (female animal) indicating that this was an hermaphroditic animal. The chronicles describe the Kirin as having the single-horned head of a dragon the body of a deer the legs and hoofs of a horse and the bushy tail of the Chinese Buddhist lion. Its body is covered with hair and its armpits discharge flakes of fire which denote its divine origin. Its colouring is mottled.

Kirin

Rhinoceros horn. Eyes in mussel pearls.
Height 11.0cm. 1975.

Exhibited & Illustrated Michael Birch, Netsuke and Sculpture Eskenazi Oriental Art London 1976.

Exhibited & Illustrated Japanese Netsuke Inro, Ojime. Kiseruzutsu at Midori Gallery Miami 1987.

The netsuke was carved longitudinally from the dark mottled section of the horn surrounding the black pigmented core of the crown.

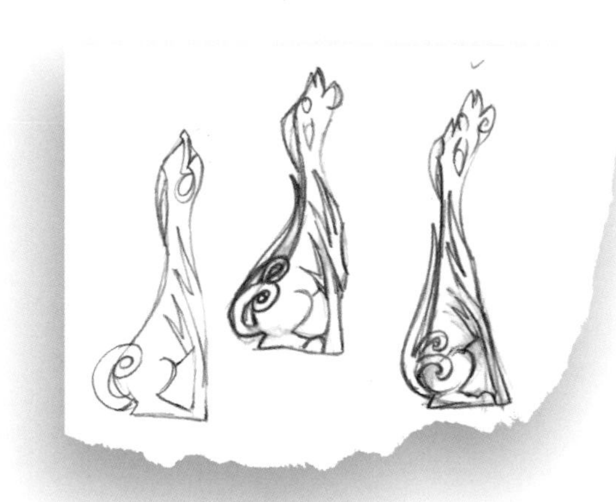

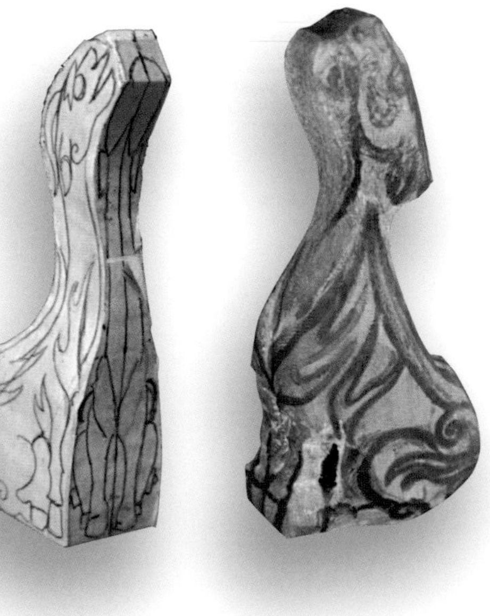

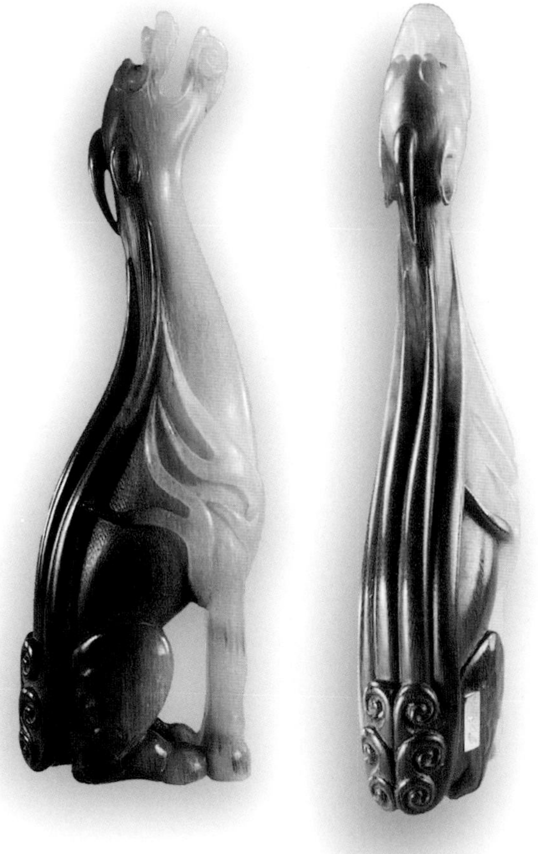

Kirin

Rhinoceros horn. Eyes double inlaid in gold and black onyx.
Height 11.8cm. 1974.

Illustrated I.N.C.S.J. Vol. 4 No. 1 1976.

Exhibited The Carvings of Michael Henry Birch I.N.C.S.C. Honolulu 1977.

Illustrated I.N.C.S.J. Vol. 9 No. 3 1981.

Illustrated Asiatika Kunthaus Zacke Vienna catalogue 1996.

Illustrated Sotheby's London, Japanese Works of Art Prints & Paintings Auction catalogue 2001.

Michael used the paler shade of this two-toned horn to depict the underside of the Kirin.

Ashinaga and Tenaga are the mythical foreigners who came to Japan from a fabled Indian kingdom by way of China and Korea. According to legend, they are skilful fishermen. Ashinaga wades through deep water with his long legs, while Tenaga, riding pick-a-back, gathers their customary diet of seafood with the help of his long arms. Thus they symbolise in Japan the mutual help which people should give to one another.

Michael believed that there was often an imbalance in the benefits derived from the mutual help partnership, that it was too often a 'front' for self-help. He depicted this inequality by the portrayal of Tenaga as significantly fatter than Ashinaga; and by showing racial differences with a perceptive choice of materials, or contemporary facial features versus those of ancient depictions.

In these netsuke the two figures have been simplified to the extent that superfluous limbs have been eliminated altogether.

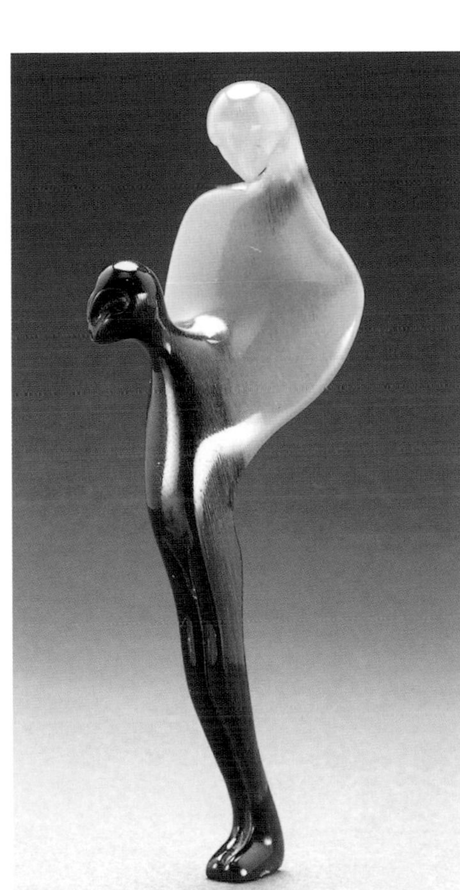

Ashinaga and Tenaga

Rhinoceros horn.
Height 10.5cm. 1975.

Exhibited & Illustrated Michael Birch Netsuke and Sculpture Eskenazi Oriental Art London 1976.

Illustrated Arts of Asia September October 1976.

Carved from a single piece of rare horn in which the heavily pigmented central core is adjacent to the translucent amber-coloured outer ring, without an intervening mottled area, symbolising the common origin of light-skinned and dark-skinned races.

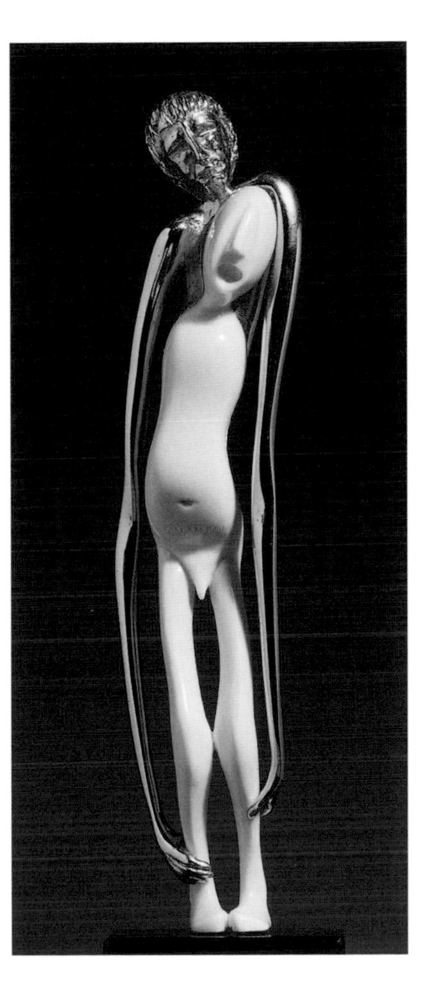

Ashinaga and Tenaga

Gold and elephant ivory (Chryselephantine).
Height 11.9cm. 1975.

Exhibited & Illustrated Michael Birch Netsuke and Sculpture Eskenazi Oriental Art London 1976.

Exhibited N.K.C. Minneapolis 1979.

Illustrated lecture Notion to Netsuke Minneapolis 1979

Tenaga is portrayed with modern features, and Ashinaga with features derived from Japanese stone carvings.

Mermaids

One of the universal myths is that of the mermaid, a beautiful woman, part-human and part-fish. All sea-faring nations have stories of these creatures. Greeks believed they had the ability to raise terrible storms if crossed; in China it was believed that a mermaid's tears turned to pearls; the Polynesians believed that mermaids could create huge storms that frightened fish away from nets; in England, mermaids were thought to have the ability both to foretell and to provoke disaster.

The explorer Christopher Columbus reported that the three mermaids he saw (probably manatees, aquatic plant-eating mammals) were 'not half as beautiful as they are painted.'

Mermaid

Elephant ivory. Hair in rhinoceros horn.

Length 8.5cm. 1976.

This commissioned piece was among those which Michael took to Tokyo in May 1977 to show to the Japanese carvers. It was seen by Raymond Bushell who refused to part with it and swapped it for one of his treasured netsuke, a Namazu Earthquake fish carved in umimatsu by Kaigyokusai.

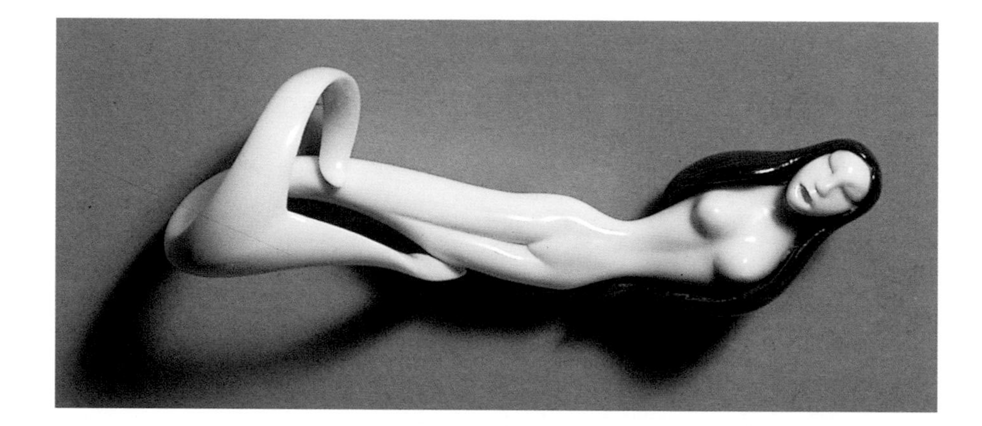

Mermaid

Elephant ivory.
Hair in rhinoceros horn.

Exhibited N.K.C. Kansas City 1977.

Illustrated Christie's New York Auction Catalogue 1985.

This Mermaid was carved to replace the commissioned one which Raymond Bushell acquired before it could be delivered.

Mermaid

Narwhal ivory. Hair in rhinoceros horn.
Length 7.0cm. 1976.

Illustrated Michael Birch (Part Duex) and Others by Nicolas Westover Euronetsuke 2009.

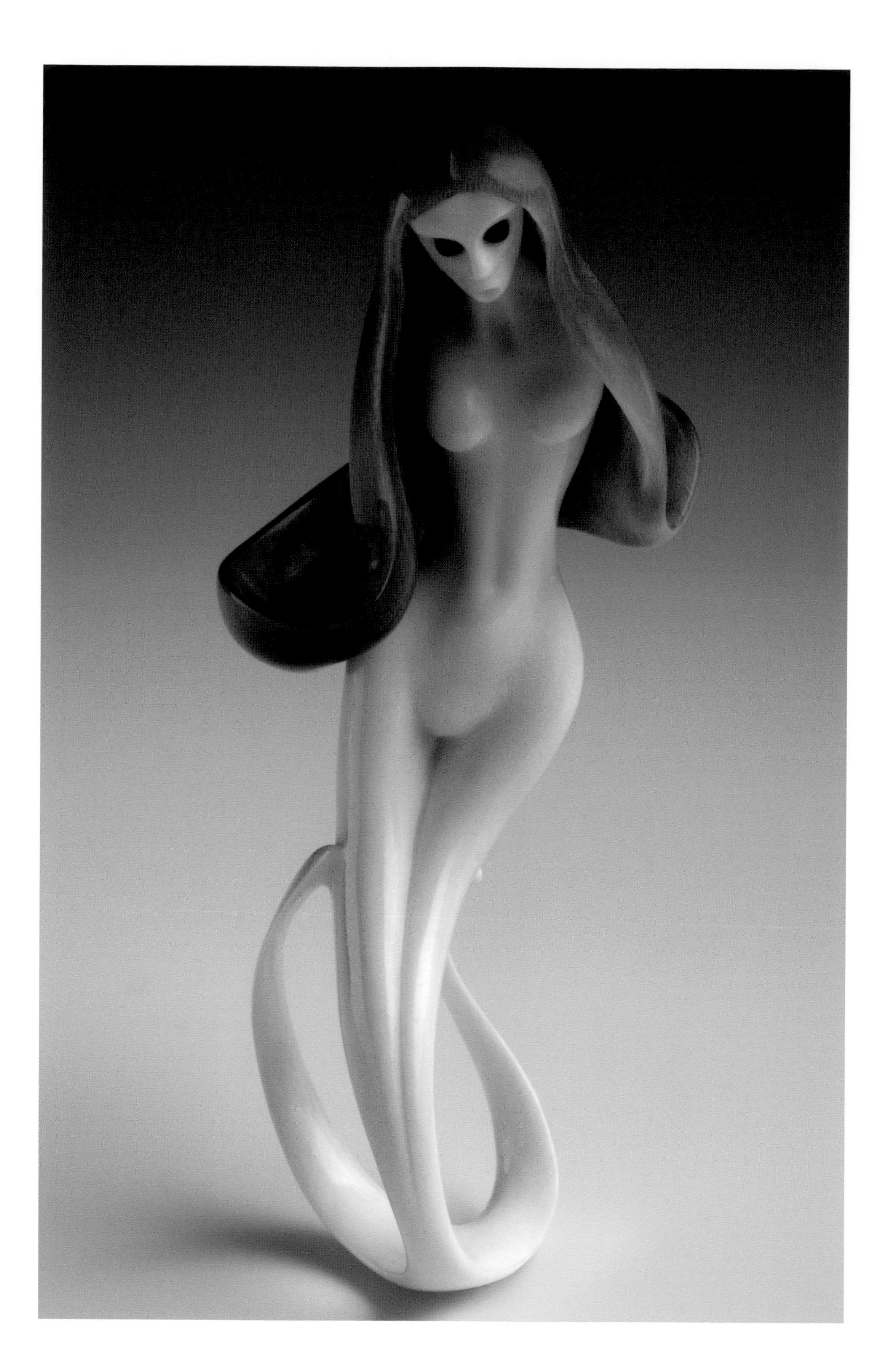

Mermaid

Elephant ivory. Hair in rhinoceros horn carved to simulate a marine plant. Eyes in drawn crystal rod.
Height 7.9cm. 1978.

Illustrated I.N.C.S.J. Vol. 6 No. 2 1978.

Exhibited & Illustrated Eighteenth to Twentieth Century Netsuke Eskenazi Oriental Art London 1978.

Exhibited Sotheby's Bond St. London 1994.

Exhibited & Illustrated Michael Henry Birch Sculptures 11th Vienna Netsuke Symposium Galerie Zacke Vienna Austria 1997.

Exhibited Michael Birch Netsuke Carver and Sculptor National College of Art & Design Dublin 1997.

ACTUAL SIZE

Mermaid

Ebony. Hair in ivory.
Eyes in drawn crystal rod.
Height 9.5cm. 1977.

Illustrated Michael Birch (Part Duex) and Others by Nicolas Westover Euronetsuke 2009.

Karashishi are the stone lions found at the gates of Buddhist temples and in gardens all over China and Japan.

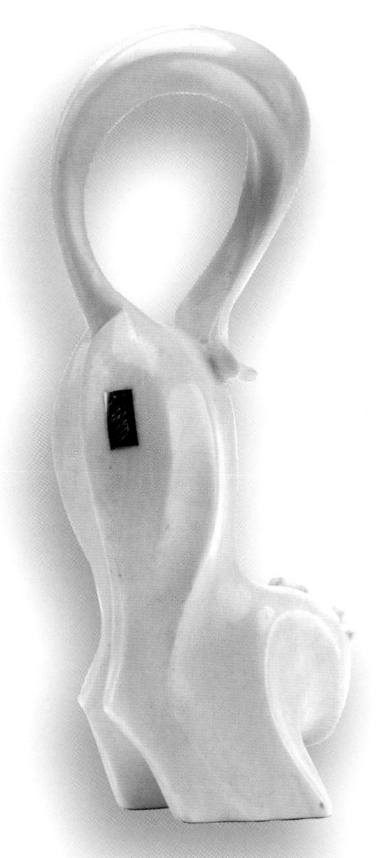

ACTUAL SIZE

Karashishi

Elephant ivory. Eyes in dark horn.
A pearl in its mouth.
Height 10.0cm. 1976.

Exhibited N.K.C. Kansas City 1977.

Illustrated Arts of Asia Vol. 8 No. 1 1978.

Illustrated Netsuke and Inro Artists and How to Read Their Signatures Vol. 1. by George Lazarnik 1982.

Illustrated Christie's New York Auction Catalogue 1985.

Shojo are mythical creatures who live by the sea. Their favourite occupation is the consumption of intoxicating liquid. Not aggressive creatures, both male and female are usually depicted either laughing and cheerful, or fast asleep after their alcoholic exertions.

Shojo Cheerfully Immersed in a Giant Saké Cup

Kagamibuta netsuke.
Lacquered Alaskan umimatsu cup. Patinated gold head. Eyes double inlaid in drawn crystal rod.
Height 4.3 cm. 1995.

Exhibited The Carvings of Michael Henry Birch N.K.C. New York 1995.

Illustrated I.N.S.J. Vol. 16 No. 2 1996.

Exhibited & Illustrated The Carvings of Michael Henry Birch I.N.S.C. Honolulu 1997.

Exhibited Michael Birch Netsuke Carver and Sculptor National College of Art & Design Dublin 1997.

The Drowning Drunk

Kagamibuta netsuke.
Pacific umimatsu cup. Gold face.
Height 3.8cm. C.1980.

Exhibited The Carvings of Michael Henry Birch N.K.C. Los Angeles 1981.

Illustrated Living Masters of Netsuke by Miriam Kinsey 1983.

Illustrated N.K.S.J. Vol. 8 No. 4 1988.

Exhibited & illustrated Contemporary Netsuke Miniature Sculpture from Japan and Beyond The Bowers Museum of Cultural Art Santa Ana California 1997.

Shojo the drunken saké drinker

Stag antler. Hair in the burl wood of manzanita. Eyes in drawn crystal rod.
Height 3.8cm. C.1994.

Exhibited Sotheby's Bond St. London.1994.

Shojo

Stag antler. Eyes in drawn crystal rod.
1980.

Exhibited The Carvings of Michael Henry Birch
N.K.C. Los Angeles 1981.

Shojo

Stag antler.
Height 4cm. 1980.

Exhibited I.N.C.S.C. Honolulu 1981.

Illustrated I.N.C.S.C.J. Vol. 8 No.4 1981.

Tanuki the Goblin

Uminatsu with marine organism inclusions. Head stripes inlaid black lacquer. Eyes in drawn crystal rod.
Length 4.6cm. 1995.

Exhibited The Carvings of Michael Henry Birch
N.K.C. New York 1995.

The Tanuki Badger, the legendary raccoon-like mischievous creature that is credited with supernatural magical powers is, in fact, a raccoon-faced dog. According to one legend it disguises itself as a monk and, feigning sleep, squats motionless by the roadside, eager to waylay and harass passing travellers. By beating its distended stomach or scrotum like a drum it frightens them away and then steals the possessions they dropped as they fled in terror.

Wherever possible Michael preferred to retain the integrity of the organic materials he used. For all the depictions of the Tanuki that follow, he polished the antler coronets but left them uncarved.

Tanuki

Molokai Taxis deer antler. Head stripes inlaid black lacquer. Eyes in drawn crystal rod.

Height 3.0cm. 1995.

Exhibited The Carvings of Michael Henry Birch N.K.C. New York 1995.

Exhibited Michael Birch Netsuke Carver and Sculptor National College of Art & Design Dublin 1997.

Exhibited & Illustrated Tactiles by Michael Henry Birch I.N.S.C. Boston 2001.

Tanuki

Highland stag antler, stained. Black lacquer features. Nose and eyes in drawn crystal rod.

Height: 4.5cm, Width: 5.5cm. C.1978.

Illustrated Michael Birch by Nicolas Westover, Euronetsuke, 2003.

Tanuki

Stag antler. Gold-rimmed cloak.
Abalone inlaid navel. Facial features and head stripes are inlaid black lacquer.
Eyes in drawn crystal rod.
Scrotum in walnut shell.
Height 5.4cm. C.1978.

Illustrated Christie's South Kensington London Japanese Ceramics and Works of Art Auction catalogue 2007.

Tanuki

Highland stag antler, stained. Black lacquer features, nose in drawn crystal rod.

Height 4.5cm Width 5.5cm. C.1978.

Illustrated Michael Birch by Nicolas Westover Euronetsuke 2003.

Tanuki Bozu

Highlands stag antler. Eye stripes inlaid black lacquer.
Height: 2.5cm. 1977.

Exhibited N.K.C., Kansas City, 1977.

Illustrated Living Masters of Netsuke by Miriam Kinsey 1983.

Exhibited Contemporary Netsuke, Miniature Sculpture from Japan and Beyond, The Bowers Museum of Cultural Art Santa Ana California 1997.

Exhibited & Illustrated Contemporary Netsuke: The Kinsey Collection Accompanied by H.I.H. Prince Takamado Collection by Robert O. Kinsey Chiba City Museum of Art Japan. 2001.

Tanuki Priest

Stag antler. Facial features and head stripes are inlaid black lacquer.
Eyes in drawn crystal rod.
Height: 4.9cm. 1979.

Exhibited Sotheby's Bond St. London 1994.

Illustrated I.N.S.J. Vol. 16 No. 2 1996.

Illustrated Contemporary Netsuke The H.I.H. Prince Takamado Collection The Tobacco & Salt Museum Tokyo Japan 2003.

Exhibited & Illustrated Netsuke The Prince Takamado Collection Tokyo National Museum Japan 2011.

Juvenile Tanuki

Dark-stained boxwood. Stag antler head. Head stripes are inlaid black lacquer. Eyes in drawn crystal rod.
Height 2.8cm Width 3.7cm. C.1994.

Exhibited Sotheby's Bond St. London. 1994.

Exhibited The Carvings of Michael Henry Birch N.K.C. New York 1995.

Exhibited & Illustrated Tactiles by Michael Henry Birch I.N.S.C. Boston 2001.

Badger Priest

Stag antler. Head stripes inlaid black lacquer. Cloak buttons in ruby cabochons. Eyes in drawn crystal rod.
1978.

Exhibited The Carvings of Michael Henry Birch, I.N.S.C. Honolulu 1979.

Tanuki

Highlands stag antler. His belt inlaid with cow horn. Head stripes inlaid black lacquer. Eyes in drawn crystal rod.
1995.

Exhibited The Carvings of Michael Henry Birch N.K.C. New York 1995.

Exhibited & Illustrated The Carvings of Michael Henry Birch I.N.S.C. Honolulu 1997.

Exhibited & Illustrated Michael Henry Birch Sculptures 11th Vienna Netsuke Symposium Galerie Zacke Vienna Austria. 1997.

Exhibited Michael Birch Netsuke Carver and Sculptor National College of Art & Design Dublin 1997.

Exhibited & Illustrated Tactiles by Michael Henry Birch I.N.S.C. Boston 2001.

Exhibited & Illustrated Netsuke Sculptures by Michael Henry Birch I.N.S.C. Honolulu 2004.

Tanuki

Stag antler carved from the base of an exceptionally large antler. The coronet decorated with coloured lacquer inlays. Facial features and head stripes are inlaid black lacquer. Eyes in drawn crystal rod.
1996.

Exhibited & Illustrated The Carvings of Michael Henry Birch I.N.S.C. Honolulu 1997.

TANUKI WITH PORCELAIN SHARDS INLAID.

Inlays of lacquer replaced the porcelain in the finished carving.

Tanuki

Roebuck antler. Facial features and head stripes are inlaid black lacquer. Eyes in drawn crystal rod. 1977.

Illustrated I.N.C.S.J. Vol. 6 No. 3 1978.

Exhibited The Carvings of Michael Henry Birch N.K.C. Los Angeles 1981.

Tanuki the Badger Priest

Stag antler, the coronet un-carved and decorated with bamboo leaf and setting sun pattern in inlaid lacquer. Facial features and head stripes are inlaid black lacquer. Eyes in drawn crystal rod.
Length 4.8cm. 1999.

Exhibited & Illustrated The Carvings of Michael Henry Birch I.N.S.C. Chicago 1999.

OF THIS PIECE THE COLLECTOR WROTE

You make good use of natural material and shape. Your creativity is excellent and the way of depicting a facial expression is superbly done by your magnificent inlay.

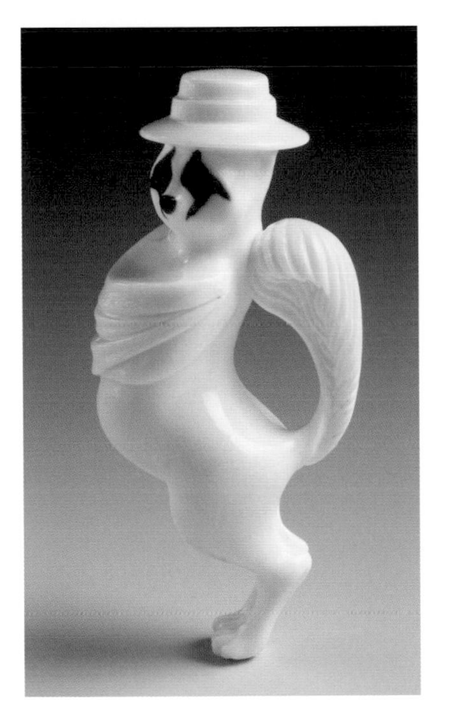

ACTUAL SIZE

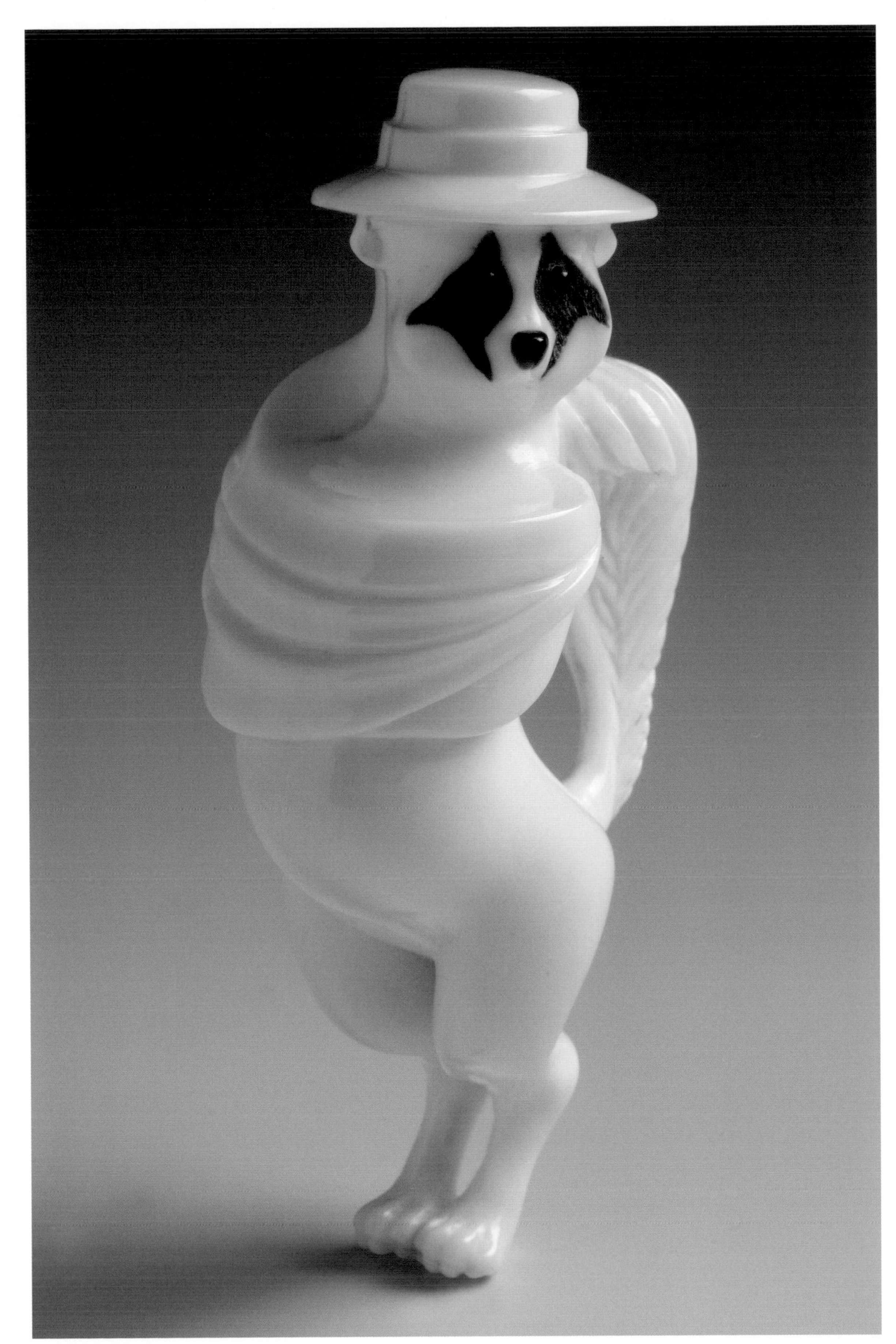

A Standing Racoon-faced Dog

Hippopotamus incisor. Facial features and head stripes are inlaid black lacquer. Eyes and nose in drawn crystal rod.
Height 8.0cm. 1996.

Exhibited & Illustrated The Carvings of Michael Henry Birch I.N.S.C. Honolulu 1997.

Exhibited & Illustrated Tactiles by Michael Henry Birch I.N.S.C. Chicago 1999.

Exhibited & Illustrated Tactiles by Michael Henry Birch I.N.S.C. Boston 2001.

The Tengu is a mythical bird-like creature that has been depicted in many legendary disguises. It has also been a model for extra-terrestrial alien figures for writers and illustrators of science-fiction.

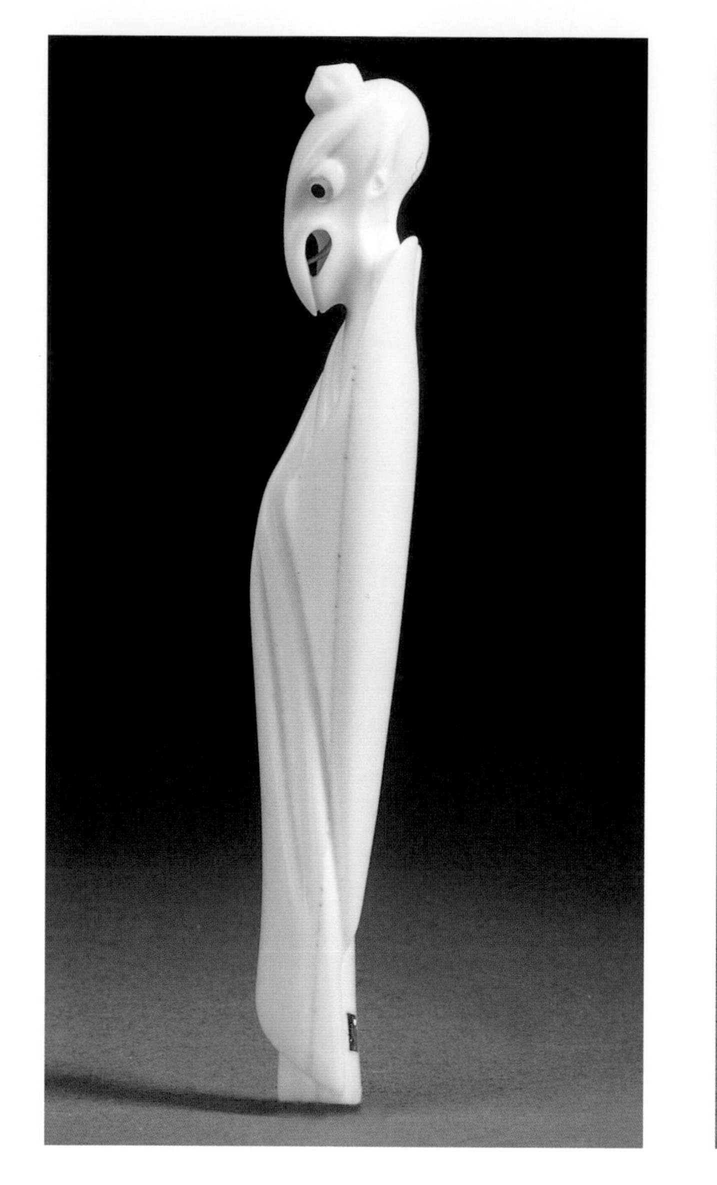

Tengu in the guise of an Immortal

Hippopotamus incisor. Gold tongue. Eyes double inlaid with amber and buffalo horn.

Height 11.7cm. 1994.

Exhibited The Carvings of Michael Henry Birch N.K.C. New York 1995.

Illustrated I.N.S.J. Vol. 16 No. 2 1996.

Exhibited & illustrated Contemporary Netsuke Miniature Sculpture from Japan and Beyond The Bowers Museum of Cultural Art Santa Ana California 1997.

Illustrated I.N.S.J. Vol. 18 No. 1 1998.

Alien bird perched on a small sphere

Hippopotamus incisor. Gold tongue. Eyes double inlaid.

Height 6.3cm. 1994.

Exhibited The Carvings of Michael Henry Birch N.K.C. New York 1995.

Illustrated I.N.S.J. Vol. 16 No. 2 1996.

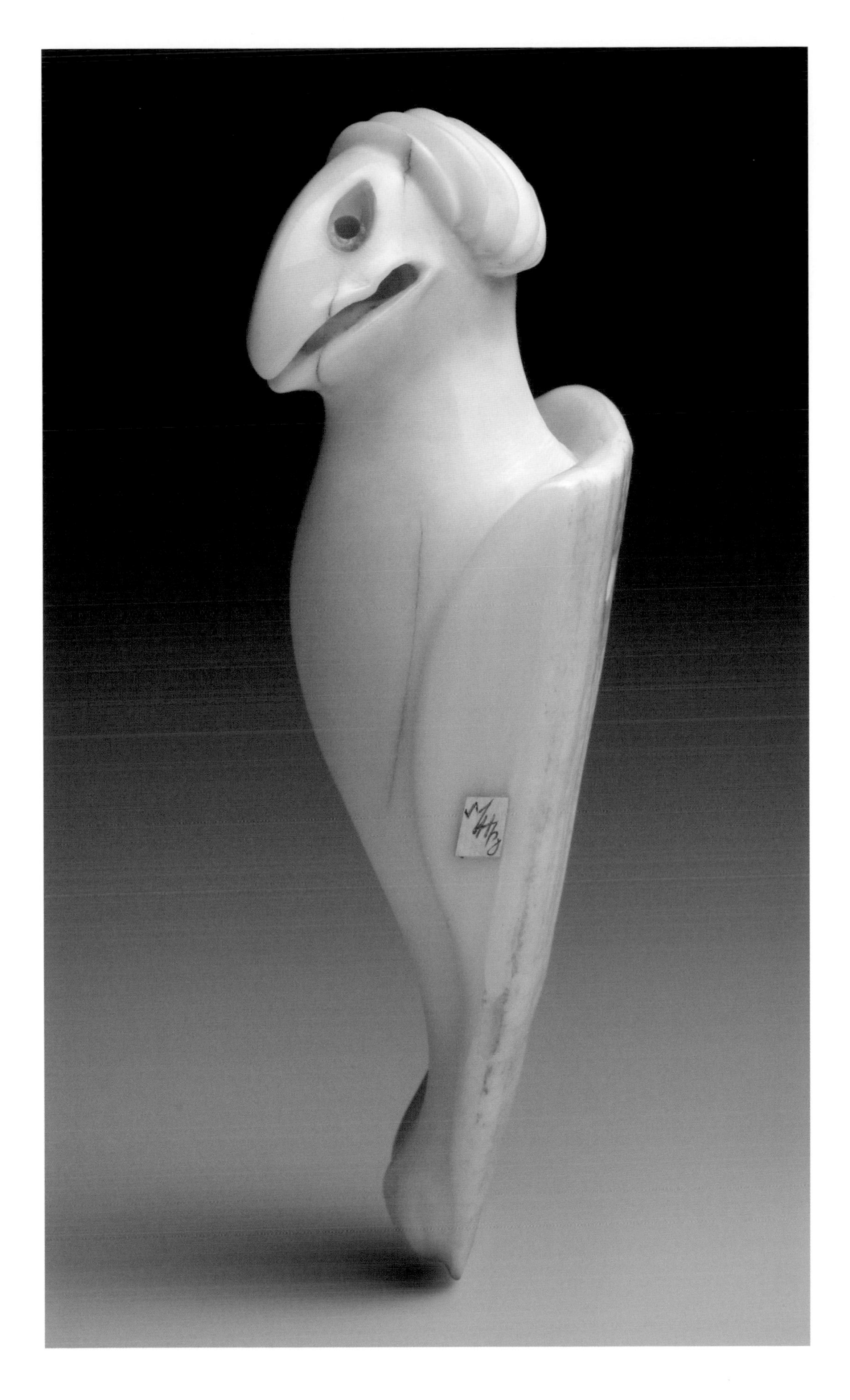

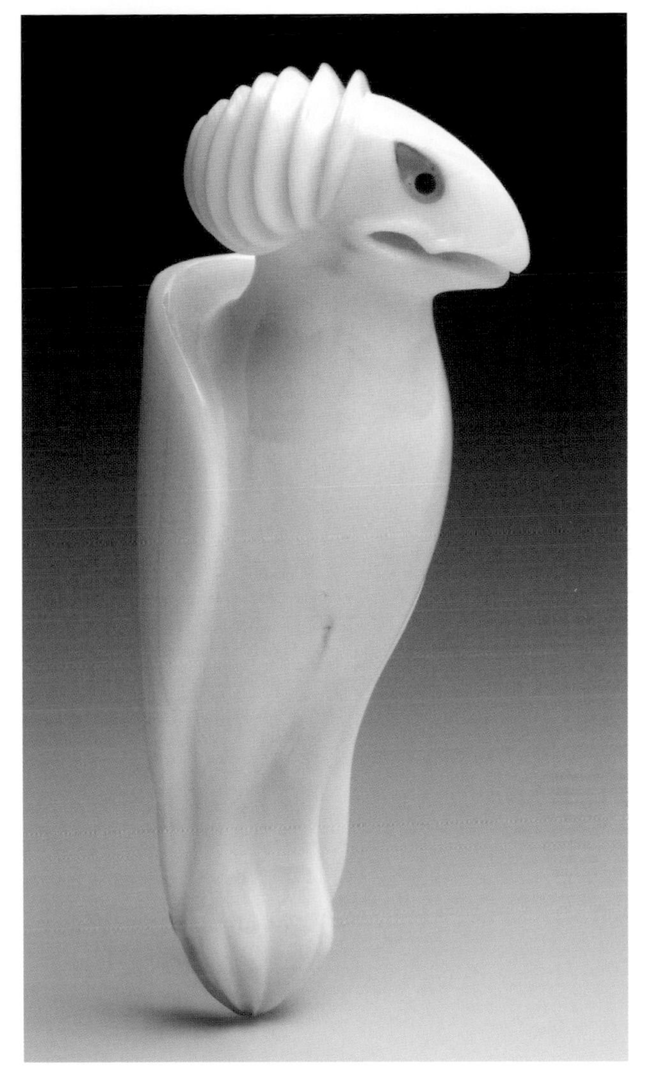

Extraterrestrial Tengu

Hippopotamus incisor. The glass-hard enamel is retained un-carved on one surface. Gold tongue. Eyes double inlaid in methyl-methacrilate and buffalo horn.
Height 7.7cm. 1995.

Exhibited The Carvings of Michael Henry Birch N.K.C. New York 1995.

Exhibited & Illustrated The Carvings of Michael Henry Birch I.N.S.C. Honolulu 1997.

Exhibited & Illustrated Tactiles by Michael Henry Birch I.N.S.C. Boston 2001.

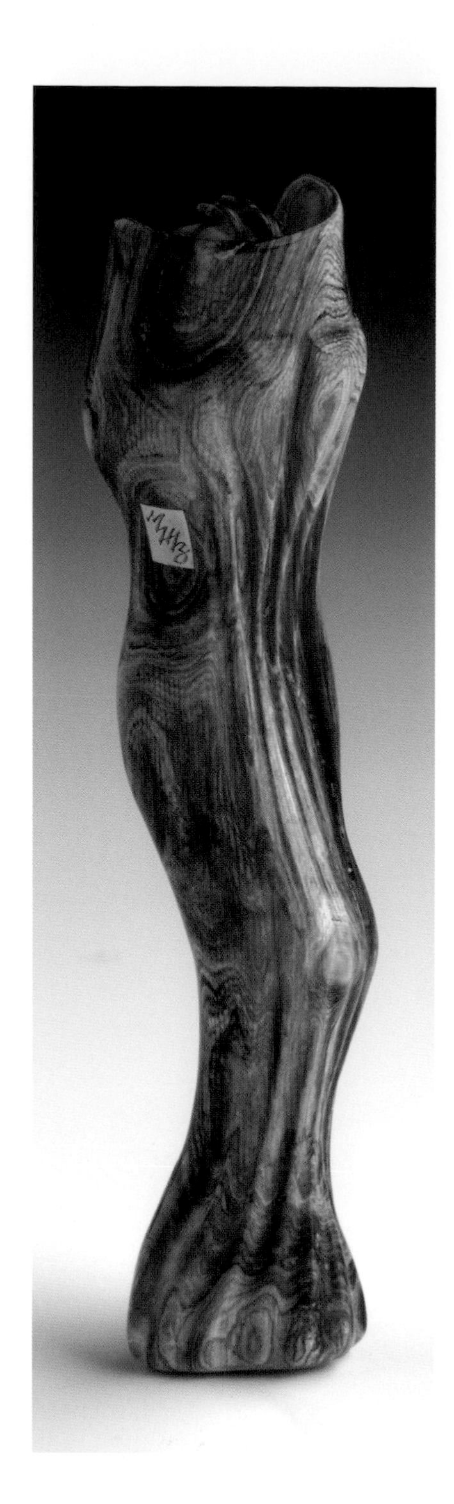

Tengu Princeling

Alaskan umimatsu. Eyes double inlaid in amber and methyl-methacrilate.
Height 9.4cm. 2002.

Exhibited & Illustrated Netsuke Sculptures by Michael Henry Birch I.N.S.C. Honolulu 2004.

I cast my raw materials upon the waters, and netsuke came back to me. Michael Birch's fabulous netsuke were fine art that I originally thought I could not afford, yet somehow I find that I now own eight netsuke carved by Michael. The material that he carved two of them from came directly from me, and it was all because of the one netsuke that got away from Michael.

He wanted to buy a plain umimatsu netsuke from me, and made the mistake of telling me that he was going to cut it up and use it for inlays. Purist that I was, I refused to sell it to him. But we were both in luck, because on a trip to Japan soon after that I found the world's ugliest vase, made of one piece of umimatsu, about 15" tall. Michael was ecstatic when I delivered it to him at the netsuke convention.

NORMAN SANDFIELD

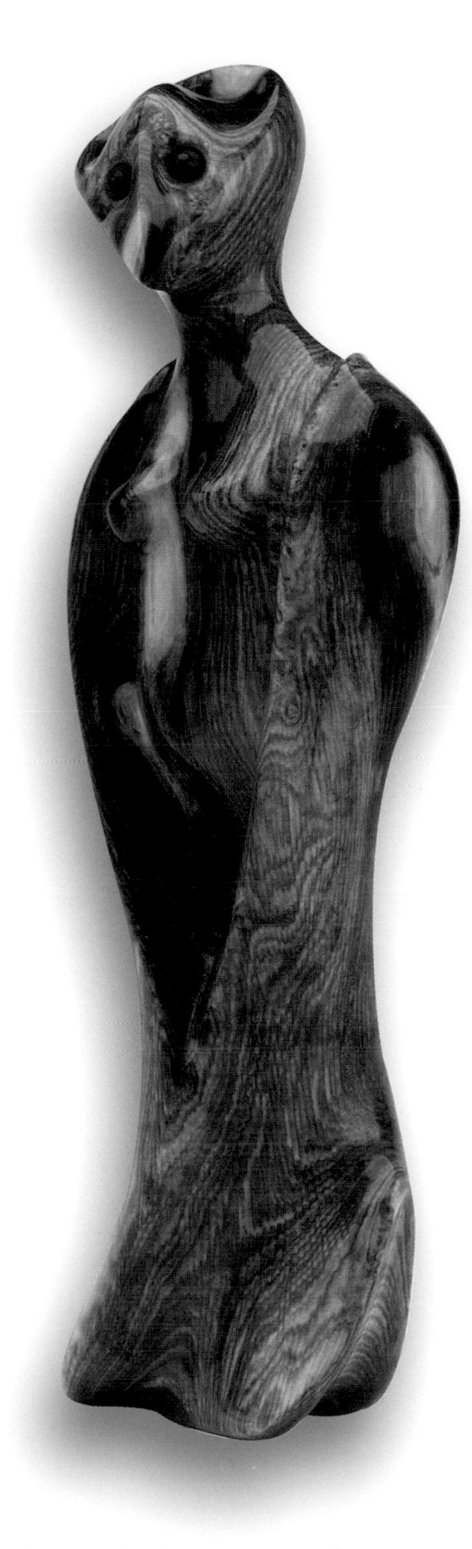

She is vulnerable in an alien Terran environment...

MHB

My Tengu Princess

Alaskan umimatsu. Eyes double inlaid with drawn crystal rod.

Height 9.5cm. 1999.

Exhibited & Illustrated Tactiles by Michael Henry Birch I.N.S.C. Chicago 1999.

Having learned that I was as much a materials aficionado as he was, Michael asked for my help in obtaining some corozo (tagua) nuts for his carving. These are commonly available in the United States, but apparently not easily available in England. I sent him a small sack full, and in return I got the generous gift of a Tengu mask ashpan netsuke (the back is hollow) which he carved. So, not only do I now own a fine group of Michael Birch netsuke, I also have the wonderful stories about this great artist and me that come with them.

NORMAN SANDFIELD

Mask of a Humanoid Tengu

Corozo nut (vegetable ivory).
Eyes in drawn crystal rod.
Width 4.0cm. C.1982.

Tengu

Molokai antler crown. Eyes inlaid with pearls from salt water mussels.
Width 4.25cm. C.1981.

Illustrated Netsuke and Inro Artists and How to Read Their Signatures Vol. 1. by George Lazarnik 1982.

Donated to the Convention Auction at I.N.S.C. Miami Florida 2007.

MICHAEL WROTE TO THE COLLECTOR:

For the Disillusioned Old Satyr, the impala horn came from one of the Natural History auctions held by Christie's in London many years ago. The horn has a keratinous black sheath, and the bony core running through four fifths of its length. It is that bony core that I carved into his head and legs. The outer black horn is simply polished. As for the subject: I decided that a stereotype satyr would not interest me – but, I reflected, surely satyrs grow old and grumpy; they must lose interest in the depraved erotic capers of their youthful prime. And yet they must somehow retain vestiges of wickedness in their elderly demeanour: the horns, the tail, the lecherous hooded eyes – Good Lord! I hope I'm not putting you off him, because, in fact, he's a harmless old pussycat, a luvvie!

MHB

The Disillusioned Old Satyr

Impala horn. Satyr's horns in cow horn.
Eyes in drawn crystal rod. 1996.

Exhibited & Illustrated The Carvings of Michael Henry Birch I.N.S.C. Honolulu 1997.

As always, your creativity and imagination, not to mention the fine craftsmanship and finishing are wonderful! Only in seeing the finished piece can I see what was obvious to you from the beginning: that it was meant to be a mask.

NORMAN SANDFIELD 1986

HE RECENTLY WROTE:

I delivered to him a relatively boring Tibetan or Himalayan ritual drinking cup made from a rhinoceros toe nail. It must have been at one of the London netsuke conventions, because he took it home and brought it back the next day.
He was so excited to show me that polishing it revealed that under the ugly burnt-wood looking exterior was a beautiful golden grain. Eventually I got the Tengu face netsuke you see here. This is probably one of the few netsuke materials of which there is only one known example, as rare as the coprolite [fossilised faeces] and moon rock netsuke.

NORMAN SANDFIELD

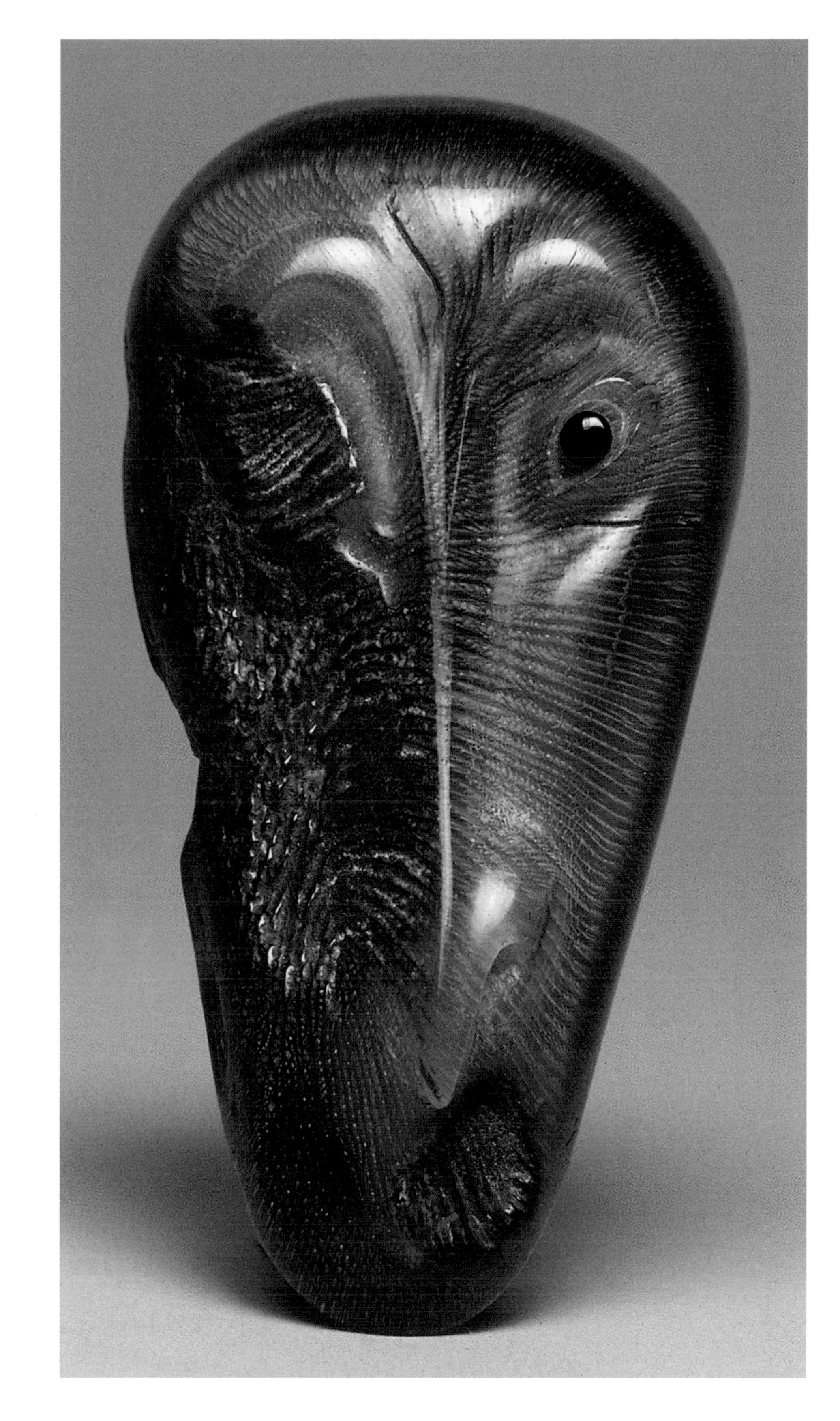

Tengu Mask

Rhinoceros toe-nail.
Eyes in drawn crystal rod.
Height 10.0cm. 1986.

Exhibited Contemporary Netsuke Masterful Miniatures Museum of Art and Design New York 2007.

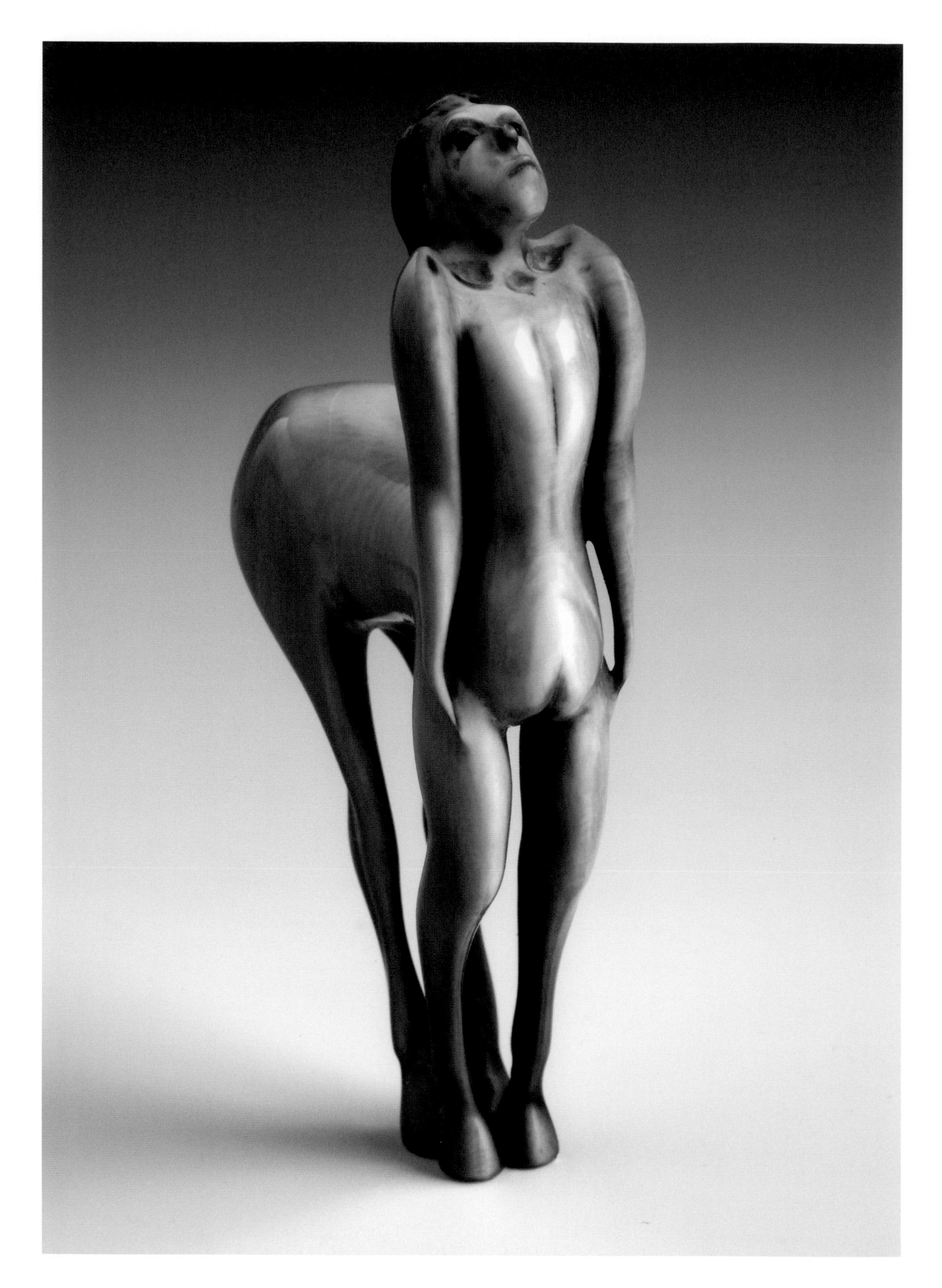

Young Centaur Paying Respectful Attention to Advice from his Elders

Siberian mammoth ivory stained.
Eyes in drawn crystal rod.
Height 7.4cm. 1994.

Exhibited The Carvings of Michael Henry Birch N.K.C. New York 1995.

Illustrated I.N.S.J. Vol. 16 No. 2 1996.

Exhibited & Illustrated The Carvings of Michael Henry Birch I.N.S.C. Honolulu 1997.

Exhibited Michael Birch Netsuke Carver and Sculptor National College of Art & Design Dublin 1997.

Exhibited & Illustrated Tactiles by Michael Henry Birch I.N.S.C. Boston 2001.

Exhibited & Illustrated Netsuke Sculptures by Michael Henry Birch I.N.S.C. Honolulu 2004.

The Male Form

Michael was acknowledged for his ability to create character in a face that is rarely any more, and often much less, than one centimetre in height. Some collectors consider many of the faces to be self-portraits, a notion which the artist strongly denied. Although he sometimes used collectors and other individuals as models for his faces, they rarely recognise themselves.

One of Michael's most popular subjects was his depiction of Dutch and Portuguese merchants who were the early traders in Japan, usually depicted in a humorous manner by Japanese artists. Other figures and masks, together with his Mobius figures are included here.

A Man wearing a Black Hat

Cloak and body in uncarved Greater Kudu horn. Legs in Siberian mammoth ivory. Head and ruff in hippopotamus incisor. Hat in stag antler stained black. Eyes in drawn crystal rod.

Height 8.0cm. 1996.

Exhibited & Illustrated The Carvinqs of Michael Henry Birch I.N.S.C. Honolulu 1997.

Exhibited & Illustrated Tactiles by Michael Henry Birch I.N.S.C. Chicago 1999.

Exhibited & Illustrated Tactiles by Michael Henry Birch I.N.S.C. Boston 2001.

Michael used this darker-than-usual bony core of the antler coronet to denote the dark skin of a trader from Goa posing as a Portuguese merchant.

The Goan Impostor

Roebuck antler. Hat in Molokai Taxis deer antler. Eyes in drawn crystal rod.

Height 6.5cm. 1996.

Exhibited & Illustrated The Carvings of Michael Henry Birch I.N.S.C. Honolulu 1997.

Exhibited & Illustrated Tactiles by Michael Henry Birch I.N.S.C. Boston 2001.

When I cut into an antler I have had for almost 20 years, I saw in my mind's eye this dandy aristocratic gentleman. I set about carving the piece without hesitation and with no preliminary sketches, It was one of those rare occasions when it all went smoothly, and when I completed the piece there was no question in my mind that there was no more I should do to it — no inlays, no staining, no embellishments.

MHB

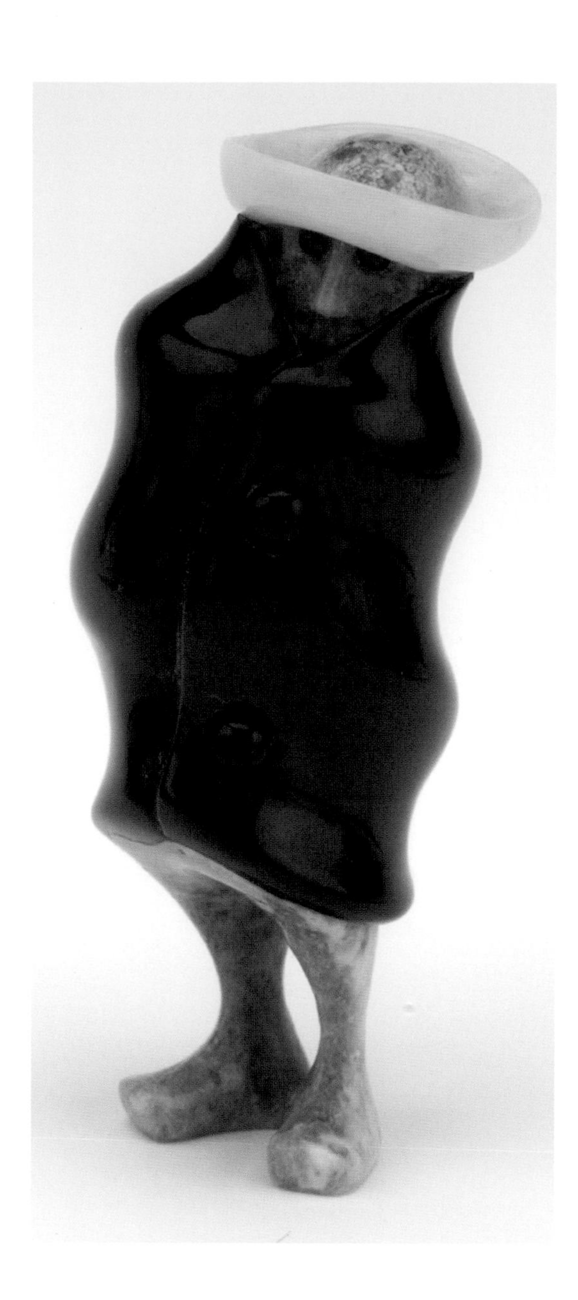

The Furtive Foreigner

Cloak and body in uncarved Impala horn. Hat in stag antler. Eyes in mussel pearls.

Height 9.5cm. 1999.

Exhibited & Illustrated Tactiles by Michael Henry Birch I.N.S.C. Chicago 1999.

Exhibited & Illustrated Tactiles by Michael Henry Birch I.N.S.C. Boston 2001.

The Portuguese Dandy

Stag antler. Eyes in drawn crystal rod.

Height 10.2cm. 1996.

Exhibited & Illustrated The Carvings of Michael Henry Birch I.N.S.C. Honolulu 1997.

Dutchman

Roebuck antler.

Height 7.4cm. 1985.

Illustrated I.N.S.J. Vol. 16 No. 2 1996.

Exhibited & illustrated Contemporary Netsuke Miniature Sculpture from Japan and Beyond The Bowers Museum of Cultural Art Santa Ana California 1997.

Illustrated I.N.S.J. Vol. 17 No. 2 1998.

Exhibited & Illustrated Contemporary Netsuke The Kinsey Collection Accompanied by H.I.H. Prince Takamado Collection by Robert O. Kinsey Chiba City Museum of Art Japan. 2001.

The Japanese with their extraordinary gift for enhancing the quality of functional objects they adopt and adapt. . . developed netsuke into an astonishing archival record of their day-to-day lives. . . their crafts, their dress. . . their religious customs, myths and legends. . . their oblique humour with which they sometimes mocked with impunity those in positions of pompous authority.

MHB 1990

It is no coincidence to me that Michael himself possessed this extraordinary gift for creating diminutive figures that he frequently observed from the world around him and which also emerged from his own fertile and artistic imagination which is certainly unique amongst the contemporary artists of today. He made some innovative netsuke figures with surprisingly idiosyncratic characters: a Conspirator with a sinister look staring furtively from under a Molokai stag antler hat, a Portuguese Merchant in Greater Kudu horn with a posture of great self-assurance, yet with a quizzical look of uncertainty, a Shojo as a delightfully idiotic drunk, a couple of Roebuck antler Dutchmen revealing undisguised disdain and this elderly stag antler Dutchman. He is turning slightly to his right with a haughty expression, a white ruff above his short coat, carved in relief with scrolls, blowing apart in a breeze. The eyes are inlaid with little specks of horn. Curiously it has an inkling of resemblance to the face of its creator.

DAVID BURDITT
CHAIRMAN OF EUROPEAN CHAPTER OF THE I.N.S.

An elderly Dutchman wishing he were somewhere else

Stag antler partially stained. Double inlaid eyes in horn and drawn crystal rod. Embroidery pattern on cloak carved 1995.
Height c.5.5cm. 1988.

Illustrated Handbook to London Netsuke Fair and Convention 1990.

Exhibited The Carvings of Michael Henry Birch N.K.C. New York 1995.

Illustrated I.N.S.J. Vol. 16 No. 2 1996.

Illustrated Sotheby's London Japanese Works of Art Prints & Paintings Auction catalogue 2006.

Illustrated I.N.S.J. Vol. 27 No. 1 2007.

A Dignified Old Dutchman

Cloak and body in Springbok horn.
Hat in Molokai Taxis deer antler.
Eyes double inlaid with drawn crystal rod.
Height 8.0cm. 1999.

Exhibited & Illustrated Tactiles by Michael Henry Birch I.N.S.C. Chicago 1999.

Exhibited & Illustrated Tactiles by Michael Henry Birch I.N.S.C. Boston 2001.

Exhibited & Illustrated Netsuke Sculptures by Michael Henry Birch I.N.S.C. Honolulu 2004.

A Dutchman with Attitude

Roebuck antler. Buttons in jade cabochons. Hat in Molokai Taxis deer antler. Eyes in drawn crystal rod.

Height 7.6cm. 1999.

Exhibited & Illustrated Tactiles by Michael Henry Birch I.N.S.C. Chicago 1999.

Exhibited & Illustrated Tactiles by Michael Henry Birch I.N.S.C. Boston 2001.

He is turning away with a grimace from what he assumes to be an unpleasant scene...

Michael explained to the collector of this piece that he had given the Conspirator a slight strabismus which gave him a more furtive expression.

THE COLLECTOR REPLIED:

I showed your 'Conspirator' netsuke yesterday to a most appreciative audience that included an American, who had lived in Japan for several years. When I mentioned that your Dutch spy was a bit strabismic, my friend informed me that in Japanese the word for "strabismus" is "ronpari", meaning Rondon/Paris, meaning that the viewer's imbalanced eye muscles can't distinguish one capital from the other. He was quite certain about the Japanese word, having his own strabismus while he lived in Tokyo.

The Conspirator

Greater Kudu horn. Cloak carved from the helical sheath of the horn, his body from the integral bony core. Hat in Molokai Taxis deer antler. Cloak buttons in black mussel pearls. Eyes double inlaid with drawn crystal rod.

Height 9.1cm. 1995.

Exhibited The Carvings of Michael Henry Birch N.K.C. New York 1995.

Illustrated Arts of Asia Vol. 26 No. 1 1996.

Illustrated I.N.S.J. Vol. 16 No. 2 1996.

Exhibited & illustrated Contemporary Netsuke Miniature Sculpture from Japan and Beyond The Bowers Museum of Cultural Art Santa Ana California 1997.

Illustrated I.N.S.J. Vol. 18 No. 1 1998.

The Proud Dutchman

Various stag antlers. Eyes double inlaid with drawn crystal rod.

Height 7.6cm. 1996.

Exhibited & Illustrated The Carvings of Michael Henry Birch I.N.S.C. Honolulu 1997.

Exhibited & Illustrated Michael Henry Birch Sculptures 11th Vienna Netsuke Symposium Galerie Zacke Vienna Austria. 1997.

Exhibited & Illustrated Tactiles by Michael Henry Birch I.N.S.C. Boston 2001.

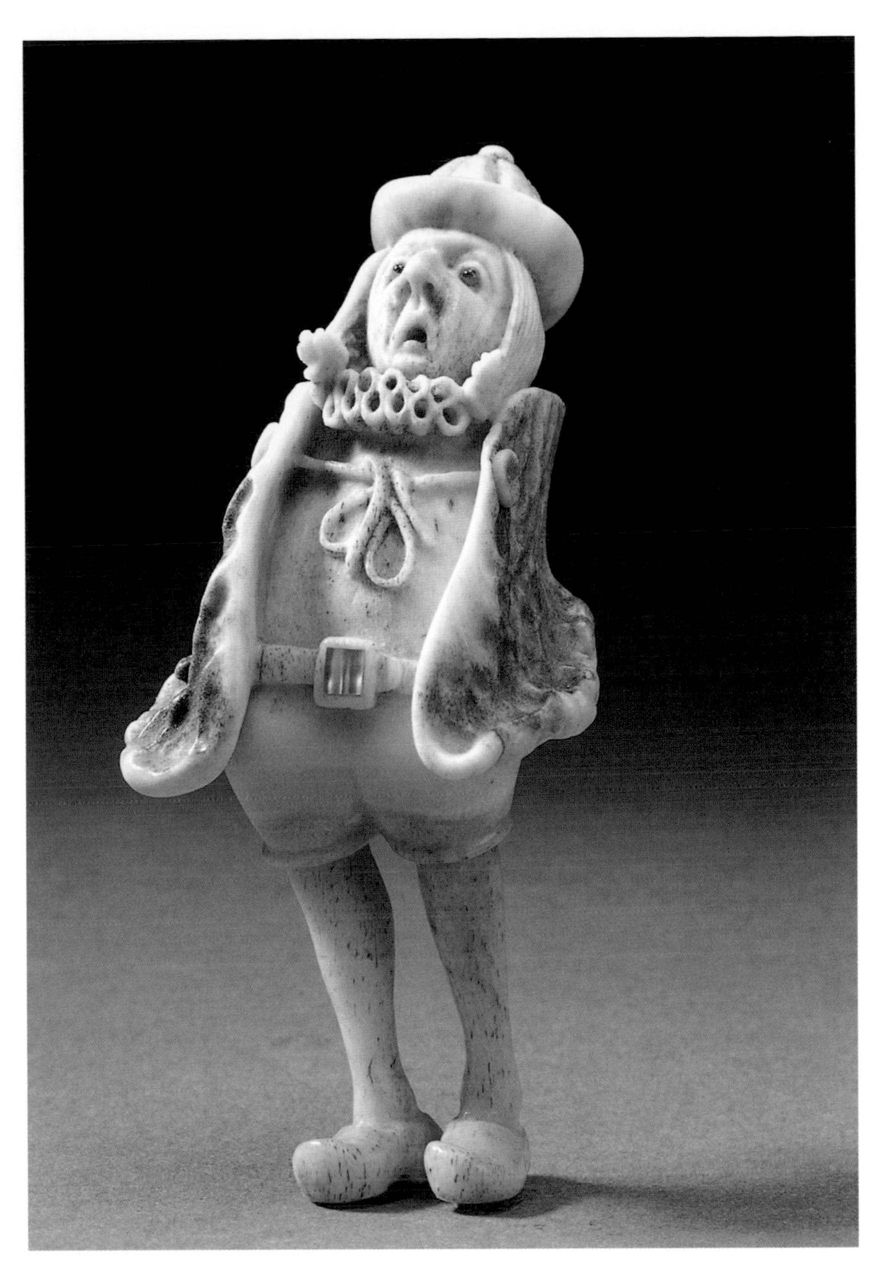

A Dutchman having been informed that he is a barbarian

Stag antler. Cloak buttons in ram's horn. Eyes in drawn crystal rod.

Height 6.7cm. 1995.

Exhibited The Carvings of Michael Henry Birch N.K.C. New York 1995.

Despite the stern face often taken as a self portrait of the artist, the collector confirmed that this Dutchman continues to make her smile.

A Dutchman displaying signs of uncertainty

Stag antler. Belt buckle inlaid with abalone shell. Eyes double inlaid in drawn crystal rod.

1995.

Exhibited The Carvings of Michael Henry Birch N.K.C. New York 1995.

Exhibited & Illustrated The Japanese Art of Miniature Carving Minneapolis Institute of Arts Minnesota 1999.

Exhibited & Illustrated The Japanese Art of Miniature Carving Herbert F. Johnson Museum of Art Cornell University Ithaca New York 1999.

ACTUAL SIZE

Dutchman

Roebuck antler. Hat in Molokai antler. Inlaid lacquer waistcoat. Drawn crystal rod eyes, waistcoat buttons and shoe studs.

Height 9cm. C.1998.

Illustrated Michael Birch by Nicolas Westover Euronetsuke 2003.

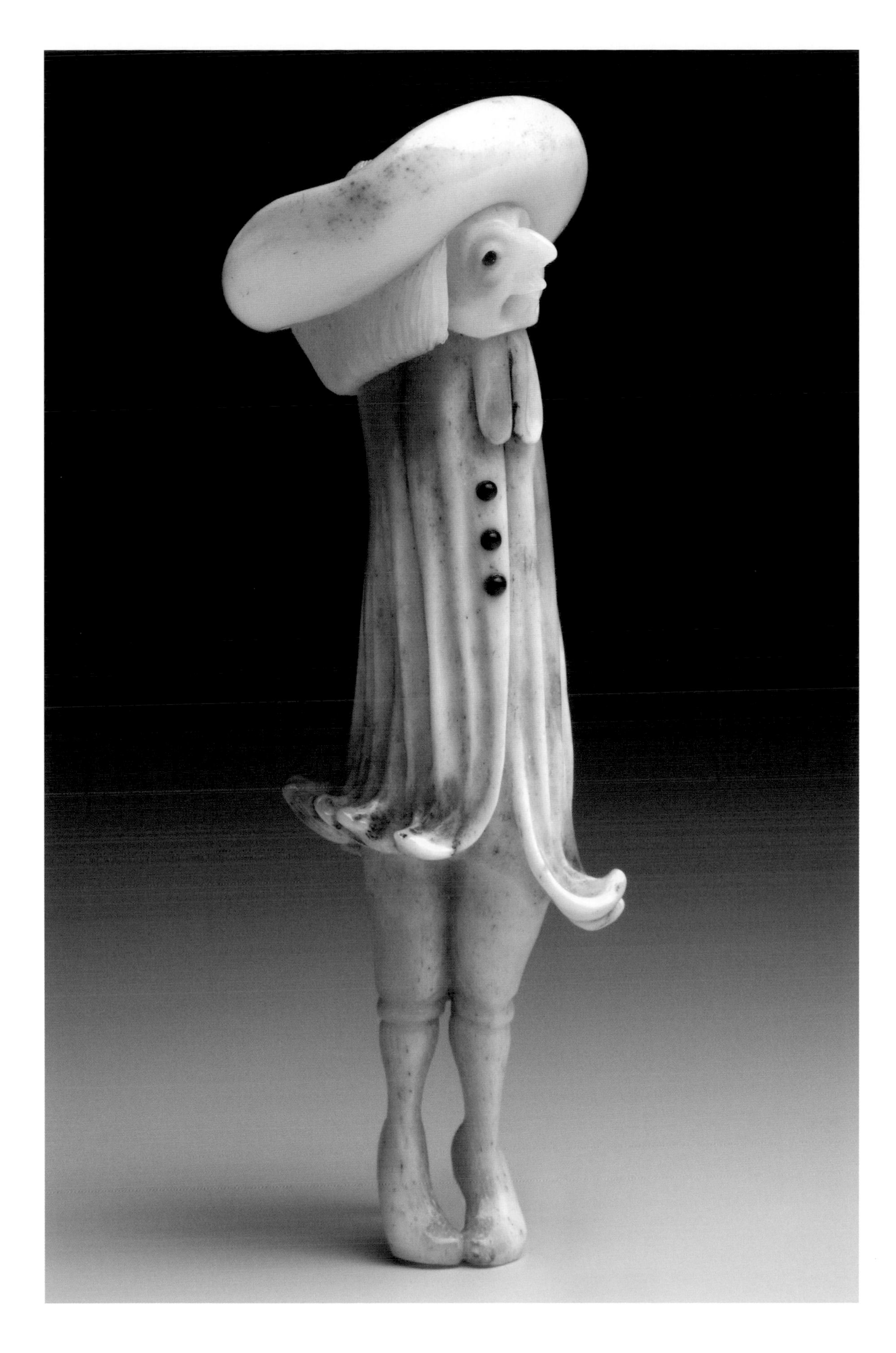

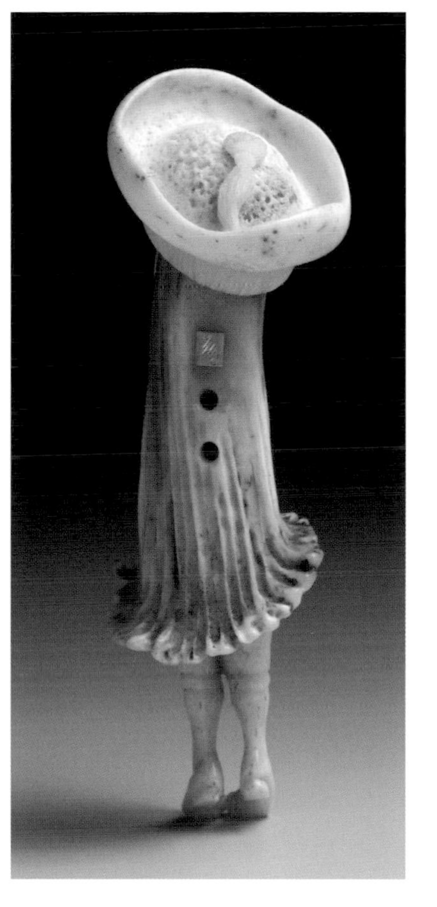

ACTUAL SIZE

A Discomfited Dutch Gentleman

Highlands stag antler. Hat in Molokai Taxis deer antler. Eyes inlaid with drawn crystal rod.

Height 10cm. 1996.

Exhibited & Illustrated The Carvings of Michael Henry Birch I.N.S.C. Honolulu 1997.

Exhibited & Illustrated Netsuke Sculptures by Michael Henry Birch I.N.S.C. Honolulu 2004.

Dialogue with a Disconsolate Dutchman

Highlands stag antler. Hat in Molokai Taxis deer antler. Belt in abalone inlaid with jade cabochon studs. Shoe buckles in pink coral. Eyes in drawn crystal rod.
Height 10.0cm. 1999.

Exhibited & Illustrated Tactiles by Michael Henry Birch I.N.S.C. Chicago 1999.

Exhibited & Illustrated Tactiles by Michael Henry Birch I.N.S.C. Boston 2001.

IN A LETTER TO THE COLLECTOR OF THE 'DON' PIECE, MICHAEL EXPLAINED:

A 'Don' is a person of more highly elevated social standing than a 'Señor', and this merchant is clearly above a mere 'mister', that is obvious from his posture of unarguable superiority.

A Dutchman crouching, possibly inspecting an object at low level

Stag antler. Porous section sealed with clear lacquer. Collar clasp in pink coral. Eyes in drawn crystal rod. 1994.

Exhibited Sotheby's Bond St. London. 1994.

Exhibited The Carvings of Michael Henry Birch N.K.C. New York 1995.

Illustrated I.N.S.J. Vol. 16 No. 2 1996.

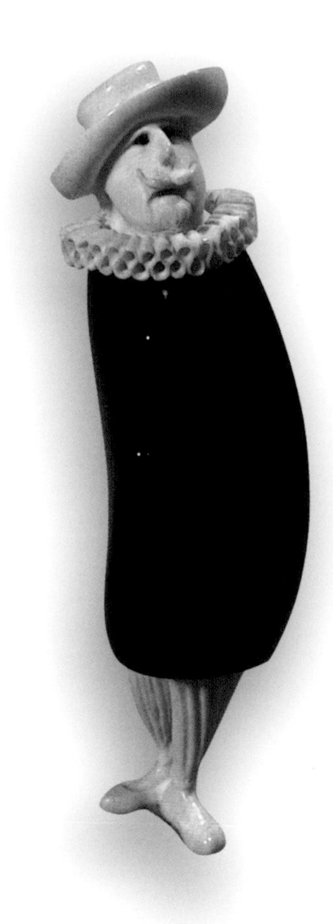

The Don, a Portuguese Merchant

Cloak and body in Greater kudu horn. Head in Siberian mammoth ivory. Eyes in drawn crystal rod.
1996.

Illustrated I.N.S.J. Vol.16 No. 2 1996.

Exhibited & Illustrated The Carvings of Michael Henry Birch I.N.S.C. Honolulu 1997.

Bearing in mind Michael's sense of humour this Dutchman is probably not inspecting an object on the ground.

Using different materials bonded together in a special way, the artist depicts an amusing figure of a Dutchman. Despite the different hairstyle, the face is almost an exact copy of the artist's.

H.I.H. PRINCESS HISAKO OF TAKAMADO

Michael's work is much appreciated for the subtle touches of humour that often appear in his carvings. Like busy cobblers who never have time to repair their own shoes, this Wigmaster's own wig requires attention. I found this American bull horn hanging on the wall of a General Store in Utah, while on a trip to the North Rim of the Grand Canyon. Michael had to show the store owner some of his netsuke before the man could be persuaded to sell it to us.

OF HIS HUMAN FORMS, LYNN RICHARDSON, THE NETSUKE ARTIST WHO WORKS IN CERAMICS WROTE:

Often times in my own art my 'hand' is clearly evident even when unintended or unwanted. So many of the pieces that I have seen of Michael's in publications or on display at Netsuke Conventions look just like him – unmistakably 'Birches'. His work – his wry humor, his intelligence, his oeuvre, all in a compact form – netsuke. That is what the carvers do, putting as much as we can into our tiny creations. 'Multum in parvo', 'much in little'. Through his hand and imagination he said a lot. I wonder if Michael actually posed in front of a mirror to catch the subtlety of a pose such as his fabulous 'Conspirator' netsuke made from kudu horn and stag antler or his 'Portuguese Merchant' also made of kudu horn and ivory, or especially his Dutchmen. His materials were chosen with such sensitivity and were, themselves, celebrated and honoured.

The Dutch Wigmaster

Cloak and body in North American bull horn. Head and hat carved in African hippopotamus incisor and legs in Alaskan walrus phallus bone. Eyes double inlaid with drawn crystal rod.

Height 10.3. 1996

Exhibited & Illustrated The Carvings of Michael Henry Birch I.N.S.C. Honolulu 1997.

Exhibited & Illustrated Michael Henry Birch Sculptures 11th Vienna Netsuke Symposium Galerie Zacke Vienna Austria. 1997.

Exhibited & Illustrated Tactiles by Michael Henry Birch I.N.S.C. Boston 2001.

Illustrated Netsuke; Have Netsuke Will Travel by H.I.H. Princess Hisako of Takamado 2008.

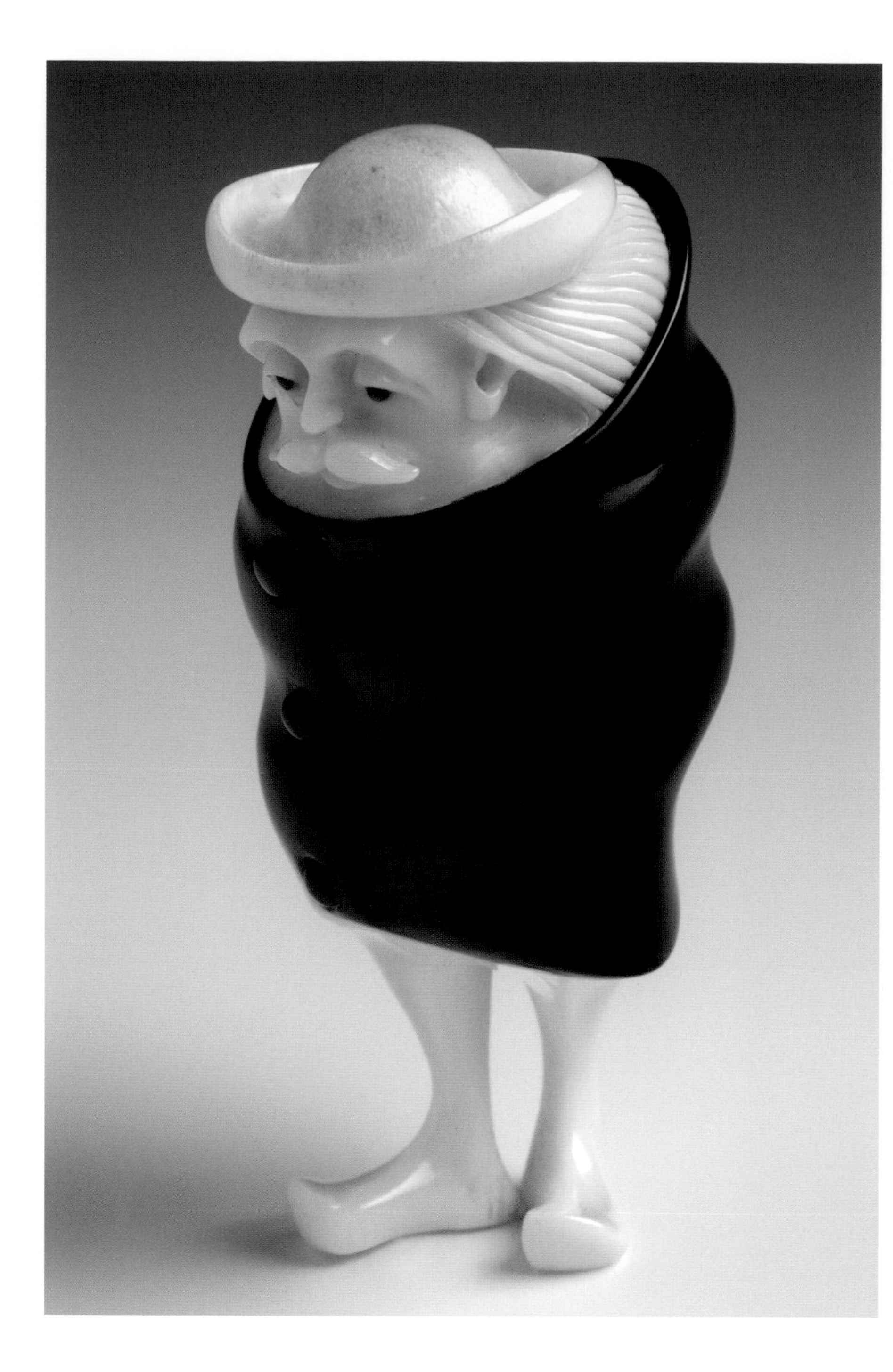

Beautifully adapted to the material, with the crown of antler as the flounced border of the Dutchman's coat, his feet beneath carved from part of the antler growing from the head of the stag. A dour face (somewhat resembling Michael's own).

VIRGINIA ATCHLEY

A Genial Dutchman

Cloak and body in Impala horn and hippopotamus incisor. Hat in stag antler. Eyes double inlaid with drawn crystal rod.

Height 7.2cm. 1999.

Exhibited & Illustrated Tactiles by Michael Henry Birch I.N.S.C. Chicago 1999.

Exhibited & Illustrated Tactiles by Michael Henry Birch I.N.S.C. Boston 2001.

Exhibited & Illustrated Netsuke Sculptures by Michael Henry Birch I.N.S.C. Honolulu 2004.

Dutchman with Long Cravat

Roebuck antler.

1985.

Illustrated N.K.S.J. Vol. 7 No. 4 1987.

Illustrated I.N.S.J. Vol. 16 No. 2 1996.

Illustrated The Virginia Atchley Collection of Japanese Miniature Arts by Virginia G. Atchley & Neil K. Davey 2006.

The Squat Dutchman

An Anamorphic netsuke.
Lignum Vitae. Eyes double inlaid drawn crystal rod.
Height 6.2cm. 1996.

Exhibited & Illustrated The Carvings of Michael Henry Birch I.N.S.C. Honolulu 1997.

Illustrated International Netsuke Society European Chapter Lecture Sotheby's London 1997.

Exhibited & Illustrated Tactiles by Michael Henry Birch I.N.S.C. Boston 2001.

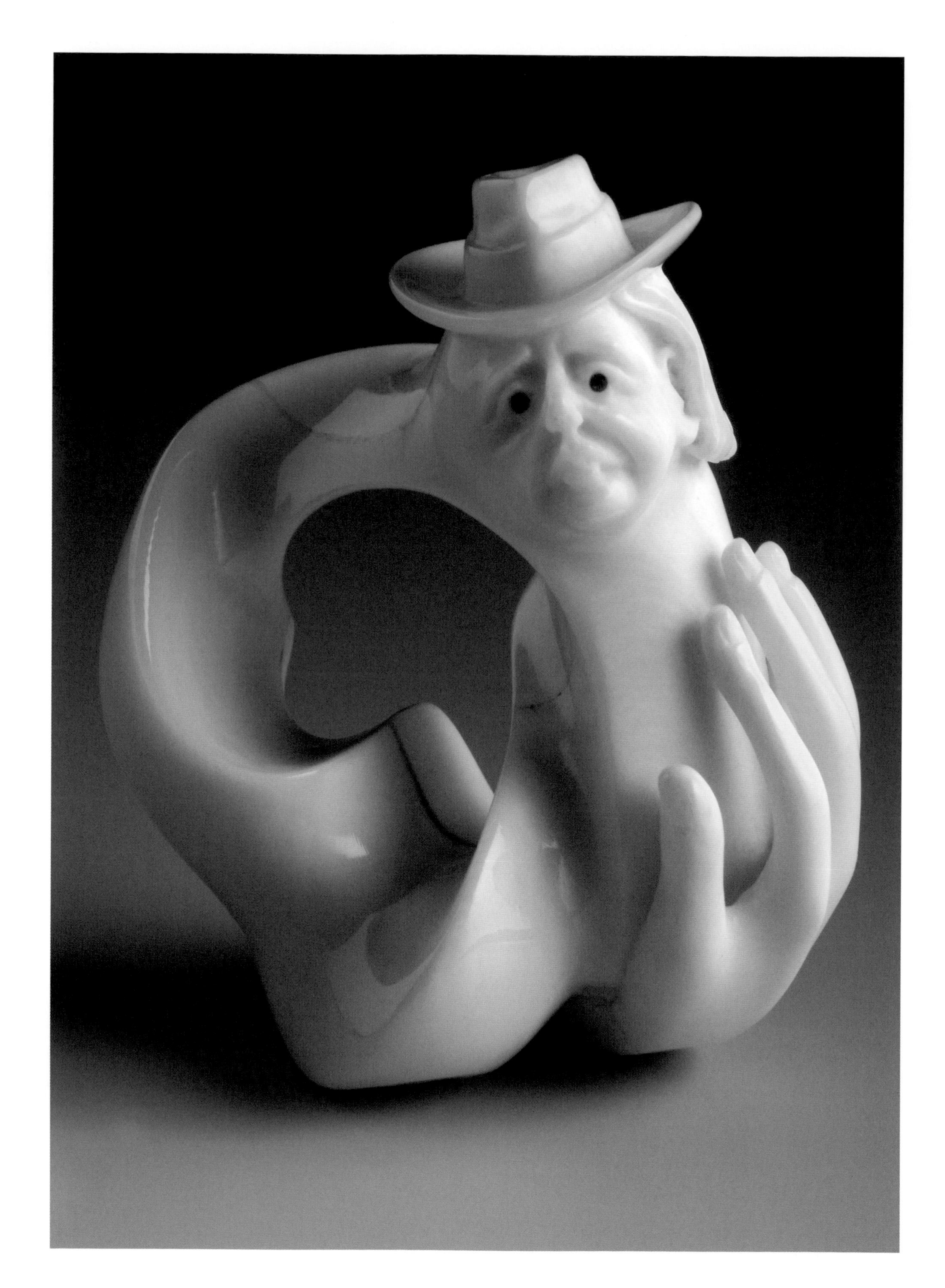

Oscar Wilde as an epigram emerging from a double Möbius

Siberian mammoth ivory.
Eyes in drawn crystal rod.
Height: 6.5cm. 1997.

Exhibited & Illustrated Tactiles by Michael Henry Birch I.N.S.C. Chicago 1999.

Exhibited & Illustrated Tactiles by Michael Henry Birch I.N.S.C. Boston 2001.

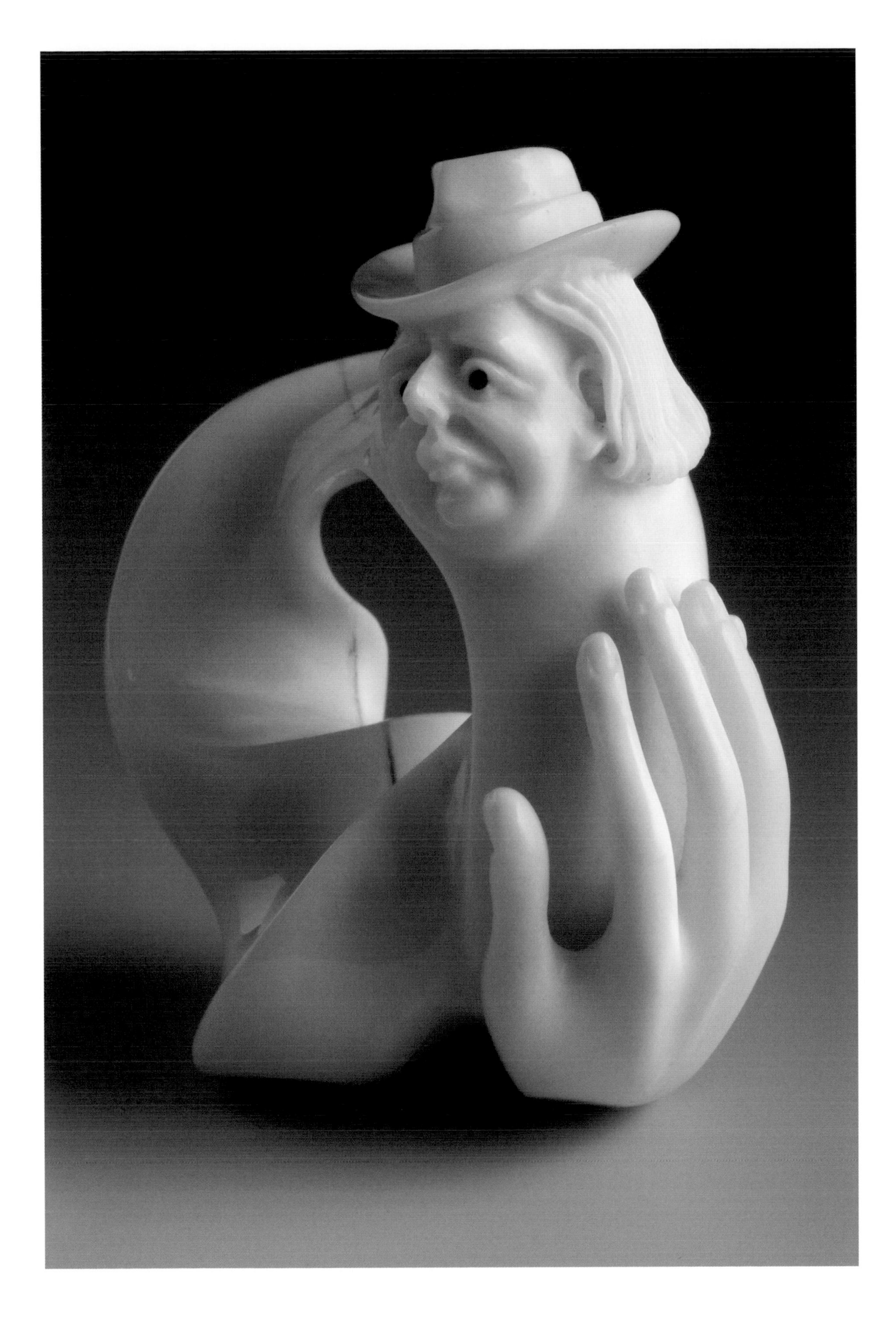

The chubby features and delicate hand are on one surface, while on the opposite featureless surface he is pursued endlessly by one of his effete epigrams. The Möbius, an unnatural form, may also be an epigram, a paradox, a pun and a twist.

MHB

ACTUAL SIZE

This netsuke represents the portrait of a fugitive alien being, who from time to time appears fleetingly in my imaginings.

MHB

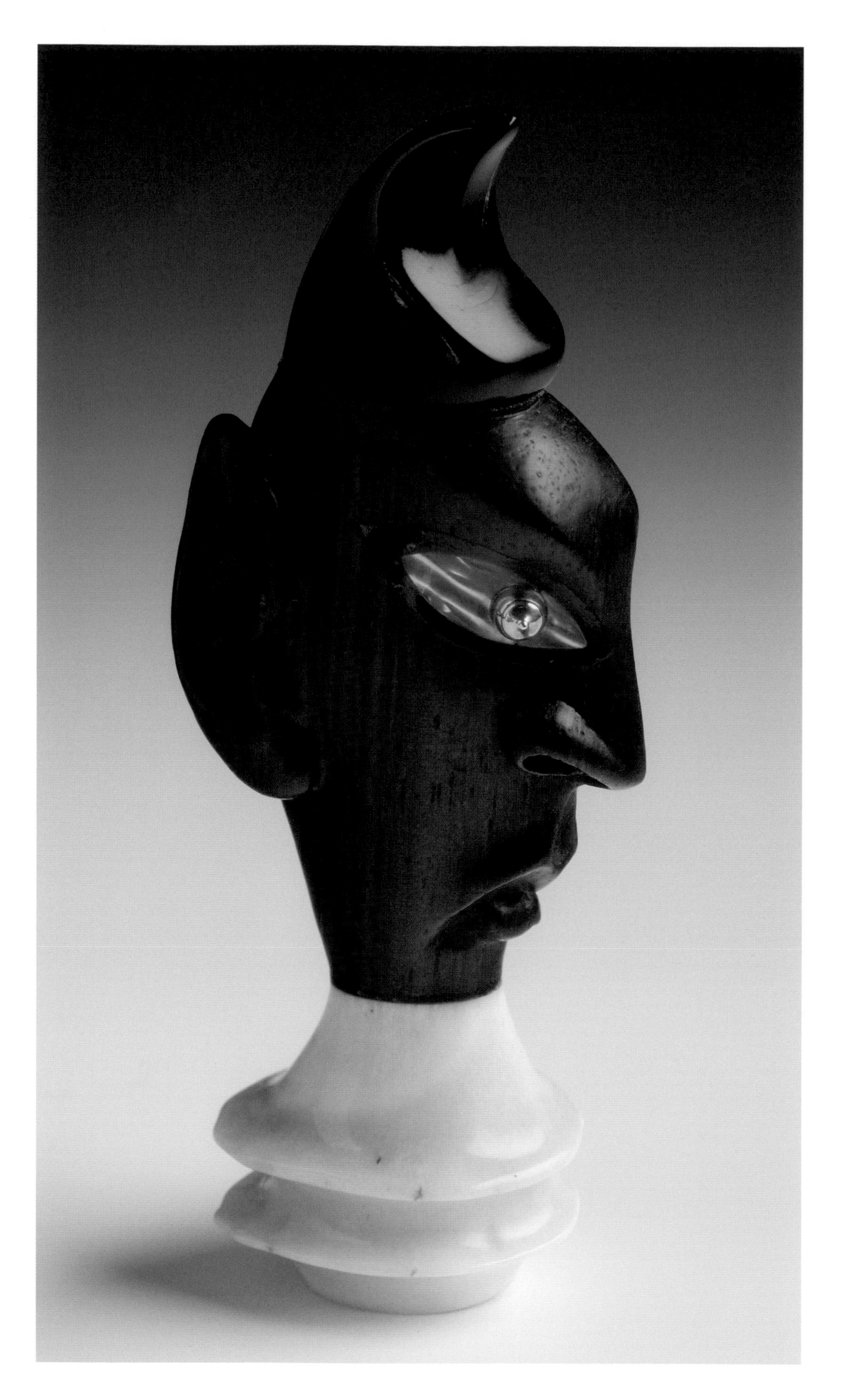

The Exotic Princeling

Head in rosewood. Eyes in blue lacquer, abalone and gold. Headgear in Hawaiian umimatsu. Stag antler plinth.

Height 9.2cm. 1996.

Exhibited & Illustrated Tactiles by Michael Henry Birch I.N.S.C. Chicago 1999.

The Samurai

Siberian mammoth ivory.

Height 3.7cm. 1994.

Exhibited The Carvings of Michael Henry Birch N.K.C. New York 1995.

Exhibited Michael Birch Netsuke Carver and Sculptor National College of Art & Design Dublin 1997.

Exhibited & Illustrated Tactiles by Michael Henry Birch I.N.S.C. Boston 2001.

Exhibited & Illustrated Netsuke Sculptures by Michael Henry Birch I.N.S.C. Honolulu 2004.

The natural patina of the outer bark has been retained on the back surface of the carving and the thickness of the tooth enamel can be clearly seen.

Masks have been used by cultures throughout history in religious ceremonies, dances and theatrical performances. In Japan, they play a vital part in representing the principal performers in Noh dramas, in their classical roles as heroes, gods, demons, ghosts, legendary animals and foreigners. Masks have long been subjects for netsuke, usually carved singly but sometimes in pairs or compact groups.

MHB 1976

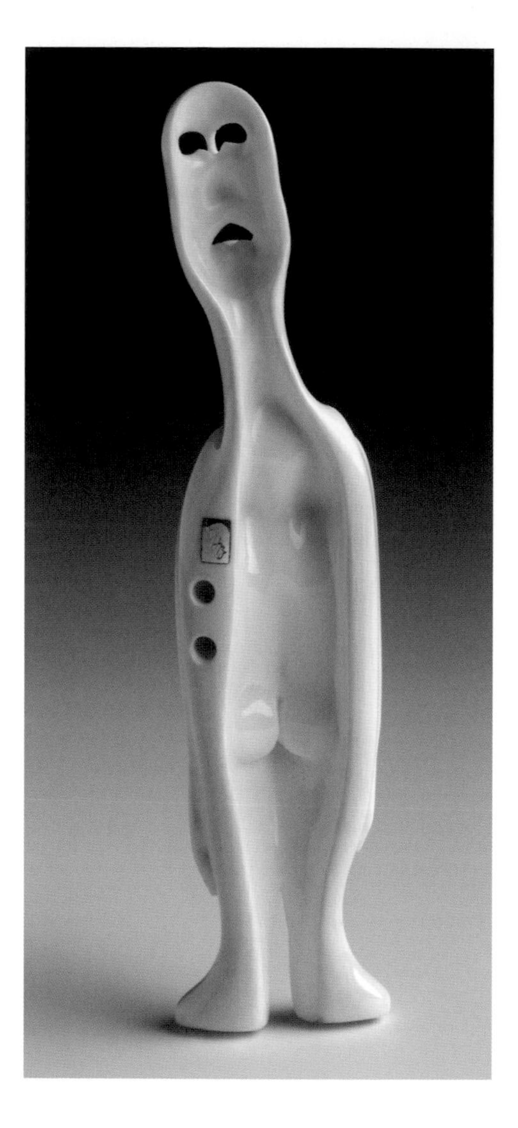

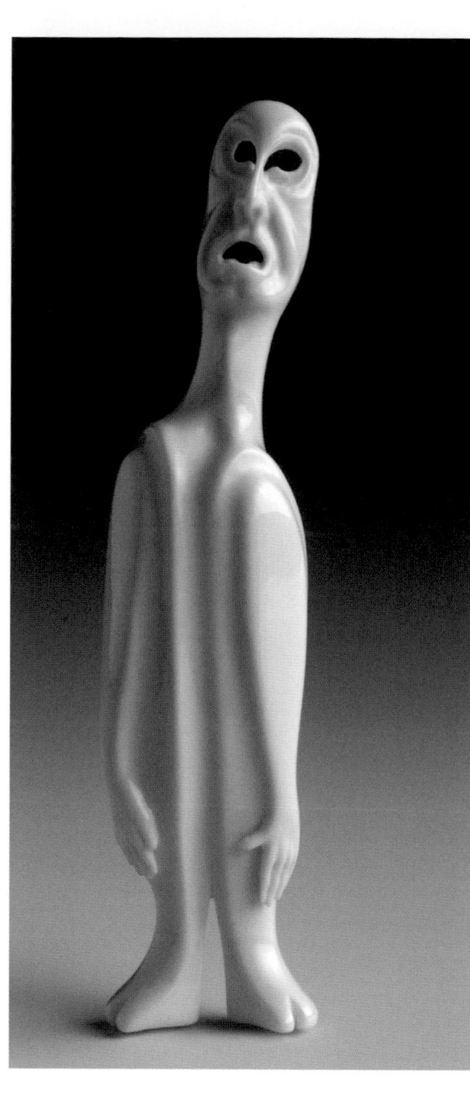

Noh Actor

Hippopotamus incisor. The un-carved unpolished enamel gives the actor's cloak its texture. Hair in rhinoceros. Eyes in drawn crystal rod.

Height 5.5cm. 1978.

Exhibited N.K.C. Minneapolis 1979.

Illustrated lecture Notion to Netsuke Minneapolis 1979.

Exhibited Sotheby's Bond St. London. 1994.

Exhibited Michael Birch Netsuke Carver and Sculptor National College of Art & Design Dublin 1997.

Standing Mask-man

Elephant ivory.

Height 9.8cm.

Exhibited Sotheby's Bond St. London. 1994.

Exhibited Michael Birch Netsuke Carver and Sculptor National College of Art & Design Dublin 1997.

Fierce-face Mask

Stag antler coronet.

Height 4.6cm. 1995.

Exhibited The Carvings of Michael Henry Birch N.K.C. New York 1995.

Illustrated I.N.S.J. Vol. 16 No. 2 1996.

Exhibited Michael Birch Netsuke Carver and Sculptor National College of Art & Design Dublin 1997.

Mask

Bamboo. 1978.

Exhibited The Carvings of Michael Henry Birch I.N.S.C. Honolulu 1979.

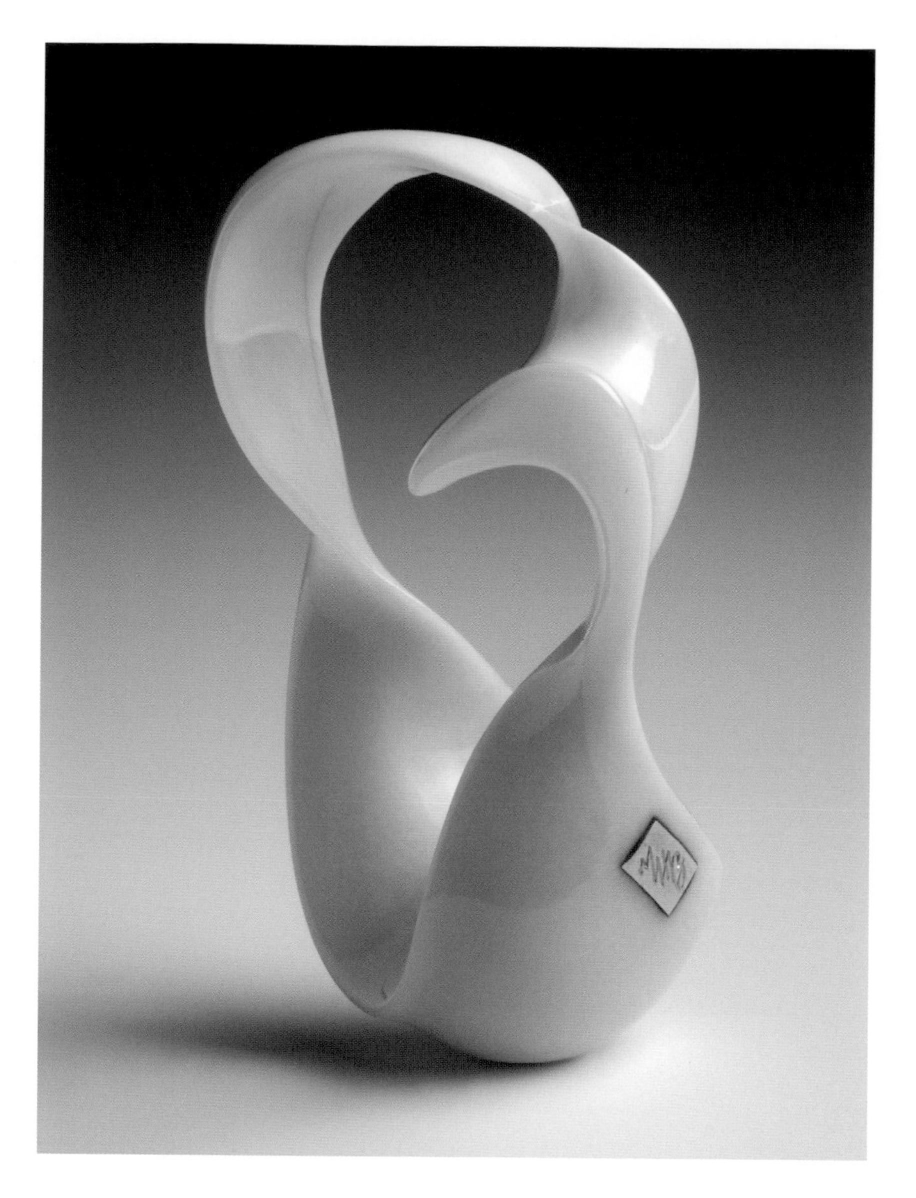

The Vanishing Guru

Hippopotamus incisor

Height 5.6cm. 1996.

Illustrated I.N.S.J. Vol. 16 No. 2 1996.

Exhibited & Illustrated The Carvings of Michael Henry Birch I.N.S.C. Honolulu 1997.

Illustrated International Netsuke Society European Chapter Lecture Sotheby's London 1997.

ACTUAL SIZE

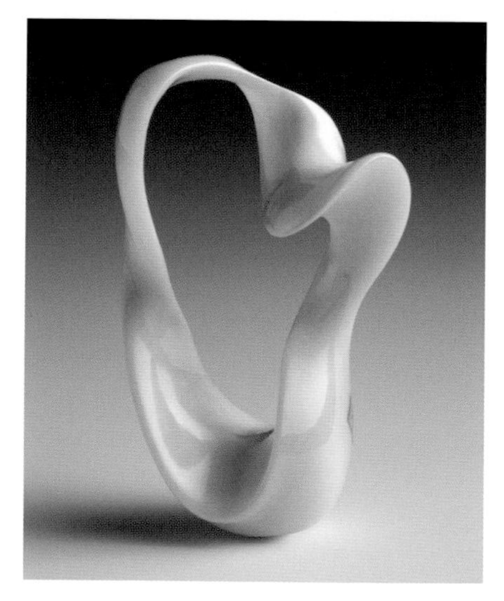

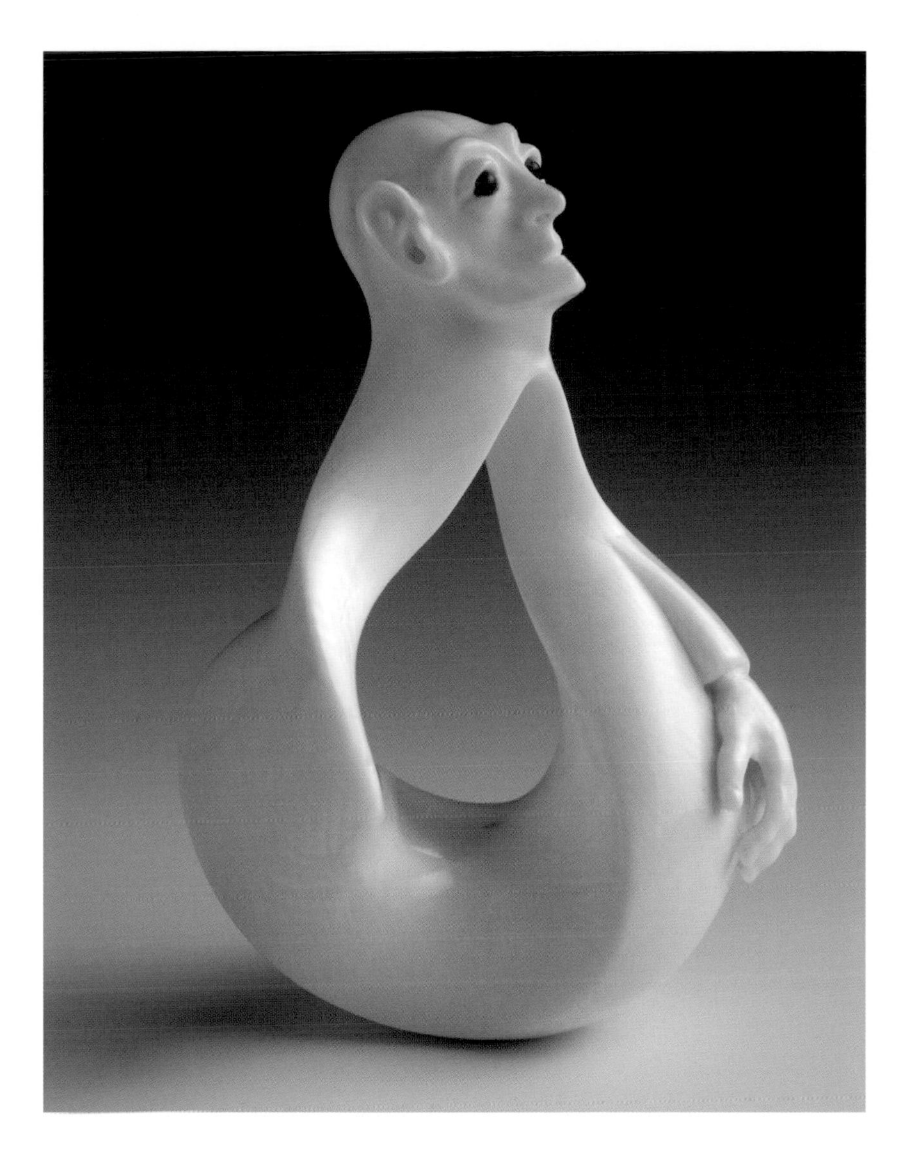

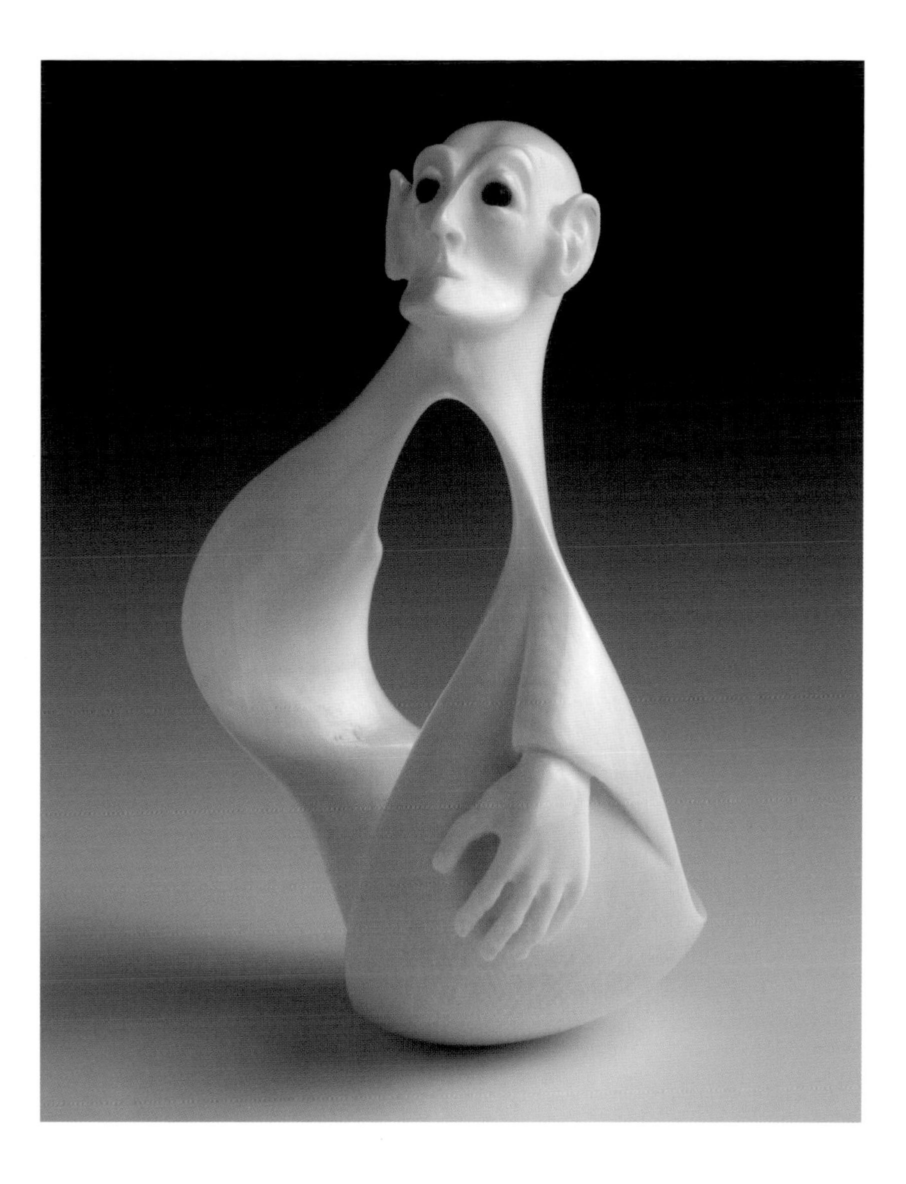

Doctor Möbius was relatively unknown until he chanced upon the phenomenon that was to bring him everlasting fame. The greatest mystery is why no one thought of it before.

MHB

ACTUAL SIZE

Doctor Möbius in Symbiosis with his own Discovery

Siberian mammoth ivory.
Eyes in drawn crystal rod.
Height 7.7cm. 1997.

Illustrated International Netsuke Society European Chapter Lecture Sotheby's London 1997.

Exhibited & Illustrated Tactiles by Michael Henry Birch I.N.S.C. Chicago 1999.

Exhibited & Illustrated Tactiles by Michael Henry Birch I.N.S.C. Boston 2001.

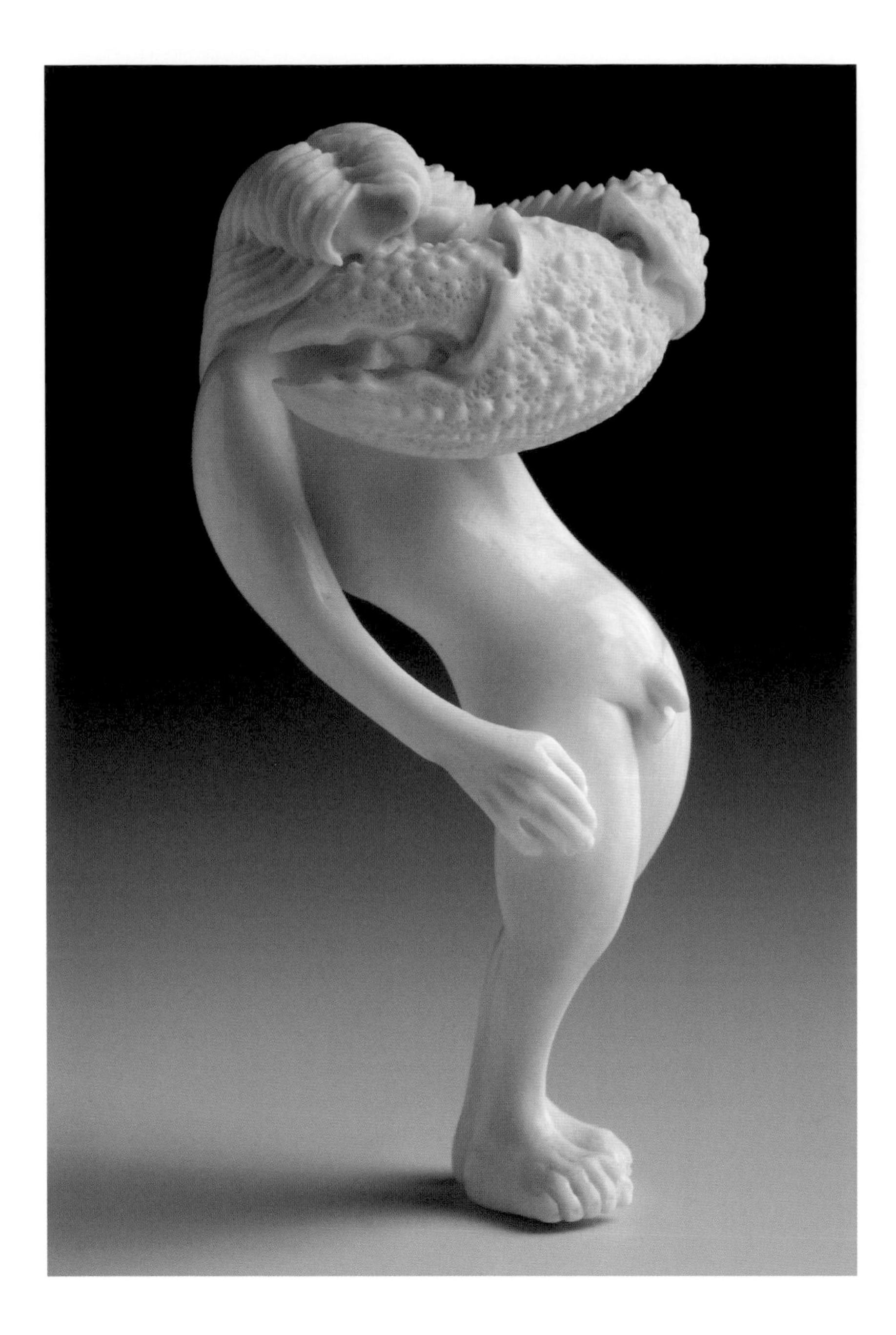

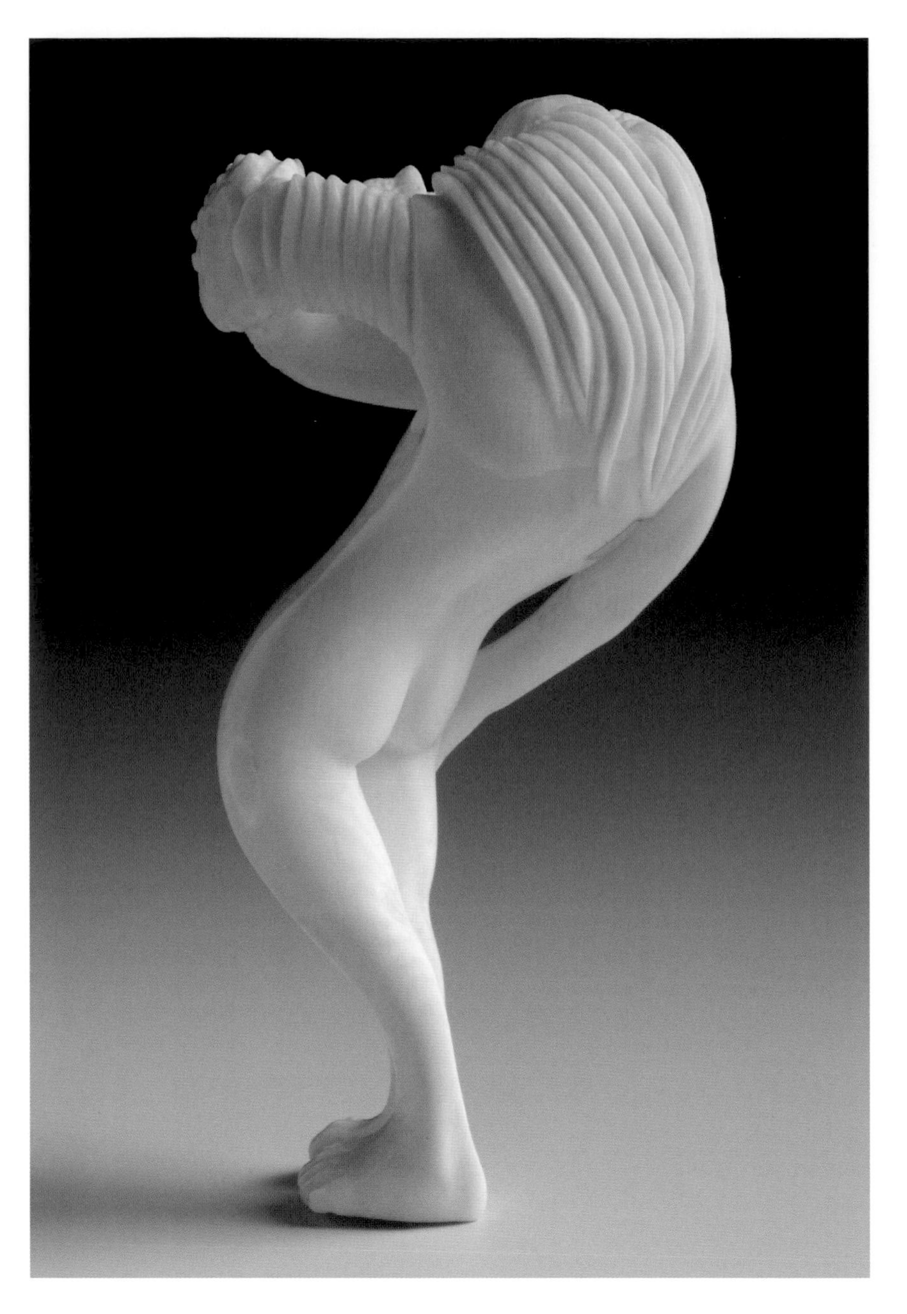

The Beckoner

Siberian mammoth ivory.

Height 8.7cm. 1996.

Exhibited & Illustrated The Carvings of Michael Henry Birch I.N.S.C. Honolulu 1997.

Illustrated International Netsuke Society European Chapter Lecture Sotheby's London 1997.

Illustrated I.N.S.J. Vol. 19 No. 1 1999

Exhibited & Illustrated Tactiles by Michael Henry Birch I.N.S.C. Chicago 1999.

Exhibited & Illustrated Tactiles by Michael Henry Birch I.N.S.C. Boston 2001.

Exhibited & Illustrated Netsuke Sculptures by Michael Henry Birch I.N.S.C. Honolulu 2004.

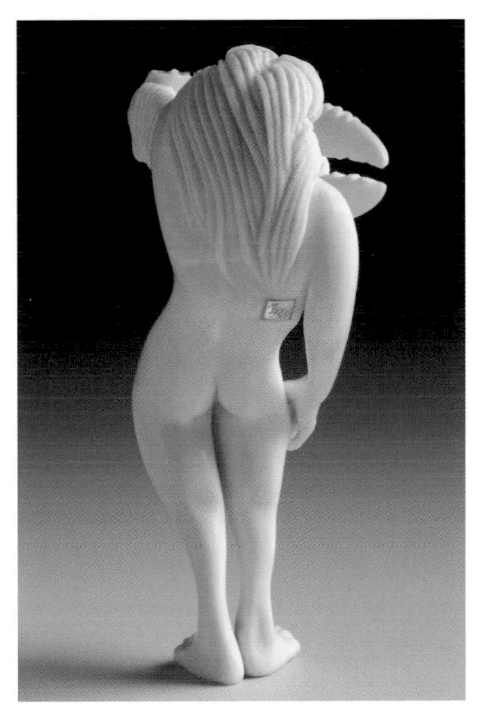

ACTUAL SIZE

This carving was inspired by the antipodean fiddler crab. He has one very small claw that he uses to feed himself and a second massive claw that is as large as the body of the crab itself. It is with this impressive claw that he beckons females during his courtship ritual. Michael told me that he had known one or two men like that.

The Female Form

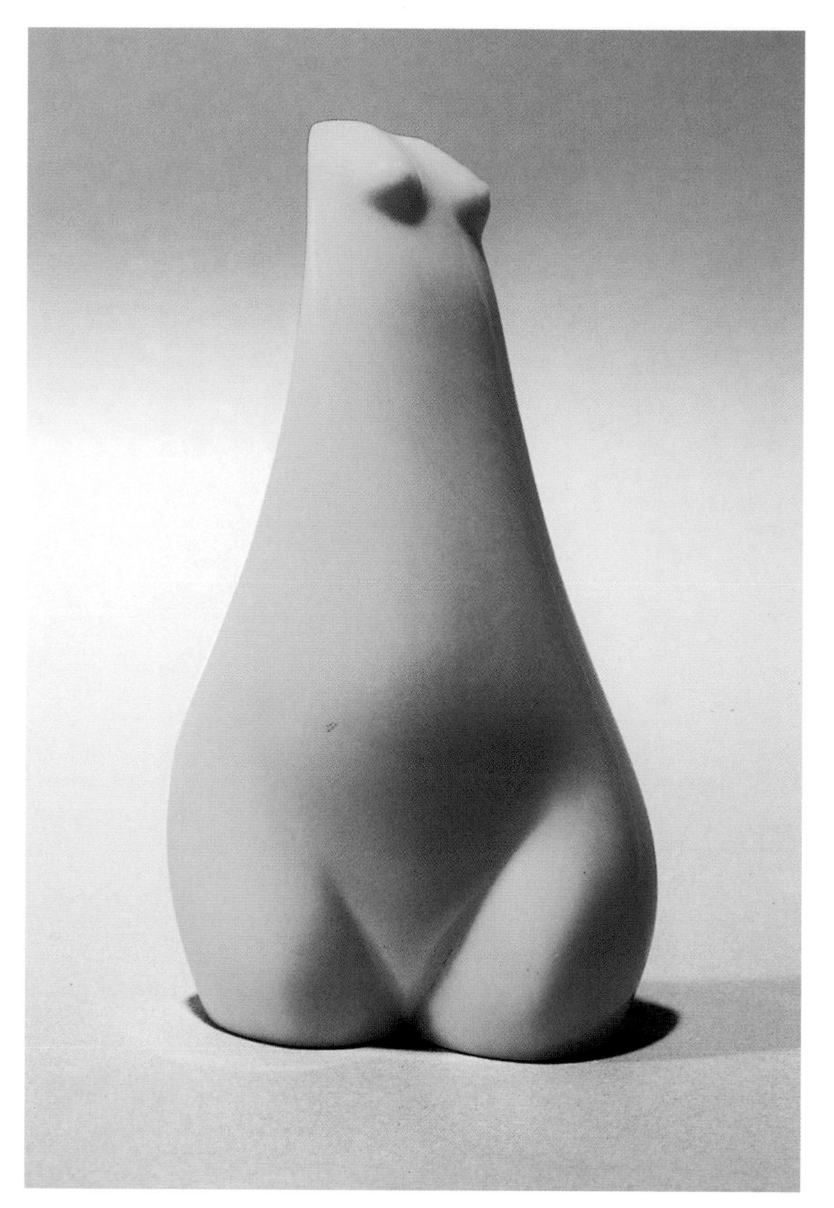

Michael Birch is foremost among European and American sculptors producing netsuke. His elegant work qualifies as miniature sculpture, whether or not it also qualifies as netsuke.

RAYMOND BUSHELL

It is early to be telling you but since the die is cast you may enjoy the anticipations as we are. Group IV (#450-#600) of our collection is scheduled for exhibition at the Los Angeles County Museum of Art from January to June 1987. No. 599 is a Michael Birch, the luscious ivory torso I got from you at the last London convention. Except for Masatoshi (Nakamura Tokisada) you will be the only contemporary carver represented.
While I am glad for you as a friend, I must assure you that our selection was based solely on artistic considerations and not at all on our personal regard.

RAYMOND BUSHELL 1986

Eve Torso

Elephant ivory.
Height 6.1cm. 1984.

Illustrated London International Convention Handbook, London 1984.

Exhibited on a rotating display The Raymond and Frances Bushell Gallery The Pavilion for Japanese Art, Los Angeles County Museum of Art.

Illustrated Netsuke The Collection of Raymond & Frances Bushell, A Legacy Los Angeles County Museum 1987.

Illustrated Handbook to London Netsuke Fair and Convention 1990.

Illustrated I.N.S.J. Vol. 16 No. 2 1996.

For Michael it was a matter of great pride that his work was included in the collection at LACMA with some of the very best netsuke from all ages.

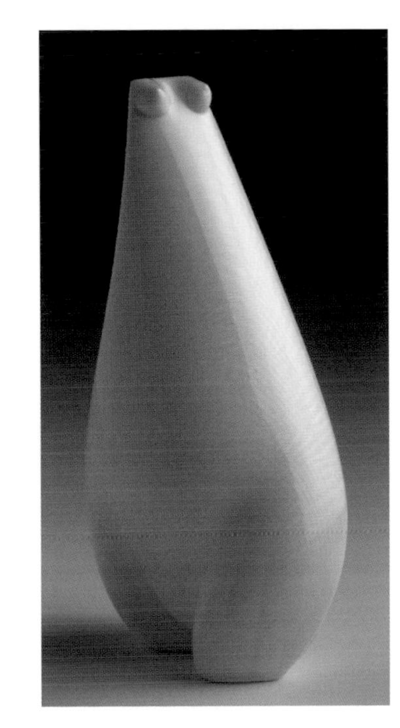

A Monument to Eve's hasty departure from the Garden of Eden

Mammoth ivory.

Height 7.9cm. 1997.

Illustrated International Netsuke Society European Chapter Lecture, Sotheby's London 1997.

Exhibited & Illustrated Tactiles by Michael Henry Birch I.N.S.C. Chicago 1999.

Exhibited & Illustrated Tactiles by Michael Henry Birch I.N.S.C. Boston 2001.

ACTUAL SIZE

When visiting the Birches in England in the late seventies, my husband greatly admired a three foot work of abstract sculpture depicting a nude torso which Michael had done. The next time we saw him he had for us a miniature replica made from black African buffalo horn. It is a smoothly tactile netsuke which my husband irreverently calls 'the lewd nude'.

MIRIAM KINSEY

The Lewd Nude

African buffalo horn.

Height 6.6cm. 1979.

Illustrated Living Masters of Netsuke by Miriam Kinsey 1983.

Exhibited Contemporary Netsuke Miniature Sculpture from Japan and Beyond The Bowers Museum of Cultural Art Santa Ana California 1997.

The Millennium Phoenix Venus

Hippopotamus incisor. Eyes in mussel pearls. Base section with inlaid red lacquer flames. Natural tooth enamel exposed at the back.

Height 9.7cm. 1998.

Exhibited & Illustrated Tactiles by Michael Henry Birch I.N.S.C. Chicago 1999.

Illustrated I.N.S.J. Vol.20 No.1 2000.

She rises wide-eyed, her skin slightly reddened from the flames of her previous existence. She bears within her present self the future incarnation that will emerge from fiery ashes at the start of the fourth millennium.

MHB

The intention to carve a coral diver is followed by the idea to use the customary and obvious materials: ebony and coral. Only the design was to be original.

MHB

Coral diver

Nigerian ebony pink coral and buffalo horn, hair tied with gold band. The himotoshi is formed by the pony-tail.
Height 9.7cm. 1977.

Illustrated Modern Carvers Antiques Trade Gazette 1978.

Illustrated I.N.C.S.J. Vol. 6 No. 2 1978.

Exhibited & Illustrated Eighteenth to Twentieth Century Netsuke Eskenazi Oriental Art London 1978.

Exhibited N.K.C. Minneapolis 1979.

Illustrated lecture Notion to Netsuke Minneapolis 1979.

Exhibited Michael Birch Netsuke Carver and Sculptor National College of Art & Design Dublin 1997.

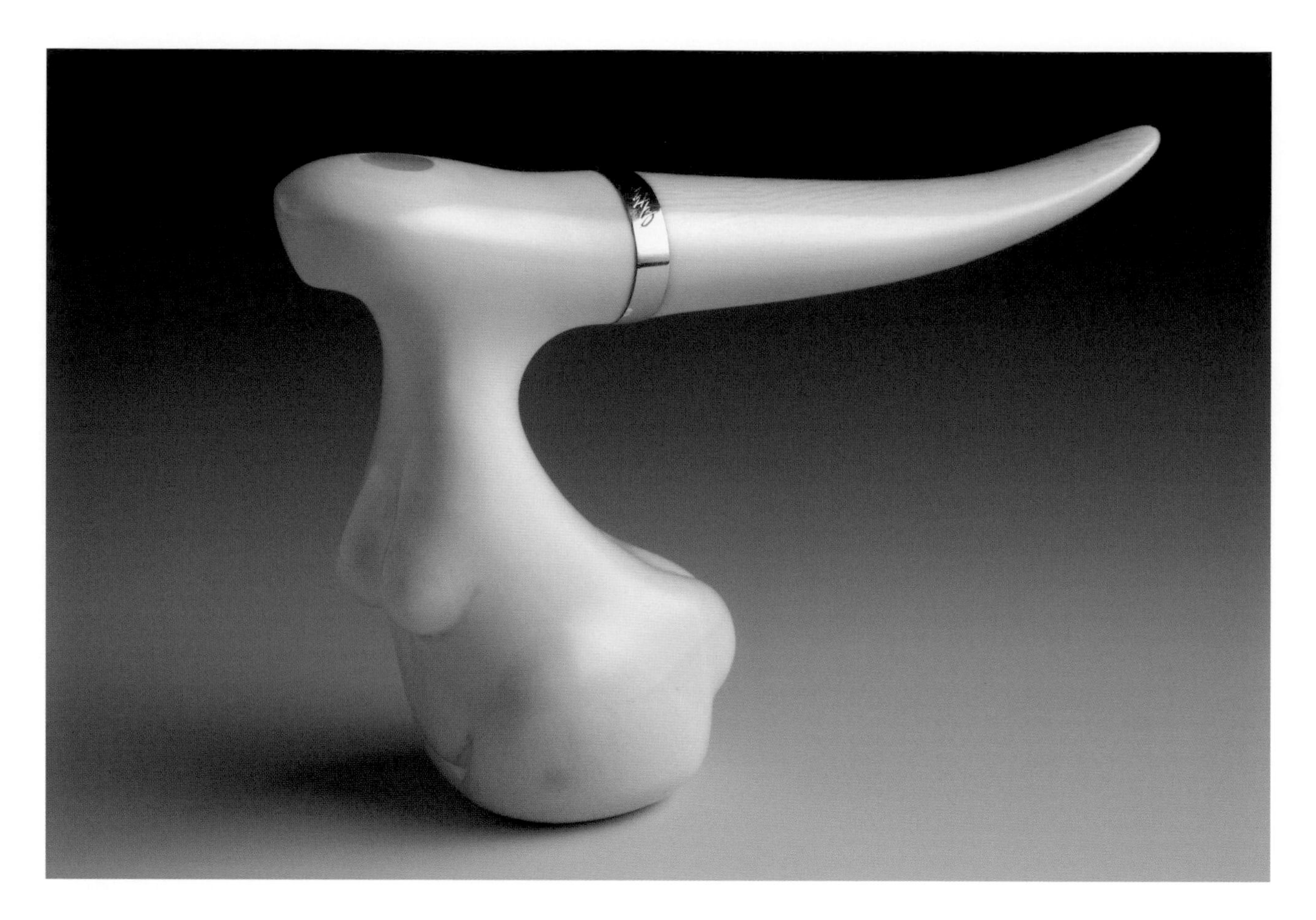

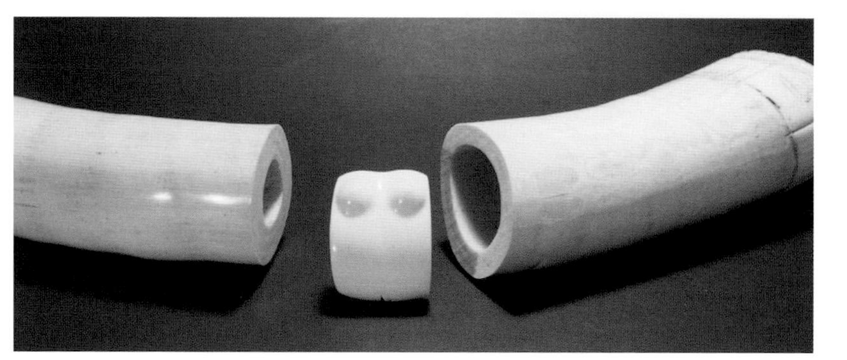

Auctioneer's gavel

Elephant ivory and gold

The hollow end of the tusk is not normally used for netsuke carving because of its thin cross section. In this case an end segment of this very old piece of ivory has been simply and effectively carved into an erotic torso of voluptuous proportions.

MIRIAM KINSEY

Toroidal Torso

The rear view shows that the spinal vertebrae and the hollow of the back have been carved.

Cow elephant ivory.

Height 4.6cm. 1978.

Illustrated Living Masters of Netsuke by Miriam Kinsey 1983.

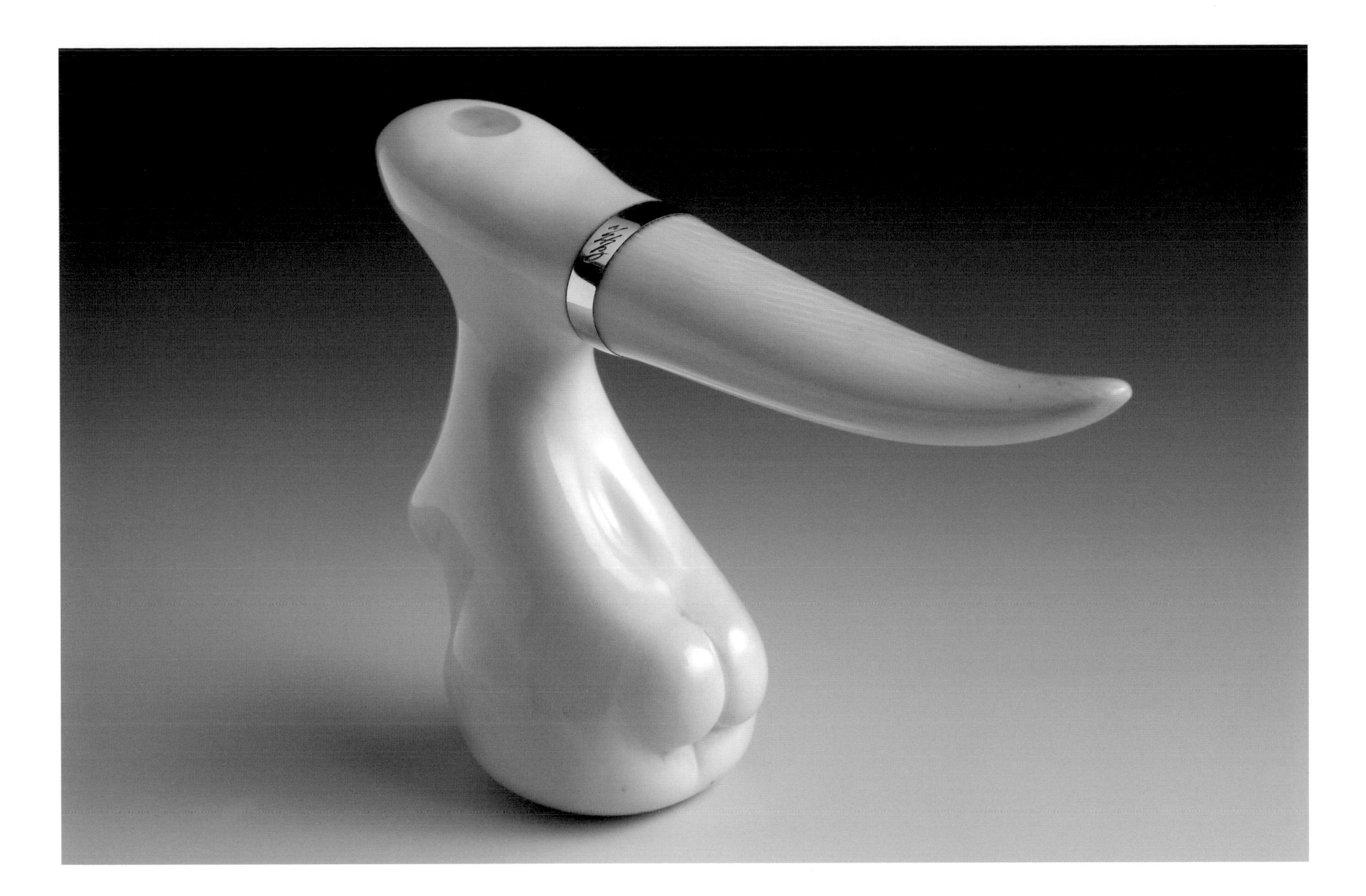

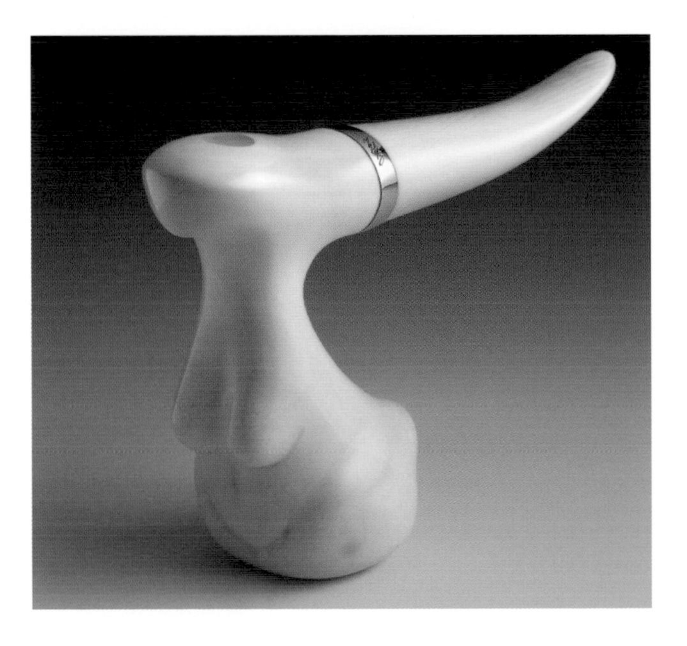

One of my most treasured objects is not a netsuke at all, but the auctioneer's gavel that Michael made for me in 1984. In this, he created a utilitarian object of great beauty, which is a joy to handle, so much so that it has, over the years, built up a patina worthy of an old well-used netsuke and has been much admired and envied by many other auctioneers.

NEIL DAVEY

ACTUAL SIZE

The Venus Torso

Pacific umimatsu and amber.
Eyes set in gold.
Height 7.5cm. 1998.

Exhibited & Illustrated Tactiles by Michael Henry Birch I.N.S.C. Chicago 1999.

Exhibited & Illustrated Tactiles by Michael Henry Birch I.N.S.C. Boston 2001.

Exhibited & Illustrated Netsuke Sculptures by Michael Henry Birch I.N.S.C. Honolulu 2004.

Umimatsu is made up of millions of microscopic polyps that can render the material friable and likely to shatter during the carving process. It comes in a variety of colours and in many pattern configurations and this often leads to a fussy or over-decorative surface which is unsuitable for many netsuke designs. These limitations mean that if such a piece of material is to be used, the subject has to be planned with strong but simple lines. Here it forms the torso carved with simple but voluptuous curves. The subtle difference between this and the piece of dark amber that Michael carved for the head and neck is not immediately obvious. It is the combination of graceful elegance and the highly decorative materials that Michael used to create this piece that made it one of his favourite sculptures.

Real Beasts

The horse in Japanese art is a creature of war and indefatigable spirit. It symbolises courage and endurance and represents the ninth hour of the day in the astrological zodiac. According to legend, the artist Kose Kanaoka painted horses with such skill that they came to life during the night and went out to graze. In Japanese paintings of horses, the maxim 'the fewest brush strokes lead to the finest work' was poignantly illustrated by Hokusai when he portrayed a horse perfectly with only eight strokes of his brush.

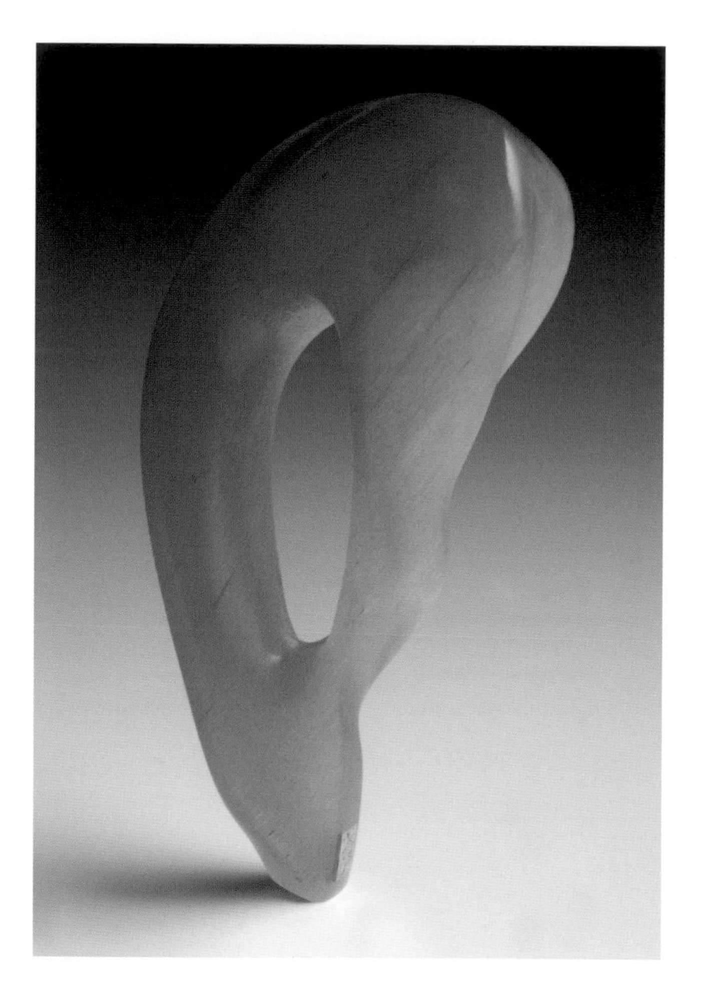

Grazing colt

Rare flawless blonde section of rhinoceros horn.
Height 7.0cm. 1980.

Exhibited Netsuke by Birch London Netsuke Convention 1980.
Illustrated Michael Birch by Nicolas Westover Euronetsuke 2003.

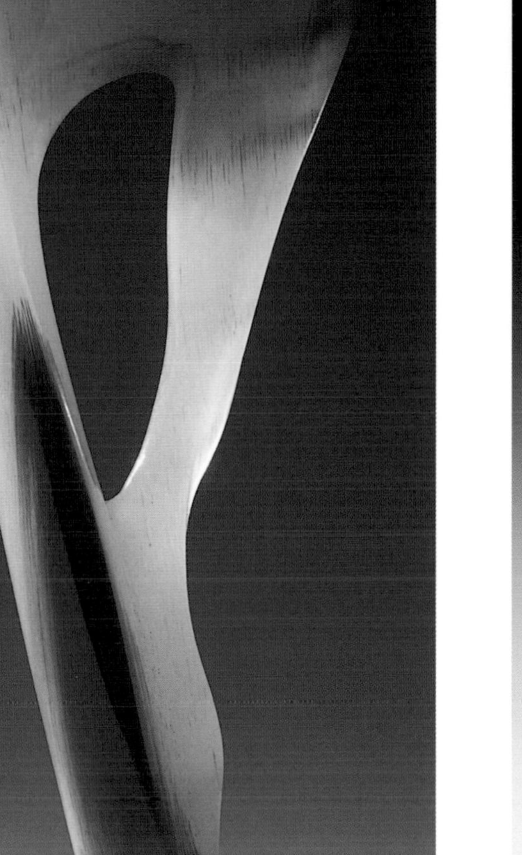

Grazing Colt

Rhinoceros horn.

Height: 11.5cm. 1978.

Illustrated: I.N.C.S.J.,Vol. 6 No. 3 1978.

Exhibited The Carvings of Michael Henry Birch, I.N.S.C. Honolulu 1979.

Illustrated Christie's New York Auction Catalogue, 1985.

This highly stylised grazing horse netsuke was carved from a flawless peripheral crown section of rare 'amber' rhinoceros horn over 100 years old.

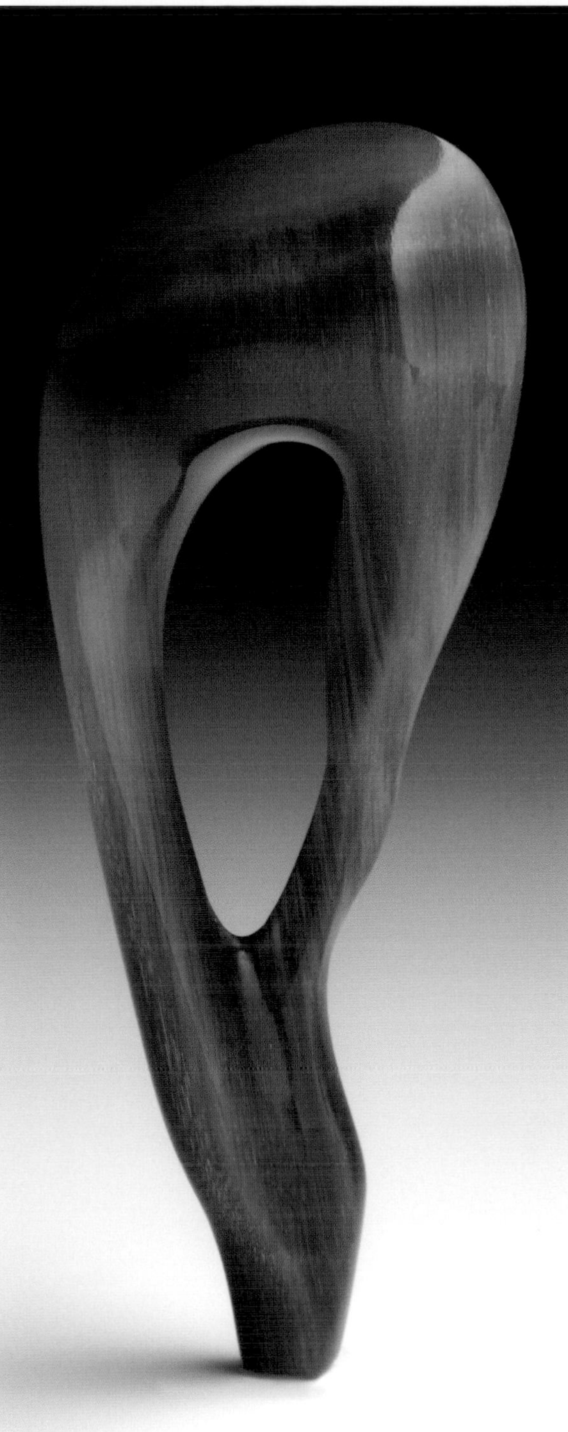

Grazing colt

Rhinoceros horn.

Height 9.6cm. 1979.

Exhibited Sotheby's Bond St. London. 1994.

Exhibited Michael Birch Netsuke Carver and Sculptor National College of Art & Design Dublin 1997.

Bear reflected on ice

Hippopotamus incisor. Eyes black onyx.
Length 6.1cm. 2003.

Dolphin

Narwhal ivory.
Length 5.0cm. Height 3.5cm.

Illustrated Michael Birch by Nicolas Westover
Euronetsuke 2003.

Despite the ravages they cause, rats are viewed by the Japanese with a measure of resignation and even some humour. Traditional netsuke rats tend, on the whole to be quite gentle attractive creatures. I really wanted this one to be tense, tough. . . a ratty rat.

MHB

This netsuke was carved from the mid-section of a stag antler from the island of Molokai Hawaii. The use of dark staining to shade the porous areas of material has produced a grey mottled texture that resembles the rodent's fur. With ears laid back and head thrust forward on an elongated neck it creates a vivid impression of alertness.

MARIAN KINSEY

Ratty Rat

Stag antler darkly stained.
Eyes in mussel pearls.
Length 7.6cm. 1978.

Exhibited N.K.C. Minneapolis 1979.

Illustrated lecture Notion to Netsuke Minneapolis 1979.

Illustrated Living Masters of Netsuke by Miriam Kinsey 1983.

Exhibited & illustrated Contemporary Netsuke Miniature Sculpture from Japan and Beyond The Bowers Museum of Cultural Art Santa Ana California 1997.

Exhibited & Illustrated Contemporary Netsuke The Kinsey Collection Accompanied by H.I.H. Prince Takamado Collection by Robert O. Kinsey Chiba City Museum of Art Japan. 2001.

Exhibited & Illustrated Netsuke The Prince Takamado Collection Tokyo National Museum Japan 2011.

Rat

Stag antler. Eyes in mussel pearls.
Length 7.0cm Height 2.5cm. 1979.

Illustrated Michael Birch by Nicolas Westover Euronetsuke 2003.

Ratty Rat

Rhinoceros horn.
Eyes in black onyx.
Length 8.3cm. c.1979.

Illustrated Contemporary Netsuke,
The H.I.H. Prince Takamado Collection
The Tobacco & Salt Museum Tokyo
Japan. 2003.

Questing Rat

Stag antler.
Eyes in drawn crystal rod. 1979.

Rat on the watch

Stag antler. Porous section sealed with clear lacquer. Eyes in black onyx. 1994.

Exhibited The Carvings of Michael Henry Birch
N.K.C. New York 1995.

Exhibited & Illustrated Tactiles by Michael Henry
Birch I.N.S.C. Boston 2001.

Exhibited Sotheby's Bond St. London 1994.

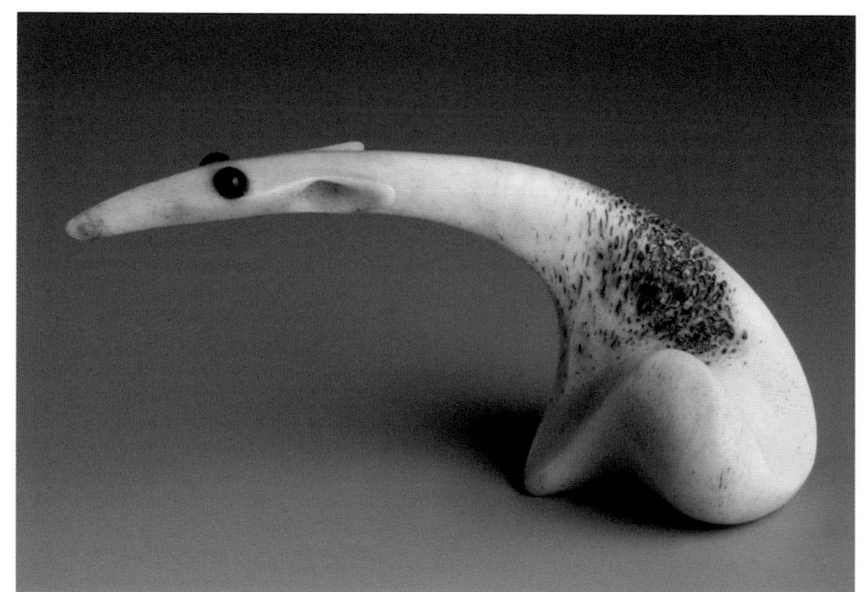

Ratty Rat

Stag antler unstained.
Eyes in mussel pearls.
Length 5.4cm. 2002.

From the Earth

In the East the bean is the symbol of renewed life. The similarity between 'mamma' the Japanese word for bean and the greeting Mamede Kurase 'I wish you health' has given beans a symbolic meaning of great strength in Japanese folklore.

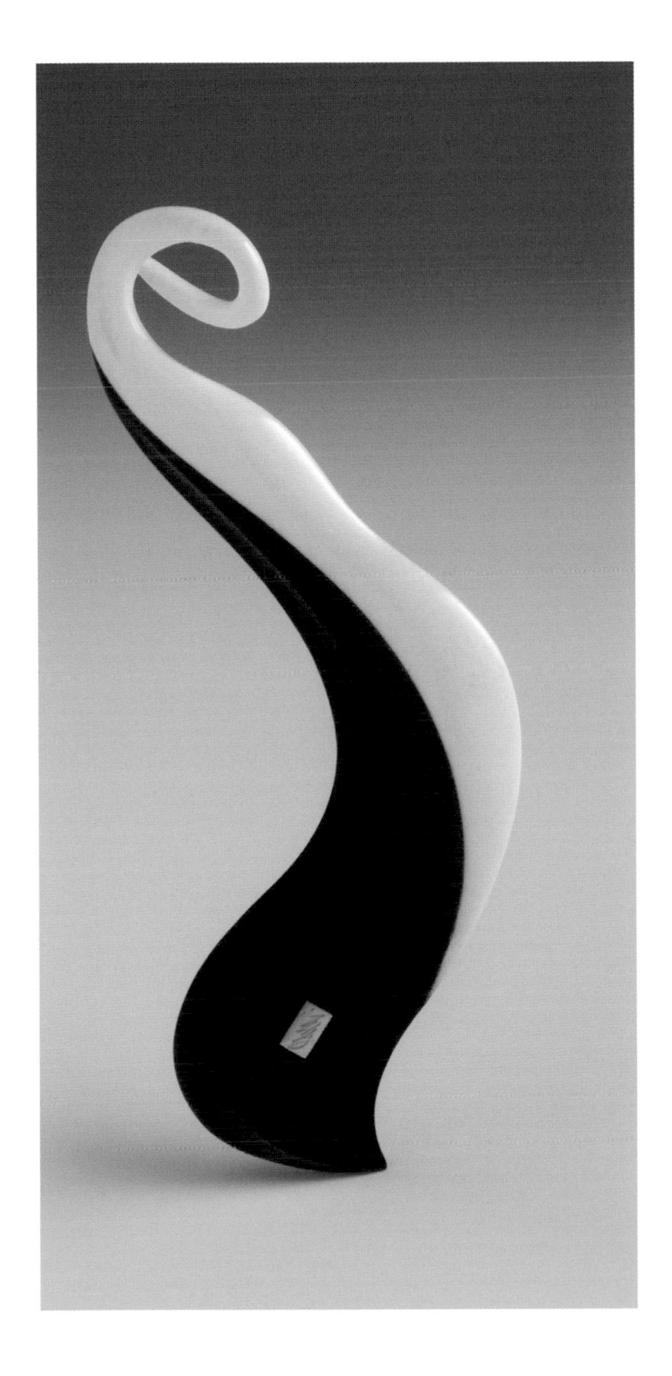

Yin/Yang Bean Pod representing the female form

Elephant ivory and ebony.
Dewdrops in oyster pearls.
Height 9.6cm. 1977.

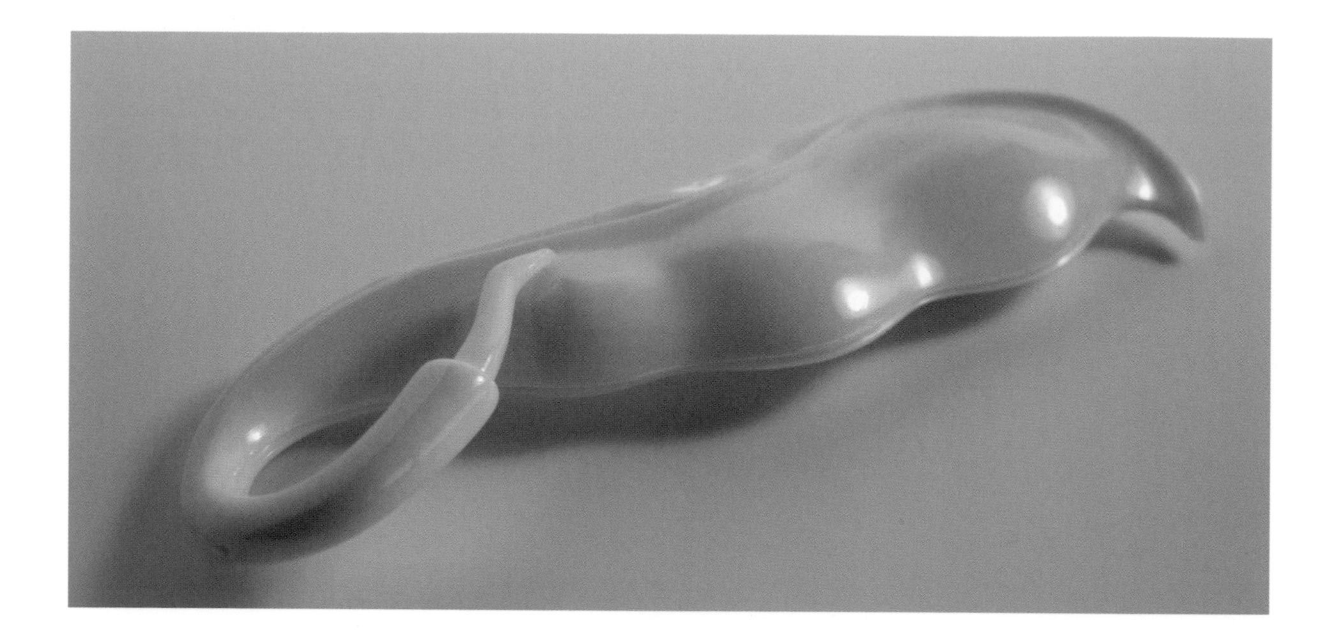

Bean Pod

Elephant ivory

Length 15cm. 1980

Illustrated Michael Birch I.N.S.C. by Nicholas Westover Euronetsuke 2003.

A single bean with a tiny gold stem nestles in a highly polished pod segment. This compact functional netsuke is an eloquent reference to the legend.

MIRIAM KINSEY

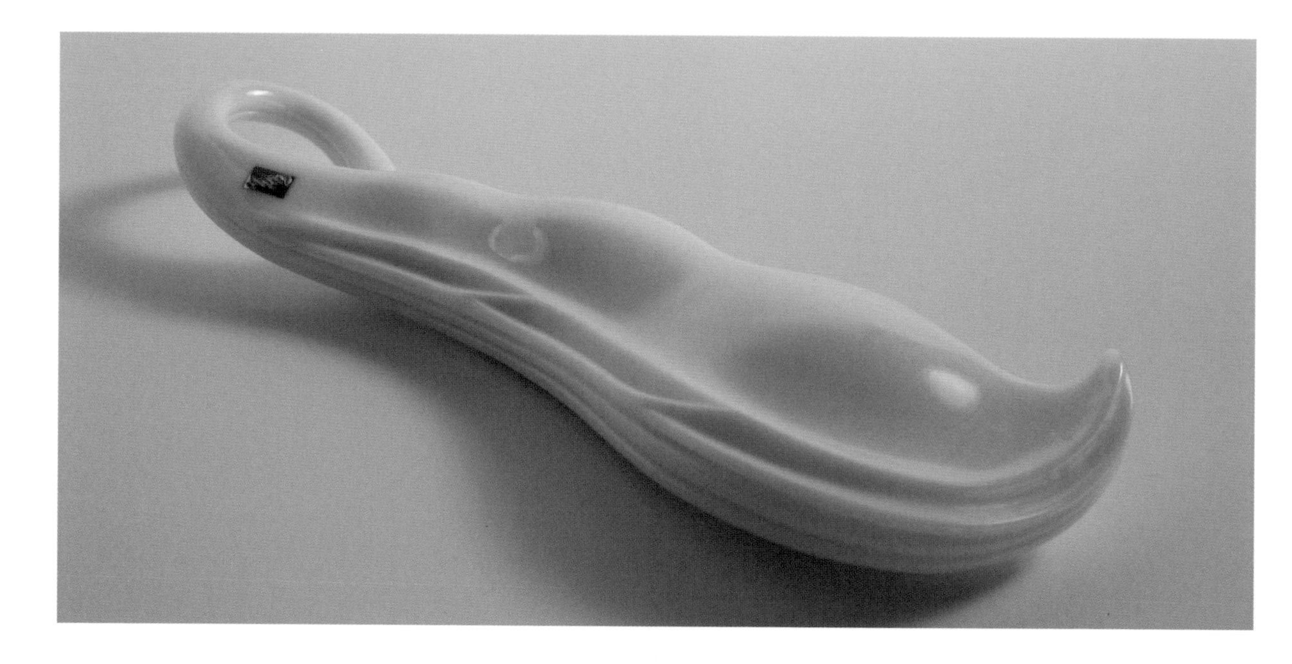

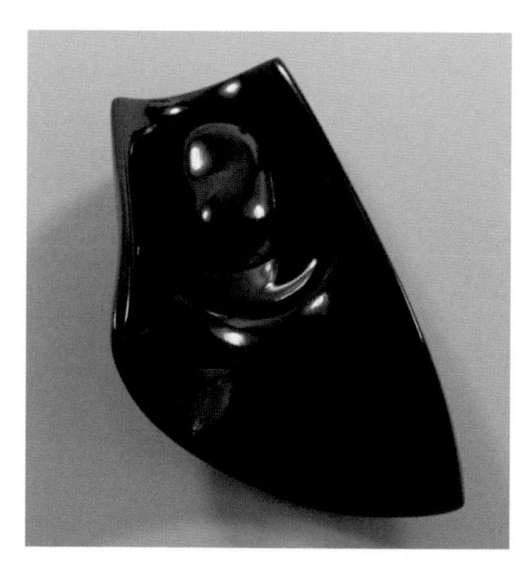

Sliced Bean

Buffalo horn and gold.

Height 5.1cm. 1975.

Exhibited & Illustrated Michael Birch Netsuke and Sculpture Eskenazi Oriental Art London 1976.

Illustrated Living Masters of Netsuke by Miriam Kinsey 1983.

The 16th century warrior Kenshin possessed an exceptionally sharp sword with magical properties which had belonged to a farmer of Echigo. According to legend this farmer held his unsheathed sword vertically above his head during a violent storm. When the storm had abated, the sword as well as his clothing was drenched in the blood of Raijin the thunder god who had carelessly spayed himself on the blade. On another occasion, the very same sword had neatly sliced each bean as it fell from a hole in the farmer's bag which he was carrying on his back.

MHB

The design of the carving is a subtly erotic analogue of the female form, the arched stem resembling the nape of the neck. . . the pod has sensuous curves and its lower half seen from the rear is suggestive of a gently provocative swing of the hips. One added feature of the netsuke is the visual illusion of bean seeds in the pod's interior when the piece is held up to the light making the carving a reference to female fecundity.

MHB

Despite being hesitant in accepting commissions Michael agreed to carve a piece for an exhibition of shunga netsuke. For his subject, shown here at right, he selected the subject of a bean pod the symbol of fecundity and fertility and carved the piece in the female form. Michael considered this one of his finest carvings and was disappointed when the subtlety of the piece was not recognised and it was rejected as not being shunga enough.

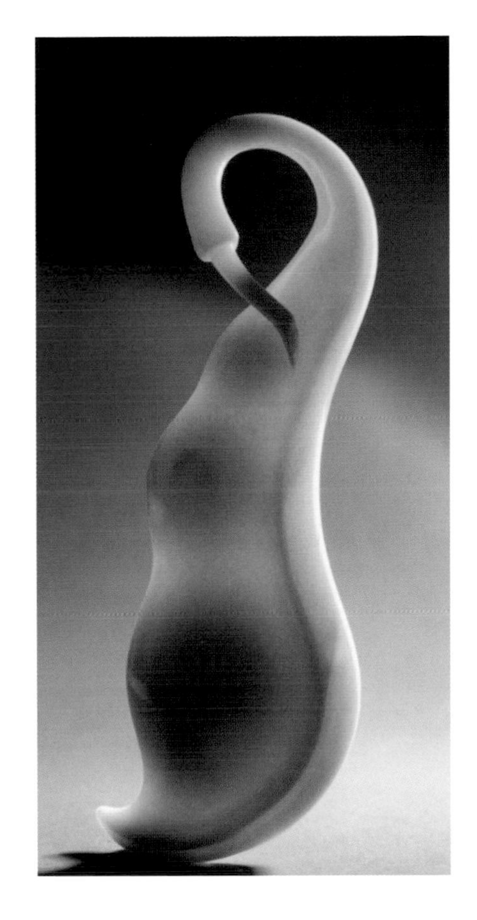

Bean pod

Elephant ivory and ebony.

Height 9.4cm 1976.

Exhibited N.K.C. Kansas City 1977.

Illustrated Living Masters of Netsuke by Miriam Kinsey 1983.

Exhibited Contemporary Netsuke Miniature Sculpture from Japan and Beyond The Bowers Museum of Cultural Art Santa Ana California 1997

This deceptively simple abstract carving is a subtle analogy to the female form. The erotic nuance can be seen in the sinuous outlines especially in the curve of the stem which suggests the provocative tilt of the female neck in Japanese art. It is also discreetly implied by the unfolding ripened pod.

MIRIAM KINSEY

The Dancing Bean

Hippopotamus incisor.

Height 10.4cm. 1997.

Illustrated International Netsuke Society European Chapter Lecture Sotheby's London 1997.

Exhibited & Illustrated Tactiles by Michael Henry Birch I.N.S.C. Chicago 1999.

Exhibited & Illustrated Contemporary Netsuke The Kinsey Collection Accompanied by H.I.H. Prince Takamado Collection by Robert O. Kinsey Chiba City Museum of Art Japan. 2001.

Bean in the shape of a Swan

Narwhal ivory.
Height 6.0cm.

Exhibited Sotheby's Bond St. London. 1994.

Exhibited Michael Birch Netsuke Carver and Sculptor National College of Art & Design Dublin 1997.

Illustrated MHB Lecture to International Netsuke Society European Chapter at Sotheby's London 1997.

For this most complicated of his Möbius Strip carvings, Michael first made a model in a narrow strip of lead to ensure that the mathematical rules would be correctly followed. To make this shape, one end should be turned five times for a total of 900º.

One has to follow the twists and turns from the stem and back to prove that the piece does follow the Möbius rules, but Michael's brain was able to see them as he carved, and this netsuke clearly demonstrates his visual acuity.

Bean pod
A Triple-Interlocking Möbius

Stained Siberian mammoth ivory.
Height 4.8cm. 1997.

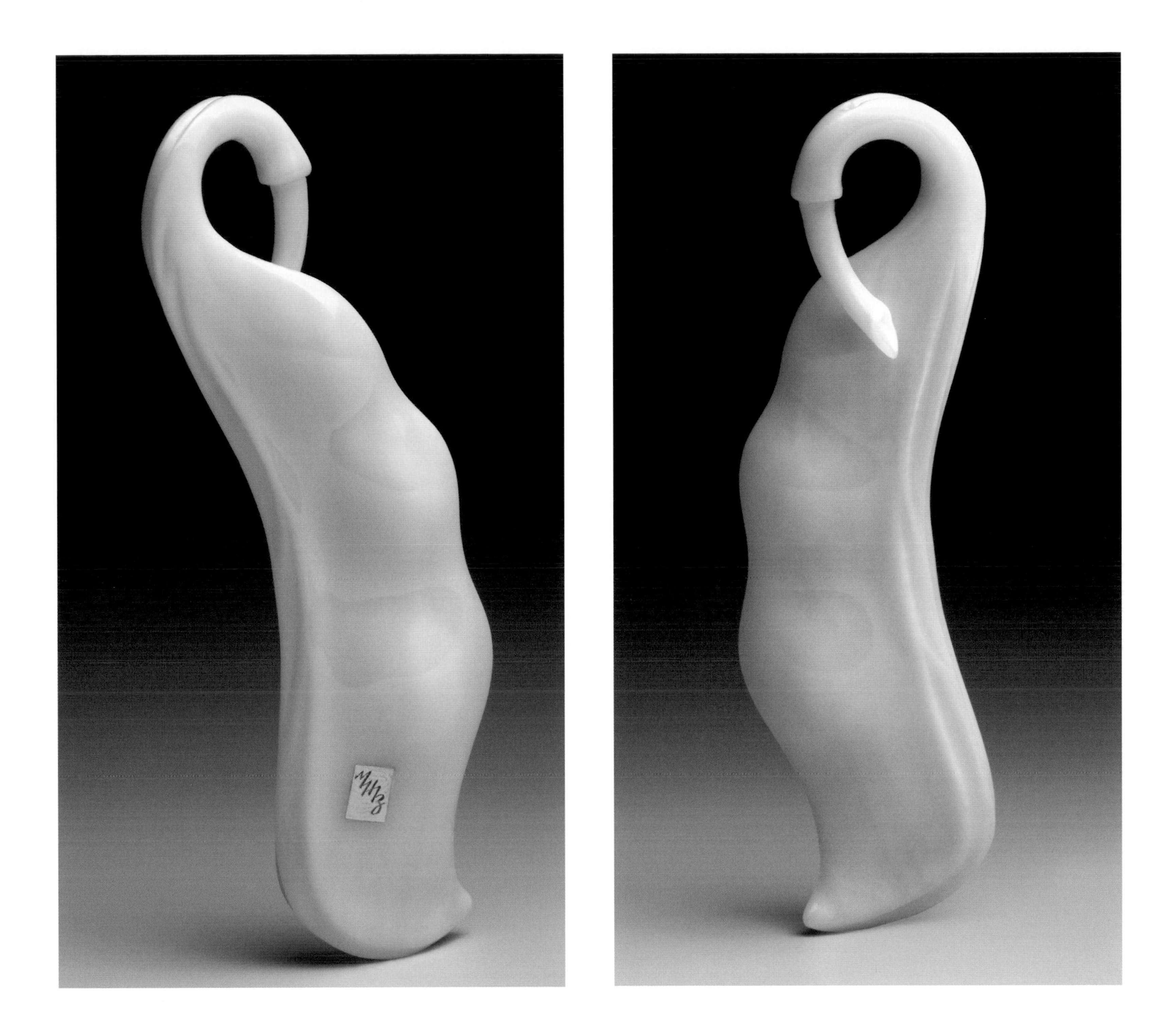

The fertile female form is suggested by the curved stem indicating the nape of the neck and the three protrusions indicating breasts, pregnant belly and rounded hips. What is not so obvious until the netsuke is held, is the curve in the spine of the bean which gives the piece a wiggle in the hips.

Bean pod

Hippopotamus incisor.
Length 9.6cm. 2002

Exhibited & Illustrated Netsuke Sculptures by Michael Henry Birch I.N.S.C. Honolulu 2004.

The Kappa is frequently epitomised in the form of a cucumber (Kappa Ni Kiuri). This netsuke represents a cucumber in flower with gold pistil.
MHB

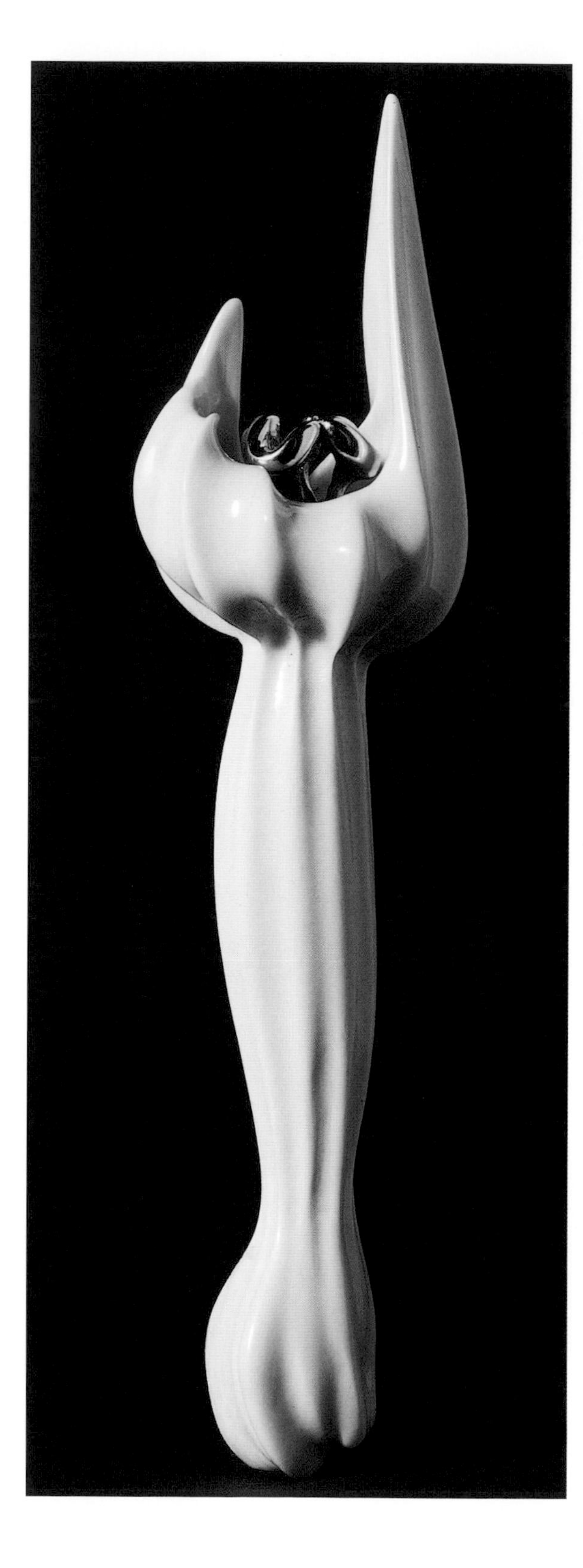

Cucumber

Elephant ivory with gold pistil (Chryselephantine).
Height 11.0cm. 1975.

Illustrated I.N.C.S.J. Vol. 4 No. 1 1976.

Exhibited & Illustrated Michael Birch Netsuke and Sculpture Eskenazi Oriental Art London 1976.

Illustrated N.K.S.J. Vol. 6 No. 2 1986.

Illustrated Christie's New York Auction Catalogue 1985.

Strawberry

Amber with insect inclusion and gold
Height 3.5cm. 1980.

Exhibited The Carvings of Michael Henry Birch, N.K.C. Los Angeles 1981.

Cape Gooseberry (Hozuki) with Spider

Clear gold amber (Ching Peh).
Ant and berry stem in 18 carat gold.
Height 3.8cm. 1979.

Exhibited N.K.C. Minneapolis 1979.

Exhibited Contemporary Netsuke Miniature Sculpture from Japan and Beyond The Bowers Museum of Cultural Art Santa Ana
California 1997.

Log with a spider guarding its refuge

Alaskan umimatsu with spider in gold.
Length 5.0cm. 1995.

Exhibited The Carvings of Michael Henry Birch
N.K.C. New York 1995.

Illustrated I.N.S.J. Vol. 16 No. 2 1996.

Seed Pod

Elephant ivory.
Height 5.0cm. 1947. Unsigned.

Exhibited Sotheby's Bond St. London. 1994.

Illustrated I.N.C.S.J. Vol. 4 No. 1 1976.

Exhibited & Illustrated Michael Birch Netsuke and Sculpture Eskenazi Oriental Art
London 1976.

This sculpture representing a seed pod is one of several small pieces carved from ivory billiard balls in the period 1946 - 1948. Readily available and the perfect size for a netsuke Michael purchased them for six pence (2½p) carved and sold them for fifteen shillings (75p).

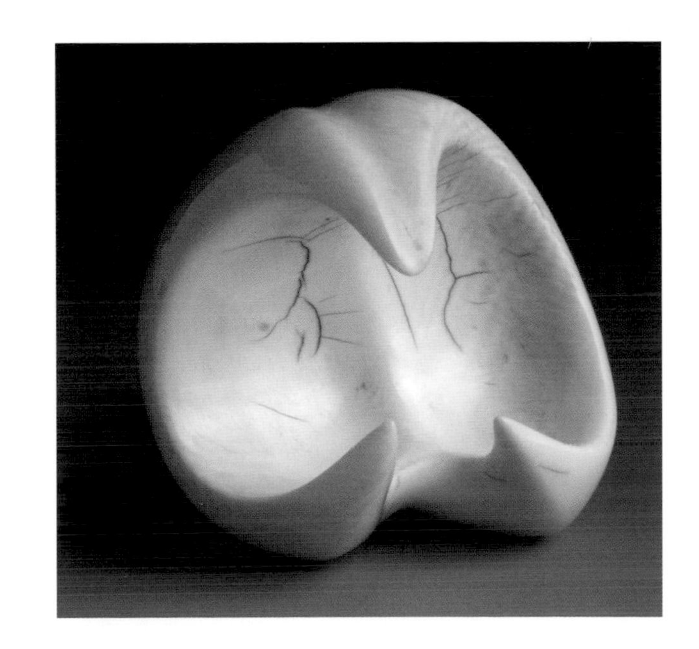

In the Air

The cicada's life cycle from egg to fully formed adult can span a period of up to seventeen years. It is not surprising, therefore, that this insect is the symbol of resurrection in a new body in Japanese mythology.

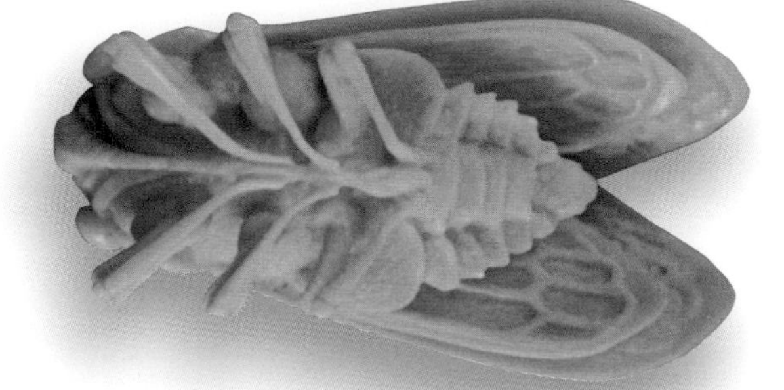

According to Richard Silverman, Michael told him that he considered this piece one of his greatest carvings. Silverman agreed. In an article written in 1977 and distributed to a small number of collectors, he stated:

I cannot end my list of the truly great carvers without mentioning the only non-Japanese whose work is equal to Masatoshi and the great masters of days gone by, Michael Birch of Britain. His netsuke have to be seen to be believed. They are exquisite in concept, form and execution.

His choice of materials is sheer perfection. I am very much a purist when it comes to 'foreigners copying indigenous art', but for Michael I had to make an exeption. His creative imagination has captured the essence of miniature sculpture and they are no less netsuke because of it. He has added a dimension to the world of netsuke that a Japanese might never be able to execute, let alone conceive. He is now working full-time as a carver, but the perfection he demands of himself allows him to create relatively few pieces and they are in great demand.

RICHARD SILVERMAN 1977

Cicada

Narwhal ivory and amber with insect inclusions.

5.0cm. 1982.

Illustrated I.N.S.J. Vol. 16 No. 2 1996.

Illustrated Sotheby's Floyd Segal Collection Auction Catalogue 1999.

Cicada

Pacific umimatsu and rare unclouded amber nugget containing several perfectly preserved Eocene flying insect inclusions. Eyes inlaid in black mussel pearls.

Length 5.4cm. Height 2.8cm. 1983.

Exhibited Sotheby's, Bond St. London 1994.

Exhibited The Carvings of Michael Henry Birch, N.K.C. New York 1995.

Exhibited Michael Birch, Netsuke Carver and Sculptor, National College of Art & Design Dublin 1997.

Exhibited& Illustrated Tactiles by Michael Henry Birch, I.N.S.C. Boston 2001.

Exhibited & Illustrated Netsuke Sculptures by Michael Henry Birch, I.N.S.C., Honolulu, 2004.

Cicada

Bois D'Arc. Eyes in mussel pearls.

1982.

The presence of a moth or butterfly in a Japanese house is often seen as a happy omen. Lepidoptera are considered to be the incarnation of souls of living persons, and when one enters the room it is an indication that the person's soul which it represents will pervade the house.

In the Japanese theatre, a dream is symbolised by the simulation of a moth fluttering about the sleeping actor's head. Moths are also widely used in coats of arms and, among the gift accoutrements in a Japanese marriage, a pair of symbolised moths or butterflies is an emblem conveying wishes for a long and happy union.

MHB

Moth

Rhinoceros horn carved across the grain. Eyes in inlaid pearls.
Width 4.5cm. 1975.

Exhibited & Illustrated Michael Birch Netsuke and Sculpture Eskenazi Oriental Art London 1976.

Exhibited The Carvings of Michael Henry Birch I.N.S.C. Honolulu 1979.

Moth

Rhinoceros horn. Eyes in inlaid pearls.
Width 7.0cm. 1978.

Illustrated Butterfield & Butterfield San Francisco Fine Oriental Works of Art Catalogue. 1981.

Discussed in The Butterfield Bulletin Issue 7 1981

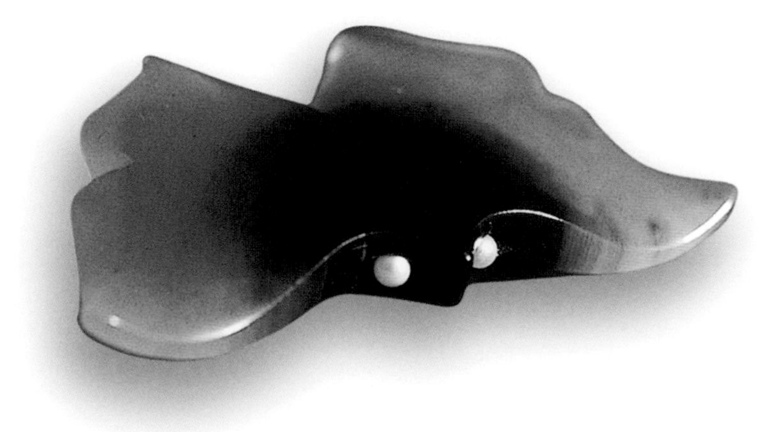

Suzume

Rhinoceros horn. Eyes in 18 carat gold.
Width 5.0cm. 1975.

Exhibited & Illustrated Michael Birch Netsuke and Sculpture Eskenazi Oriental Art London 1976.

The sparrow is an emblem of gracefulness and gentleness in Oriental art. It is generally represented in stylised form squatting with outstretched wings and rounded tail. A symbolic subject in heraldry as well as in children's toys the sparrow features in a number of legends such as the children's fable of Shitakiri Suzume (tongue-cut sparrow) which tells the tale of Bidori, the pet sparrow whose tongue is cut off for stealing starch from the wicked Arababa.

Another popular legend relates to the spirit of the exiled Fujiwara Senekata, who starved to death on the island of Oshu and was transformed into a flock of sparrows which flew into the courtyard of the Imperial palace. In Japan the image of sparrows walking in single file is the symbol for a prosperous or very rare occurrence.

MHB

My wife, Miriam, and I first met Michael in 1974 in Honolulu, during a convention of the International Netsuke Society. It was soon after he had focused his talents on the creation of netsuke and ojime. Somewhat timidly, he showed a few of his carvings to seasoned netsuke collectors. He was surprised and delighted by their interest and applause.

Soon after he returned to England, I wrote Michael a letter, asking him to create a netsuke for me to give my wife as a very special present: any subject, design, and material that he himself might decide. It was his first commission.

He arrived at our home in California with his netsuke masterpiece in August of 1975. For material he had selected rhinoceros horn. His subject was a stylised, very tactile sparrow. He had carved the horn across the grain so that the hair fibers acted as light ducts to give it a sparkling texture when held at certain angles.

Michael explained that: 'When I carved this netsuke, the tactile quality was uppermost in my mind. I felt that the hand, like the bird, is not earthbound. It can move about, flutter, hover, land, take off again, signal, or remain motionless – and that is where the piece belongs, hand-held in space.'

Of course for Miriam and me, this superb netsuke was love at first sight, and it promptly became one of our highly prized favourites.

ROBERT O. KINSEY

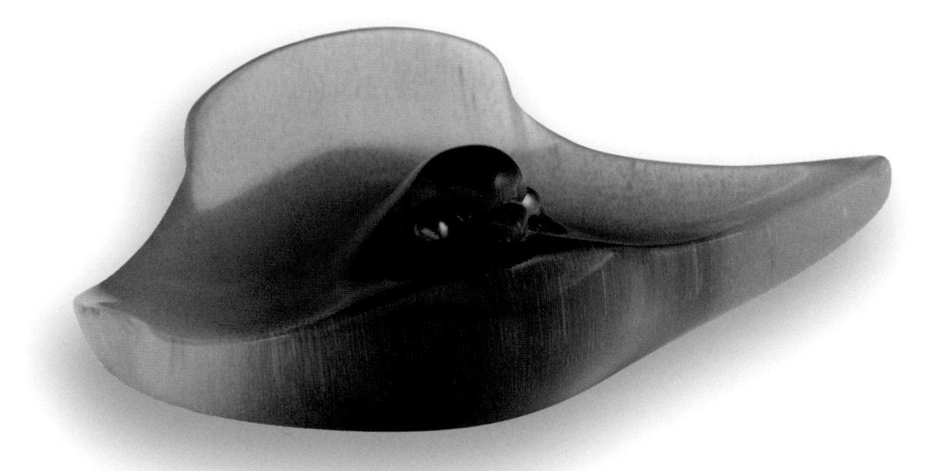

This simple pebble-like form, not much larger than a silver dollar, is one of Michael Birch's most tactile netsuke.

MIRIAM KINSEY

Suzume

Rhinoceros horn. Eyes in gold.
Width 4.9cm. 1975.

Illustrated Living Masters of Netsuke by Miriam Kinsey 1983.

Exhibited Contemporary Netsuke Miniature Sculpture from Japan and Beyond The Bowers Museum of Cultural Art Santa Ana California 1997.

This Fukura Suzume (puffed-up sparrow) netsuke was carved from the centre of the crown of an exceptionally large rhinoceros horn over one hundred years old. The contrasting tonal configuration was achieved by cutting the horn across the grain. Rhinoceros horn is composed of hair consolidated with keratin and the diffraction of light by the hair fibres is vividly apparent when this netsuke is held up to the light.

MHB

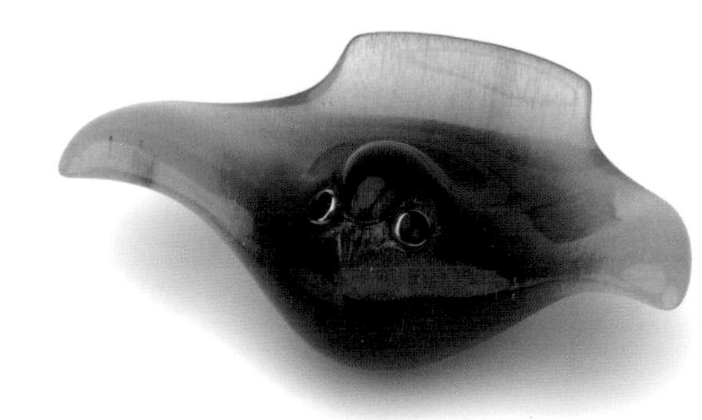

Suzume

Rhinoceros horn. Horn eyes double inlaid n horn & gold.
Height 2.5cm Width 6.0cm 1976.

Exhibited The Carvings of Michael Henry Birch I.N.C.S.C. Honolulu 1977.

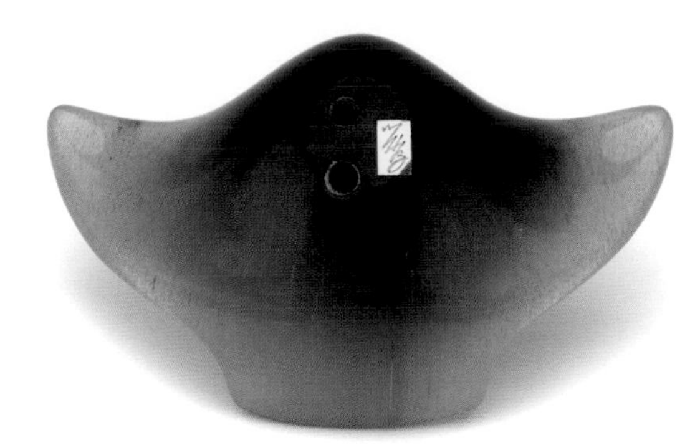

Fukura Suzume

Rhinoceros horn. Eyes in black horn.
Width 5.5cm 1975.

Exhibited & Illustrated Michael Birch, Netsuke and Sculpture, Eskenazi Oriental Art London 1976.

Illustrated The Virginia Atchley Collection of Japanese Miniature Arts by Virginia G. Atchley & Neil K. Davey 2006.

This netsuke is from a peripheral section of the crown of the horn, with the grain running longitudinally, thereby creating a tonal pattern.

MHB

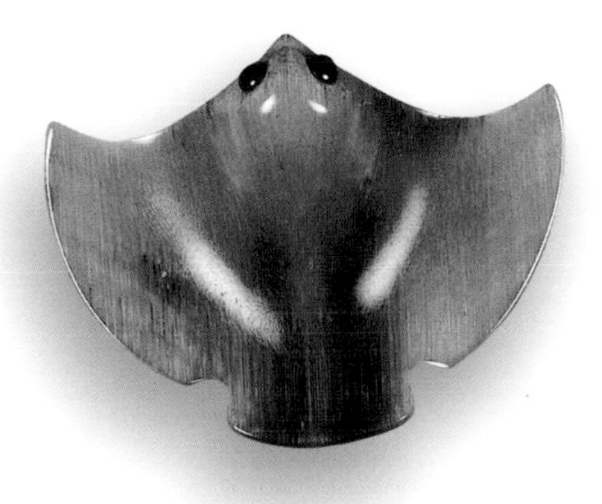

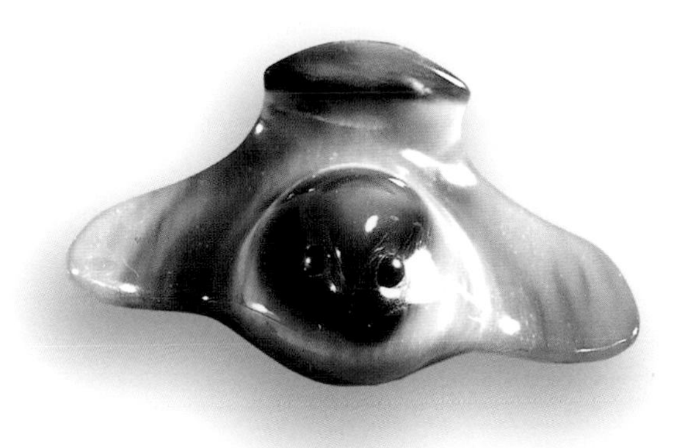

Sparrow

Nile water-buffalo horn.
Eyes in black mussel pearls.
1996.

Exhibited Michael Henry Birch Sculptures, 11th Vienna Netsuke Symposium Galerie Zacke Vienna Austria 1997.

Exhibited & Illustrated Tactiles by Michael Henry Birch I.N.S.C. Chicago 1999.

Exhibited & Illustrated Tactiles by Michael Henry Birch I.N.S.C. Boston 2001.

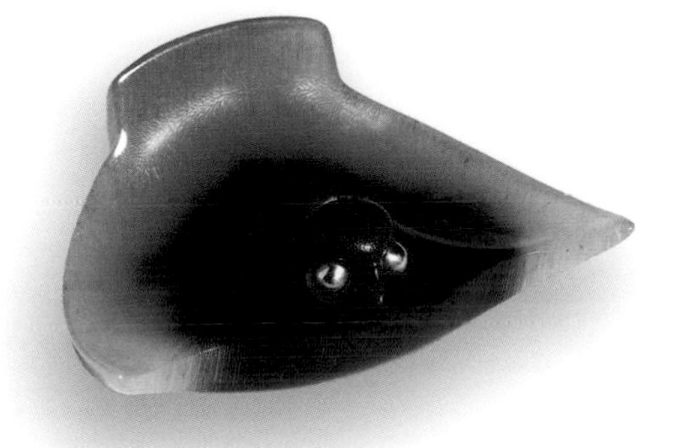

Suzume

Olive wood. Inlaid eyes in mussel pearls.
Width 8.0cm 1977.

Exhibited N.K.C. Kansas City 1977.

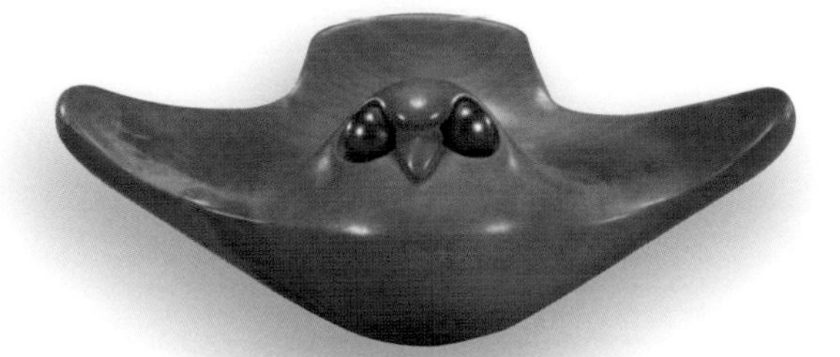

Suzume

Rhinoceros horn. Eyes in 18 carat gold.
Width 5cm 1975.

Exhibited & Illustrated Michael Birch, Netsuke and Sculpture, Eskenazi Oriental Art London 1976.

This Fukura Suzume (puffed-up sparrow) netsuke was carved from the centre of the crown of an exceptionally large rhinoceros horn over one hundred years old. The contrasting total configuration was achieved by cutting the horn across the grain. Rhinoceros horn is composed of hair consolidated with keratin and the diffraction of light by the hair fibres is vividly apparent when this netsuke is held up to the light.

MHB

Owl

Stag antler. Eyes in drawn crystal rod.
c.1983.

Illustrated lecture Notion to Netsuke, Minneapolis 1979.

The portion of uncarved bony core of the antler suggests feathers.

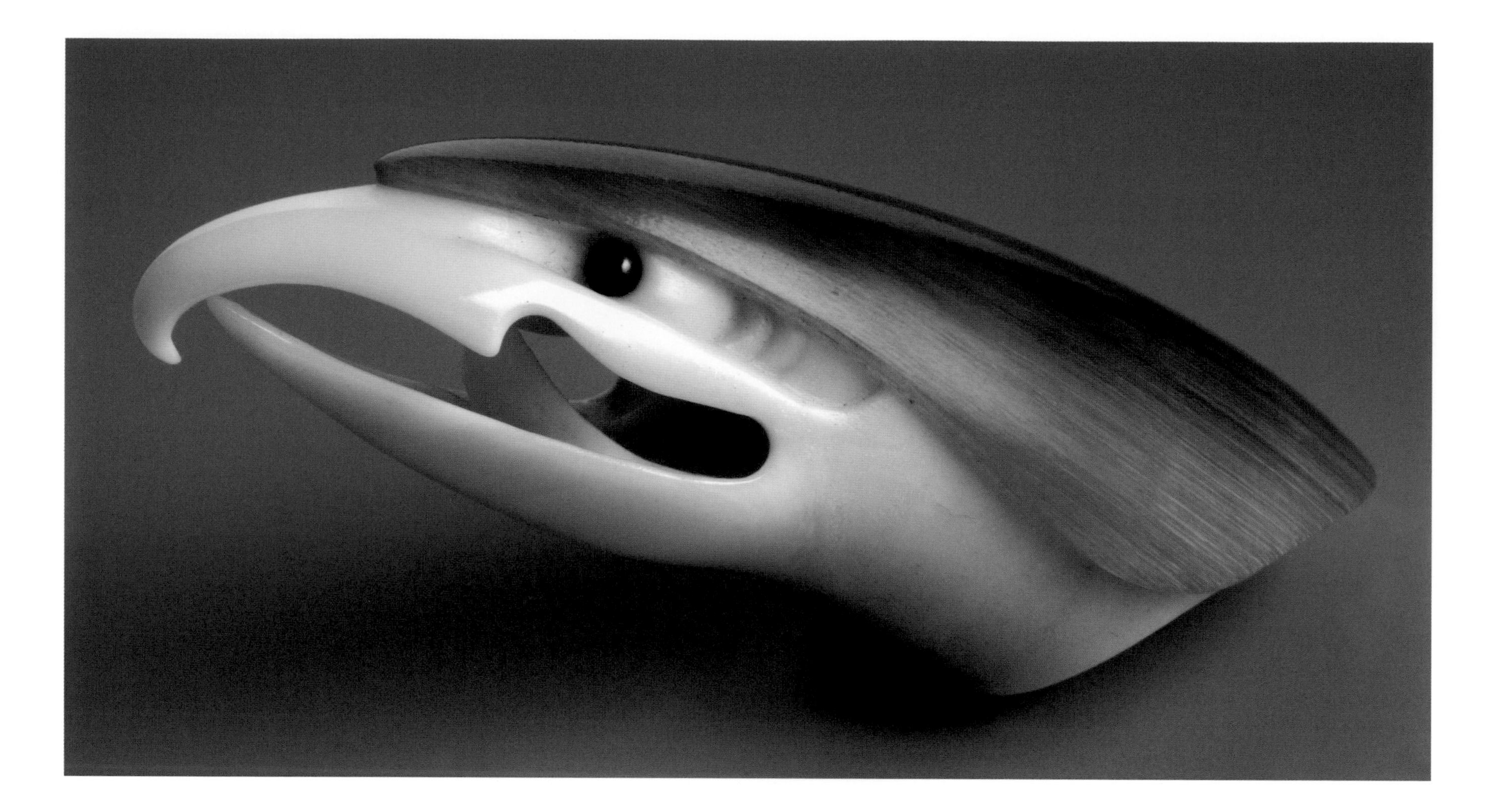

Eagle Head

Rhinoceros horn and whale tooth.
Eyes in mussel pearl.
Length 8.3cm. 1977.

Exhibited N.K.C. Kansas City 1977.

Illustrated Arts of Asia Vol. 8 No. 1 1978.

Exhibited N.K.C. Minneapolis 1979.

Illustrated lecture Notion to Netsuke Minneapolis 1979.

Illustrated Contrasting Styles by Robert G Sawers.

Illustrated Netsuke and Inro Artists and How to Read Their Signatures Vol. 1. by George Lazarnik 1982.

Exhibited Sotheby's Bond St. London. 1994.

Illustrated I.N.S.J. Vol. 16 No. 2 1996.

Exhibited Michael Birch Netsuke Carver and Sculptor National College of Art & Design Dublin 1997.

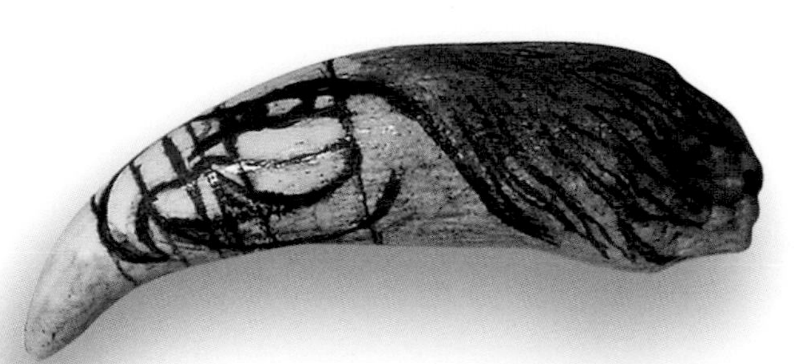

Like many carvers, Michael sometimes marked out his design on the raw material before commencing the carving.

Fallen Icarus Bird

Seasoned corozo nut with part of the dark husk retained. Stag antler claws. Pink coral tongue. Eyes in drawn crystal rod.

Width 4.7cm. 1994.

Exhibited The Carvings of Michael Henry Birch N.K.C. New York 1995.

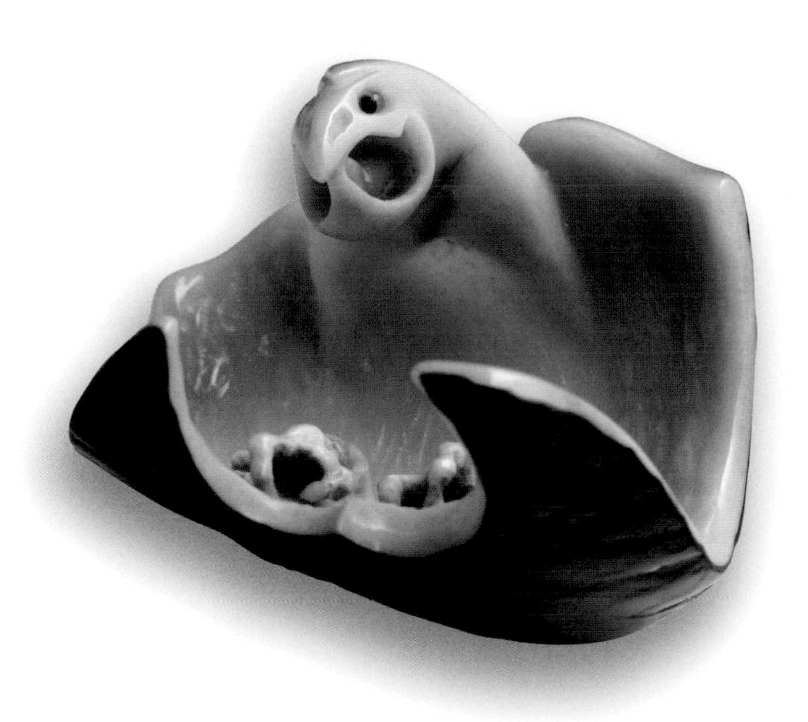

The Phoenix bird, having lived for a thousand years, was due to go up in flames in the year 2000.

In this netsuke it has been re-born carrying with it some mementoes from our millennium.

MHB

ACTUAL SIZE

The Millennium Phoenix Hatchling

Lacquered Pink Ivory wood. Eyes in ebony. Inclusions – beetle, crab's claw, seashells, coral, pearls, semi-precious stones, steel springs, computer parts.

Height 6.0cm. 1996.

Exhibited & Illustrated The Carvings of Michael Henry Birch I.N.S.C. Honolulu 1997.

Illustrated International Netsuke Society European Chapter Lecture Sotheby's London 1997.

In the Water

Namazu is the giant catfish which has the power to cause earthquakes. The monster carries the islands of Japan on its back and, when annoyed, it wriggles violently from head to tail, thereby creating awesome seismic disturbances. It is said that the god, Kadori Myojin, makes somewhat ineffectual attempts to subdue this intemperate behaviour with his gourd. Hence the Japanese saying 'a gourd against a Namazu' – to describe a futile effort.

MHB

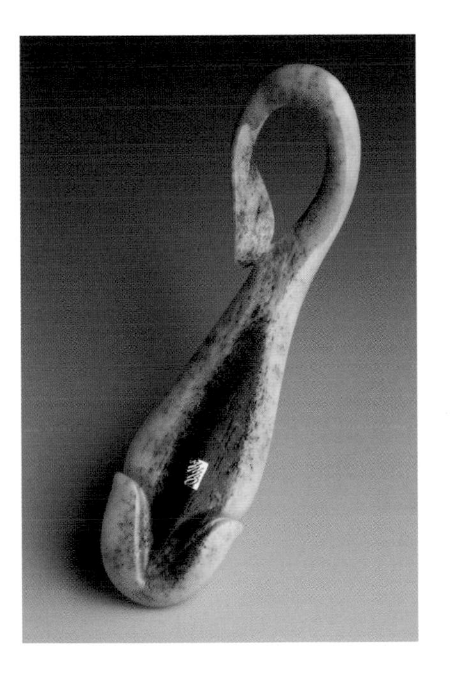

ACTUAL SIZE

Traditionally, once a year local fishermen in bays around the coasts of Japan's islands sailed out to offer the Namazu a drink of saké in the hope that it would calm the turbulent waters for the following year.

Namazu

Stag antler. Eyes double inlaid with mother-of-pearl and drawn crystal rod.
Length 6.5cm. 1978.

Exhibited: Sotheby's, Bond St., London. 1994.

Exhibited: Michael Birch, Netsuke Carver and Sculptor, National College of Art & Design, Dublin, 1997.

Exhibited & Illustrated Tactiles by Michael Henry Birch, I.N.S.C. Boston 2001.

Michael left a portion of the antler uncarved to suggest the dorsal fin. The colour variation through the antler can be clearly seen on the underneath.

Namazu

Burl wood of manzanita and elephant ivory. Eyes double inlaid with mother-of-pearl and drawn crystal rod.

Length 3.5cm. 1980.

Exhibited Netsuke by Birch London Netsuke Convention 1980.

Exhibited I.N.C.S.C. Honolulu 1981.

Namazu

Stag antler. Eyes double inlaid with mother-of-pearl and drawn crystal rod.

Length 11.0cm. 1979.

Exhibited N.K.C. Minneapolis 1979.

Illustrated lecture Notion to Netsuke, Minneapolis 1979.

Namazu

Umimatsu with inlaid eyes.

Length 9.5cm. 1980.

Exhibited Netsuke by Birch London Netsuke Convention 1980.

Exhibited N.K.C. Honolulu 1983.

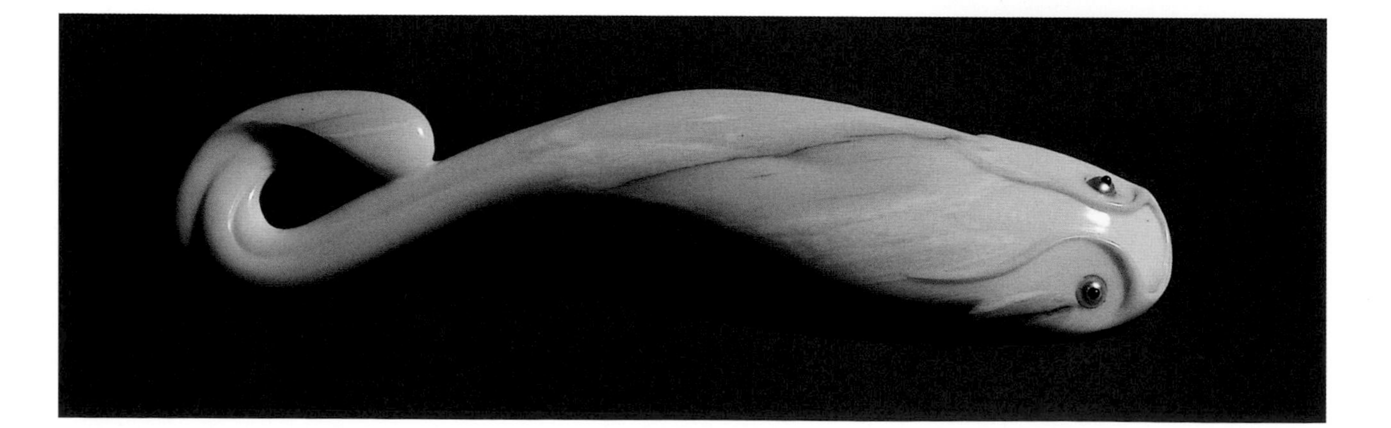

Namazu

Narwhal ivory. Eyes double inlaid with mother-of-pearl and drawn crystal rod.

1978.

Exhibited The Carvings of Michael Henry Birch, I.N.S.C. Honolulu 1979.

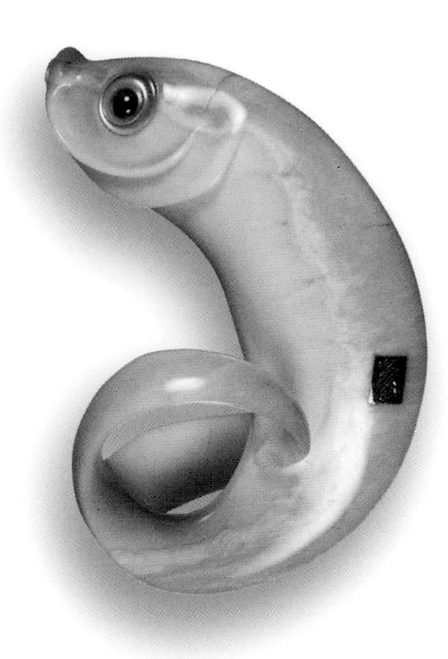

Carp

Narwhal ivory. Eyes inlaid in cabochon rubies and mother-of-pearl.
Length 5.2cm. 1976.

Illustrated Living Masters of Netsuke by Miriam Kinsey 1983.

Exhibited & illustrated Contemporary Netsuke, Miniature Sculpture from Japan and Beyond The Bowers Museum of Cultural Art Santa Ana California 1997.

Carp

Boxwood. Eyes double inlaid with mother-of-pearl and cabochon rubies. 1979.

Exhibited N.K.C. Minneapolis 1979.

ABOUT THIS PIECE, MIRIAM KINSEY WROTE:

This stylised netsuke invites the fingers to explore its pierced curves, and the fluid movement of its form is remarkable in a work of such small dimensions. The contrasting grains of the inner and the outer layers of narwhal tusk have been used to define the separate textures of the body. Its eyes, inlaid in mother-of-pearl and rubies, are focal points of colour on the well-detailed head.

Leaping Carp

Boxwood. Eyes double inlaid with mother of pearl and gold. 1977.

Exhibited N.K.C. Kansas City 1977.

Illustrated Arts of Asia Vol. 8 No. 1 1978.

Illustrated I.N.C.S.J. Vol. 6 No. 3 1978.

Illustrated Netsuke and Inro Artists and How to Read Their Signatures Vol. 1. by George Lazarnik 1982.

Leaping Carp

Narwhal ivory. Eyes double inlaid with ruby cabochon and mother-of-pearl.
Height: 3.8cm. 1980.

Exhibited Netsuke by Birch, London Netsuke Convention 1980.

Exhibited The Carvings of Michael Henry Birch, N.K.C. Los Angeles 1981.

Exhibited & Illustrated Netsuke, The Prince Takamado Collection, Tokyo National Museum Japan 2011.

Fish taking refuge in a sunken log

Fish in Pacific umimatsu. Log in Alaskan umimatsu. Eyes in cabochon rubies.
Length 6.7cm. 1999.

Exhibited & Illustrated Tactiles by Michael Henry Birch I.N.S.C. Chicago 1999.

Exhibited & Illustrated Tactiles by Michael Henry Birch I.N.S.C. Boston 2001.

Exhibited & Illustrated Netsuke Sculptures by Michael Henry Birch I.N.S.C. Honolulu 2004.

Carp backing into its refuge

Pacific umimatsu log. Fish in narwhal ivory. Eyes double inlaid in amber.
Length 9cm. 1980.

Fish backing into a log

Pacific umimatsu log. Fish in Siberian mammoth ivory with double inlaid eyes of amber & Pacific umimatsu.
Length 6.8cm. Carved 1999

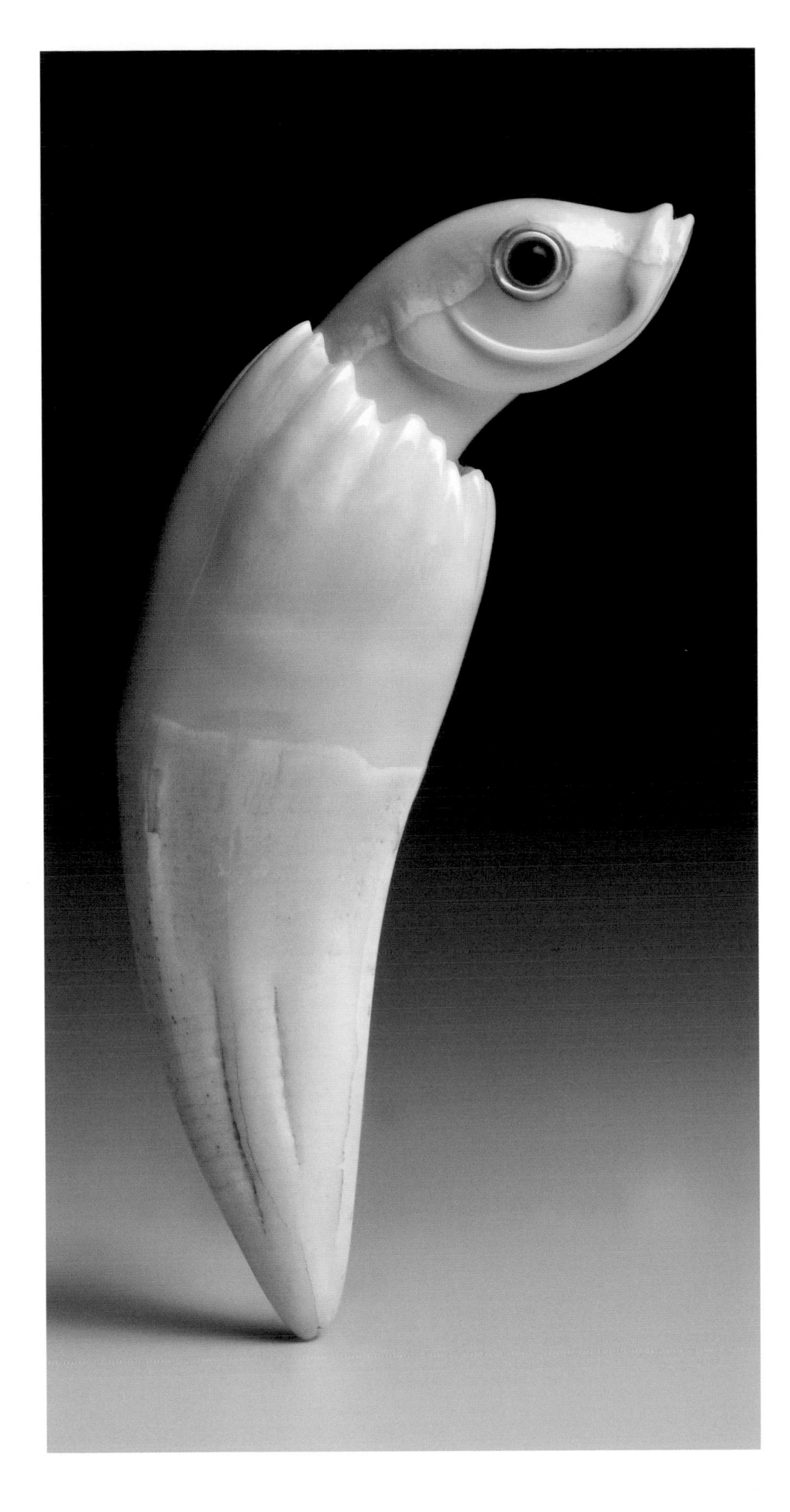

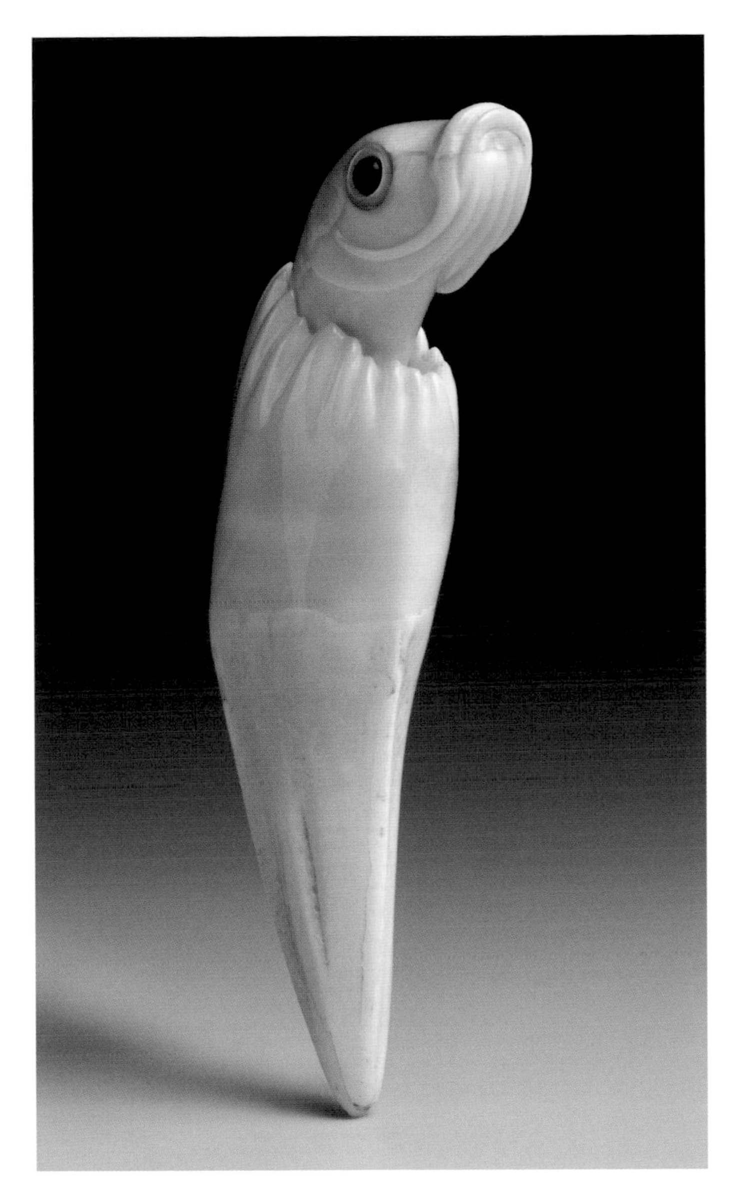

Small fish in shark tooth

Narwhal ivory and shark tooth.
Eyes in mother-of-pearl and black onyx.
Length 9.8cm. C.1980.

Crab and Seaweed

Hog's tooth, 18 carat gold and abalone shell.

Length 9.0cm. 1979.

Exhibited Netsuke by Birch London Netsuke Convention 1980.

Exhibited Michael Birch Netsuke Carver and Sculptor National College of Art & Design Dublin 1997.

Exhibited & Illustrated Tactiles by Michael Henry Birch I.N.S.C. Boston 2001

I saw this in London in October 1984 in an unfinished state. Michael said that he didn't like it and was going to discard it. I urged him to finish saying I liked it. "So does Maggie [Michael's first wife]" he replied. "I'll finish it and you shall have it." When he came to Los Angeles in late May 1985 (his first trip after Maggie's sudden death in November 1984) he had it with him and presented it to me. He remarked that Maggie was a better judge of his work than he was himself.

VIRGINIA ATCHLEY

Small Crab on driftwood

Ram's horn.
Crab's eyes in black coral.

1985.

Illustrated The Virginia Atchley Collection of Japanese Miniature Arts by Virginia
G. Atchley & Neil K. Davey 2006

Broken Shell with Crab

Whale tooth and 18 carat gold.
Carved from the tip of a very large tooth.

1980.

Exhibited Netsuke by Birch London Netsuke Convention 1980.

Exhibited I.N.C.S.C. Honolulu 1981.

Illustrated I.N.C.S.J. Vol. 8 No. 4 1981.

Illustrated Netsuke and Inro Artists and How To Read Their Signatures Vol. 1. by George Lazarnik 1982.

Illustrated I.N.S.J. Vol. 16 No. 2 1996.

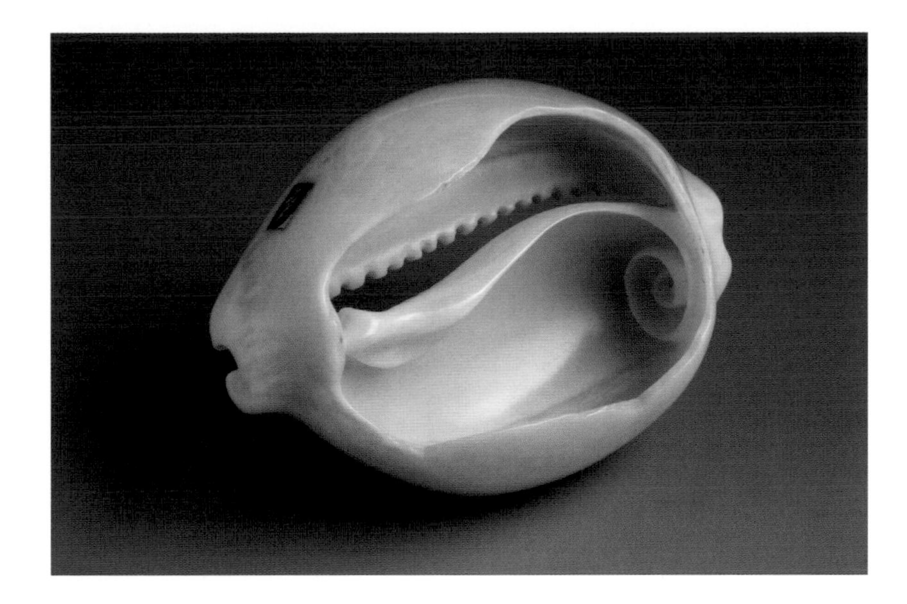

Broken Cowrie Shell

Whale tooth.
Width 5.9cm. 1980.

Exhibited The Carvings of Michael Henry Birch N.K.C. Los Angeles 1981.

Exhibited Sotheby's Bond St. London. 1994.

Exhibited & Illustrated The Carvings of Michael Henry Birch I.N.S.C. Honolulu 1997.

Exhibited Michael Birch Netsuke Carver and Sculptor National College of Art & Design Dublin 1997.

It's very realistic but it's not carved from shell. The infinitely subtle difference between the natural object and the object made by a human being, is barely perceptible. It's that difference that becomes so vast once you have appreciated and understood that it was not produced by nature – it was produced by a human being. And that is the definition of art. . . For me there is something very dramatic about an object that is so realistic that it can fool the eye.

MHB

Crab's claw

Narwhal ivory.
Length 9.0cm. 1974.

Illustrated I.N.C.S.J. Vol. 4 No. 1 1976.

Exhibited & Illustrated Michael Birch Netsuke and Sculpture Eskenazi Oriental Art London 1976.

Exhibited Michael Birch Netsuke Carver and Sculptor National College of Art & Design Dublin 1997.

This netsuke symbolises the crab which features in several legends. One of the best known is the characteristically violent children's fable (Saru Kani Kassen) in which the monkey tricks the kindly crab into parting with his rice cake.

Following a number of episodes involving at one stage a war between an army of crabs and the simian race the wretched monkey is crushed to death and the crab is avenged.

MHB

When carving the following three pieces from the thin hollow end of the incisor, Michael left the crystal-hard enamel un-carved on the underside of each to denote ripples on a sandy seabed beneath the waves.

The Sea Waves at Dawn

Hippopotamus incisor.
Length 14.0cm. 2000.

Exhibited & Illustrated Tactiles by Michael Henry Birch, I.N.S.C. Boston 2001.

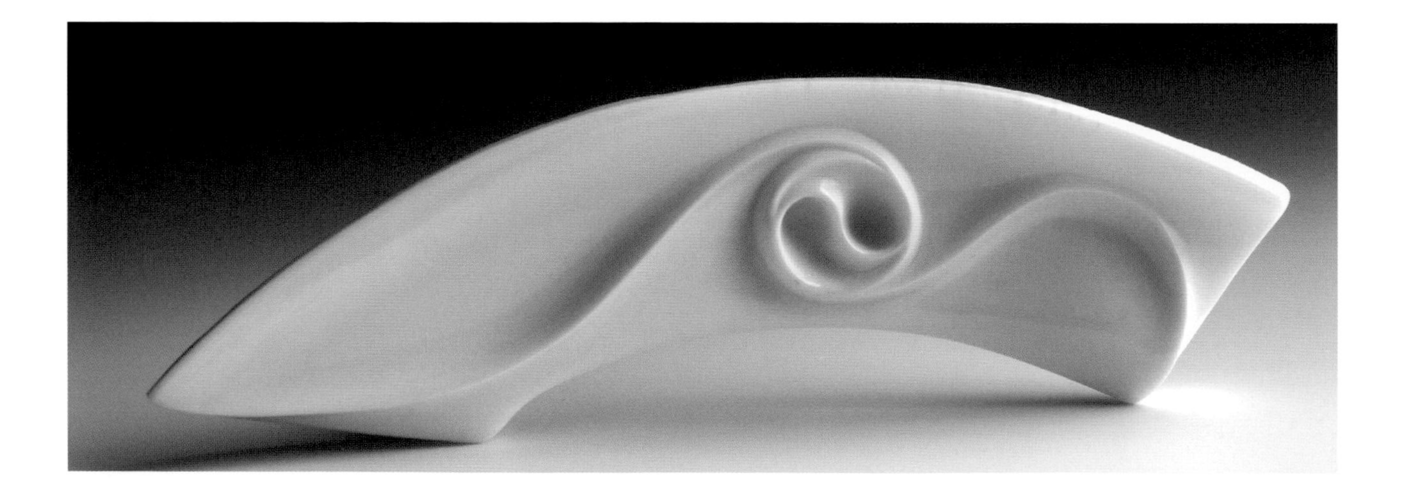

Large Whirlpool

Hippopotamus incisor.
Length 14.0cm. 2000.

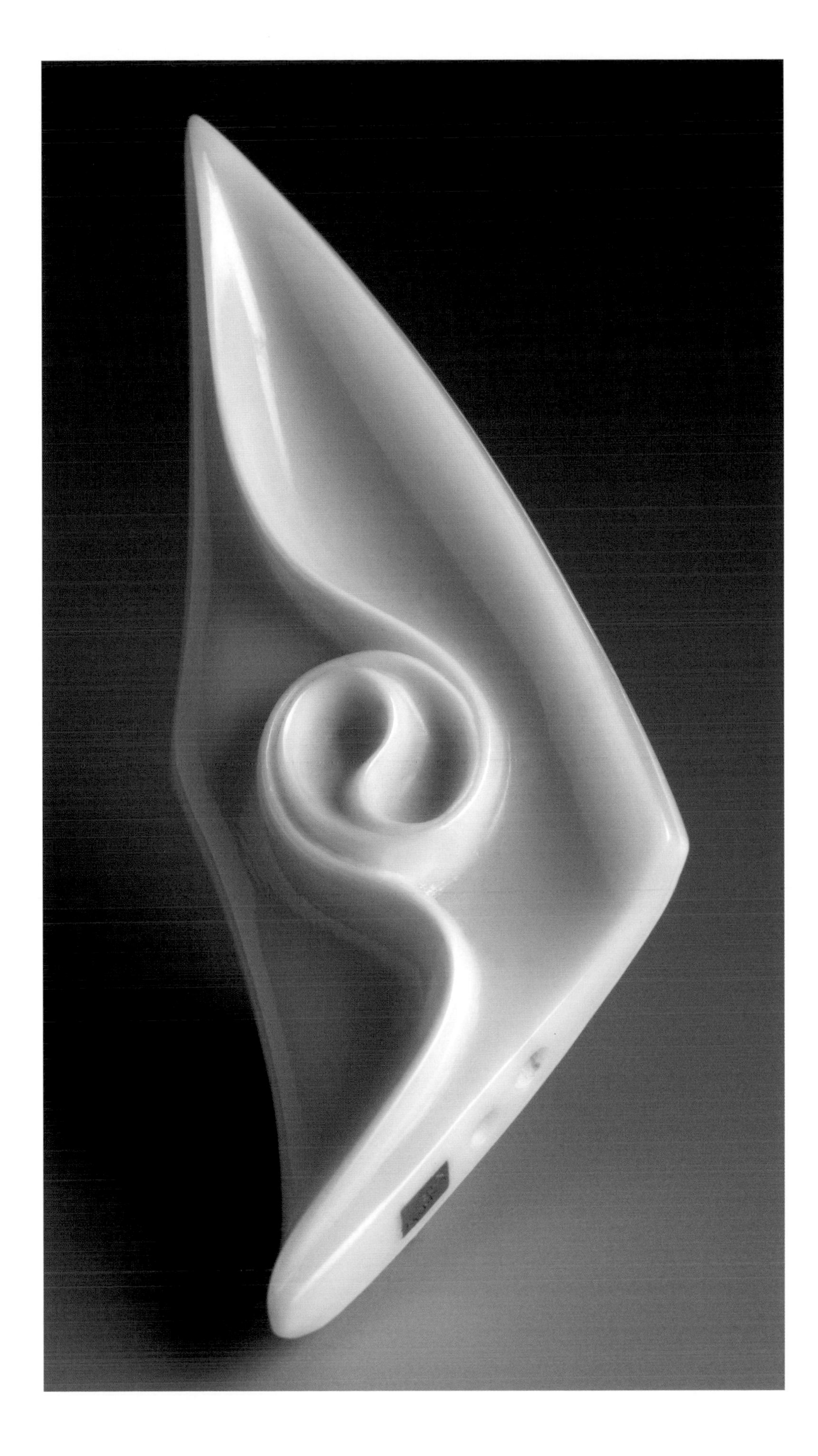

The Magic Whirlpool with Yin/Yang symbol

Hippopotamus incisor.
Length 8.5cm. 2000.

Exhibited & Illustrated Netsuke Sculptures by Michael Henry Birch, I.N.S.C. Honolulu 2004.

Squid Beak

Rhinoceros horn.
1979.

MATERIAL SELECTED

THE OUTLINE DRAWN

Squid Beak

Rhinoceros horn. 1979.

Exhibited N.K.C. Minneapolis 1979.

Illustrated lecture Notion to Netsuke Minneapolis 1979.

Illustrated I.N.S.J. Vol. 16 No. 2 1996.

Exhibited Michael Birch Netsuke Carver and Sculptor National College of Art & Design Dublin 1997.

Miscellaneous subjects

This netsuke represents several thoughts, some interconnected in the chambers of the mind.

Such thoughts are often riddles without answers.

MHB

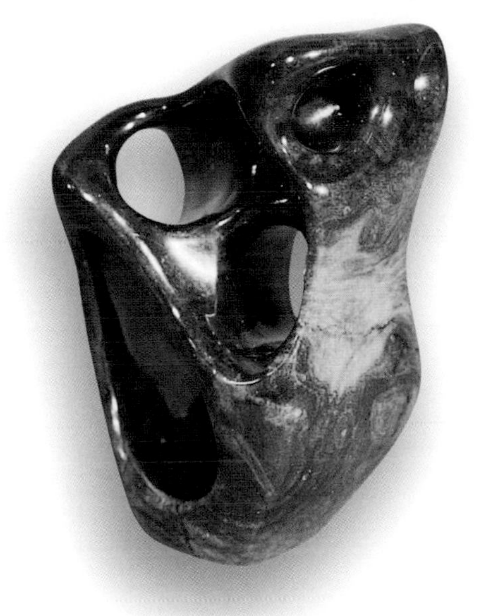

Thoughts & Riddles

Lacquered burl wood of Mexican Manzanita.

Height: 6.0cm. 1996.

Exhibited & Illustrated: The Carvings of Michael Henry Birch, I.N.S.C., Honolulu, 1997.

Exhibited & Illustrated: Tactiles by Michael Henry Birch, I.N.S.C., Chicago, 1999.

Illustrated: Contemporary Netsuke, The H.I.H. Prince Takamado Collection, The Tobacco & Salt Museum, Tokyo, Japan. 2003.

Exhibited & Illustrated: Netsuke, The Prince Takamado Collection, Tokyo National Museum, Japan, 2011.

Levels of the Mind

Lacquered Olive wood (Olea Europea).

Height 7.2cm. 1996.

Exhibited & Illustrated The Carvings of Michael Henry Birch I.N.S.C. Honolulu 1997.

Exhibited & Illustrated Tactiles by Michael Henry Birch I.N.S.C. Boston 2001.

This netsuke is a highly stylised representation of the legendary castle of Ryujin king of the dragons. This is the 'castle in the air' of Japanese children's fables and is often depicted nestling in the interior of a half-open clam shell.

While walking on a beach in Hawaii with the English collector Edward Wrangham, Michael claimed that the most unlikely materials could be used to make netsuke. Ted bent down and picked up pieces of mother-of-pearl and coral that were lying in the sand at his feet. Passing them to Michael he challenged him to make good his word. These netsuke are the result of that wager.

Ryujin's Palace

Hawaiian white coral and mother-of-pearl.
Height 4.7cm. 1975.

Exhibited Sotheby's Bond St. London. 1994.

> *This picture is of a most allusive netsuke, the subject being Ryujin's undersea Palace of Shinkiro in a clam shell. It is made from two pieces of mother-of-pearl that enclose a small chunk of coral from a beach in Hawaii. It is the result of a joke when beachcombing during the first Netsuke Convention in Hawaii. The carver is a genius.*
>
> EDWARD WRANGHAM

Nameplate

Elephant ivory stag antler mother-of-pearl narwhal ivory buffalo horn walrus ivory and rhinoceros horn.
Width 5.3cm 1979.

Illustrated Living Masters of Netsuke by Miriam Kinsey 1983.

Illustrated International Netsuke Society European Chapter Lecture Sotheby's London 1997.

Ojime

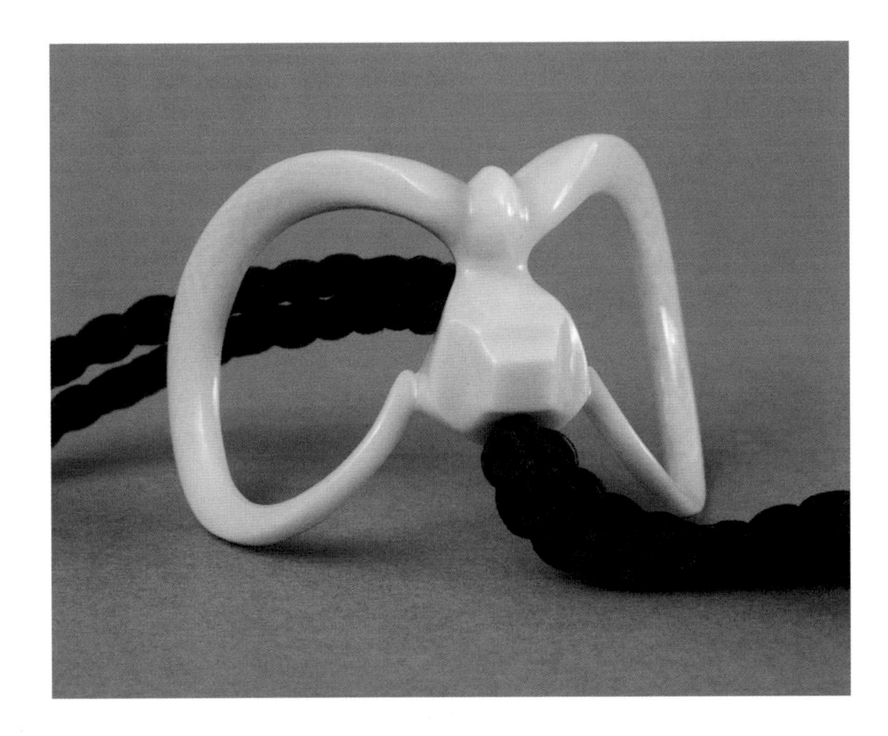

Ram

Elephant ivory.

Width 5.1cm.

In this depiction of the Ram's head, it has been abstracted to just a few lines, but immediately identifiable, nonetheless.

Ojime are an art form of stunning aesthetic qualities rather than merely enchanting beads. The word 'art' in its Western meaning does not exist in the Japanese language. The closest one gets to it is the word 'katachi' which means form and design. But more than that katachi implies that art is synonymous with living, with its functional purpose, and even with spiritual serenity.

The importance of the art of ojime does not lie just in the extraordinary technical skill and patience required to carve these tour-de-force pieces, but also in the same quality by which we judge any sculpture, regardless of size. When all is said and done, size surely has little to do with importance, or artistic merit. Every known culture has produced very small works of art.

Human beings are fascinated by miniature artefacts, perhaps because objects that can be held in the hand are, in a sense, more intimate extensions of ourselves and in our control, while things that are much larger are sometimes enveloping and often overpowering.

Ojime and netsuke are essentially tactile objects – a feast for the eyes, true, but also offering a range of sensations to the touch that is without equal. Not only do they give us the chance to explore a multitude of textures, both natural and carved, and actually to feel the subject matter, but also the opportunity to enjoy the materials by their warmth or coolness, their 'hardness' or 'softness', and their lightness or heaviness – a compendium of tactile stimuli – as we touch them with our eyes and see them with our fingertips.

There is no doubt in my mind that the original users in operating an ojime to tighten the sagemono cord, invariably, if only subliminally, received a sensory reward.

MHB

For this commissioned ojime Michael's brief was to record the Chinese year of the goat in any way he saw fit. This carving shows that textures and fine detail can still be carved on a piece of such small scale.

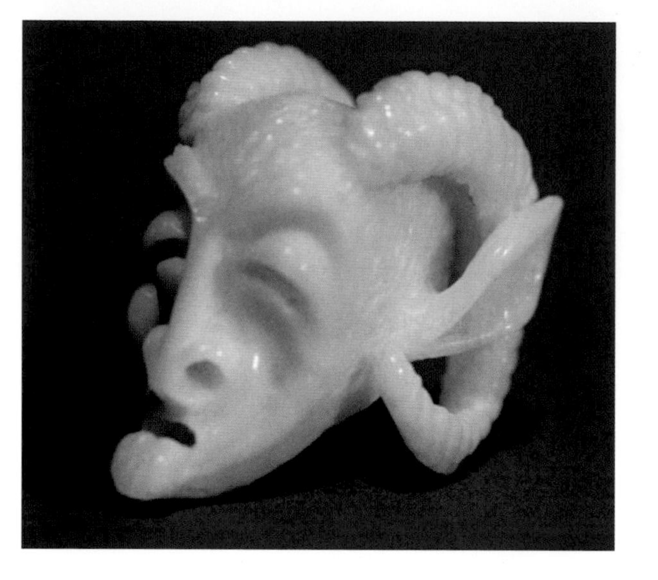

Pan as Ram's Head

Hippopotamus incisor.
Height 2.0cm. 1996.

I have chosen to carve a head of Pan — half man half goat. It was quite a challenge — probably one of the most difficult subjects I have ever attempted.... The material is hippo tooth, over 150 years old, and a beautiful specimen, quite small in fact. I used the centre section to obtain the most translucent 'milky' quality and, if you hold the piece up to the edge of an opaque lampshade, you will see what I mean. The slight discolouration on the right horn is simply a characteristic vein in this kind of material and not a fracture. I believe that this emphasises the organic origin of the material and thereby makes it all the more interesting.

MHB

FROM THE COLLECTOR

Your face on the goat continues to amaze and delight us!
The more we look at our ojime the more we marvel at your textures and fine detail.

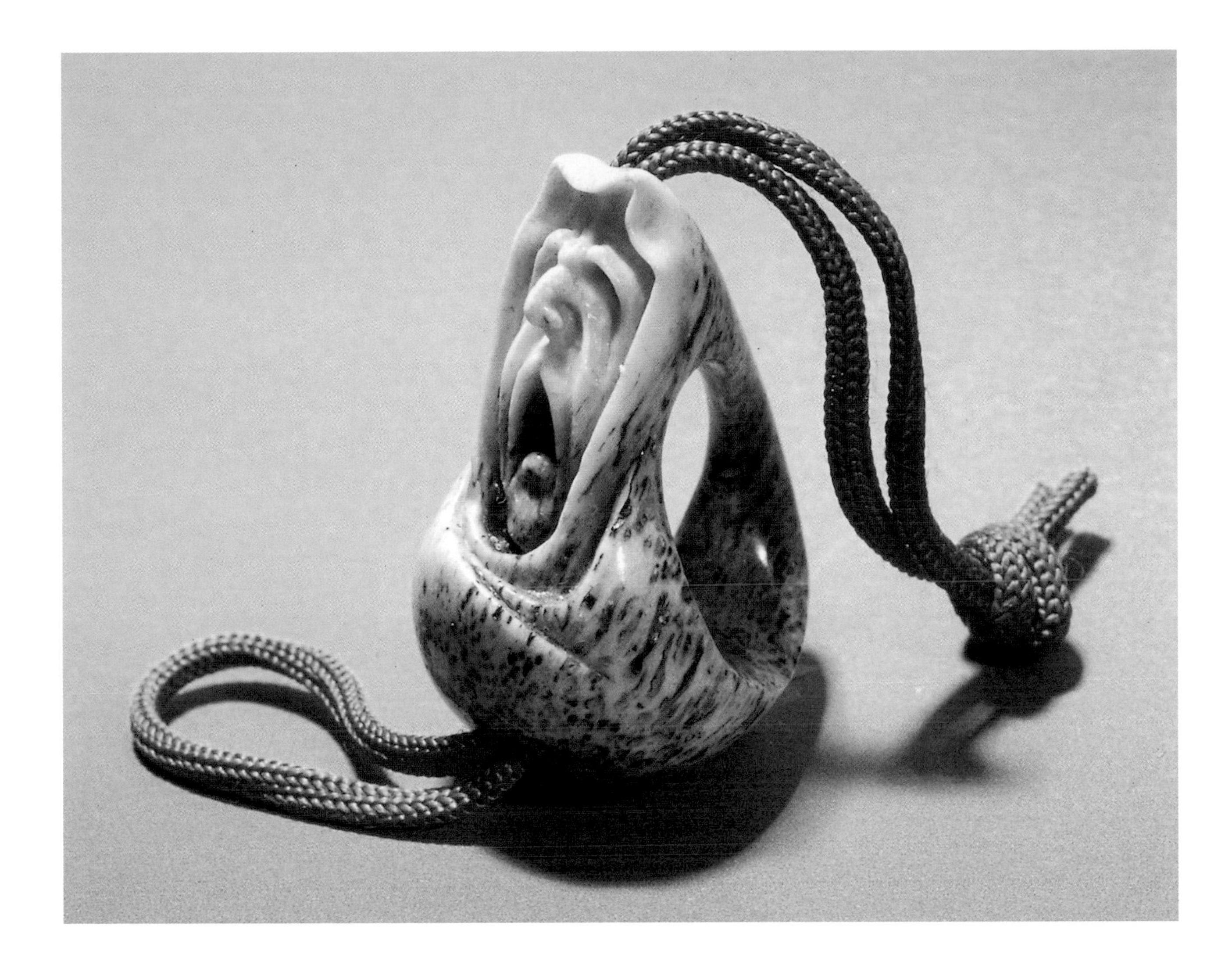

Portrait of Daruma Yawning

Stag antler the porous section sealed with clear lacquer.
Height 3.8cm. 1995.

Exhibited The Carvings of Michael Henry Birch, N.K.C. New York 1995.

Daruma is seen yawning as he emerges from the surface of a Möbius at the end of his nine years' solitary contemplation.

Tanuki

Highlands stag antler. Eye stripes inlaid black lacquer.
Height 1.3cm 1977.

Exhibited N.K.C. Kansas City 1977.

Illustrated The Soken Kisho and Ojime by Misao Mikoshiba & Raymond Bushell in Arts of Asia Vol. 9 No. 4 1979.

Exhibited Real and Imaginary Beings The Netsuke Collection of Joseph and Edith Kurstin Yale University Connecticut 1980.

Illustrated I.N.C.S.J. Vol. 8 No. 1 1980.

Illustrated Ojime Magical Jewels of Japan by Robert O. Kinsey 1991

Exhibited Contemporary Netsuke, Miniature Sculpture from Japan and Beyond, The Bowers Museum of Cultural Art Santa Ana California 1997.

Exhibited & Illustrated Contemporary Netsuke The Kinsey Collection Accompanied by H.I.H. Prince Takamado Collection by Robert O. Kinsey Chiba City Museum of Art Japan. 2001.

A Rare Collaboration

The following is an article written by Michael and published in the I.N.S.J., Vol.24, No.3, Fall 2004. It tells of a rare collaboration between two artists, Michael Birch, the carver, and Tomiso Saratani, the Japanese lacquer artist, and how two Hako netsuke came to be created.

In 1979 Raymond Bushell sent me the gift of a copy of his recently published book 'The Inro Handbook'. It is a remarkably comprehensive and colourfully illustrated work, which I read and studied and consistently enjoyed from start to finish. It became abundantly clear to me that the complexity of the art of lacquer graphic decoration of inro required not only a massive body of knowledge and technical information, but also infinite patience, dedication, many years of practise and, not least, a clear mind and a controlled and steady hand. I was aware that, above all, what is required of the experienced lacquer artist is a conscious sense of katachi, the Japanese word meaning design, form, sensitivity and the art of living.

On a warm spring day in 1984 I received a telephone call from my friend Luigi Bandini. He asked me if I would accommodate a Japanese lacquer artist as my guest for a month in the unoccupied cottage on my property, and I readily agreed. The artist, previously unknown to me, was Tomiso Saratani. He moved in and that evening I prepared a sushi dinner for both of us, washed down with liberal cupfuls of hot saké. He was thirty-five years old and I was fifty-eight – but the difference in our ages mattered not at all. We very soon shared the degree of kindred spirit that two like-minded artists develop with instinctive ease. Tomiso's main task was the restoration of some valuable inro.

Now Ray Bushell's book was being transformed into a reality for me as I watched Tomiso mixing pigments to achieve perfect colour matches and textures. He sprinkled with dexterity tiny flakes of abalone shell, pulverised pearl, crushed egg-shell, powdered gold and silver, and gold leaf into, where appropriate, the surface of the newly lacquered areas. (He told me that there are over six hundred different lacquer techniques – a staggering number – and more still to be discovered.)

The lacquer medium, filtered ki-urushi, is the toxic sap of a rare gum tree and must be handled with caution. Tomiso demonstrated that the applied lacquer would set to a durable hardness when cured for two or three days in a hot moist atmosphere inside a pinewood cabinet. I observed with fascination as Tomiso matched the original patterns of the inro using the powdered metals, shell flakes, and other design features with breath-taking skill and accuracy. He used sable brushes that consisted of only three or four hairs for painting fine lines, and employed larger brushes to re-create areas of colour to match the original.

Several days later I invited Tomiso to come to my studio and examine my method of carving netsuke. He showed great interest in my techniques which are, in the main, different from the ones employed by Japanese netsuke-shi. He showed particular interest in my work-in-progress and in the wide range of materials I use; and he asked many questions. It suddenly occurred to me that it would be an interesting collaboration if Tomiso and I would join our minds in the creation of

Tengu

Hako (box) netsuke.
Lacquered boxwood with aogai and silver foil inlay. Signed for the carving MHB. Signed for the lacquer Tomiso Saratani.
Height 3.0cm. 1984.

Illustrated Handbook to London Netsuke Fair and Convention 1990.

Illustrated I.N.S.J. Vol. 16 No. 2 1996.

Illustrated I.N.S.J. Vol. 24 No. 3 2004.

two netsuke incorporating both our skills – mine as a netsuke artist and Tomiso's as a lacquer artist. I asked him what he thought of the idea and he agreed with enthusiasm. We decided that we would create two hako netsuke — not the customary small square boxes, but sculptured figurative subjects based on well-known legends. And so we chose Tanuki, the badger priest, and Tengu, the mythical bird-faced creature. The following day I started my preparations for the carvings. Using sections of well-seasoned century-old English boxwood, I carved the two subjects with great care.

Following Tomiso's guidelines, I paid particular attention to the uniform spacing of 1.5 millimetres between the overlapping rim of the lid and the outer edge of the box base. This would allow clearance for the lacquer and create a near-airtight fit. To achieve the best degree of bilateral symmetry for the oval bases, I shaped several acrylic templates 3mm in thickness. A cord hole in the bottom of each base would enable the inro cord to be threaded into the interior of the netsuke and then through the small ring (the himotoshi) carved inside the lid.
In the case of the Tengu, I fitted a pair of ruby cabochons for the eyes. After a number of days of concentrated effort, I was ready to show my carvings to Tomiso for his comments.

He examined the carvings carefully, turning them over several times, checking the interiors and the spacing between the lids and the bases. Finally he looked straight at me and quietly said, "Perfect". A week later Tomiso called me and showed me his completed lacquer work on the two netsuke. I could scarcely believe my eyes. He had transformed my carvings and brought them to life with his consummate artistry. The illustrations merely provide a pictorial impression of what Tomiso achieved and I shall not attempt to put that achievement into words.

We agreed that he should keep the Tengu and that I would have the Tanuki, and we were both delighted that we could now share the fruits of our collaboration. We each signed the two pieces with a kakihan (artist signature) and promised each other that we would never part with our unique lacquered netsuke. It is not surprising to learn that Tomiso Saratani, now recognised as one of the world's great lacquer artists, has kept his promise. And, for that matter, so have I.

MHB

Tanuki the Badger priest

Hako (box) netsuke.
Lacquered boxwood with aogai and silver foil inlay. Signed for the carving MHB. Signed for the lacquer Tomiso Saratani.
Height 3.0cm. 1984.

Illustrated Handbook to London Netsuke Fair and Convention 1990.

Exhibited The Carvings of Michael Henry Birch N.K.C. New York 1995.

Illustrated I.N.S.J. Vol. 16 No. 2 1996.

Exhibited Michael Birch Netsuke Carver and Sculptor National College of Art & Design Dublin 1997

Paintings

Although best known as a sculptor, throughout his life Michael was also a painter. In his youth in Cairo as a member of a surrealist group, his work was predominantly in oils. After it was favourably received, he was commissioned to complete five large murals. Although he continued working in oils, he later produced work in watercolours and crayons.

Self Portrait I

Self portrait Unsigned. Undated c.1972

Self Portrait III

Oil on Canvas.
Size 68cm x 56cm.
Unsigned. Undated c.1973.

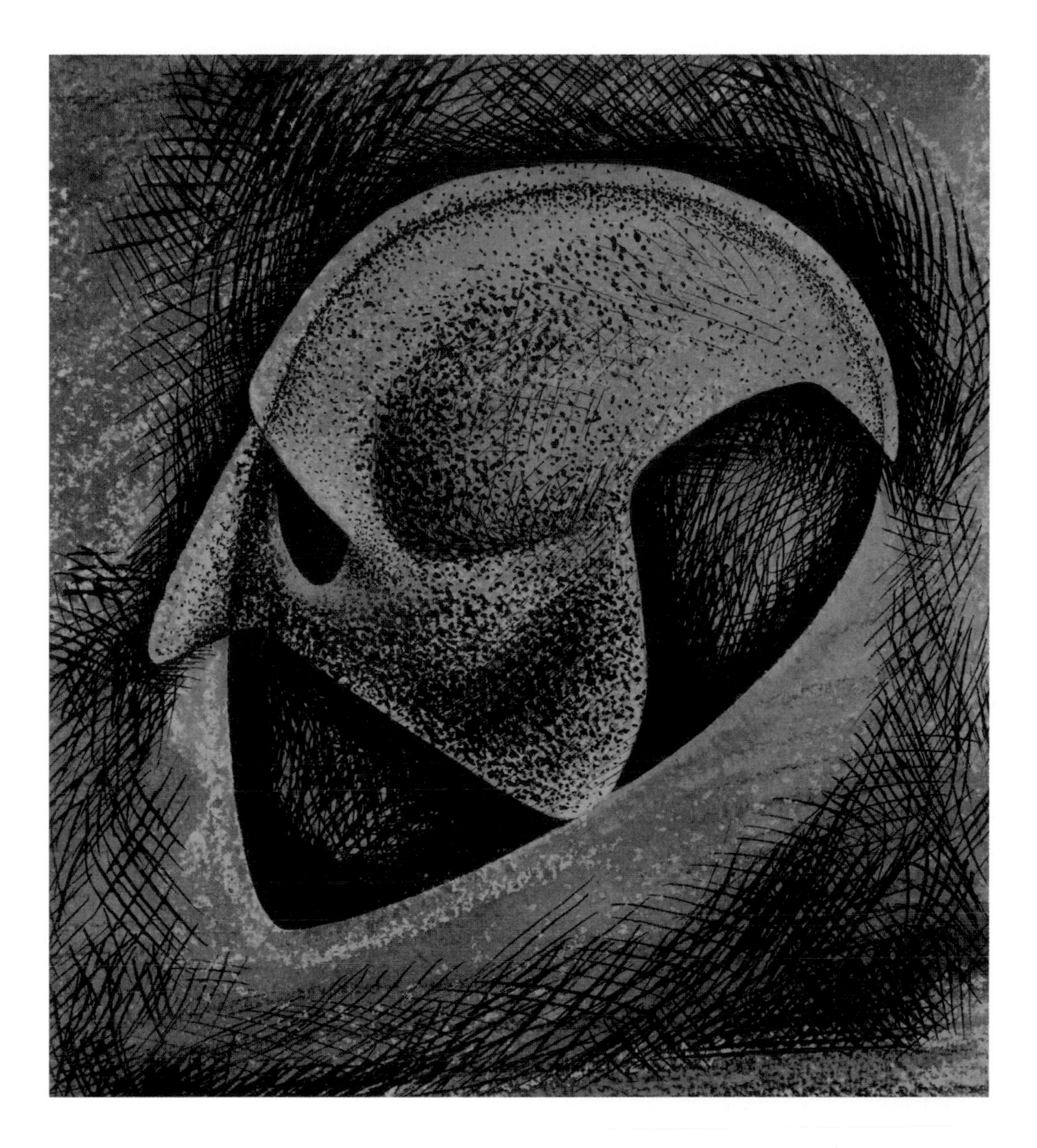

Head I

Watercolour, ink and crayon on card
Size 21cm x 18cm.
Unsigned. Undated.

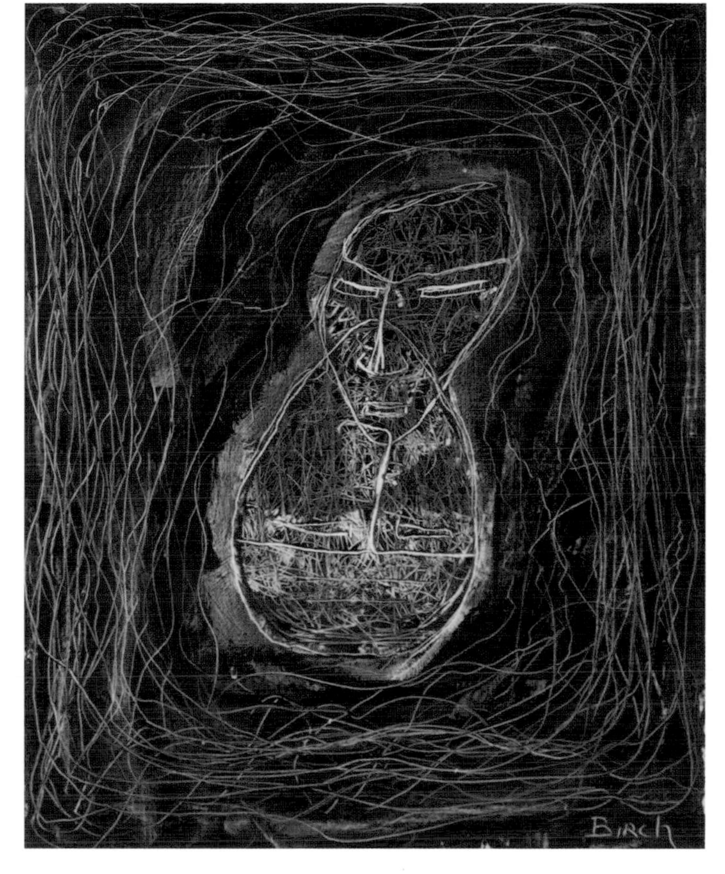

Self Portrait II

Oil on Canvas.
Size 81cm x 66cm.
Signed Birch. Undated c.1973.

Head II

Watercolour, ink and crayon on paper
Size 16.5cm x 11.9cm.
Unsigned. Undated.

Clown 1

Oil on Canvas.
No measurements available.
Signed Birch. Undated c.1970.

The Fox Ghost

Oil on Canvas.
No measurements available.
Signed Birch. Undated.

Clown II

Oil on Canvas.
Size 51cm x 61cm
Signed Birch Undated c.1970.

Red Fish I

Oil on Canvas.
Size 24.5cm x 30cm.
Unsigned. Undated c.1956.

Inner Worlds

Oil & Watercolours on Paper.
Size 32.5cm x 24.5cm.
Unsigned. Undated c.1947

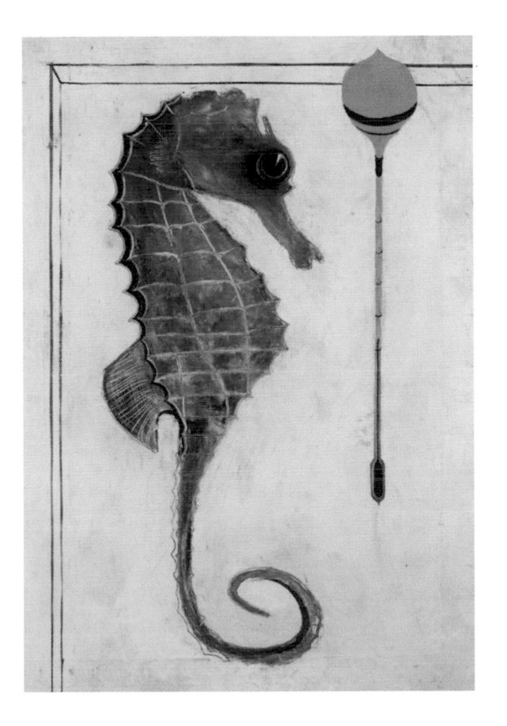

The Seahorse

Oil on Canvas.
Size 40cm x 30cm.
Unsigned. Undated c.1953.

Iris

Oil on Canvas.
Size 60cm x 51cm.
Signed Birch. Undated c.1953.

Chrysanthemums

Oil on Canvas.
Size 60cm x 51cm.
Unsigned. Undated c.1954.

Rectangles

Oil on Canvas.
Size 76cm x 50.5cm.
Unsigned. Undated c.1957.

Fired Earth

Oil on Canvas.
Size 76cm x 63.5cm.
Unsigned. Undated c.1955.

Sumi-e Paintings

During his trip to Japan in May 1977, Michael purchased brushes, inks and hand-made paper so that he could begin to work in the traditional calligraphic style where a single stroke can display tonal variations from palest grey to black. A technique that is difficult to master, he would produce the same few brush strokes over and over again until satisfied with the result.

After discovering that his work, originally intended as wrapping paper, had been pressed, mounted and framed by a collector into traditional wall hangings, he began to extend his subjects.

Katachi
Sumi-e ink on Paper.
Size 48cm x 35.5cm.
Titled. Initialled MHB. Dated 1979.

The Bulb
Sumi-e ink on Paper.
Size 45cm x 30.5cm.
Initialled MHB. Dated 1980.

The Rabbit

Sumi-e ink on Paper.
Size 37cm x 53.5cm.
Initialled MHB. Sealed.

Inscribed 'A bunny in five, eat your heart out Hokusai. To Bob & Miriam with love, Fatsuo'. Fatsuo was a nickname given to Michael by Robert O. Kinsey.

Ghost Head

Sumi-e ink on Paper.
Size 47.5cm x 37cm.
Titled. Initialled MHB. Dated Aug 79.

Ghost Leaf Procession

Sumi-e ink on Paper.
Size 45cm x 31cm.
Titled. Signed Michael Birch.
Initialled MHB. Dated Aug. 95.

Leaping Carp

Sumi-e ink on Paper.
Size 52cm x 32.5cm.
Initialled MHB. Undated c.1981.

Baby Tanuki

Sumi-e ink on Paper.
No measurements available.
Initialled MHB. Undated c.1981.

The Seal

Sumi-e ink on Paper.
Size 36cm x 49cm.
Titled. Initialled MHB. Dated 79.

Tanuki and Cherry Blossom

Sumi-e ink on Paper.
Size 29cm x 40cm.
Signed Michael Birch. Undated C.1982.

Tanuki the Priest in Harlequin robes

Sumi-e ink on Paper.
Size 42cm x 30cm.
Signed Michael Birch.
Initialled MHB.
Undated c.1982.

Tanuki the Badger in Monk's Robe

Sumi-e ink on Paper.
Size 40cm x 29cm.
Signed Michael Birch. Dated 1980.

The Three Crows

Sumi-e ink on Paper.
Size 42cm x 94cm.
Initialled MHB. Undated c.1979.

After spending an evening in the Hawaii apartment of Michael and his wife, a collector who was eager to own this painting of the lucky symbol of three crows, removed it from the wall as he left.

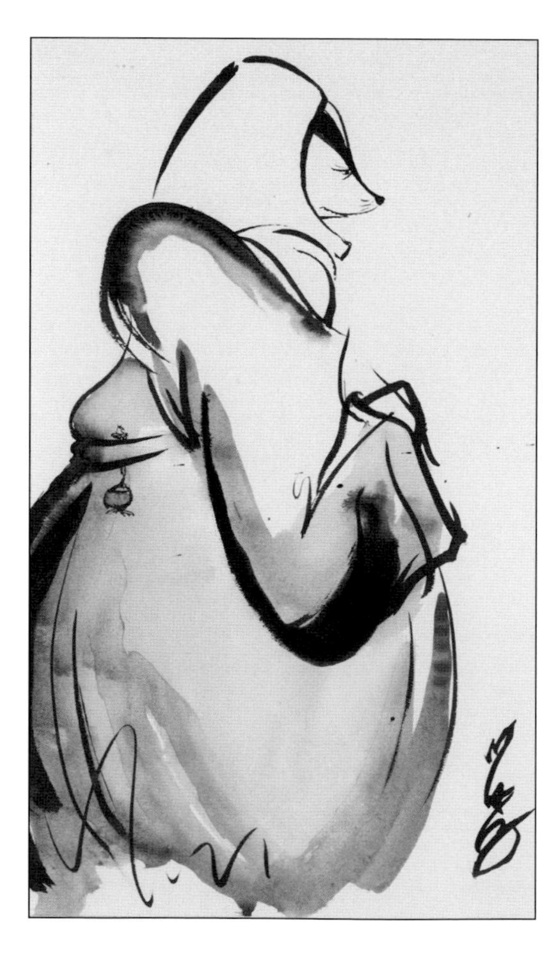

Daruma

Sumi-e ink on Paper.
No measurements available.
Unsigned. Undated c.1981.

Illustrated Michael Birch 1926-2008
Euronetsuke 2009.

The Matronly Tanuki

Sumi-e ink on Paper.
Size 52cm x 34cm.
Initialled MHB. Undated, c.1981.

Futen, The God of the Winds

Sumi-e ink on Paper.
Size 40cm x 22.5cm.
Signed Michael Birch. Dated 1980.

Hair-Raising Ghost II

Sumi-e ink on Paper.
Size 59cm x 32cm.
Initialled MHB. Undated, c.1981.

The Wind

Sumi-e ink on Paper.
Size 28cm x 20cm.
Unsigned. Undated, c.1980.

Shojo

Sumi-e ink on Paper.
Size 52cm x 36cm.
Sealed. Undated c.1982.

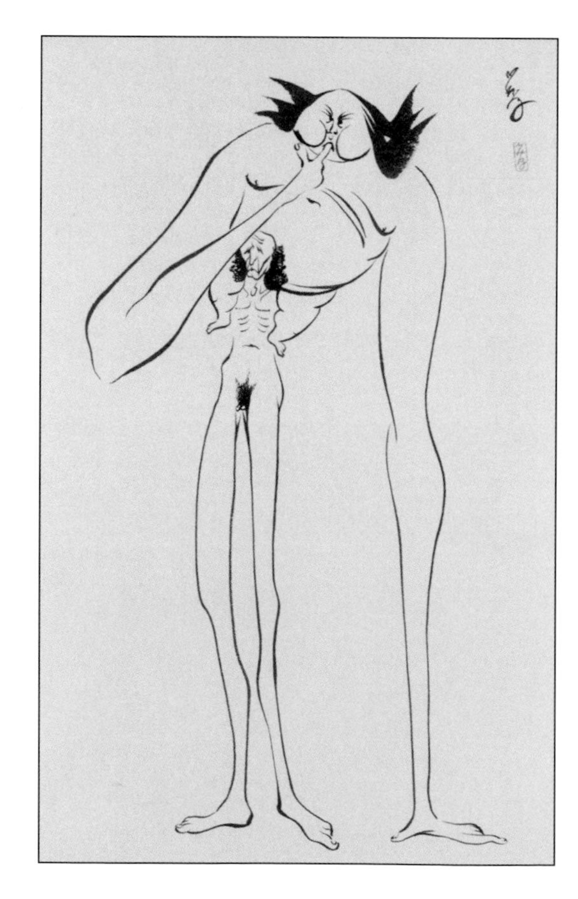

Ashinaga and Tenaga

Sumi-e ink on Paper.
Size 51cm x 35cm.
Initialled MHB.
Sealed. Undated c.1982.

Ghost

Sumi-e ink on Paper.
Size 51cm x 24.5cm.
Initialled MHB. Sealed. Dated '79.

Teruko, Princess Moonbeam

Sumi-e ink on Paper.
Size 51cm x 38cm.
Initialled MHB.
Sealed. Undated c.1982.

Mask I

Sumi-e ink on Paper.
Size 52cm x 37cm.
Titled. Initialled MHB.
Sealed. Undated c.1981.

Sculpture & Pottery

Although interested in netsuke from the age of nine, Michael created a number of larger sculptures. Also included here is his pottery, although not his first choice of artistic expression, his talent was recognised by Pablo Picasso for whom he created works in 1946/1947.

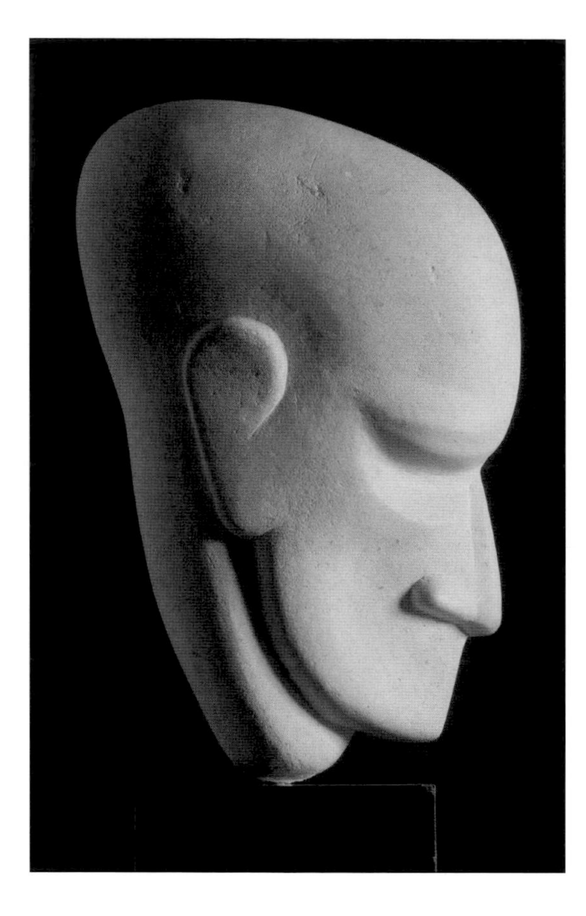

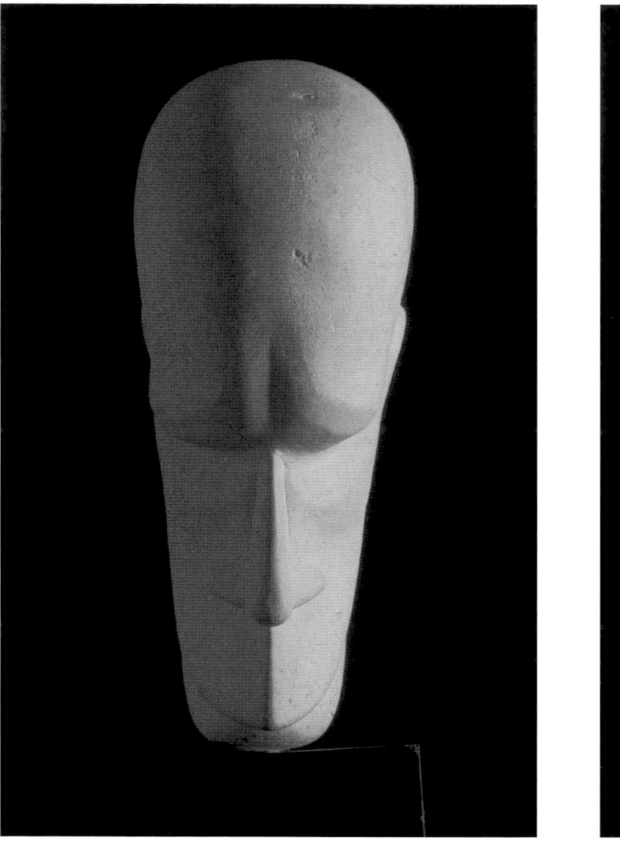

Head of the artist's father

Portland Limestone.

Height 38cm. 1946.

Exhibited & Illustrated Michael Birch Netsuke and Sculpture Eskenazi Oriental Art London 1976.

This head was created while Michael was at Camberwell College of Arts & Crafts. The sculptor Henry Moore purchased a plaster cast of the piece for which he paid five guineas (two weeks' pay for the average man at the time), after Michael refused to sell him the original.

This piece was also created while Michael was at Camberwell College of Arts & Crafts. The sculptor Henry Moore watched him working on it and commented: 'Ah, a Henry Moore, and a damned good one at that'.

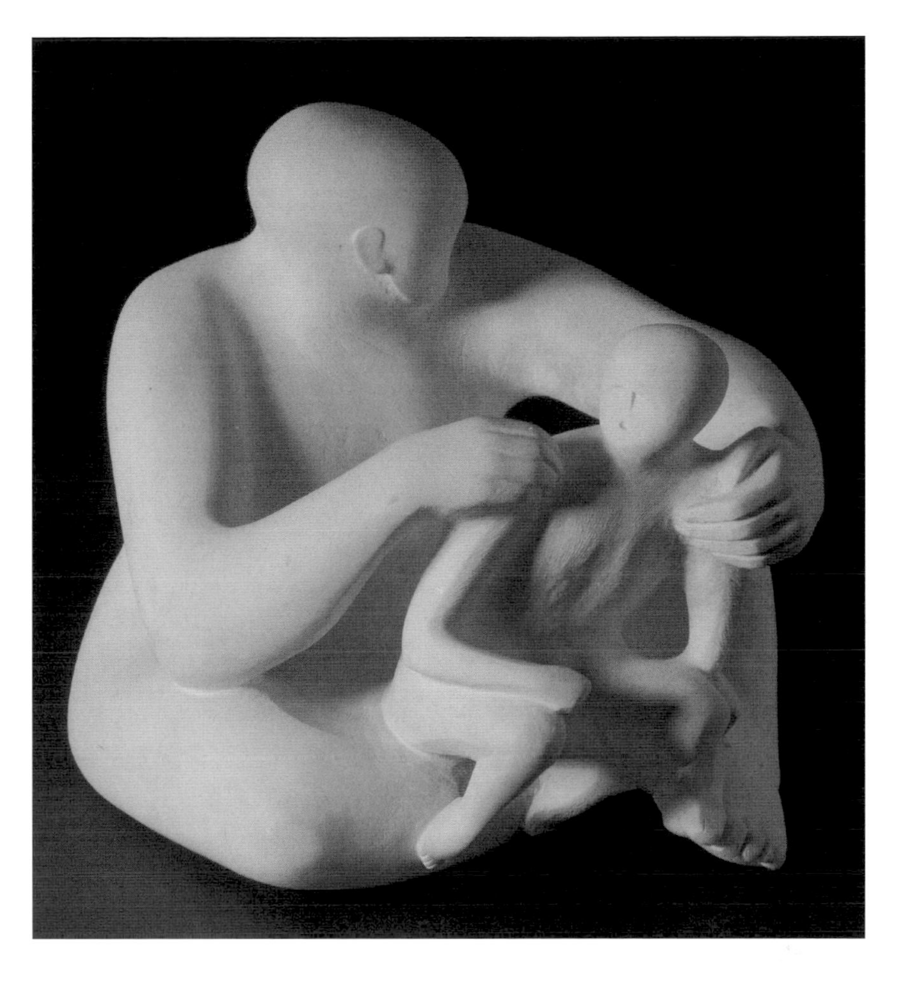

Father & Son

Palombino marble.

Height 24cm. 1947.

Exhibited & Illustrated Michael Birch, Netsuke and Sculpture, Eskenazi Oriental Art, London 1976

In the late 1970's three large sculptures were commissioned for a newly designed garden in Southern California. They were to be cast in acrylic, not usually the first choice of material for a sculptor, but Michael rose to the challenge. He created three designs: a female torso shown from the shoulders to just below the hips; a double Möbius, shaped with organic curves; and a stylised representation of the beak of an octopus.

The first stage was to create the masters from which the moulds would be made. Rough outlines were created from large blocks of expanded polystyrene.

Eve Torso

Epoxy Resin.
Height 85cm. C.1978.

Möbius

Epoxy Resin.
Height 62cm. C.1978.

The blocks were 2ft. x 2ft. x 4ft. in height, and the first cuts for the outline shape were made with a chain-saw, before being gradually refined by increasingly fine rasps and files.

Once he was certain that he had developed the expanded polystyrene to the correct design shapes, they were covered with layer upon layer of epoxy resin. Each layer was rubbed down and polished before the next layer was applied, and over forty layers in all were processed until the required smooth finish was achieved. Michael was helped in this process by his son Jonathan who remembers that both he and his father became intoxicated (or worse) by the fumes of the chemical resin.

Octopus Beak

Epoxy Resin.
Height 63cm. C.1978.

Octopus Beak

Test Acrylic casting.
Height 63cm. C.1978.

Head of Jonathan Michael Birch

Bronze

Width 16.5cm Height 13cm. c.1966.

Eve Torso

Bronze.

Height 85cm. C.1978.

Michael arranged for the Eve torso to be cast in bronze.

Dosojin

Bronze
Size 12cm x 8cm.
Signed with monogram.

Exhibited & Illustrated Michael Birch
Netsuke and Sculpture Eskenazi Oriental Art
London 1976.

Octopus Beak

Bronze
Size 10cm x 9cm.

Head

Forest green marble
Size 21cm x 10.5cm. c.1946

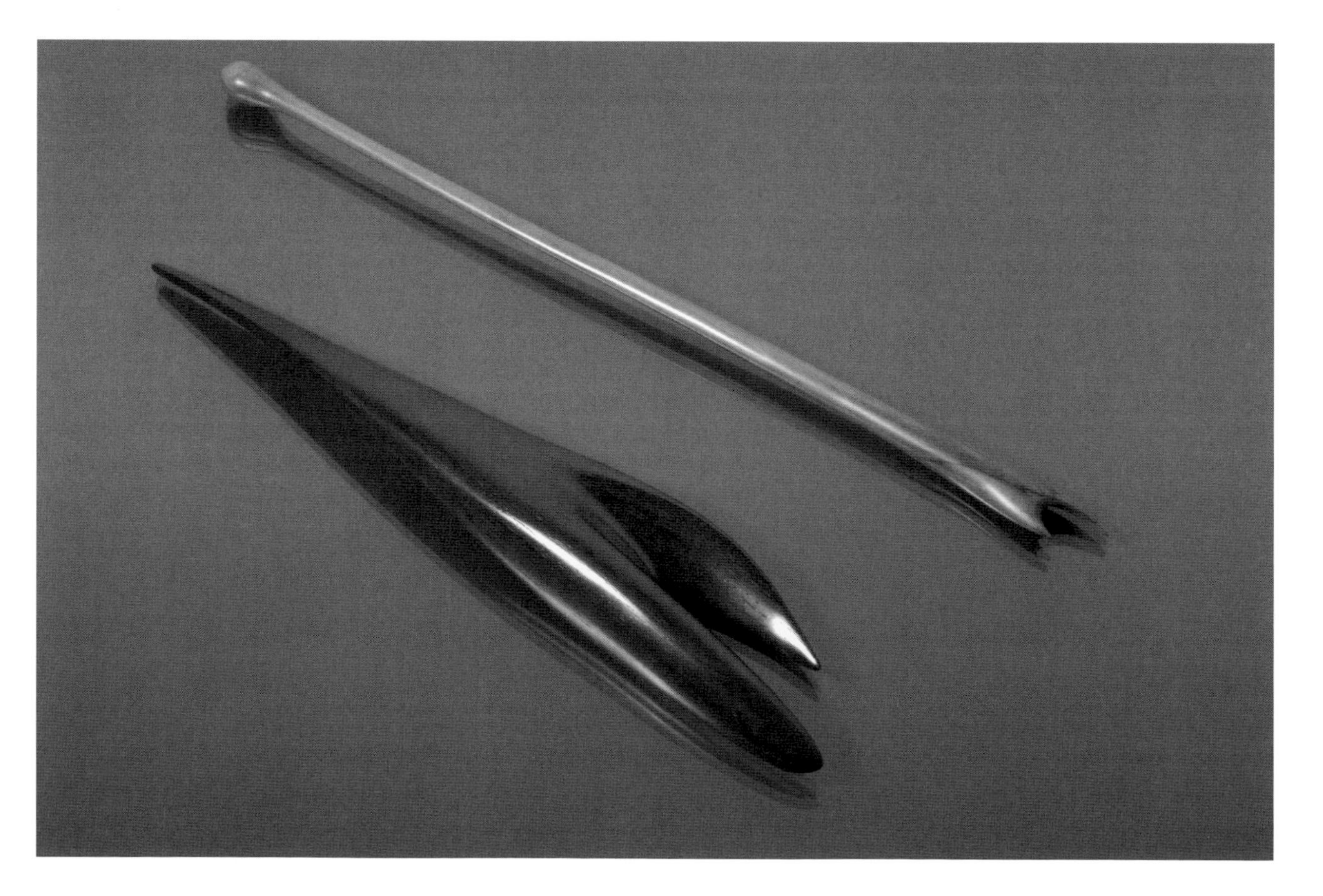

An Organic Shape & a Rod

Left: Brazillian Rosewood.
Length 44.5cm.

Right: Olive Wood.
Length 53cm.

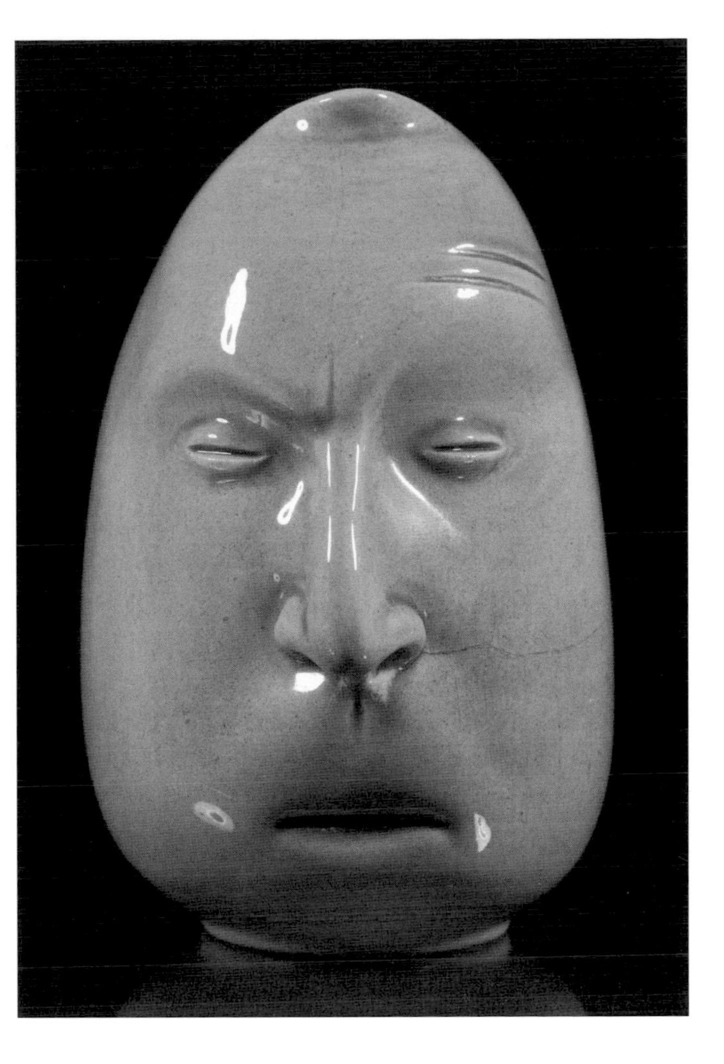

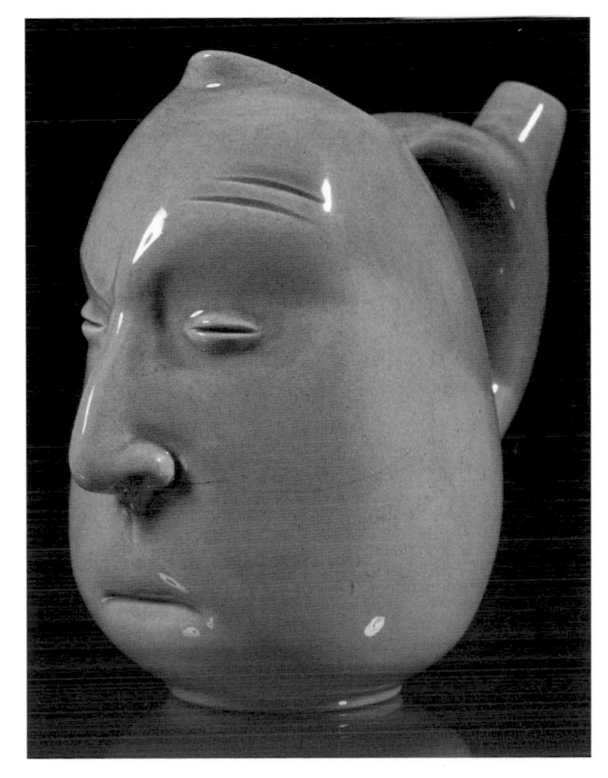

Toby Jug with hollow handle

Glazed.
Height 16cm. 1947.

Queen Victoria
Unglazed.
Height 11.5cm. c.1947.

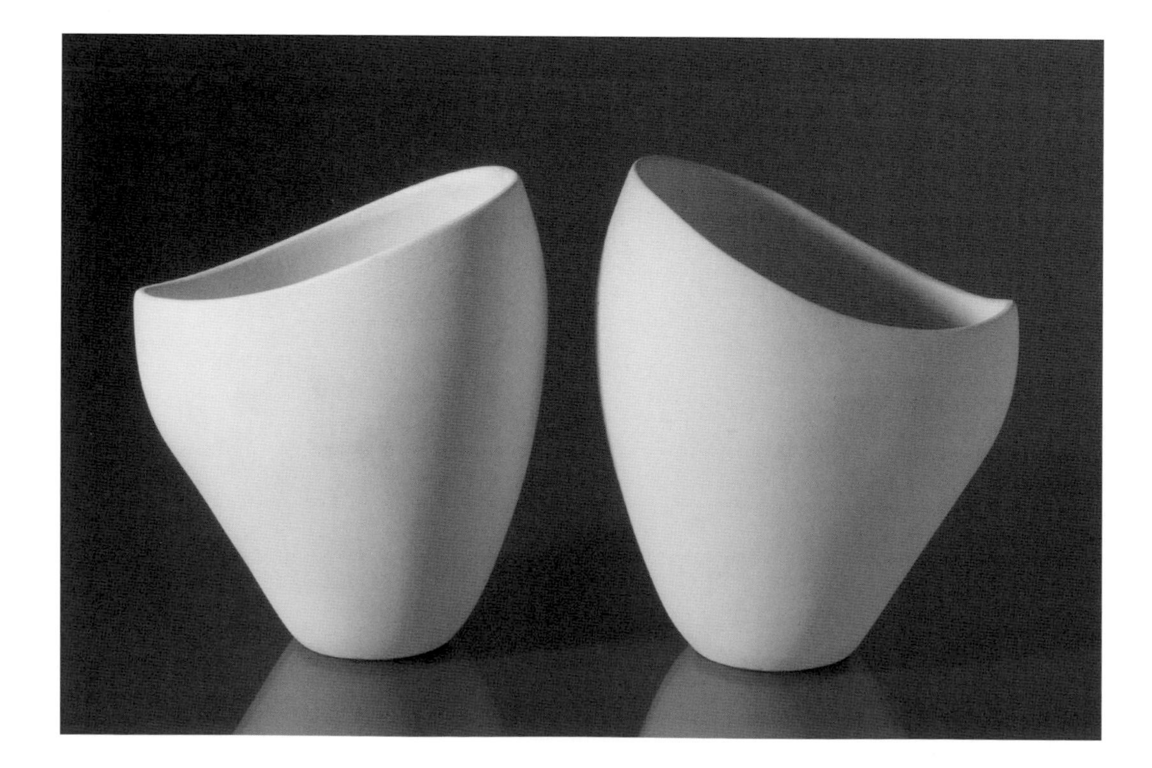

Two Vases
Unglazed.
Height 14cm & 14.5cm. c.1947.

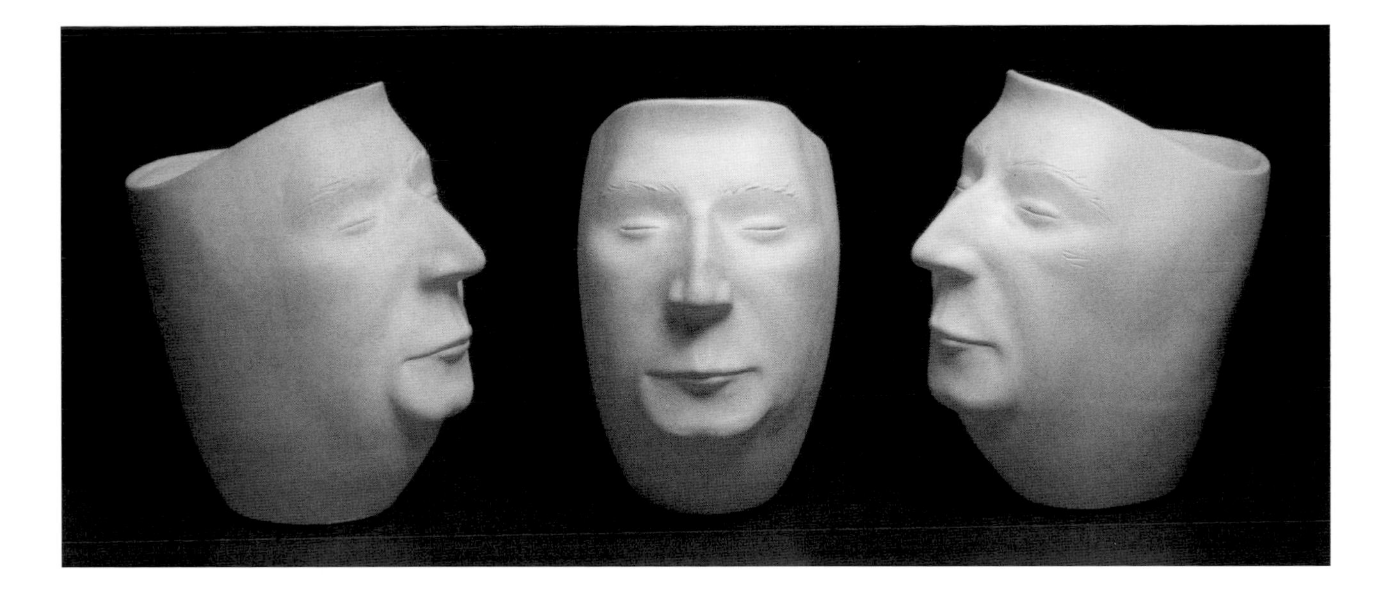

Three (of seven) self-portrait vessels

Unglazed.
Various Heights 14.5cm to 15.5cm. c.1947.

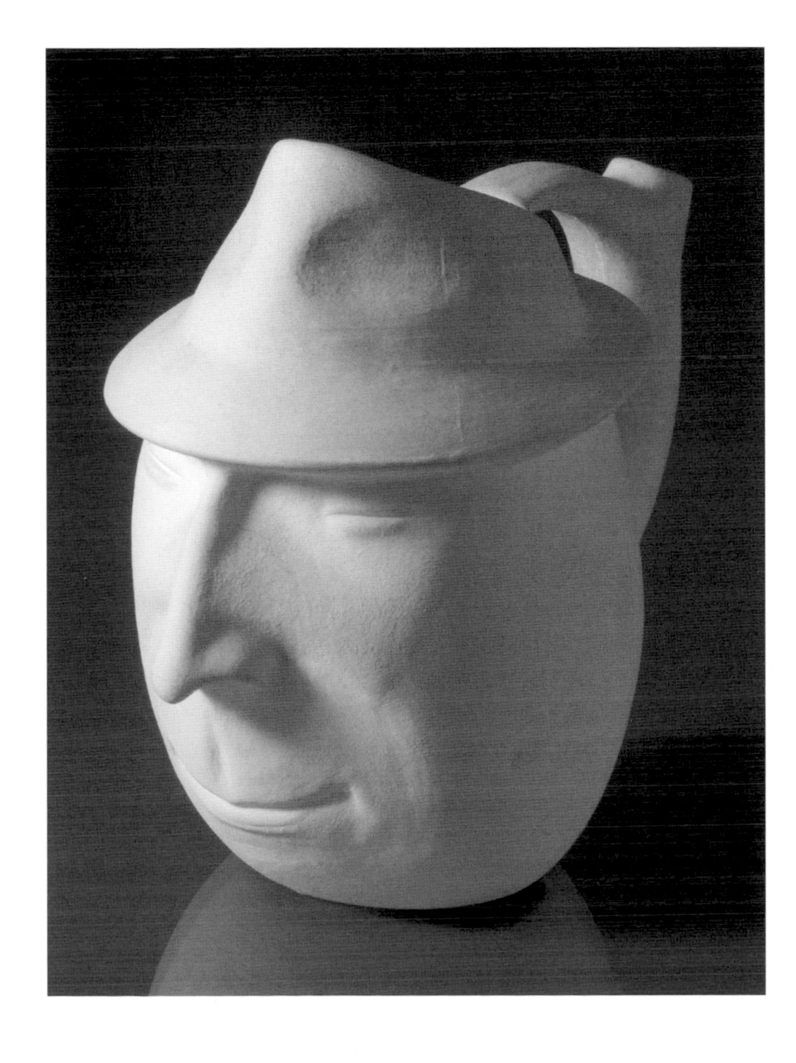

Toby jug with hat & hollow handle

Unglazed.
Height 13.5cm. c.1947.

Chronology

1926	Born 16th December in Alexandria, Egypt of Anglo-French parentage.
1936	Given three netsuke for his ninth birthday by his father.
1939	Family moved to Cairo where he attended the English School as a boarder.
1943	Obtained a position with British Overseas Airways Corporation as skipper of the mail launch with responsibility for overseeing the loading, unloading and delivery of mail to and from the flying boats that landed on the Nile.
	Became a member of a surrealist/anarchist group of artists.
	Took a part-time job playing the Hammond Organ for pin money in a house of ill repute.
1944	Served in RAF before being seconded to the United States Army Air Force at Payne Field where his aircraft loading experience was utilised.
1945	Sailed to England for the first time on troopship RMS Britannic.
1946	Settled in London sharing a flat with fellow artist Howard Pickersgill.
	First met Margaret Elizabeth Goldfinch.
1946–1947	Offered a place at Camberwell School of Arts & Crafts and applied for a grant. Began attending lectures by Henry Moore, William Coldstream, Johnnie Minton, Ben Nicholson, Victor Pasmore & Claude Rogers. Sold plaster cast of a sculpture of his father to Henry Moore for five guineas. After his grant application was refused, he continued to attend lectures on an unofficial basis until expelled as a non-paying student.
	Carved netsuke from billiard balls purchased for 6d and sold for between fifteen shillings and one pound.
	Went drinking in Bloomsbury with James Broome-Lynne, Theodore Bikel and Dylan Thomas. Played piano in a band with Humphrey Lyttleton.
1947-1948	Extended trip to France where he drew portraits in Parisian cafes. Visited his parents in Grasse. Worked at the Madoura Pottery in Vallauris throwing pots for Picasso.
1948	Returned to London and passed audition as tap-dancing chorus boy in the pantomime Cinderella with actor Leslie Phillips and director Patrick Cargill.
	Married Margaret Goldfinch.
1949	Birth of daughter Belinda Danae.
1949-1952	Unable to earn a living to support his family as a painter or sculptor, he took a series of jobs: late-night cabaret artist; managed a junk shop; washed dishes; made ice cream; laboured on a building site.
1951	Birth of daughter Susan Louise Marguerite.
1952	Obtained a permanent position at the International Telephone Exchange in London.
1953	Birth of daughter Louise.
	Obtained a position with Marylebone Optical Company where he made spectacles by hand and began to design frames. Offered a job by Stanley Unger, a manufacturing optician based in Tunbridge Wells, to design and make stylish frames.
1954	Sacked by Stanley Unger.
	Formed a business in his home with start-up capital of £15, repairing spectacle frames. Took on his first employees.
	Began designing frames and producing them under Michael H. Birch (Designs) Ltd.
	Moved to own premises and employed more staff.
1955–1969	Continued to expand the business. Won a Courtauld's Industrial Design award.
	Played charades with Michael Wilding and Elizabeth Taylor.
	Met Albert Falco, lead diver with Jacques Cousteau and was invited to dive with Cousteau and his team in the Mediterranean Sea, the Red Sea and the Gulf of Mexico.
	Began collecting quality netsuke.
	Paid his only post-war visit to Alexandria.
	Purchased a Rolls Royce which was painted to match a purple rhododendron flower from his garden.

1957	Purchased Stanley Unger's company. Early research & development of injection-moulded plastics was a success and the first trays for chocolate boxes were produced as well as tableware.
1958	Birth of daughter Kelly Margaret.
	His company expanded rapidly and would eventually include a factory area of approx. 285,000sq.ft. (6.5acres), for the manufacture of frames and lenses and injection-moulded plastics. Amongst the Group's other interests were: Stowe Electronics; Vox Amplifiers Company; Hammond Organ Company; and CAPS (Commercial Aid Printing Services) Microfilm. Company continued expansion into Europe and North America.
1959	Birth of son Stephen John.
	Sentenced to 8 month prison term for motoring offence.
1961	Birth of son Jonathan Michael.
1962	Birth of son Patrick Michael.
1963	Involved in proceedings which set a British legal precedent when the Comptroller General of Patents ruled in favour of Michael H. Birch (Designs) Ltd. and against the Minister of Health at an Arbitration Hearing.
1970	Made the decision to sell the company through the bankers Schroder Wagg and regretted that the relationship became one of barely concealed animosity. Company shares sold to Pilkington Glass. Agreed to act as a consultant for a period of 2 years.
	Cleared his debts, set aside funds for his wife and children, and made an ex-gratia payment to staff pension fund.
	Continued to purchase top quality netsuke as well as damaged and fake netsuke to repair and re-carve.
1971-1974	Agreed to act as an art expert for entrepreneur Willy Stern, before they went into partnership as property developers. A planned major hotel/casino development was cancelled after Michael was threatened by gangsters in Bermuda. The Stern Group collapsed owing over £100 million. As Stern had made cross-company guarantees without his partner's knowledge, Michael lost his initial investment and the expected profit of £500,000.
	Continued to enlarge his collection of top quality antique netsuke and to develop his own netsuke carving skills.
1975	Attended the first International Netsuke Collectors Society Convention and began to show his work to collectors.
1976	Held his first one-man show of netsuke at Eskenazi Oriental Art, in London.
1977	Paid his only visit to Japan where he spent time with the Japanese carvers; leading collector Raymond Bushell swapped a Namazu by Kaigyokusai for a mermaid Michael had carved; and he decorated plates with the potter Shoji Hamada.
1977-1984	Continued carving netsuke and attended Netsuke Conventions where he gave lectures and workshops and was admired for his after-dinner talks.
1978	Began creating sumi-e (ink wash paintings) for wrapping paper.
1984	Sudden death of wife Margaret.
1984-1993	Wrote, produced and self-published his seven books: Cursory Rhymes, a book of satirical verses which had been written for his wife over a thirty year period. Lemon Yellow & Pistachio Green, a science-fiction novel. The Teller of Tall Tales, a semi-autobiographical novel. Like Some People Do, a collection of short stories: including The Imperfect Spouse, winner of the H. E. Bates Best Short Story of the Year Award. Suspended Tales, a collection of short stories. The Death of Pinocchio, a 20th century 'fin de siècle' novel. My Head on the Line, a collection of 100 poems.
1984-1993	Finished only 7 netsuke during the eight years following Margaret's death.
1989	Met Janet Martin, whom he married in 1991.
1994	Began carving netsuke again.
1995	Returned to the netsuke scene with an exhibition at the Netsuke Kenkyukai Convention in New York.
1999	H.I.H. Prince Norihito Takamado and his wife paid a visit to view his work and personal collection.
2001	Suffered a dislocated shoulder following a 12ft fall down a garden bank. The resulting permanent damage made it increasingly difficult for him to carve.
2002-2008	Gradual deterioration in health following a series of small strokes.
2008	Died on 16th September at the age of 81.

The Years 1926 to 1945

Like so much that was unusual about Michael, even a question about his date of birth was not without its complications. He was born on 16th December in either 1926 or 1928, depending on which of his two birth certificates you were looking at. They both, however, showed that he was born in Alexandria, Egypt of Anglo-French parentage.

His paternal grandfather was Lewis Henry Birch, a talented businessman whose wide interests varied from cotton trading and financial services to property, civil construction and mining. In 1872 he married his cousin, Isabella Murray Peel who was related to England's Prime Minister Sir Robert Peel,[1] and the couple had moved from Staffordshire to India and then to Alexandria. There they were heavily involved in the local commercial, political and social life and placed great emphasis on the importance of education and philanthropy.

Michael's father, Louis, was the youngest of the couple's ten children. He was seventeen and at school in England when his father died suddenly of typhoid at the age of fifty-nine. He returned home in time to attend the state funeral awarded to his father by Egypt's ruler, Khedive Abbas, where, alongside the formal military procession, the cortege was completed by a troop of Bedouins on camels with bridles jingling with bells. Although the family expected to inherit a very large fortune, they discovered that Lewis's assets had been reduced by a downturn in the world's stock markets; and that he had sacrificed a substantial part of what remained of his own fortune to safeguard the investments of those who had trusted him with their wealth.

After an early failed marriage, Louis met Marguerite Angele Sapet in 1923. A singer who had started her career in the same Parisian show as a young performer named Maurice Chevalier;[2] she was on tour in Egypt when the theatrical variety company was left stranded after the impresario absconded with the box-office takings. She found a job managing a small hotel where she met Louis, one of the tenants. He was a quiet Englishman with impeccable manners who fell instantly in love with her and remained so for the rest of his life.

Marguerite's father was French and came from Nice and her mother was Italian from a town north of Genoa. Margot, as she was usually called, was eight years younger than Louis and had been married twice before. Widowed during WW I, in 1919 she had married a man who one day left their home and failed to return. Until he could be found, Margot was unable to obtain a divorce.

1. Sir Robert Peel, 2nd Baronet, 1788-1850. Twice UK Prime Minister 1834-1835 and 1841-1846. Best known for leading the repeal of the Corn Laws which maintained high prices for grain in favour of landowners to the detriment of the poor and hungry; and for forming the modern police force (known as 'Bobbies' in England, and as 'Peelers' in Ireland).

2. Maurice Auguste Chevalier, 1888-1972. French actor, singer and popular vaudeville entertainer, best known to non-French audiences for his part in the 1958 film *Gigi*.

Michael, the couple's only child, was born in 1926, his birth was notarised by the hospital in an Arabic-language certificate. Later, when Margot's husband was finally traced and a divorce obtained, Louis and Margot were able to marry in September 1928. To alleviate the stigma of illegitimacy, it was then that Michael's birth was registered at the British Consulate. As a result, Michael Henry Birch had two birth certificates showing that he was born on the same day in two different years.

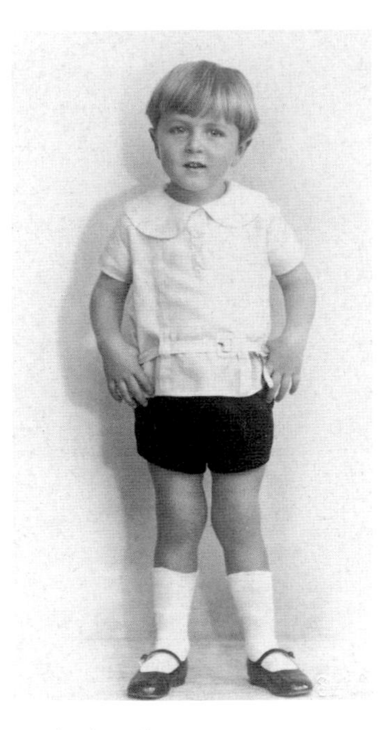

Michael aged 3

After a stressful business career, Louis obtained a post teaching English at a small private school in Alexandria. As Margot's English was negligible, she and Louis, always a gentleman, spoke to each other in French and Michael was raised in a French-speaking family. As the only European child in the area, he spent much of his time with the young members of the local Bedouin family, often sleeping with the children on a rush mat in their tents. He learned to speak Arabic and their Bedouin dialect, eat their food, and take part in their adventures. He came to love his second family and never forgot some of the characters in the group. Speaking English was a very poor third language. It improved when he began to attend Victoria College[3] in 1931 where there were pupils of English, French, Italian, Egyptian, Turkish, Greek and Maltese backgrounds, and of the Protestant, Catholic, Greek Orthodox, Muslim and Jewish faiths; a true reflection of the cosmopolitan nature of the city of Alexandria.

When Michael was eight, Margot suffered from one of her recurring bouts of deep depression; at the same time, Louis's mother Isabella, who was now in her late 80's, became seriously ill. Louis arranged for Michael to stay with a Greek widow who lived nearby while he nursed the two patients. Banished from the family home and cut off from his parents, Michael became a sad little boy who spent time hiding under the dining table. Eventually, it was time to go home but, while still finding it difficult to adjust back into family life after the confusion caused by his parents' apparent rejection, Michael was dealt another blow to his self-assurance when he overheard his aunt reflect her sadness that: *'Mickey is a nice little boy, but he will never amount to anything'.* For the rest of his life Michael would strive to prove her wrong.

Louis believed that if his son was eventually to go to an English university, his comprehension of the language should be improved. He gave Michael a brand new copy of Dickens's *Martin Chuzzlewit,* Rudolph Raspe's *The Surprising Adventures of Baron Munchausen*, his own leather-bound set of the plays of William Shakespeare, and *The Concise Oxford Dictionary.* For Michael, the result was an unusually extensive, if somewhat idiosyncratic English vocabulary.

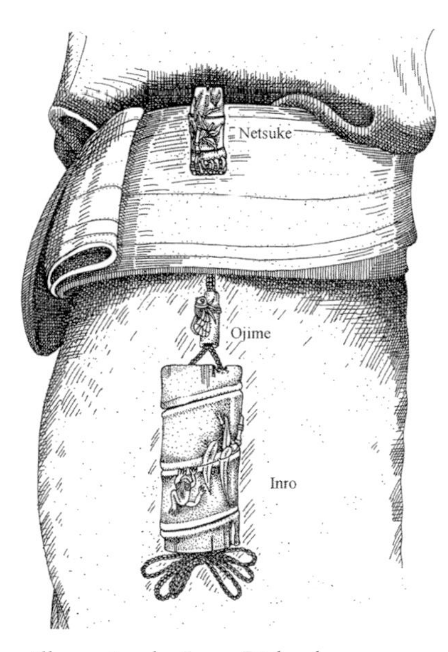

Illustration by Lynn Richardson

On the chest of drawers in his bedroom, Louis kept a collection of small Japanese ivory carvings which had been part of his father's collection of oriental art; on 16th December 1935 he gave Michael three netsuke.[4] Louis explained that traditional Japanese garments, robes called *kosode* and *kimono*, had no pockets, but a place to keep personal belongings such as pipes, tobacco, money, seals, or medicines was still needed. The elegant solution was to place such objects in small containers *(sagemono)* or cases *(inro)* fastened with a bead *(ojime)*, suspended on cord from the sash *(obi)* of the robe, and kept in place by the button-like toggle, the *netsuke.*

3. Notable alumni of Victoria College during Michael's time there include internationally recognized politicians, academics and artists. Perhaps the most famous are the late King Hussein of Jordan and Michel Shalhoub, now better known as the actor Omar Sharif.

4. Chambers Dictionary definition: Netsuke, a small Japanese carved object, once used to fasten small objects to a sash, now collectors' pieces. Pronounced: net'ské .

Three Bedouin Heads by Michael, aged 9

Their utilitarian use determined the rules of size, shape, design and materials used, and it was that combination, together with the important sense of touch and the entrancing myths behind the pieces, that fascinated Michael. In later years he sometimes used the game of tennis as an analogy to define the appeal of carving the netsuke form. Without the court lines to define the boundary, the game becomes meaningless. The most skilled players are those able to place the ball on the very edges of the court, while remaining within the lines. Likewise, the most skilled netsuke carvers are those able to create imaginative pieces that push at the very edge of the boundaries, while remaining within the rules of functionality, size and form.

It is not often that a ninth birthday present from a father to his young son has a profound effect on the child's creative mind and an enduring impact on his future adult life, but that was result of the gift. It set in motion a life-long interest in netsuke. Having decided that he would grow up to become a carver of such fascinating objects, within a very short time Michael was attempting his first netsuke carvings.

The Sandpiper

Wood on steel rod. Eyes depicted by small painted nails.

Height 6.8cm, Length 8.8cm. 1937.

Michael carved this for his mother, and shows that at ten years of age he was quickly developing his skills.

In the spring of 1939 Louis was appointed lecturer in English at the Fuad el Awal University, and the family moved to Cairo. Michael transferred to the English Mission College in Heliopolis, and then to The English School[5] as a boarder. There he had difficulty adjusting to the differences between the curriculums, and more particularly to the prevalent use of capital punishment. He described a somewhat troubled school-life, which culminated in his being made 'a non-person' after an example of mild scatological humour. Sos Green, one of his fellow pupils, recalled decades later that:

Michael is still remembered for his version of Midsummer Night's Dream's Pyramus and Thisbe, presented during a short interlude between the house plays which were put on every year. He wrote, directed and played in it and brought down the house, as well as the Headmaster's ire.

He had used a toilet roll as a scroll from which his character, Chorus, read his lines, and the headmaster was so angered by the schoolboy's humour that, according to Michael, he decided that a beating was insufficient punishment. Declining to expel a boy whose father was attached to Military Intelligence and serving as Chief Postal Censor of British Armed Forces, he determined that the boy should be ignored. What the headmaster failed to take into account was that if Michael did not exist, neither could he be punished for any wrong-doing. Needless to say, the teenager took full advantage of the situation until he left the school. Michael was saddened that at an old-boys' school reunion over thirty years later the headmaster maintained a steadfast refusal to shake his hand.

Another memory, that several of his school friends shared more than sixty years later, was their certainty that Michael would develop as an artist. One told me that if he was missing from any lesson, meal or leisure activity, he could always be found sitting on the steps leading to the main entrance with a knife and a piece of wood, carving an animal or a bird. Even so, Michael remembered those years as the unhappiest period of his life.

Schooldays, Heliopolis 1942

5. Also attending the school at the same time, was the slightly older George Blake (born George Behar), 1922- . An MI6 agent who worked for the Russians, who in 1966, after having served five years of a forty-two year sentence, escaped from Wormwood Scrubs Prison and fled to Moscow.

After leaving school in 1943, he obtained a position with British Overseas Airways Corporation (BOAC) as skipper of the mail launch, for which he had to undergo a strict vetting procedure where, apparently, his father's important position reinforced the personable young man's credentials. He was responsible for overseeing the loading, unloading and delivery of mail, which included diplomatic pouches, to and from the flying boats from England which landed on the Nile at Rod-el-Farag, before the onward flight to Baghdad and Karachi. While learning the techniques for safely loading luggage and cargo into the baggage compartment of the flying boats, he took advantage of his position to occasionally take a spare seat on flights; and it was on one of these that he caught the eye of Noël Coward,[6] who invited Michael to dinner. The invitation was refused; Michael might be young but was not unknowing.

He rented a flat in Ezbekyieh and became a member of a surrealist/anarchist group of artists. He painted abstract forms in oils which he burnt in patches; and, using the pseudonym 'Espaycel', his exhibited paintings were favourably reviewed in the *Egyptian Gazette*. He had two particular friends among the group. Antoine (Tonton) Hettena, a favourite of Margot, was to die of heat exhaustion while sitting in the pilot's seat of a plane at Payne Airfield in 1944. The other was Hassan el-Telmisani,[7] whose particular talent lay in the medium of watercolour paintings, and who specialised in the depiction of erotic, if not pornographic, scenes. He had a ready market for his work and all the pieces he could produce were, ironically, bearing his political beliefs in mind, collected by the chauffeur of a Rolls Royce in the red and black livery of King Farouk, whose collection of pornography was extensive.

Kamboora

Oil on canvas.
No measurements available.
Signed ESP" [Espaycel] Birch.
Undated C.1944

While still only seventeen, in his spare time Michael was earning pin money playing a Hammond organ and singing at a house of ill-repute in Ezbekyieh. There he made friends with the dwarf, Kamboora, whose job it was to supply hot water and towels for the girls in each of the rooms. Although strictly off-limits to British and US officers and men, among the visitors to the top-class bordello were members of the Glenn Miller Orchestra, led by the saxophonist Tex Beneke. Michael invited them back to his flat for a drink, and spent the early hours playing his piano in a jam session with them. Asked what he would like to hear, Michael replied that he would be happy to hear anything and never forgot the thirty-minute improvisation of God Save the King that followed.

After a brief period serving in the RAF where his experience of loading aircraft for BOAC was valued, Michael was seconded to the United States Army Air Force in the autumn of 1944 to fulfil the same function. His tour of duty mainly involved the transportation of supplies to USA and Canadian forces and, like many young servicemen, he sometimes took advantage of spare seats on flights. He was based just outside Cairo at Payne Field and was often able to return to Cairo at the end of the day.

6. Sir Noël Pierce Coward, 1899-1973. Flamboyant English playwright, composer, actor, director and singer. His best works, *Hay Fever, Private Lives* and *Blithe Spirit* remain part of the repertoire of many theatres.

7. After the war, Hassan el-Telmisani and other members of the Surrealist group were arrested by the Egyptian secret police. In the late 1950's Michael met Hassan in Blvd. Saint-Germain in Paris. He was a physical and mental wreck, living from hand to mouth. He had been tortured and his finger nails torn out. Michael gave him all the money he had in his pockets.

Gezira Lido, Egypt 1942

Always a talented swimmer, he spent time at weekends at the Lido at Gezira where his talent for putting on a show was displayed. His school friend, Sos Green recently recalled:

The other memory that we all have is Michael (on Sunday mornings when the Lido at Gezira was particularly full of officers and girlfriends) climbing to the top (4.5 metre) board and, having waited until the audience was ready, diving off, making a graceful swallow dive and landing flat on his belly with a great splash. An hour or so later he would repeat the performance. The second time round there would be complete silence for the dive but roars and roars of applause after. Years later I asked him how he managed to do it without hurting himself. "Don't be silly, it hurt like blazes but the applause was worth it!!" It became quite a Sunday feature and people would come to the Lido just to watch.

There are just two stories which Michael told that I have been unable to verify; but as his life could be described as full of extraordinary and unlikely events, and all the others have been proved to be true, I include these, the first of which he told on several occasions.

It relates to his being aboard a USAAF plane which crash-landed in the desert after running out of fuel and failing to land successfully, with the wheels only half deployed. Michael, a young eighteen year-old, was unable to stop his fellow crew-members from leaving the damaged aircraft and setting out in full sunlight across the desert; none of them survived. After waiting for two days by the plane without rescue, the following night he began walking in the direction of the Suez Canal. Seriously weakened by his injuries, he walked until found by a group of Bedouins. Most servicemen found wounded in the desert would have been relieved of their clothing and valuables and left, but, recalling memories of his childhood he was able to mutter in their dialect: 'I am a Bedouin'. His wounds were dressed, he was fed dates that the women softened by chewing before placing them in his mouth, and he was given camels' milk to drink. After about a week, the Bedouins reached a French military camp and handed Michael over to the authorities.
He was flown to a hospital in Cairo where his facial injuries were operated on by the famous war-time plastic surgeon, Professor McIndoe[8] who happened to be in the city at the time treating seriously burned airmen.

8. Sir Archibald Hector McIndoe, 1900-1960. New Zealand surgeon who pioneered techniques in plastic surgery. Based at the Queen Victoria Hospital at East Grinstead, West Sussex, he is particularly noted for his work on badly burned RAF pilots during WW II.

The second event about which Michael spoke relates to a brief marriage in 1944. It was a rash move for a young man, serving in the armed forces and spending frequent periods away from home, to have contracted a marriage that was secret from her family, and from his own. Michael wrote that his wife had been:

. . . abducted by her two brothers during one of my absences on active duty, and I had not been able to trace her whereabouts. It had been the final drastic move by her wealthy and powerful Egyptian family which confirmed the fact that I was not considered a suitable or permanent match for their only daughter. There was a war on and they may, after all, have been right. It had been a secret wedding, and neither of my parents was aware of that aspect of my life since I had not wanted to cause my mother unnecessary concern. In view of her nervous condition it might have precipitated the most dramatic migraine of all time. Or perhaps the main reason had been that I was unwilling to receive any advice which did not suit me.

The quotation comes from his book *A Teller of Tall Tales* which is part autobiographical and part fiction. It is just one paragraph, disconnected from the surrounding text; and if this marriage were fictional it seems remarkably out of place. During a frank admission, he was very clear that there had been a marriage. He told me that he was unsuccessful in all his attempts to contact his wife; and when he tried to obtain a copy of the marriage certificate from the Egyptian authorities, he discovered that the relevant pages had been removed from the Marriage Register with a razor blade. He finally had to accept that he was in no position to take the matter further. The marriage is not mentioned in any of his other work, nor did he mention it to friends. It is true, however, that although events in Michael's life often seem improbable at the very least, this is not the only personal action which he did not discuss with others.

By the end of the war, Michael was certain that his future lay in the arts, and in December 1945 he packed his luggage, which consisted mainly of the paintings and carvings he hoped would lead to a place at a reputable college to study art, and sailed to England on the SS Britannic. He landed in Southampton on his nineteenth birthday, 16th December 1945 but, unfortunately, the luggage on which he had pinned his hopes did not arrive with him and, despite all his attempts, was never found.

The Years 1946 to 1953

Michael needed somewhere to live that would also provide space for him to work, and obtained lodgings in a small maisonette flat in Bayswater with another aspiring artist named Howard Pickersgill. There was not much room, but they were young and ambitious and soon became good friends. Michael worked hard to produce paintings and carvings to replace those lost on the journey from Egypt, and then applied for a place at Camberwell School of Arts and Crafts where Pickersgill was studying. With just a small allowance from Louis, he found London an expensive place to live, but he produced works for his artistic portfolio and continued his studies at the London galleries and museums. He was particularly interested in the Pre-Columbian, Byzantine, Etruscan and Mongolian collections of small items at the British Museum.

He was delighted to be offered a place at Camberwell and began attending classes while his grant application as an ex-serviceman was being processed. Unfortunately, somewhere between BOAC in Egypt, the RAF in England and USAAF in America, Michael's service record had gone missing and his application for an education grant was refused. He felt that his English, still spoken with a strong Middle-Eastern accent, the fact that he was underage when enlisting, and serving with the Americans rather than the British at the end of the war, all contributed to the refusal.

Without a grant he certainly could not afford the fees at Camberwell, but Pickersgill persuaded him to continue to attend the lectures there on an unofficial basis. The college was rich with the greatest artistic talent of the time. Among the prominent lecturers were William Coldstream, Johnnie Minton, Ben Nicholson, Victor Pasmore, and Claude Rogers.[9] In an interview he gave to Aoife Burke at the National College of Art and Design in Dublin, Michael told her:

I was gate-crashing the Camberwell College of Arts and Crafts — I couldn't afford to pay for tuition — and I found the conservatory at the back of the college where they kept the clay and it had a gas ring. So I used to go there every day. The tutors came down and the sculptor tutor saw me and asked who I was. He assumed I was some kind of lone maverick sculptor belonging to some part of the school. By that time I was making tea and brewing a better cup than the canteen. So I used to get very individual tuition from the tutors.

But as far as Michael's artistic development was concerned, the most important figure was the sculptor Henry Moore.[10] Michael showed Moore his latest netsuke, carved from a second-hand ivory billiard ball purchased for sixpence (2½p), which he would sell for one pound, and they discussed the challenge of remaining within the rules and restrictions of the form while pushing those boundaries as far as possible. Moore reached into his trouser pocket and pulled out a small carving of his own which would have fulfilled all the requirements of a netsuke. Moore explained that he enjoyed carving small pieces, that he kept them close and handled them often, and that he called them 'feelies'.

9. Sir William Menzies Coldstream, 1908-1987. British realist painter and war artist; visiting teacher at Camberwell School of Arts & Crafts, London, 1945–1949. Founder member of the Euston Road School movement.

Francis John Minton, 1917-1957. British teacher of portraits and landscapes, and theatrical designer.

Ben Nicholson, 1894-1982. Influential English painter.

Victor Pasmore, 1908-1998. Influential British abstract artist; Director of Painting at Camberwell School of Arts & Crafts, London; founder member of the Euston Road School movement.

Claude Rogers, 1907-1979. Teacher of portrait and landscape painting at Camberwell School of Arts & Crafts, London, 1945-1949. Founder member of the Euston Road School movement.

10. Sir Henry Moore, 1898-1986. Pre-eminent English sculptor, most famous for his monumental bronze sculptures which are displayed around the world as public works of art.

Michael, 4th right with college friends

Michael explained to Aoife Burke:

Henry Moore told me that for a piece of sculpture to be important it has to be large. To which, with all the arrogance and pertinence of youth I replied that I think that something small can be even greater.

According to Michael, they finally compromised with the assertion that while publicly important sculpture should be large, it was perfectly acceptable, in some ways preferable, for personally important sculpture to be small.

His evenings were spent with Pickersgill and friends, discussing art and literature over pints of beer at the Goodge Street basement flat of the artist James Broome-Lynne.[11] Among the group were the rising character actor Theodore Bikel,[12] who urged Michael to join him on a trip to Hollywood, where he was sure they would make their fortunes; and the poet Dylan Thomas,[13] who always had a notebook in his jacket pocket in which he recorded any overheard unusual words, phrases and smart comments. (Famous for his capacity to consume alcoholic beverages, Thomas was occasionally found fast asleep in the bath when overcome, with his notebook resting on his chest.) Always a keen pianist, Michael spent some of his evenings playing the piano in a group led by fellow student, Humphrey Lyttelton[14] who, at that time, still played the clarinet, rather that the trumpet for which he later became much better known. Nor was female company ever in short supply; the flat below Pickersgill's was rented by a young dancer, so plenty of late nights were spent with a steady flow of girls from London's many stage shows, and an ample supply of drinks and music.

At Camberwell one morning, Moore noticed Michael working on a marble sculpture of a father and son, and commented: *"Ah, a Henry Moore, and a damned good one at that."* Later, he praised a sculptured head in Portland limestone that Michael was working on, and asked to purchase it. Michael refused as it was a portrait of his father and intended as a gift. Moore settled on a plaster cast of the piece, for which he paid the large sum of five guineas (£5.25pence), twice the average weekly wage at the time. All was well at the college until, in the early spring of 1947, the College authorities caught up with him, and Michael was firmly invited to leave the building, never to return.

11. James Broome-Lynne, 1916-1995. Graphic designer and illustrator.

12. Theodore Bikel, 1924- . Austrian/Jewish actor, singer and musician whose film debut was *The African Queen* and who was nominated for an Oscar for his supporting role in *The Defiant Ones*. Prominent in the actors unions, he was also a human rights activist.

13. Dylan Marlais Thomas, 1914-1953. Welsh poet and writer, most famous for the play *Under Milk Wood*.

14. Humphrey Lyttelton, 1921-2008. English jazz musician and writer and broadcaster.

When Louis retired, Margot, never a good linguist, was keen to return to her native France. They had purchased a small property in a village near Grasse, about twenty-five miles west of Nice, where they farmed jasmine for the perfumery trade. Michael thought it would be a good idea to visit his parents before deciding his next step and on his way south, he stopped in Paris. It was his first visit to the city to which he would often return for the rest of his life. He stayed in a small cheap hotel on the Left Bank and visited as many of the museums and galleries as possible, absorbing the styles and techniques of both the classical and the contemporary artists. When his funds finally out he caught a train to Nice. He enjoyed a brief holiday period with his parents before he began looking for a job, ideally one that utilised his artistic talents.

Just ten miles from the family farm was the village of Vallauris, famous for its ceramic and pottery crafts. Michael was delighted to obtain a position with one of the major potteries in the village, Georges and Suzanne Ramie's Madoura Pottery. He began creating pots that reflected his interest in Pre-Columbian art, which were soon noticed by the famous new resident in the village, Pablo Picasso.[15]Known to have had an interest in the same art form for many years, he appreciated Michael's skill in producing the hollow handles so indicative of the vessels they both admired. Michael prepared thrown pots ready for Picasso to deftly mould the soft clay into the simple shape of an animal or a bird. Picasso referred to Michael as *'le petit Anglais'* and often included him in invitations to have lunch, at the end of which Michael watched him pay for everyone's meal by folding an empty Gauloises cigarette packet into the shape of a cockerel, or making a small sketch on a napkin.

When Michael returned to London in 1948, he stayed with his friend Howard Pickersgill in Bayswater; and it was there that he renewed his friendship with an attractive young dancer named Margaret Goldfinch whom he had first met two years before. He and Margaret married on 4th December 1948, and the following year, on 6th September, they had celebrated the birth of their first daughter. He discovered that full-time work was difficult to find, but his outgoing personality and musical abilities gave him an advantage and, through a contact of Margaret's, he heard of auditions for the job as a tap-dancing chorus boy. He was successful and appeared in the *Cinderella* pantomime production at Duke of York theatre, where he worked with a young Leslie Phillips[16] under the direction of Patrick Cargill.[17] When the pantomime season finished Michael obtained a job in a late-night cabaret show, during which time he worked with composer/actor Burt Rhodes.[18] His last engagement as a cabaret artist was at a smart nightclub in Grosvenor Square, which came to an abrupt halt in October 1949. The owner, Max Setty, went into hiding after his brother Stanley was murdered;[19] the night-club was closed and Michael's late nights as a cabaret singer were over. Now that he was unemployed, it seemed a good time for a brief trip to introduce his new family to his parents in Grasse.

15. Pablo Picasso, 1881-1973. Prolific Spanish-born artist who lived and worked in France. His work included painting, sculpture and collage. With fellow artist Braque he developed the cubism movement. One of his best known works is *Guernica*, a depiction of the horrors of the destruction of the Basque capital during the Spanish Civil War.

16. Leslie Phillips, 1924 - . English comedy actor who made a successful transition to character parts.

17. Patrick Cargill, 1918-1986. British stage and television actor and director.

18. Burt Rhodes, 1923-2003. Highly successful British musical director who worked on stage in London and on Broadway with, among others, Judy Garland, Cliff Richard, Johnny Mathis, Frankie Vaughan, Lovelace Watkins, The Supremes, Eartha Kitt and Howard Keel. His film credits include the orchestration of the Bond theme in *Dr. No*. On television his credits include the theme music for the highly successful television series *The Good Life*.

19. Stanley Setty, 1903-1949. Part of London's seedy underworld, he was stabbed five times, his body dismembered, and wrapped in felt parcels. The packages were dropped from a light aircraft, but it was not long before parts of the body were left stranded by a low tide off Essex's coastline. No murder conviction was obtained.

On the family's return, Michael had to accept that there was little hope of earning enough in the visual or musical arts to support a family, so he took a job managing a junk shop in Bayswater which provided a small flat above the shop. In February 1951, after a second daughter was born, the family's financial position became difficult. The landlord of the tiny flat they were renting wanted it made vacant for members of her own family. Michael and Margaret could find nowhere else to rent in a city still recovering from extensive bomb damage and suffering an acute housing shortage, and they finally had to accept the break-up of the family. Margaret, with their two daughters moved into a hostel, while Michael joined the ranks of the post-war homeless population.

He took whatever job he could find. He washed dishes at a central London restaurant; worked in a vanilla ice-cream factory in Kentish Town; and laboured on a building site in Cheapside where he found a six feet tall block of Portland limestone and, during his breaks, carved a stone head. It was a desperate situation for a few weeks until the family's luck changed. Finally, his perfect French came to the rescue, and he was successful at an interview for a position as an overnight operator at the International Telephone Exchange in London. The couple were able to rent a flat in Marylebone and be together again.

While secure in his new job, Michael was keen to spend more time with his young family and to find work that would use his artistic talents. He eventually found a position making spectacle-frames by hand for Marylebone Optical Company where he had a creative outlet and the opportunity to use his hands; and he was able to make spectacle frames to his own designs.

In February 1953 Margaret was pregnant with their third child. Born at home with a young and inexperienced midwife present, the baby was starved of oxygen prior to her birth and the couple were devastated to discover that she had suffered severe brain damage. She has lived in the same Rudolph Steiner residential facility for nearly forty years, she is happy, loves music, and recently had her first holiday abroad.

Later that year Michael's talents were noticed by Stanley Unger, a manufacturing optician based in Tunbridge Wells. He offered Michael a job to design and make stylish prototype frames by hand. While many are familiar with his netsuke and may be aware of his larger sculptures and his paintings, most will not have seen the extraordinary spectacle frame designs Michael produced. Some went into production, and some did not.

He was working on a wide range of designs when, in the early summer of 1954, Unger called Michael into his office and told him to design a pair of spectacles that was orbital. Michael always maintained that he did not understand, and that Unger's voice became louder and his face redder as he described the shape with his fingers. Michael, still confused by the shape in the air that looked like every other pair of glasses, continued to protest that he did not understand what was being asked of him.

Finally, exploding with fury, Unger said: *"Fuck off!"* Michael, even more confused, asked: *"Fuck off? Out of your office? Out of the building?"* Unger: *"Fuck off out of my office, out of the building, and out of my life!"*

Some of Michael's designs for the Stanley Unger manufacturing company

20. Rudolph Steiner, 1861-1925. Austrian philosopher whose theories on education place an emphasis on the changing needs of a growing child to develop all three areas of their physical, mental and emotion well-being.

The Years 1954 to 1969

Few individuals have been fired in such a dramatic fashion. But with a wife and three daughters, Michael once again had no job and no support for his family. Desperate for work he began repairing spectacle frames for his old employers Marylebone Optical Company and for the local opticians he had got to know while working for Unger. He and Margaret cleared the front room of their home and Michael set to work in the makeshift workshop. Michael H. Birch (Designs) Ltd. was started with a total investment capital of fifteen pounds. It was all he and Margaret could scrape together with a loan from his parents after the bank had refused him a loan of fifty pounds. (Just a few years later, at a meeting with the Directors of Barclays Bank, he was asked if the one hundred thousand pounds he was asking for, was going to be enough.) Soon he needed help. His first employee was John Sullivan, a sixteen year-old who had quickly become disillusioned with working for Unger. Next, came the more experienced Brian Green, also from the Unger workshop. It was not long before they were not just repairing frames but making them from Michael's designs. By the end of that year the company had become so successful that larger premises were needed, as well as more staff; the equipment was moved to a building belonging to the defunct Silverdale Bakery, and additional staff were engaged.

As will be seen, Michael was one of those fortunate individuals who happen not only to be in the right place at the right time, but also in a position to take advantage of whatever opportunity arose. One such event occurred in late 1955 at the dancing salon in Chelsea of Margaret's sister and her husband, Betty and Philip Buchel. He and Margaret met the actor Michael Wilding,[21] who was taking lessons before having to dance in a film, and his wife, Elizabeth Taylor.[22] The three couples got on well and spent an evening playing charades. (Wilding's effort to portray the film and song *I Cover the Waterfront* by placing his hands over his genitalia was not forgotten.) More such social occasions followed.

When he began the business, Michael spent as much as he could afford on advertising; creating a top quality product with some exclusive touches, he was eager for his frames to be recognised as the best available. Although still short of funds, he contacted the Advertising Manager at the fortnightly published trade magazine *The Optician* and requested a full page advertisement for every issue for six months, but stated that he could not make any payment until the end of the period. It says much for Michael's persuasive skills that the man agreed.

'The Best in the World' advertisement

In 1955 he placed an advertisement in the trade papers which showed a Rolls Royce with the *Spirit of Ecstasy* ornament against which was resting *Baby Doll*, his most recently designed frame which was described as 'The Best in the World'. The motor manufacturer threatened to sue Michael for infringing their copyright. Michael, who had hired the car for just one hour, (all that he could afford at the time) replied that Rolls Royce should be grateful that he had used their vehicle as a prop, rather than that of any other manufacturer. Rolls Royce was not happy about it, but decided to withdraw their legal action.

In early 1957 Michael was surprised to learn that Stanley Unger was asking for an appointment to see his erstwhile employee. Unger explained that he wished to retire and, despite the way they had parted three years before, he hoped that Michael would buy his company. Michael promised to

21. Michael Wilding, 1919-1979. English stage and film actor most successful in light comedy roles. He married four times, most notably to actress Elizabeth Taylor 1952-1957.

22. Elizabeth Taylor, 1932-2011. Anglo-American child star, who, after appearing in *National Velvet* at the age of twelve, went on to become one of Hollywood's most recognised actresses. The much-married actress was as famous for her off-stage glamorous life-style as for her on-screen performances.

BABY DOLL and FIESTA

consider the proposal after reviewing copies of the company accounts, which were duly delivered. On examination, it was clear that Unger's company was insolvent. Another meeting was arranged and Michael made the position clear: he would take over the company, staff and stock, and pay nothing for it, but in return he would clear all of Unger's debts. Unger agreed, deciding that, with no prospect of any funds, at least his 'good name' would be protected. Michael contacted each of Unger's creditors and his promise was accepted that, although it might take him six months, all debts would be paid. One unexpected benefit of the transaction was that Michael regained the intellectual property rights to the designs he had created while employed by Unger.

He soon learned, however, exactly what value could be placed on Unger's 'good name' when, only a few weeks later, Unger's wife arrived at Michael's office and asked what had happened to her pay cheque. For years, her errant husband had paid her a monthly sum for housekeeping from the company's petty cash; but he had recently left the country with his former secretary, leaving his wife abandoned and destitute. She was now living in a caravan in a field with no services, no food, and no money. Michael asked her if he could, if necessary, sometime in the future, talk to her about Unger's business dealings and confirmed that, in the meantime, he would pay her a monthly retainer for her possible potential assistance. It was a typical act of generosity of the sort which would be repeated over the years to come.

By June 1957, even together the old Silverdale Bakery premises and Stanley Unger's workshop had become too small, and a major change was necessary. More space and more staff were essential if he was to maintain the standards he had set. Michael was fast becoming a major employer in the town and had big plans for enlarging his manufacturing base. He approached the local Town Hall Clerk, Jack Girling, and took a building lease on open land on the north-eastern edges of the town that was suitable for development for a new factory complex. In the spring of 1958, as the new factory was completed, he purchased Stigmat Ltd., a lens manufacturing company, and moved its staff from London to Tunbridge Wells, providing deposits on houses for key staff and temporary accommodation for whole families where necessary.

Much of his manufacturing processes were so innovative that none of the machinery required was available for purchase. It all had to be designed and manufactured in his brand new tool room, the largest in the south of England, and the envy of British, German, American and Japanese companies, all of whom sent management teams to review his working practices.

Michael, appearing in an advertisement for his frame design *Lady In Mink,* 1957

One morning in May 1958 he was in the accounts department of his new office/factory complex discussing some change to the accounting procedures with his book-keeper. Brian Green, by now one of his managers, interrupted them. Michael turned and explained that he would not be long and that Green was to wait patiently. Again Green tried to interrupt and was again instructed, this time a little more tersely, that he was to wait. When he had finished his discussion Michael turned and asked what had been so important. He was told that the whole of the old Unger factory was on fire. It was, but fortunately no one was injured; the fire brigade had been called and limited production would soon be restored. Despite this, Michael continued to insist that interruptions are neither polite nor permissible, whatever the circumstances. He had been aware of the occasional dangers of restrained politeness years before, when, as a small boy, he had almost drowned. His grandmother had waited until her son had finished his sentence before pointing out that Michael might be in some kind of difficulty. He had fallen into the garden pond and only his hat could be seen floating on the surface.

The fire at the Unger factory

The Birch-Stigmat Group now manufactured spectacle frames and lenses; had developed injection moulded plastics; made the first shaped trays for the inside of a box of chocolates; and made tableware in jewel colours which was displayed at the Design Centre in London, the premier showcase for contemporary design, and sold at Harrods and Selfridges.

Not all was well, however, outside the factory which had been built on agricultural land. The poor drainage services were unpredictable and there were many failed attempts to get the problem sorted out; it was only when Michael threatened to purchase a container of farm manure and have it tipped on the steps of the Town Hall, that the sewage system was finally replaced. Despite this, Michael remained on good terms with Girling, the Town Clerk, who some years later chose the names Birch Close and Birch Way for a new development of residential properties. Michael always enjoyed the irony that both these roads were cul-de-sacs.

In 1959 Michael was sentenced to eight months in prison for a motoring offence after the local magistrate decided to make an example of him. Nearly four years after his death, I mentioned to

The replacement factory in Lamberts Road

The first stage factory in full production

his old school friends that I had found no evidence of his story. From their response it was clear that Michael's claim that it was 'a fit up' was shared by those who were in the car at the time. It was the wartime service in RAF that he shared with the 'main man' in the prison, who gave him the nickname 'Posh', which protected him from the aggressive prison population. However, his well-spoken voice did not protect him from a small group of prison wardens who took him to an isolated cell, and showed him what they thought of his accent. Michael continued to run his business from his prison cell and was truly grateful to be released at the end of his sentence. Just a few weeks later, a security guard knocked on his office door late one evening to check that there was no problem. It was one of the prison wardens who had beaten him while in prison. The guard suggested that everything was now OK, and that the past could be forgiven. Michael was sure everything was not OK, nor would it be forgiven. The following morning, the security company was informed that if that particular guard ever appeared on the Birch Group premises again, their contract would be cancelled immediately.

Margaret gave birth to their fourth daughter in August 1958, and, in October 1961 she gave birth to their only son. (Michael's other two sons, Stephen and Patrick, were born in July 1959 and November 1962.) With their family rapidly growing up, it was clear that he and Margaret needed more space. The couple viewed Rust Hall, originally a small seventeenth century house; now little remained of the original property which had been altered and enlarged by almost every generation since then. It was again in sore need of modernisation, but there was a large garden for the children to play in, and spectacular views across a valley of wooded areas interspersed by farm land for about twelve miles. The Birch family made their contribution to the enlargement and moved in.

The first machine to manufacture injection moulded trays

The much envied Birch-Stigmat tool-room

Presentation box for Michael H. Birch (Designs) Ltd.

CANDIDA

In 1963 Michael's access to an established market for a popular design called *Candida* was blocked. The British National Health Service funded approved spectacles for those in need, and the officials at Department of Health (DoH) had rejected the frame as it did not, in their view, meet the required DoH Regulation 12 specifications for approval. Michael felt otherwise and believed that the Department was pursuing their objections because the price of his frames was higher than those of his competitors. He decided to appeal the decision. Although his appeal was rejected, Michael felt strongly enough to commence a law suit against the Secretary of State for the Health Service. It was unprecedented in legal history for a Minister of the Crown to be sued in that way, and at the first court hearing Michael was offered a choice: the case could either be heard in High Court with a judge and jury or by a judge sitting alone in an arbitration court for the Comptroller of Patents. Michael chose the latter, where he could be represented by his family solicitor Philip Langford, for whom he had great respect, rather than the unhelpful QC he had seen earlier. It was the correct decision. The judge deemed that the frame fulfilled the necessary DoH criteria and that the Minister had exceeded his authority in his rejection.
Both the legal case and the frame were a great success.

Next, Michael faced a challenge from union representatives. At their request, he arranged a free afternoon in the factory for them to make a presentation to his staff. At the end of the meeting a vote was held to confirm union representation in the factory. It was not carried. The stunned and angry union representatives blamed Michael for the rejection, accusing him of threatening his staff if they joined a union. Michael explained that, as a young man he had held communist views, and that the package being offered to his staff by the union was significantly less than their current employment contracts gave them. It was, he told them, a lesson of the importance of preparation. He maintained liberal employment conditions, high rates of pay and, extremely unusual for the times, equal pay for his female employees. Forty years later he was still being recognised by ex-employees, who confirmed that he was a demanding man to work for, but that he was always scrupulously fair.

Now, in addition to the manufacturing opticians, prescription lens house, prescription spectacle frames, sunglasses for recreational use, safety spectacles for industrial use, and injection plastic mouldings, the Birch Group had developed interests in Stowe Electronics, and applied for patents

Modelling one of his own frames. c. 1968

In 1968 Michael launched an extensive advertising campaign, all using the same slogan: The Best in the World. One example referred to the frame *Rhanee* which he had designed for Stanley Unger in 1952. The text of the advertisement read:

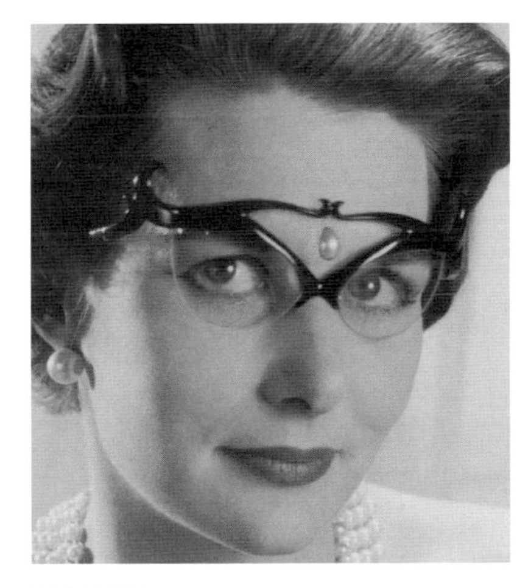

RHANEE

Michael Birch designed this kooky creation back in '52. Any day now some kinky couturier may design it all over again. Ah well, that's the price you pay for being THE BEST IN THE WORLD.

His words were not too far from the truth although it was his own designs which would achieve the 'designer' status he mentioned. As one of the earliest 'designer labels' of spectacle frames, Michael Birch designs are now available as collectors' items on the Internet.

The continuing huge success of the Birch Group of companies led to the obvious next step in the expansion programme: to purchase the sales outlets for the manufacturing output of the spectacle division. The purchase of one group was troubled by a recent manufacturing problem with a metal frame. The solution, when it was discovered, did not help. It was learned that the recently retired forge-master chewed tobacco and had for years been spitting his tobacco juice-ridden saliva into the barrel where the frames were being polished. Without the added ingredient the whole process failed to reach the expected standard, and the purchase of the group fell through. Next, Michael negotiated a merger with a chain which fell through at the last moment because at 67, the younger of the two brothers in the partnership decided that he had 'another ten years in me, and I'm not ready to retire'. The purchase of third group dragged on for months. In 1969 the fourth attempt related to a chain that had been purchased by the British bank: Slater Walker. Michael negotiated and agreed a purchase price of ten million pounds. After a brief trip to USA, he learned that Slater Walker had increased the price to fourteen million pounds. Despite the willingness of his investment bank to proceed with the deal, Michael walked away. He said later that it was the moment that he began to form his decision to sell the Birch Group and return to being an artist.

The Years 1970 to 1974

One morning in the autumn of 1970 he awoke to spend yet another day attending business meetings. He now ran a highly successful multi-national and multi-million pound group of industrial companies, with almost one thousand employees. Despite the financial success of the company, or perhaps because of it, Michael increasingly spent his time with bankers, accountants and lawyers. It was not how he had planned to spend his adult life, and it was time to return to youthful ambition, time to return to being an artist.

London's premier merchant bank was given the responsibility of disposing of the shares of the Birch Group of Companies. All did not go well. There was a clash of personalities between Michael and Gordon Richardson,[26] the Chairman of the bankers Schroder Wagg. As he left a meeting in the city, Michael overheard Richardson ask one of his managers if Michael was a hippy, a communist, a homo-sexual, or something? Michael didn't object to any of the first three, but 'something'? Anyway, he didn't see what relevance any of them had to the sale of his companies. At another meeting, Richardson asked why Michael was selling the business. He was shocked when told that it was no longer fun, and angrily responded that business was not supposed to be fun; he was mystified when Michael told him that was where he was wrong.

Self portrait
Unsigned. Undated C.1972

Michael's working relationship was no better with Richardson's assistant in charge of the day-to-day activities in the interim period. John Bayley made it clear that he was determined to find something against Michael. The auditors he sent to review the company accounts were overheard challenging each other to look for discrepancies: 'Just ten bob (50p) and we've got him'. At the same time, Michael was trailed by two private detectives who were looking for gossip and scandal. In another example of the unfortunate deterioration of the relationship, Bayley called a Directors' meeting in London (40 miles from Tunbridge Wells) for 4pm on Christmas Eve. Michael told his directors to go home to their families for the holiday and went on his own to the Schroder Wagg flat near the Ritz Hotel. At first Bayley was angry and blustered; said that he felt threatened by Michael's equanimity in the face of all that had been thrown at him; then he broke down, cried, and attempted to excuse himself with stories of how difficult his life was with a handicapped son. Michael was stunned by the man's behaviour, and told him to pull himself together and to go home to his family; he made no mention of his own daughter's difficulties.

The Group's shares were provisionally placed with blue chip investment companies and pension schemes, then became an unquoted public company before being purchased for £5,000,000 by the pre-eminent British manufacturer and supplier of glass products to architects and vehicle manufacturers: Pilkington Glass Ltd. Michael was disappointed with the lack of efficiency shown by Schroders. Their failure to follow his verbal and written instructions caused a loss of £60,000 on some investments in just a few days.

With the funds he received from the sale of the business, Michael paid off his bank loan, (his bank overdraft limit had been one million pounds on the security of just his word); paid off his mortgage; and put aside money to purchase homes for each of his children and enough capital to secure an income for Margaret in the event of his death. Then he paid a significant sum into the Birch-Stigmat Group Staff Pension Fund, (the latent communist in him argued that, without them he could not have acquired the assets available, and that his employees were as entitled to their share of the profits as he was).

25. Gordon Richardson, Baron Richardson of Duntisbourne, 1915–2010. British banker, former lawyer, Governor of the Bank of England 1973-1983.

Michael was retained to act in an advisory consultancy capacity for Pilkington's for the next two years. It was a frustrating period, as he found the new owners unwilling to accept any suggestions regarding the financial or the marketing decisions for the business, and as a result Pilkington made a loss for each of the next two years. So it was particularly galling when a half-page article appeared in *The Guardian* newspaper denigrating Michael for the losses made by the company. Supposedly by an investigative reporter, the author had not contacted Michael first, nor understood that the losses were made in the years when he no longer owned the business, and was acting on a consultancy basis only and not able to make any decisions.

As it transpired, the sale of the Birch Group to Pilkington Glass was a disaster for the company, and for the employees. By 1974, Pilkington Glass had closed the factory and made the staff redundant. Michael's reputation in the optical industry was still recognised, however. In an article in *The Optician* about the two major influences since the end of the Second World War, Michael was described as:

. . . an artist of outstanding merit in his own right, who brought fashion into British frame manufacture. . . Michael Birch was an intuitive designer who gave British optics a fillip into the realm of glamour.

He would be proud to reflect that, forty years after he sold the business, there are still opticians who remember his contribution to the industry. An assessment of his contribution to the glasses frames industry recently appeared on the website of *The Vintage Optical Shop.*

One of the most fascinating aspects of the history of vintage eyeglasses – besides all the strange, fantastic shapes and creative designs produced over the years – is the association of various eccentric people with the world of vintage eyewear. Benjamin Franklin, Teddy Roosevelt, Mahatma Gandhi, John Lennon, and Leon Trotsky are all associated with certain styles of glasses. The history of cat eye glasses frames from the 1950s and 1960s is closely associated with another highly colorful individual – Michael Birch. He left his mark on the design of cat eye glasses frames during their heyday and his success had an undoubted effect on the global fashion scene as it related to vintage cats-eye glasses.

A fanatically driven artist and designer, Birch produced his own designs through a long, painstaking process. Rather than relying on design teams and just selling the product, the British designer would draw an initial concept, then erase it repeatedly, attempting to draw a further refined design each time until he was finally satisfied that the glasses had been honed to perfection.

Peppery and temperamental, Michael Birch once trampled a defective batch of cat eye glasses frames after moulding, smashing them under the soles of his shoes in outrage at their poor quality. His design genius shone through in the numerous innovative, dramatic cats-eye glasses frames that were produced at his firm, including a number of models that achieved international notoriety.

His manufacturing techniques always showed an experimental urge – his first attempt was to make fiberglass cats-eye glasses frames. However, vacuum-forming, another leading Birch technological adaptation to glasses manufacture soon displaced fiberglass. Later on, moving into the 1960s, Birch started using acetate and aluminium in many of his creations, thus encouraging their use among imitators. Though half a century has passed since Michael Birch began designing and manufacturing cat eye glasses frames, many of them are designs so bold that they almost look like the creations of a modern fashion house and given Birch's fanatical insistence on high quality, large numbers have survived to be collected and worn today.

Michael had retired from the business world at the age of forty-four. He went from being responsible for nearly one thousand employees and their families one week, to the next week sitting alone at home at his workbench carving netsuke. Then, in the spring of 1971, he was asked if he would act as an art expert for the wealthy businessman William Stern,[27] who wanted to form an important art collection. Michael had left the business world, but this was a different challenge. During a seven minute appointment, timed precisely with an alarm, Stern set up an off-the-shelf company with an account at Moscow Narodny Bank, and with funds of up to £10,000,000 available. Michael was to have free reign in the choice of media, subject and artist and he spent the next few months reviewing the current art markets, attending auction previews and sales, and visiting major galleries. Then he received a call from Stern, who informed Michael that he was no longer interested in art but that he was happy to continue working with Michael jointly on property purchase and development projects. Michael agreed to the formation of a property investment partnership.

Stern had recently made contact with a Kuwaiti prince who had a $15,000,000 plan to build a 1,000 bed hotel, casino and conference centre in Freeport, Bahamas. The Hyatt Hotel group had agreed to manage the property, and the logo and house style for carpets, china and cutlery had been designed. What was urgently needed was the government license for the casino, to make it financially viable. Michael flew to Nassau by the prince's private jet for meetings with Prime Minister Lynden Pindling and his Tourism Minister.

He presented a package which included details of thousands of new jobs; good rates of pay; strict working hours; a full health insurance programme; and a well-funded pension package. Pindling informed him that the Constitution set a limit for the number of casinos that were allowed to operate in the county at any one time and that currently there were none available for issue. If the developers were to go ahead with this new project, and the Government was very keen for them to do so in the light of the impressive employment potential and the staff welfare scheme proposed, a license would have to be withdrawn from someone else when renewals were due.

Further meetings were held during the year before existing licences came up for renewal, until one evening during his trip to the island in November 1971. While having a drink by the pool, Michael was joined by two gentlemen in charcoal grey silk suits with under-arm bulges. One placed an envelope in front of Michael, who was suspicious and asked what it was. He was told in an Italian-American accent that it was a first class ticket to Heathrow. Michael explained that he already had one, but was told that the ticket he had been given was for the following morning. It was not Michael's flight, but he was told that he was to be on it. Threats were made against construction workers and against the building itself, and promises made that the hotel would never be completed. After physical threats to himself and his family, Michael used the ticket given to him. All plans for the hotel and casino were dropped following his report of that trip in which he tactfully stated:

There is an awkward political situation involving the other hotel and casino owners. This fact, coupled with the unfavourable economic climate in the Bahamas led me to recommend that we should not proceed with the project.

27. William George Stern, 1934 - . Bergen-Belsen survivor whose business assets were predominantly based in property and insurance and who was Britain's largest bankrupt to date in 1978, when he owed £118 million.

Michael's venture into property development was working well until there was a crash in property prices and Willie's Stern Group empire collapsed amid accusations of impropriety, and questions in the Houses of Parliament about the bankruptcy valued at nearly one hundred and twenty million pounds. Michael was certain that his part in the Group would pull through, but the liquidator discovered that Stern had occasionally made cross-company guarantees without the knowledge of his partners. It was no consolation when Michael was told in 1975 that his company was the only one in the Group to be in profit, but that the cross-guarantees had wiped out all of his initial significant investment, and the expected profits of half a million pounds.

Draft pop concert poster. C.1972

Another business opportunity which failed to develop was when Michael was introduced to Jeffrey Archer[28] in the early 1970's. At a meeting in Archer's office close to Trafalgar Square the young politician snapped and clicked his fingers, and Michael remained unimpressed by his manners. A cautionary aside from the young man at the desk in the outer office (probably David Mellor[29]) only confirmed Michael's suspicions that Archer was not a man he was prepared to trust in business.

During the 1960's and 1970's Michael had purchased plots of land adjoining and close to his home. These included a small public house/restaurant which Michael upgraded, modernising the property and installing a new chef. Occasionally, just for fun, he acted as a waiter or sommelier, leaving local customers to wonder if the largest employer in the town was in financial difficulty. Another venture was a small farm where a prize cattle herd was developed. Always keen to embrace new practices, the decision was made to raise the animals on hydroponically produced feed, to provide better quality feed in less space all year round, for animals which then produced better quality meat and a higher price at market.

In 1972, his love of all forms of music led him join John Sullivan, his very first employee, as pop concert promoters. Success at local venues led to more concerts at increasingly important venues including the Royal Albert Hall, among others. This developed into a brief period in band management, included *The Anti-Nowhere League* whose line-up included his son Jonathan on drums.

In July 1974 he contacted a reclusive netsuke collector who lived nearby. Collingwood Ingram did not usually receive visitors, but he recognised Michael's name and, intrigued that a local businessman was carving netsuke, was pleased to show his collection to an appreciative audience. Ingram was an authority on Japanese flowering cherry trees, and is famous in horticultural circles for re-introducing into Japan the Great White Cherry, 'Tai Haku', which had been believed to be extinct. Michael admired the way that the Major, by then ninety-four years old, was continuing to start new projects, which would not flower for another fifteen years. Later, he learned that the Major's family had been friends with his grandparents in Alexandria in the first years of the 20th century. 'Cherry' Ingram's antique netsuke now form part of the British Museum collection.

28. Jeffrey Howard Archer, Baron Archer of Weston-Super-Mare, 1940 - . Best-selling British author and former politician whose political career ended with his conviction and subsequent imprisonment for perjury and perverting the course of justice.

29. David John Mellor, 1949 - . British politician, non-practising barrister, broadcaster, journalist and football pundit. Worked for Archer while studying for the bar.

The Years 1975 to 1984

In order to develop his sculptural skills, Michael had continued to purchase top quality netsuke and now he began to buy a large number of secondary, damaged and fake pieces. He believed that one needed to compare good with bad to appreciate the best. Just as he had polished his carving craft in the spectacle frame business by repairing damaged items, and then making them by hand, so he set about repairing and re-carving minor netsuke pieces. He was able to practise his craft while learning precisely how the best examples of netsuke carving were created, all of which stood him in good stead as he came to his own creative process.

In 1975, Michael attended the first International Netsuke Collectors Society Convention in Hawaii and began to show his work to a few collectors. George and Verna Lazarnik were among the first to appreciate his work, and they offered to exhibit some of Michael's pieces in their home. When the prestigious gallery Eskenazi Ltd., in London's Piccadilly, agreed to hold a one-man show the following year to introduce his work to the wider world market of netsuke collectors, Michael began a period of twelve months of concentrated work, determined to produce sculptures which obeyed the functional rules of the netsuke art form, while pushing the boundaries of those rules. The exhibition opened in June 1976, and displayed some of his stunning designs in a wide range of organic materials. It was an enormous success.

In his Preface to the exhibition catalogue, Luigi Bandini commented on Miriam Kinsey's view of Michael's work that:

. . . you have completely caught the essence of Japanese beauty and culture. And your netsuke have shibui. . . Shibui is the Japanese notion of an artist's ability to convey, by the most perceptive and elegant economy of means, the essence of what he wishes to convey.

The noted English collector Edward Wrangham commented:

. . . The exhibition introduced the work of an English sculptor, Michael Birch, whose netsuke and other small sculptures are becoming widely known and evidently much appreciated, judging by the eagerness with which many were snapped up at substantial prices.

In the following International Netsuke Collectors Society Journal, Bernard Hurtig wrote:

. . . Michael's work is simply superb miniature sculpture. He is a master of the utilization of materials, with a remarkable ability to marry ivory with wood or gold. He carves extensively in rhinoceros horn and his new interest in stag horn leaves little doubt that he is a man with great imagination and imposing ability. He exhibited some exciting work at Eskenazi's with an original approach to Japanese subject matter spiced with Occidental flavour.

There was one sour note to an opening evening of success. Michael overheard another artist declaring firmly that although, of course, a good carver, Michael could not carve hands. In truth, Michael has no such problems, as the purchase by HIH Prince Norihito Takamado of Japan of a netsuke by Michael proves. It depicts a small head and torso figure with a perfectly carved oversized pair of hands with fingertips touching.

Illustrated in the Eskenazi catalogue for the exhibition are seven pieces cast in gold. A limited edition of five of each piece was produced but the complete set of thirty-five pieces was stolen shortly before the exhibition opened. None were ever recovered.

Octopus Beak
Gold. Signed with monogram.
Height: 3.6cm. 1976.

Secretary Bird
Gold. Signed with monogram.
Height: 9.5cm. 1976.

Masks
Gold. Signed with monogram.
4.0cm. 1976.

In the spring of the following year Michael met film director Karel Reisz[30] at a dinner. Reisz was planning the production of *Who'll Stop the Rain* in America, and offered Michael a small part. It was a second opportunity for Michael to go to Hollywood and make his fortune, but he again declined; he had other travels in mind. He and Margaret were planning their first visit to Japan. It was to be a memorable trip, although it did not have the most auspicious start. As they arrived at their hotel he realised that he had left his briefcase containing all his carvings on the ground at the taxi rank queue at the airport. After some language difficulty, he persuaded the taxi driver to return to the airport and was impressed to find that his briefcase was exactly where he had left it.

With Ichiro, May 1977

Michael was pleased to be invited to share time with a few of the artists in their home, and enjoyed an evening spent with his fellow-carvers, during which he drank a great deal of saké, while his hosts drank mostly whisky. He was proud to be made an honorary member of the Japanese Netsuke Carvers Kenkyukai, the first non-Japanese to be given the honour. Among the netsuke artists Michael met during this trip were: Ichiro, Masatoshi, Kodo, Ryushi, Bishu, Hodo, Shodo, Mitsuyuki, Kangyoku and Hideyuki.

About the trip to Japan, Robert O. Kinsey wrote:

Michael accompanied my wife and me on one of our major three-week trips to Japan, and we thoroughly enjoyed introducing him, and some of his netsuke, to dozens of Japan's leading netsuke artists and collectors. They were astonished to discover that a 'foreigner' could so remarkably distinguish himself in Japan's centuries-old field of netsuke carving.

Shoji Hamada, May 1977

A special trip was made to the estate of the potter Shoji Hamada.[31] He spoke good English and took Michael aside to a long line of plates and dishes awaiting decoration. Hamada walked down the line with a pot of paint and a brush and almost flicked the brush at each plate in turn. At one point he handed the brush to Michael and said that he should take a turn. Somewhere, in valued Hamada collections, there may be a few pieces decorated by Michael Birch.

A highlight of the trip was an evening spent, together with Robert and Miriam Kinsey, at the home of Raymond and Frances Bushell. The American lawyer had formed one of the world's largest collections of netsuke and after dinner he brought out a few of his treasures. Michael was invited to show his own work which Bushell admired. One piece in particular caught his eye: it was a mermaid carved in elephant ivory and rhinoceros horn and the lawyer kept hold of it for the rest of the evening. Following Bushell's death and the disposal of part of his collection, Michael wrote to the new owner about the mermaid:

In 1977 I took the mermaid, together with several other carvings, to show to the Japanese carvers in Tokyo at their request. Ray Bushell and Bob and Miriam Kinsey were present when we carvers met and showed one another our latest work. That evening, after the Kinseys and I had dinner as the guests of Ray and Frances in the Ginza, we went on to the Bushell's house for coffee. Ray, to our delight, spread some of the finest pieces from his superb netsuke collection on to the dining-room table for us to examine and enjoy. At some point, Ray asked me if he could examine the mermaid that he had seen briefly that afternoon. I took it out of my briefcase and handed it to him. He looked at it from every angle and then enclosed it tightly in his left hand.

30. Karel Reisz, 1926-2002. Czech-born British Film Director whose early film credits include: *Saturday Night and Sunday Morning* and *This Sporting Life*. His most successful film was *The French Lieutenant's Woman*.

31. Shoji Hamada, 1894-1978. Japanese potter who had a significant influence on international studio pottery after spending three years with the English potter Bernard Leach.

To my amazement, he waved his right hand over the table in a gesture that clearly indicated that I could take my pick. Assuming that this may be a joke on Ray's part, I boldly pointed at an exquisitely carved umimatsu namazu by Kaigyokusai. Ray pocketed the mermaid and gestured to me to do the same with the namazu. No words were spoken during that extraordinary transaction.

In the taxicab on the way back to the hotel, Bob Kinsey asked me if I fully appreciated 'the unique implications of what had taken place'. There were to be other instances of Ray's acts of generosity toward me in the future.

Michael was always grateful to Raymond for his encouragement. It was a matter of great pride for him that, among the contemporary netsuke artists, only his work and that of Masatoshi are represented in the Raymond and Frances Bushell Collection of Netsuke at the Los Angeles County Museum.

On his return to England, Michael's first priority was to carve another mermaid to replace the one retained by Bushell and then to complete the second commission from the same collector. It was for a depiction of Ashinaga and Tenaga, the two long-limbed fishermen. He carved Ashinaga in ivory with features derived from primordial Japanese stone carvings, and Tenaga was portrayed in 18 carat gold with modern features. With his usual sense of humour, Michael decided to make an addition to the composition in the form of an octopus, a subject often portrayed in shunga netsuke and sometimes depicted by Japanese artists in satirical and unexpected situations. In this carving Tenaga held the octopus by one tentacle, while the octopus grasped Ashinaga's testicles. Michael's ability as a great storyteller was recognised and this piece was to become the source of one of his famous 'instant myths' that amused his fellow artists, collectors and dealers alike. Lynn Richardson, the artist who creates netsuke in ceramics wrote:

Michael was a person with whom once you got into conversation you learned a great deal, not only the 'hows' and 'whys' of his pieces and his materials but you would find yourself participating in the telling of the most amazing stories, very eloquent, very historic, thoughtful, even mythic in proportions.

Although the piece was carved in plenty of time, Michael had, as usual, left the final polish until the last minute. At 1am on the morning of his departure to New York he wrapped the piece in a soft cloth for the final polish. Suddenly there was a small 'crack'. Even without opening the cloth, he knew what had happened. Carefully he opened the duster but a small piece of ivory dropped to the studio floor. Ashinaga had lost his masculinity. Margaret found Michael on his hands and knees; and when questioned he explained that he was searching for the small piece of ivory. When asked what he planned to do with it when it was found, Michael admitted that he had no idea.

The following evening, in a suite at the Waldorf Astoria Hotel, the client sat at the head of a long boardroom table, snapping his fingers in impatient anticipation. Michael removed the wrapped carving from his jacket pocket and started to explain that he had amalgamated two legends: 'that of Ashinaga and Tenaga and that of the octopus. And. . . ' The client could wait no longer. He almost snatched the silk pouch, opened it, and stared. It was only then, in the clear light of day, that Michael realised that the addition he had fashioned in gold in the early hours of the morning, was at least twice the expected size and that Ashinaga was now very well endowed.

32. Kaigyokusai Masatsugu, 1813-1892. Pre-eminent nineteenth century Japanese netsuke carver.

Although he was surprised by the netsuke being waved in his direction, his storytelling abilities came to his rescue. He told the client: 'And . . . to them I have added the Japanese myth of the foreigner with the golden penis.' He feigned surprise that the client had not heard of this legend but assured him that it did, indeed, exist.' Far from being disturbed by the late addition, or by the brand new legend, the client was delighted.

That should have been the end of the story, but some weeks later, still thrilled with his 'three-legend' netsuke the collector took the new, and now highly valued addition to his collection with him to Japan where he had an appointment with the curator of a major Tokyo museum. He hoped that the curator would be as excited by the piece as he was, and tell him more of the rarely discussed legend of 'The Foreigner with the Golden Penis'.

The curator, who seemed as disturbed by the size of the appendage as the collector had been, shook his head and frowned. Through the interpreter he was told the 'three-legend' explanation for the piece, but he found himself in a difficult position. The legend was new to him and he was confronted by an excited American collector who was convinced by all the legends depicted in the netsuke he had brought for the curator to examine and admire. The collector assured him that the existence of such a legend had been confirmed to him by an Englishman in New York. The curator remained unconvinced but promised to investigate the matter.

Rather abruptly he left the room. The collector waited. And waited. About twenty minutes later he was still waiting, and unsure if the meeting was over or if the curator would return. Eventually the door opened and the curator spoke for a few minutes to the interpreter who then explained that the records had been checked, reference books examined and other museum staff consulted. The curator regretted to inform the collector that no trace could be found of a Japanese legend concerning a foreigner with a golden penis. The collector was crestfallen. 'No, no' said the interpreter reassuringly, 'the curator says that it is not an ancient Japanese legend, it is a Korean one.'

When, sometime later, Michael was told of his mistake, he was unable to determine if Korea did, indeed, have such a legend, or if the curator, unwilling to lose face, had laid the blame at the door of Japan's old adversary. He finally confessed to the part a duster had played in the creation of an instant legend; and both he and the collector recounted the story many times.

The following year, in September 1978, Michael and Margaret paid a visit to South America; and it was during their visit to Brazil that a collector introduced them to the landscape artist Roberto Burle Marx.[33] The two artists got on well together and the Brazilian swapped one of his brush and ink landscapes for one of Michael's netsuke.

At home, Michael had renovated a cottage for his parents close to his own home, and often had the opportunity to sit and talk with his father. It was shortly after their return home from Brazil, that Louis Birch died at the age of eighty-seven. He had always been proud of his son's achievements and Michael was glad that he had lived long enough to see him become a professional artist of netsuke sculptures. Michael was sad to learn that three men he admired died that year: his father Louis; the netsuke artist, Ichiro; and the potter Hamada.

33. Roberto Burle Marx, 1909-1994. Brazilian landscape architect (whose most familiar work is probably the decorative 4km long pavement promenade at Copacabana), painter, print maker, ecologist, naturalist,artist and musician.

Carvers, from left: Susan Wraight, Lee Youngren, Nick Lamb and Michael, Miami, Florida, December 1978

Following her husband's death, Margot spent more time with her son. She would join him in his studio and, while he was working, she talked quietly about her life. Their conversations were always in French, even though she had lived in England for almost thirty years, she was still not fluent or relaxed when speaking English. Michael was happy that the earlier turbulent years of their relationship were finally settled. Margot died in 1980 after being hit by a motor-cyclist barely one hundred yards from her home.

Michael's talents were becoming increasingly recognised. In 1978, George Lazarnik wrote:

Birch's use of material, his impeccable taste and great ability result in work of fine quality. And Michael Birch's original designs are carried out with adroitness at combining various materials, and great ability at incorporating natural forms such as the crown or the point of stag antler into his work.

Michael had always been a great admirer of the wood-block paintings by Hokusai,[34] and the work of other sumi-e or ink wash painters. While in Tokyo he had purchased the necessary inks and brushes, and after his father's death he began to study the works in detail. He found that, like calligraphy, it takes years of practise to develop even the simplest brush strokes where a single stroke reveals variations in tone from deepest black to palest grey. It was not unusual for him to produce anything up to one hundred paintings of the same small group of brush strokes, one after another in a single afternoon, before being satisfied with the result. Thousands of sheets of Japanese handmade paper were destroyed in the pursuit of perfection.

It was not until two years later that he felt confident to show his work, and found a novel method to do so. He was having difficulty purchasing the small bamboo boxes which are traditionally used to hold netsuke, so he painted the same subject, although not the carving, and used it as wrapping paper. During a visit to a collector's home, Michael was surprised to see that a piece of his wrapping paper had been pressed, mounted and framed and was hanging on the wall.
He began to create paintings for hanging rather than as wrapping paper and they became quite popular. So much so, that on one occasion a sumi-e painting of three crows sitting on a branch of cherry blossom was removed, frame and all, from the wall of Michael's apartment in Honolulu, by a collector who was determined to own it. One Japanese netsuke carver was so taken with one of Michael's paintings that prompted poignant memories, that it was placed in the *kami-dana*, the family shrine area, in his home.

34. Katsushika Hokusai, 1760-1849. Leading Japanese artist, most famous for the wood-block series *Thirty-six Views of Mount Fuji* which includes *The Great Wave* print used by advertisers all over the world.

In the late 1970's three large sculptures were commissioned for a newly designed garden in Southern California. They were to be cast in acrylic, not usually the first choice of material for a sculptor, but Michael rose to the challenge. He created three designs: a female torso shown from the shoulders to just below the hips; a double Möbius, shaped with organic curves; and a stylised representation of the beak of an octopus.

The first stage was to create the masters from which the moulds would be made. Rough outlines were created from large blocks of expanded polystyrene. The blocks were 2ft x 2ft x 4ft in height, and the first cuts for the outline shape were made with a chain-saw, before being gradually refined by ever increasingly fine rasps and files.

Once he was certain that he had developed the expanded polystyrene to the designed shapes, they were covered with layer upon layer of epoxy resin. Each layer was rubbed down and polished before the next layer was applied, and over forty layers in all were processed until the required smooth finish was achieved. Michael was helped in this process by his son Jonathan who remembers that both he and his father became intoxicated (or worse) by the fumes from the chemical resin.

Octopus Beak prior to its first coat of epoxy resin

Michael continued to attend the bi-annual International Netsuke Society Conventions, (where he was an accomplished and popular after-dinner speaker and lecturer), and always had new carvings to show. Although Luigi Bandini acted as his agent for a short time, he was fortunate to be able to develop his style without recourse to the demands of a dealer who might promote certain subjects, styles or materials.

There was, of course, always a demand for the traditional subjects, but Michael tried to add his own unique style of simple lines and organic shapes to his pieces. Since being sacked by Stanley Unger in 1954, he had maintained control of his own work and his reluctance to relinquish that meant that he was careful when accepting commissions. Although only one commissioned piece was ever rejected, all too often a collector's vision of a subject was not the same as that of the artist. When he did accept a brief, it would be on the broadest terms possible. I once heard him say that, for him to accept another commission, the collector may choose the subject or the material, but that he would determine everything else, and that the collector would pay for the piece, whether he liked it or not.

By 1982, with their children rapidly growing up and leaving home, and Rust Hall now too large for their needs, Michael and Margaret took the decision to convert the brick-built indoor swimming pool into a residential property. The pool was filled in, except the deep end which became a cellar; and the spectacular views which had been such an asset to Rust Hall were bettered by the new home's position closer to the edge of the ridge of the High Weald, overlooking woodland and small farms in the valley below.

It was an immense shock when Margaret died suddenly at the age of fifty-seven in the autumn of 1984. They had been married for almost thirty-six years and, devastated by grief; Michael began a long period of reflection and introspection.

The Years 1985 to 1993

He read publications about grief, becoming angry that they were about widows; he could find nothing about the grief of widowers. Family and friends became concerned about his well-being until Michael was persuaded to travel to Israel with his old friends, Sos and Gillian Green, to celebrate their daughter's wedding. The time away from the family home, away from constant reminders of Margaret, helped him to begin facing life again.

There followed a period of nearly eight years when he barely entered his studio. His records show that he completed only seven netsuke during that period, and no paintings. His father's enthusiasm for the English language, and his own unusual introduction to it, had given Michael a love of its rich vocabulary, and he had always enjoyed the writing process. He found it a useful tool in settling personal turmoil, and wrote long letters to family and friends, sometimes even those he considered enemies, often with the intention of never posting or delivering those letters.

He compared the compact nature of netsuke and the skill required to carve them, with the abbreviated structure of poetry, and the discipline that was required to write poems and short stories. Writing became his single creative outlet and, as one would expect, many of the poems he completed at this time were related to loss and to grief but, as his emotions finally calmed, he decided to commit his time to writing. It was a talent that was to flower.

Always erudite and entertaining as a speaker and in letters and published articles, he had long nurtured the idea of writing a book. During the years that he had been running the business, and later when he was carving netsuke, he often worked late into the night. Margaret would sometimes wake to find him still in his studio. She would make him a cup of tea and then return to bed. As a 'thank you', Michael would leave a poem on her bedside table for when she awoke. After her sudden death in 1984, he had found a cardboard box in a cupboard containing thousands of these rhymes that he had written over the years. Margaret had kept them all, and Michael felt that her dedication should not be forgotten.

He spent many hours reviewing the verses, and finally selected about four hundred and fifty poems that he entitled: *Cursory Rhymes*. It was clear that the topics and styles covered in the poems in the box were so varied that it was difficult to sort them into groups or topics. Michael's way of overcoming this was to create an extended family of thirty individuals. Each family member was given an identity; a psychological profile, a rounded character with foibles; and a biographical history. He even made a pencil sketch, a face for each of them. Next, he allocated each family member a group of verses that would reflect their disparate characters. Even so, there remained a number of verses which did not fit into the profiles, so some individuals were portrayed as not always telling the truth, and, to make things more complicated, some were also given alter egos. The family was introduced by their sometimes mystified psychiatrist, himself an invention of the author, who was apparently treating most members of the family, and who let the reader into his private and professional view of each. A draft was submitted to Liz Calder, co-founder of Bloomsbury Publishing, who wrote:

CURSORY RHYMES — It is certainly an original work and very enjoyable, but I can't see a way of publishing it successfully.

Despite the rejection letter, Michael was encouraged by her comments. He put *Cursory Rhymes* to one side and moved on to his next project. In his first novel Michael combined two of his long-standing interests: science, particularly physics, and science fiction writings. The science fiction book which was eventually titled *Lemon Yellow & Pistachio Green*, has as its lead character, John Sheldon Fischer, one of the family members first portrayed in *Cursory Rhymes.* Michael's strong interest in the sciences led him to take the unusual step of adding an appendix to this science fiction novel. Not entirely happy with the completed manuscript, he put this book to one side with *Cursory Rhymes* for a period of reflection, and moved on, confident that he was refining his writing skills.

For his next book, he turned his attention to his childhood. *The Teller of Tall Tales* was written as a semi-autobiographical novel. It tells the story of when, in the late 1920's and 1930's, he had listened to stories told by a travelling teller of tales while seated at a camp-fire at a Bedouin encampment near his home in Alexandria. As a boy he was enthralled by this man's extraordinary performance and decided that he, too, would become a storyteller when he grew up. As the book progresses the factual content is overtaken by Michael's ability to tell a story. Although there is no doubt that the majority of the book is factual, he was unwilling to reveal to his readers exactly which parts of the book were true, and which were not.

I am not clear what sparked another interest: magic. Not the occult but the entertainment variety. Always an entertainer, he took on the challenge to learn how to perform the Chinese linking rings tricks, looping up to eight rings with the clash of steel. He was very proud of having been accepted as a member of Britain's Magic Circle, which is obtained by audition at their headquarters in London where a performance has to be given in front of an audience consisting entirely of professional magicians.

I first met Michael on a wet and miserable evening in November 1989 as a result of a set of lost keys. The collection of a spare set should have taken less than a minute — it took more than twenty. Two days later he telephoned and asked me out to dinner. Separated from my then husband, and with every intention of never becoming involved with men, any man, ever again, I was surprised to hear myself saying: 'Yes'. I learned that he was older than me by eighteen years; had been a widower for five years; and that cooking was his favourite form of relaxation. As he prepared the meal and we ate, he related anecdotes from his past to entertain me.
When I returned home I made a list of the extraordinary claims he had made. Names such as Sir Henry Moore, Dylan Thomas, Pablo Picasso and Jacques Cousteau had all featured in his stories. I came to the conclusion that the man I had spent the evening with was either the biggest liar I was ever likely to meet, or that he was the most interesting man I was ever likely to know. Over time I learned that almost every story he told me was true. (Not that it was proved that some were fictional, just that I have not seen the evidence to prove the story.) He was a master storyteller, a raconteur who may well have embellished and exaggerated, but the kernel of the story would be true, if he said it was. For those who knew him it was clear that the lessons in the art of storytelling learned as a child from an itinerate teller of tales, seated at the fireside in a Bedouin encampment, had not been forgotten.

Before our first dinner together, I asked a Japanese expert I had worked with for nearly fifteen years what he knew of a Michael Birch. His response was immediate — "He's mad". At the time I wasn't sure if he meant that literally or figuratively. The 'artistic temperament' is such a hackneyed expression, but I found that it held some validity in Michael's case. It is true that he suffered occasional bouts of depression; there were periods when he lay in bed for days, only rising

a meal before swiftly returning to bed. He often sat up, looking at drawn curtains which shut out the sunlight and beautiful scenery, thinking — about life; philosophy, both religious and political; about his writing; about his carving. However difficult he could be on occasion, and he certainly could be difficult, life with Michael was never dull; and worth every ounce of effort it sometimes took. We were married in 1991.

On my first visit to his home, however, there was no indication that Michael was an artist. There were no paintings on the walls, other than one in the dining room; no netsuke on display; just three sculptures in a reception room that I did not enter during my first visits. During the early period of our relationship and marriage, he was writing, not carving. It was while writing his semi-autobiographical third book, *The Teller of Tall Tales*, that he became aware that, like all writers, his books required the attention of an editor. Although I had no such experience, after we had discussed the problem, I offered to look at his manuscripts and make some suggestions.

Like many first-time authors he had included far too many ideas in his book, *Lemon Yellow & Pistachio Green.* There were so many that the narrative often digressed from the plot in order to include topics about which he felt strongly. I believed that, if edited, many of these subjects were eminently suitable for the short story format, and the collection *Like Some People Do* was the first of his books to be published. It included the story *The Imperfect Spouse*, which was the winner of the 1993 H. E. Bates Best Short Story of the Year Award.

Even as his writing was becoming recognised, there remained another area that required some thought. He was determined to have the design and production of his books under his own control. Just writing the text was not enough. The early 1990's were the infant years of self- or home-publishing. Michael pestered his computer consultant for the latest technology, and quickly progressed from his original Amstrad (not much better than a typewriter) to one of the first personal computers. Next he pestered for some bespoke software that would allow him to see a page of text in its print layout (now an industry standard, but then an option not available to personal computers). Then along came desk-top publishing. Now he was able to select fonts, and to design and print the pages. Occasionally he re-wrote a paragraph, tightening and refining the text to ensure that it was not broken at the bottom of a page. To complete the artwork for the covers, he acquired some early graphics software, then added binders and a guillotine. Now, he had personal control while his books were written, designed, printed, bound and finished.
So pleased was he with the results that he formed a company that aimed at providing other writers with the same facilities needed to produce their own books. It was not a success; the capital outlay required at that time was still too high for most aspiring authors.

Michael continued to allow me to edit his books, always appreciative of my suggestions, even though we argued more about punctuation than anything else. Soon, *The Teller of Tall Tale*s was completed, followed by *Suspended Tales*, another collection of short stories, this time covering the themes of fantasy, science fiction, mystery and fable. Next, came a redesigned *Cursory Rhymes*, followed by the re-written science fiction *Lemon Yellow & Pistachio Green*, and then the last of his novels, *The Death of Pinocchio,* which investigated the dangers of power on the human psyche.

Finally, I compiled a collection of his poetry, some of which had been written after Margaret's death. At first, Michael was unwilling to publish them, but I persuaded him that the powerful force of emotion portrayed in these poems made them an important part of his writing and that the collection would be the poorer if they were omitted. I was pleased when he agreed, although

the title, *My Head on the Line*, indicates just how close to the personal limit he felt some of these poems came.

In all he completed seven books: two collections of short stories, three novels, a selection of satirical verse, and a book of poetry. There were two additional books in preparation. One was as a result of a wager that he could produce in the space of one month a romantic novel set in eighteenth century Japan; it was to be titled *Another Time, Another Love*. The other was a collection of Japanese myths and legends for children.

In September 1993, looking over his studio workbench, with its tools and trays of raw materials all set ready for work, he rather offhandedly assured me that the studio would soon be cleared, and the tools and materials would be disposed of because he would never carve again. By that time I had seen the catalogue for the exhibition of his work at the Eskenazi Gallery in London in 1976, together with many of the pieces in his personal collection. I was shocked by his decision. With an exaggerated stance I told him that I loved him but, if he refused to carve again I thought I would probably divorce him. I explained that I wanted to watch him carve, to see the pieces grow and develop from the material. It was a rather extreme response, but I not only longed to see the creative process in action, I also felt that it would be a waste of a great creative talent if Michael never carved again. I think, perhaps, he had secretly hoped for some encouragement.

The Years 1994 to 2008

Michael at home in his garden, Summer 1995

Around the walls of Michael's studio were rows of shelving containing materials, some untouched, some scraps; whole antlers, logs of boxwood and blocks of exotic woods, horns and teeth seemed to explode from every shelf, while on the floor were more boxes of bone and tooth; trays holding tins of dry dyes; and bottles of mixed liquids of bespoke colours. But his studio was dominated by his large workbench. He had built it himself; welding together an eight-foot long metal frame with a lower shelf, and finishing it with a three-inch deep mahogany hardwood top made from the treads of a recycled staircase. It held two dental drills of different specifications, and the bits for each that he was currently using were lined up on a magnetic strip and immediately to hand. There were several angled lamps, and at the other end of the bench were two electric polishing machines with cowl covers that had been adapted from those used in the lens manufacturing department of his factory. Below, were trays of different mops and polishing soaps and an old vacuum cleaner that he had adapted to extract toxic dust from the carving process.

He had a high sprung chair on castors and was able to pull himself along the length of the bench by handles set along the front edge. Secured to the workbench was a metal peg covered in chamois leather and cloth, and a large wooden block, approximately fourteen inches by ten inches by four inches tall, against which he rested the pieces as he worked on them.

Lined up along the back was an assortment of old small bookcases full of a jumble of contents. There were trays containing work in progress; half carved and then rejected netsuke in varying stages of completion; resin and plaster materials and models of completed pieces; and working models that had been discarded half way through the creative process. More boxes and tobacco tins stored small items such as precious and semi-precious stones and shells; scraps of wood, ivory, antler and horn; pieces of broken jewellery which had been raided for inlays; and the sheets of gold from which he cut the rectangular tablets which would display his initials. Pots held an assortment of riffler files; there were packets of new drill bits and files; trays of literally hundreds of used drill bits, each of a different shape and degree of sharpness; sheets of different grades of sandpaper; rolls of graded wire wool; pieces of cloth; paper, pens and pencils; various toothbrushes cut to the required shape and size; and paint brushes of varying sizes, some with full heads, others with just a few wisps of natural hair.

He started to carve again in early 1994, as well, if not better, than he had ever carved before. Always a late riser, he sometimes worked in the afternoon, and usually went to his studio after dinner, often working until three or four in the morning. While working he wore a pair of extended magnifying glasses and played background music.

The most frequently asked question about his working practices was about the length of time it took to complete a piece. It was an unanswerable question. He never worked on a single piece from start to finish and always had several pieces at different stages of completion, some pieces were not finished until four or more years after work commenced. As an exhibition approached it was usual for Michael to review which pieces to take, and then for each stage to be completed on all the unfinished netsuke before proceeding to the next stage. He left time for his friend Rodney Rigby to engrave the MHB kakihan on each piece, and for the netsuke to be photographed. The final polish was often left until a few days before departure.After an extended absence from the netsuke scene, Michael returned to show his latest pieces at the I.N.C.S. Convention in New York in 1995 and was thrilled by the enthusiastic response to his latest work.

He had been carving netsuke for more than fifty years when he wrote the Preface for the catalogue for the exhibition *Contemporary Netsuke, Miniature Sculpture from Japan and Beyond*, at the Bowers Museum of Cultural Art in California in 1997; in it he summed up the appeal of his favoured art form, for himself, and for other artists:

Artists who choose to create netsuke are attracted to the art form for the same reason that it has appealed irresistibly to generations of collectors. It is a superbly crafted miniature form of sculpture, with a limitless range of fascinating subject matter and which, when held in the hand, is endowed with a vibrant tactile quality. Netsuke confirm that small can be truly beautiful, and we respond with pleasure and wonderment to their powerful aesthetic resonance.

The innate reason, however, why a number of very fine artists have chosen to express themselves in the netsuke art form can be found in their instinctive and resolute desire to work within a clearly defined discipline and, at the same time, to explore and to test the boundaries of the rules that govern that discipline. This may, at first, seem a constraint on the artists' freedom of creativity until one realizes that it is strict rules that make chess, for instance, so challenging a game, with its endless variations and surprises, its elegant construction and its opportunities for flashes of inventive genius.

I believe that without a necessary degree of discipline, all art becomes vacuous, repetitive, and ultimately sterile. The discipline we artists observe when we call our carvings by the generic term 'netsuke' relates to this art's classic rules of functional size and compactness — these are the criteria which establish its unique identity. Such a discipline does not deprive us of mystery and invention. It certainly does not determine our subject matter or the materials we use. On the contrary, it allows consummate craftsmanship to be wedded to aesthetic creativity of an order unmatched in richness of content by any other sculptural art form past or present.

An increasing number of Contemporary Netsuke artists from many countries are now, in concert with their Japanese fellow-carvers, creating a genuinely original compendium of international cultural concepts and fresh images through their work. . .

During his years as a netsuke carver, Michael used a large number of different organic materials, and the selection of the right piece of horn, antler or wood was never taken lightly. Antique shops, auctions, junk shops and jumble sales worldwide; walks in the countryside, and on the beaches;

Working in his studio, July 2001

all provided raw materials. Wherever possible, he retained the integrity of the material used, often leaving a part of it uncarved; and his name became synonymous with his use of the coronet of antlers in his depictions of Dutchmen and Tanuki. Art, literature, museums and galleries; his own studio; and the world around him; all provided a surplus of ideas for subjects and treatments, and the netsuke form remained a continuing artistic challenge for the rest of his life.

The artist Clive Hallam recorded his thoughts about Michael:

I first met Michael just as I set out on my own carving journey over 20 years ago. He was always a tremendous inspiration, teacher and friend. As is clearly evident in this magnificent Catalogue his works covered a vast and diverse range. Michael was a consummate master of many of the things that are characteristic of great artists, but it was as a carver's carver that I personally feel is his most enduring artistic legacy. He knew how to enter into an intense and uniquely personal dialogue with a raw material that only another carver can truly understand. Such a dialogue leads the carver to tease out that which is particularly special about a specific piece of material. I will always miss my old friend, but he lives on through the extraordinary body of work he gifted us all.

In her *Thoughts of Michael Birch*, the noted dealer Sharen Chappell recently wrote:

When I think of Michael Birch, I recall the twinkle in his eye and his puckish smile. He had such a sense of fun and exuded a wonderful 'joie de vivre'. This special spark was like a magnet that drew people to him. Anecdotes and stories flowed from him and his vivid imagination. The stories he wrote came alive when he read them aloud to those of us lucky enough to be part of his gatherings in the early days of netsuke conventions. Who could forget the cast of the Fischer family chronicles? [See Cursory Rhymes]. As a netsuke collector, Michael had a discerning eye for conformation and the careful execution of detail. As a carver he favoured uncluttered designs with graceful lines and curves. His well developed sense of humor breathes life into his subjects and the techniques he perfected brought out the properties and promise of the materials carved. He gave a finish and polish to his works which led some of us to call him 'The Mitsuhiro of the Modern Carvers' after the mid 19th century artist known for the exquisite finish he imparted to his netsuke. Michael Birch has a place alongside the best netsuke artists of the 18th, 19th and 20th centuries.

Never short of ideas for his carvings, he was already into his seventies when we spent a day in January 1997 combing a beach north of Santa Monica with his friend the late talented carver Guy Shaw. Asked if, after so many years, he ever ran out of ideas for carvings, Michael reflected sadly that he would never have the time to use all the materials he had collected over more than sixty years, or to carve all the ideas in his head or on scraps of paper. (Indeed, after his death I found dozens of sketches showing ideas for netsuke which he never had time to carve.) I was not surprised that he expressed anger when he saw artists' work which had been copied from others, even as 'an homage', as one young carver told him after copying a distinctly 'Birch' carving. For the forty years from the mid 1960's, he continued to discover copies of his work, both his spectacle frame designs and his netsuke, mostly manufactured in Hong Kong.

Throughout his artistic career he had continued to develop his skills and was keen to encourage young artists, and began to have an influence on their work. He was also a strong supporter of the International Netsuke Society and, while there remained a few die-hard advocates of the theory that 'only antique Japanese netsuke could truly be considered as real', Michael was encouraged by the increasing acceptance of the work of living artists.

He was honoured to be included in the collection of H.I.H. Prince Norihito Takamado, and to see that an illustration of his Double Möbius Daruma was selected as the frontispiece of the 2003 exhibition catalogue entitled *The H.I.H. Prince Takamado Collection* produced by the prestigious Tobacco & Salt Museum in Tokyo. In the catalogue for the exhibition, the President of the Japan Ivory Sculptors' Association, Jushō Kobari, wrote:. . . *Unlike in other years, [H.I.H. Prince Takamado] lent us 11 works by a foreign carver, Michael Birch, whose works were abstract experiments that drew the line at traditional modes of expression – a point of view that the Japanese did not possess. Through our being touched by, and actually seeing the daring and vividly striking sensibility of his works with our own eyes, His Highness wanted us to be challenged by a new sensation, and through his collecting of works, His Highness's feelings were being known to us carvers – we felt that the group of Mr. Birch's works expressed that most eloquently.*

The word often used to describe Michael's pieces was 'subtle'. Whether representational or abstract; in his sculpture or his paintings; it is his perceptive and deceptively simple smooth lines that portray an elegance, and at the same time, an implied movement, which captivates collectors. The free-hanging nature of netsuke means that they are always carved in the round and that sight is always the first sense to respond. But perhaps of greater appeal is their tactile quality, the sense of touch that is so important to all humans; their small size means that, with only a few exceptions, netsuke can be held in the palm of the hand, and fingers are able to explore the design, the texture, the weight and even the temperature of the material. The viewer is also able to add his own contribution to a work: that of recognition, a recollection or a fleeting memory; and it is this which often results in an emotional response from a collector to a particular carving. Michael was not alone in believing that no work of art was complete without a contribution being made by the viewer, and that their contribution was essential.

After Michael's death, the eminent collector of netsuke and ojime, Robert O. Kinsey, wrote: *Michael earned well-deserved recognition among the foremost netsuke artists of the latter half of the 20th century and the opening years of the 21st century. He was one of the first and most prominent non-Japanese artists to achieve pre-eminence in the field of netsuke. Early acceptance of his work by collectors throughout the world was phenomenal. Some of his carvings are now included in virtually every important collection. Fully appreciated and highly valued are the originality of Michael's netsuke designs, his consummate carving and polishing skills, the tactile and visual appeal of his sculptures, his mastery of using so many beautiful and exotic materials, and his ultimate achievement of attaining a certain flair and elegance.*

With hindsight I recognise that Michael first became unwell in October 2001 after falling twelve feet down a steep bank in our garden. It was the result, I now believe, of his first small stroke. He dislocated his left shoulder and it took some time for him to be rescued with ropes and ladders. Despite surgery the damage was considerable; a strong grip is essential to hold small netsuke during carving, and it became increasingly difficult for him to hold the material or the tools as he needed. Slowly, but inexorably, his health deteriorated. By 2005 the deterioration in his health was obvious to all. He had a major stroke on 11th July 2008 and spent five weeks in hospital. He died, at home as he had always wanted, on 16th September 2008 aged eighty-one. These pages have, I hope, shown the versatility and originality that Michael was able to display during his long career as an artist.

The Great Netsuke Myth

The text of a lecture given by Michael Birch to the International Netsuke Society at their Convention in Chicago in July 1999.

What is The Great Netsuke Myth? It is the delusion that only 'antique' Japanese netsuke are authentic netsuke, and that Contemporary Netsuke are not 'real' netsuke.

I first tried to dispose of the Myth in January 1975, when I gave a lecture in Honolulu at the first netsuke convention. Here is a short passage from the transcript of that lecture:

If netsuke fall exclusively under the category of Japanese antique toggles, then there is clearly no place for contemporary netsuke under that heading. But if netsuke are recognized as an important sculptural art form that is universal and timeless, it is obvious that contemporary netsuke should be judged in the context of that art form by their quality alone and not by where or when or by whom they were created. . . . There has been a somewhat futile controversy in the last few days over the status of contemporary netsuke. In other words, whether or not they are 'real' netsuke. It has been suggested that they should only be described as miniature sculpture. But that is playing with words. All netsuke are works of art, whether good, bad or indifferent in quality. It makes sense that the word netsuke should be accepted as a generic description for all these unique sculptural creations — whether old or new, antique or contemporary. They are, and will always remain netsuke so long as they obey the basic rules of the art form.

I was convinced that I had persuaded the die-hard believers in the Great Netsuke Myth to accept reality. But I was wrong. The Myth is still with us. So I have returned to the subject almost twenty-five years later to remove any confusion and doubt that may still exist about the fundamental nature of the netsuke art form.

The ancestral toggle

I shall start with a brief description of the origins of the ancestors of netsuke, the toggles. These were in use several thousand years before the Japanese became aware of their existence.

In the northern hemisphere, men wore tunics with belts. Pockets were unknown, so men suspended small articles and pouches on rawhide thongs attached to the belts. It is not hard to imagine that a prehistoric man once picked up a small object, say, a small piece of gnarled root, and attached it to the top end of the thong to prevent it from slipping through the belt. And so the first toggle came into being, possibly in the forested region of Northern Asia.

The distribution of toggles then spread in several directions by way of travellers and migrating tribes. Aboriginal toggles have been found in pre-Eskimo Alaska and among the Chukchee of north-eastern Siberia. The use of toggles spread in several other directions, always where the climate was cold. From Mongolia they were passed to the Huns on the Black Sea and to the early Turkish tribes. They found their way to the Bactrians in Afghanistan and by the 13th century their use had spread eastward right across northern China to northern Korea. By the 14th century, toggles were widely used by the Chinese who called them *chui tzu,* meaning 'pendulum' or 'counterweight'. In his book, *Substance and Symbols in Chinese Toggles,* Schuyler Cammann described them as: 'symbolic expressions of profound religious ideas or of deep-felt human needs and desires.'

Toggles reach Japan

In the 16th century the Japanese sent an expeditionary force to China and the troops returned to Japan with trophies including quantities of finely carved toggles. The Japanese called these toggles *karamono*, which means, literally, 'Chinese things'. They were to have a dramatic influence on Japanese culture for the next two and a half centuries. It was not until the 17th century, as far as we know, that the Japanese coined the name *netsuke*, which means 'root fastening'. It is possible that the description harked back to the much earlier root toggles which had been part of the ancient Chinese folk-art tradition.

Netsuke: The Golden Age 1780 - 1850

The art of netsuke carving in Japan grew steadily over the years until in the latter part of the 18th century came the start of the Golden Age of Netsuke. It was an art form that could lead one into a world of reality and of make-believe. Occasionally anecdote and invention were combined in works of matchless fantasy. Netsuke also became an important archival microcosm of every aspect of a whole culture – all this in compact functional sculptures you can hide in your hand.

The Golden Age lasted for seventy years, from 1780 to 1850. Then in 1853 Commodore Perry's American fleet anchored in the Bay of Tokyo (Edo). He persuaded Japan to remove all trade barriers against foreigners and to allow their free entry into the mainland. Soon after this event Japanese men adopted the Western style of clothing, and the kimono and the netsuke were abandoned.

The netsuke carvers enjoyed a brief period of prosperity as netsuke became export trinkets, (as they were described by some Western collectors). And after the Shogun was deposed in 1868, the history of netsuke follows their distribution among foreign collectors.

After The Golden Age

Some great collections were formed in England and France. As supplies of good quality old netsuke declined, hurriedly-produced new pieces destined for export became increasingly shoddy. They were the subject of contempt and derision. The general opinion was that OLD IS GOOD AND MODERN IS BAD.

In 1883, the French collector and scholar Louis Gonse published a large volume on Japanese art. In his chapter on netsuke he wrote as follows:

There are no art objects in which the Japanese gave greater free rein to their taste for invention and to their imagination than the Netsuke art form. . . It is an infinitely tiny world whose variety surpasses anything we know. . . Some netsuke, with such miniature dimensions, belong to the realms of truly great art. There have indeed been Michelangelos in the netsuke world. . . . But some ghastly specimens, artificially aged by soaking in an infusion of tea, have recently flooded the market. These are modern pieces, destined for the cheap market trade. Neophyte collectors should be on their guard and not be beguiled by their spurious charm.

Louis Gonse also quoted his friend, Monsieur Edmond de Goncourt, another famous collector, who said:

It was during the Golden Age of fine netsuke production that Japanese ivory carvers used the finest ivory with a milky translucency which, with the passage of time, acquired a beautiful patina. Not to be confused with the pickled staining of modern netsuke which... when heaped in bowls, are redolent of discarded old molars in a dentist's spittoon.... The Japanese no longer carve netsuke for their own use. All current production is destined for our market... Today, there are no more good netsuke from Japan and there will be no more to come.

No more to come... those sad words were written in 1883. Luckily, Monsieur de Goncourt was wrong. Geniuses like Kaigyokusai, Tokoku, Masaka, Ryo, and quite a few others were still to come. And some of the So School carvers were not even born.

Six years later, in 1889, the well-known English collector Mr. Seymore Trower wrote an article for a publication called The Magazine of Art. In it he made the following comment:

There is no short cut to Netsuke collecting; it takes time, study, and patience. The market is flooded with utterly worthless rubbish, and one may look over hundreds without finding one to repay the search.

Origins of The Great Netsuke Myth

So far, we have heard some harsh yet fair criticism of the poor quality of what were then, over a hundred years ago, badly made contemporary netsuke. But none of the writers questioned whether or not the pieces were 'authentic' or 'real' netsuke until I came across the printed report of a lecture about netsuke, given by Mr. Marcus Huish, at the Japan Society in London in 1895. This is what he said:

"In subject matter there was no class of article, the world over, which could compete with netsuke." Then he declared: *"The netsuke of today is in no sense of the word a netsuke.!"*

Mr. Huish made it clear that 1868 was the cut-off point, after which date 'real netsuke' were no longer produced. And the seeds were sown of what was to become The Great Netsuke Myth.

Netsuke: the art form

Netsuke the toggle had, to all intents and purposes, ceased to exist. But netsuke the art form, which had existed right from the start, in fact survived successfully to the present day.

I have used the word 'art' several times and it is important that I should define what I mean. Art is one of the least understood words in the Western world — a word that is generally misused and on which narrow and false interpretations have been imposed by the Western world for centuries. For example, the spurious notion of Fine Art in painting and sculpture, as opposed to craft, is a 17th century European invention. It was a concept that was welcomed by those artists with delusions of grandeur, who eagerly went along with the idea that their creations were divinely inspired and were therefore spiritually superior to all mundane human endeavors.

The 20th century has been the experimental playing field for many *isms* in art — Impressionism, Expressionism, Surrealism, Dadaism, Futurism, Vorticism, Cubism, Abstractionism, Minimalism,

Super-realism, and many more. All were radical and controversial in their day. Some were exciting, but even the most successful became, in the fullness of time, artistic dead-ends.

But that is not what I am talking about. The Oxford English Dictionary defines art as: *Made by humans as opposed to nature.* That is a remarkably profound definition, and it is uncannily close to the Japanese and Far Eastern cultural perception of art, which is defined as design and form, and which is synonymous with living.

Art is the most reliable archival record of a civilization; indeed, the true history of humankind is to be found in its sublime creations. It is what separates us from all other species on this planet. Art is a product of human personality that is inherent in all humans. It is a continuous and intensely personal way for all human beings, without exception, to express their responses to the world as they see it. The fact is that no two persons express in exactly the same way that ineffable quality called art. It is an intrinsic part of what we are. It is like a fingerprint of the spirit – mysterious and unique to each individual.

The great artist Henry Moore once told me that sculpture must be big to be important. *Publicly important*, perhaps. But he then agreed that netsuke can be perceived as being privately important. A netsuke does not dominate you, and it is not out of reach like most sculpture.
On the contrary, it can be held captive in your hand and explored with fingertips that have the most sensitive nerve ends in our bodies. Our fingertips can follow the form of a netsuke while our vision can examine it from every angle. And when that sensory duality, the tactile and the visual, combine in our brains, they set up a special resonance in our minds that cannot be matched by any other art form.

About function

There has always been a primary element of functionalism in all art. In the ancient past, prehistoric cave paintings served as guides to hunters. For several millennia, the function of sculpture was to memorialize the gods and to serve in the performance of ceremonial religious rites. And for many centuries, religious paintings and effigies were aimed at enthralling worshippers. In the 20th century some well-hyped modern art serves an important function as a monetary instrument of investment, rather like stocks and bonds.

The Chinese toggle also served several other functions: as a talisman with magic powers to bring good luck, and as an amulet to ward off evil. Scrapings from certain toggles also served as a handy supply of medicaments. Early netsuke had the same functions and later the Japanese gave netsuke many other intriguing uses.

Underlying the apparent functions of all art forms throughout human history, is to be found the basic role of art — and that is as a medium for the artist's self-expression and, at the same time, as an outlet for the viewer's faculty of interpretation. The viewer's existence has always been crucial to the artist's work, for without the viewer no work of art is complete.
In 1898, the French poet Stéphane Mallarmé got to the heart of the matter when he wrote: *"Art is a process that involves the artist, the art object, and the viewer in an open-ended game of mutual creation and interpretation."* This has never been more true than in the case of netsuke.

Netsuke go international

In June 1976, the exhibition in London of the carvings of a non-Japanese professional netsuke artist added a new dimension to the netsuke art form. It was the revolutionary first step toward netsuke becoming an international art form. Suddenly, netsuke were no longer the exclusive province of Japanese artists who, to their credit, willingly accepted the reality of that new situation and took the unprecedented step of inviting the foreigner to become a member of their guild. Edward Wrangham, the great collector and respected scholar, made the following comment in his introduction to the exhibition catalogue:

The Japanese took to wearing European dress after the overthrow of the feudal regime in 1868. So perhaps the purist should reject all netsuke made after that date and out of the window would go a number made by such superb artists as Kaigyukusai, Zeshin, Mitsuhiro and Sosui. Even the great early collections. . . would be suspect, since they all contained some of the later pieces.

Believers in The Great Netsuke Myth were furious when they heard about the success of the Englishman's exhibition. The message that hit their grapevine was that this artist was masquerading as a netsuke carver and passing off his creations as real netsuke. But as a number of enlightened collectors must have realized at the time, and as collectors and fellow-artists and scholars and some sensible dealers have understood to this day, the artist was not carving imitation Japanese toggles at all. He was, and still is, creating his works within the aesthetic boundaries of the netsuke art form.

The Great Netsuke Myth debate

In 1979 a Mr. Robert Dee addressed a letter to the editor of the International Netsuke Collectors Society Journal in which he asked: *". . . are the obviously gifted contemporary carvers really carving netsuke per se. . . or were they born too late? Contemporary Netsuke, are they anachronistic? – are we kidding ourselves or are we being kidded?"*

Victor Israel, later to become one of the presidents of our Society, replied to Mr. Dee: *"I feel that contemporary netsuke can qualify equally with antique netsuke."*

In his reply to Mr. Dee, Paul Stidham, a gentle and scholarly collector, said: *"When I consider the purchase of a netsuke I ask myself the following questions: Do I like it? Is it well carved? Does it feel good? Is it an interesting subject? It is not important to me when it was carved."* Later in his letter he said: *"Many of the contemporary artists are talented, dedicated, serious, imaginative, hard-working, and are breathing new life into what was a declining art form and some are even surpassing the old masters. Are we to deny ourselves the pleasure of these beautiful pieces?"*

And Miriam Kinsey with her wonderful gift for arriving swiftly at the central point had this to say: *"I start from the premise that netsuke is an art form. There was really no distinction made between art and crafts in the early years of netsuke carving. Craftsmanship was demanded of works of art; and perfect craftsmanship was art."* Miriam ended her letter with this definitive statement: *"Time will be the final judge, but I predict that in centuries to come, netsuke history will record a twentieth century renaissance in netsuke carving and list a number of its carvers among the great netsuke artists of all time."*

Last Gasp of The Great Netsuke Myth

Well, you would think that The Great Netsuke Myth would have been discredited by now. But in the last decade of the 20th century, it still has under its spell a cross-section of apparently sane and educated persons. I shall give you some actual examples of its hallucinatory effect before disposing of it once and for all.

1. In 1998, during the viewing soirée at a smart gallery in London, an elderly gentleman is in conversation with the wife of an English netsuke artist. The gentleman said: *"I am a great admirer of your husband's brilliant carvings but, of course, I only collect antique netsuke."* The words 'of course' have, of course, a depth of meaning.

2. An anguished letter from a Dr. Neil Barton was published in the Society's Spring 1995 issue of the Journal. He starts by admitting that he is *"somewhat aghast"* to find an advertisement for contemporary netsuke in the Journal. He asks ironical questions such as: *"Will an Andy Warhol type artist be the next netsuke artist?"* – and – *"Will some graffiti artist decorate a modern Shuzan piece?"* Clearly, the worthy doctor is telling netsuke artists what they are *not* permitted to carve.

This next example demonstrates how blind faith in The Great Netsuke Myth can lead to a state of high anxiety. In a letter to the Society's Journal, Mr. E.C.Gaddis Jr. declared: *". . . true netsuke were made only in the Edo period in Japan by the Japanese for the Japanese. All this contemporary outflow of small carvings which are touted in this publication don't belong here. They are not now, and never will be netsuke in the classical definition."* He ends his letter with a solemn request: *"Keep the International Netsuke Society Journal as a forum for netsuke, please."* We can observe that Mr. Gaddis Jr. is making an impassioned call for a policy of aesthetic cleansing — of throwing out of the International Netsuke Society those so-called netsuke-shi who corrupt the ethnic purity of our Society's Journal.

4. At the Honolulu Netsuke Convention in 1997 a strolling gentleman is invited by the English artist's wife to see some of her husband's latest work. He replies with a dismissive wave of his hand: *"No, it is a hundred years too late."* Puzzled by that unexpected response, the lady asks: *"When will my husband's work not be a hundred years too late?"* The gentleman replies, over his shoulder as he strolls away: *"Your husband's work will always be a hundred years too late."*

The expression 'a hundred years too late' was, no doubt, an oblique reference to the word 'antique' which has a fiscal definition of 'over 100 years of age', and a dictionary definition of 'belonging to antiquity'. Since I and my fellow artists do not produce antiques, the strolling gentleman was, it would seem, expressing the view that my work cannot be called netsuke because only antique Japanese netsuke are 'real' netsuke.

Several months after making those remarks in Honolulu, our strolling gentleman travelled to Japan where he paid a visit to Mr. Kengo Sekido, President of the Japanese Netsuke Society and a notable collector of fine netsuke, to view his collection. He subsequently wrote a report of his visit for the Society's Journal. He stated: *"Soko Morita is probably the most popular carver among Japanese collectors and the Sekido collection includes two remarkable works by this artist. Sekido-san indicated that they were carved in the 1930s, when the artist was in his prime."*

It may be interesting to note that I carved my first netsuke in 1935 when I was nine years old and a little short of my prime. I still have the piece, although I daresay the quality may not compare with the masterpieces of my fellow-carver Soko Morita.

Netsuke: a new golden age

It was the very same Mr. Kengo Sekido who, in 1994, had this to say about contemporary netsuke: "*While clinging to the traditional techniques of several centuries and adhering to the essentials of the creation of netsuke, new work imbued with completely new ideas have begun to be produced. The techniques of carving have continued to improve such that today the genre of 'contemporary netsuke' is established as a most excellent art form. . . and the quality rivals – and even in some cases excels that of the Edo period works dating from netsuke's Golden Age.*"

A few believers in the Great Netsuke Myth continue to set aside reality by questioning the validity of the contemporary netsuke artists' role in the dynamic growth of the art form. It is an attitude that is lacking in human dignity, and it undermines the unity that should exist between all members of the International Netsuke Society. It also damages the integrity and the fundamental purpose of the Society, which is clearly stated in Article II of the bylaws: *"The purpose of the Society is to promote the study of netsuke and their related appurtenances, the artists who created them, and the society from which they evolved."* The bylaw does not say dead artists — it is referring to all netsuke artists including 150 from all over the world who happen to be very much alive.

Contemporary Netsuke: The Sculptural Art Form of the 21st Century

A growing number of mainstream art collectors are truly surprised to discover the conceptual originality and the disciplined quality of design of contemporary netsuke. They are seduced by the sensitive expression of emotions, as well as the remarkable range of styles from super realism to the most subtle abstractions. They are also deeply impressed by the consummate skill and patience that the creation of netsuke demands and, not least, they are intrigued by the imaginative use of a wide variety of materials to best suit the subject, These qualities are to be found in greater measure in today's netsuke than in any sculptural form from any period in human history. This is not an exaggerated claim, it is a demonstrable fact.

Scholars and writers like William Winkworth, Raymond Bushell, Miriam and Robert Kinsey and Richard Silverman to name but a few — and notables like Robert Singer, curator of the Japanese Department at the Los Angeles County Museum of Art; Toshio Yamazaki, the Japanese Ambassador in London who is an important netsuke collector; Lawrence Smith, who was Keeper of Japanese Antiquities at the British Museum in London, and many others have all praised without reservation the work of the living netsuke artists and judged many of their works to be masterpieces of the netsuke art form. It is wholly understandable that none of these well-informed and deeply perceptive persons has questioned the right of contemporary netsuke artists to describe their work accurately and truthfully as netsuke.

In 1984 Neil Davey wrote, with great insight:

It has been recognized by knowledgeable collectors and dealers that a number of modern carvers are not, as was thought 'fly-by-night' artisans, but serious artists in the media of painting and sculpture. . . they show artistry and originality that place them on a level equal to that of the finest traditional Japanese carvers. Carving netsuke is not necessarily an art of past times. It is much in evidence today and appears to show no signs of abating in the foreseeable future.

His Imperial Highness Prince Norihito Takamado wrote in 1994: *Netsuke, once the treasured art of the Japanese, are now being carved by people all over the globe, and the number of non-Japanese carvers is growing rapidly. With the appearance of these foreign netsuke, which display the heritage and customs of other lands, the art of the netsuke has truly become international, not only on the level of appreciation but on the level of creation as well. This is something that gives me great pleasure.*

The International Netsuke Society has a great responsibility. It has under its guardianship the future progress of the unique Netsuke art form. It is an art form that continually reveals fresh subject matter, fresh ideas.

Netsuke are mirrors of the times in which they are created and it is the art form most likely to maintain its consistent high quality of creativity and to move successfully into the 21st century. I believe that it will achieve this with the continuing support of forward-looking members of the International Netsuke Society.

Exhibitions & Lectures

Exhibitions

2013	Liverpool Museum, Liverpool, England
2012	Tokyo National Museum, Tokyo, Japan
2007	Museum of Art and Design, New York
2004	Honolulu Academy of Arts, Hawaii
2003	The Tobacco and Salt Museum, Tokyo, Japan
2002	The Matsumoto City Art Museum, Matsumoto, Nagano, Japan
2001	Chiba City Museum of Art, Japan
1999	The Minneapolis Institute of Arts, Minnesota
1999	The Herbert F. Johnson Museum of Art, Cornell University, Ithaca, New York
1997	National College of Art & Design, Dublin, Eire
1997	Galerie Zacke, Vienna, Austria
1997	Museum for East Asian Art, Berlin, Germany
1997	The Bowers Museum of Cultural Art, Santa Ana, California
1995	The Tobacco and Salt Museum, Tokyo, Japan
1994	Sotheby's, Bond St., London
1989	Galerie Zacke, Vienna, Austria
1987	Pavilion for Japanese Art, Los Angeles County Museum of Art, California
1987	Midori Gallery, Miami, Florida
1987	Galerie Zacke Netsuke Symposium, Vienna, Austria
1986/7	Lowe Art Museum, University of Miami, Florida
1982	Kunsthandel, Klefisch, Cologne, Germany
1980	Yale University Art Gallery, New Haven, Connecticut
1978	Eskenazi Oriental Art, London
1976	Eskenazi Oriental Art, London

From 1974 Michael also exhibited his work at twenty-two of the bi-annual Netsuke Society Conventions held at various times in Boston, Massachusetts; Chicago, Illinois; Honolulu, Hawaii; Kansas City, Kansas; Los Angeles, California; Minneapolis, Minnesota; New York, New York; Washington, D.C. in USA and in London, England.

In addition, a number of collectors and dealers have used illustrations of Michael's work in their lectures which have been held in museums in Anchorage, Alaska; Los Angeles, Pasadena, Santa Barbara, Santa Ana and San Diego, California; Chicago, Illinois; Honolulu, Hawaii; in Tokyo, Kyoto and Chiba City in Japan; and in England, Austria, France and Germany.

Lectures

In addition to lectures and talks at I.N.S. Conventions since 1979, Michael also lectured at museums and galleries in London, Dublin, Paris and Vienna.

Selected Bibliography

Battie, David, *Ivory, an International History and Illustrated Survey,* Contemporary Carvers, New York: Harry N. Abrams, Inc., 1987

Burke, Aoifa, *Michael Birch, A Western Master of an Eastern Art,* Dublin, Eire, 1997

Cammann, Schuyler, *The Substance and Symbols in Chinese Toggles,* USA, 1962

Gonse, Louis, *L'Art Japonais,* Paris 1883

Huish, Marcus, *Japan Society Magazine,* London, 1895

Kinsey, Miriam, *Living Masters of Netsuke,* Tokyo, Japan; New York, New York: Kondansha International, 1983

Kinsey, Robert O & Miriam, *Contemporary Netsuke: Miniature Sculpture from Japan and Beyond,* Santa Ana, California, Bowers Museum of Cultural Art, 1997

Kinsey, Robert O., Ojime: *Magical Jewels of Japan,* New York, New York: Harry N. Abrams, 1991

The Poetry of Netsuke, Santa Barbara, California: Robert O. Kinsey, 2004

Contemporary Netsuke: The Kinsey Collection accompanied by H.I.H. Prince Takamado Collection, Chiba, Japan: Chiba City Museum of Art, 2001

Kurstin, Joseph and Ortega, Maria L., *Masterworks of Netsuke*: and other Japanese Miniature Art from American Collections, Coral Gables, Florida: Lowe Art Museum, University of Miami, 1986

Lazarnik, George, *The Signature Book of Netsuke, Inro and Ojime Artists in Photographs,* Honolulu, Hawaii: Reed Publishers, 1976

Netsuke & Inro Artists, and How to Read their Signatures, Honolulu, Hawaii: Reed Publishers, 1982

Okada, Barbra Teri & Neill, Mary Gardner, *Real and Imaginary Beings: The Netsuke Collection of Joseph and Edith Kurstin,* New Haven, Connecticut: Yale University Art Gallery, 1980

Sandfield, Norman L., *The Ultimate Bibliography: An annotated Guide to Miniature Japanese Carvings.* Chicago, Illinois: Art Media Resources and Norman L. Sandfield, 1999

Sawers, Robert G, *Contrasting Styles,* Somerset, England: Robert G. Sawers Publishing, 1980

Trower, Seymore, *The Magazine of Art, Vol. 12,* London & New York, 1889

Welch, Matthew & Chappell, Sharen Thane, *Netsuke: The Japanese Art of Miniature Carving,* Minneapolis Institute of Arts, 1999 and Herbert F. Johnson Museum of Art, Cornell University, 1999

See also articles by various authors in the following:

Arts of Asia: Vol. 6/5, 1976; Vol. 7/3, 1977; Vol. 8/1, 1978; Vol. 8/5, 1978; Vol. 9/4, 1979; Vol. 12/3, 1982; Vol. 22/1, 1992; Vol. 25/5, 1995; Vol. 26/1, 1996. Arts of Asia, Hong Kong. 1971 - To date

International Netsuke Collectors Society Journal: Vol. 3/1, 1975; Vol. 3/2, 1975; Vol. 4/1, 1976; Vol. 4/2, 1976; Vol. 4/4, 1977; Vol. 6/2, 1978; Vol. 6/3, 1978; Vol. 7/2, 1979; Vol. 7/3, 1979; Vol. 8/1, 1980; Vol. 8/2, 1980; Vol. 8/3, 1980; Vol. 8/4, 1981; Vol. 9/1, 1981; Vol. 9/3, 1981; Vol. 10/3, 1982; Vol. 10/4, 1983; Vol. 11/1, 1983; Vol. 11/3, 1983; Vol. 12/3, 1984. International Netsuke Collectors Society. 1973 - 1985

Netsuke Kenkyukai Society Study Journal: Issue 3, 1980; Issue 4, 1981; Issue 5, 1981; Vol. 3/2, 1983; Vol. 3/3, 1983; Vol. 3/4, 1983; Vol. 4/1, 1984; Vol. 4/4, 1984; Vol. 5/1, 1985; Vol. 6/2, 1986, Vol. 7/4, 1987; Vol. 8/1, 1988; Vol. 8/3, 1988; Vol. 8/4, 1988; Vol. 9/1, 1989; Vol. 9/2, 1989; Vol. 10/1, 1990; Vol. 10/3, 1990; Vol. 14/1, 1994; Vol. 14/2, 1994; Vol. 14/4, 1994; Vol. 15/3, 1995; New York City Convention Handbook, 1995; Vol. 15/4. Netsuke Kenkyukai Society, 1980 - 1995

International Netsuke Society Journal: Vol. 16/2, 1996; Vol. 17/2, 1997; Vol. 17/3, 1997; Vol. 18/1, 1998; Vol. 18/2, 1998; Vol. 19/1, 1999; Vol. 19/4, 1999; Vol. 20/1, 2000; Vol. 20/3, 2000; Vol. 20/4, 2000; Vol. 21/4, 2001; Vol. 24/3, 2004; Vol. 27/1, 2007; Vol. 29/1, 2009; Vol. 30/1, 2010, International Netsuke Society, 1996 – To date

Euronetsuke: Vol. 23, 2003; Vol. 33, 2009; Vol. 34, 2009. European Chapter of the International Netsuke Society, 1995 - To date.

Netsuke materials

In the past, most carvers used just a few materials: elephant ivory, rhinoceros horn or a few selected woods such as boxwood or ebony. A survey of his records shows that Michael used over seventy different materials, and most not just for inlays.

Among those materials he used are a number which were banned in 1989 under the Convention on International Trade in Endangered Species of Wild Fauna and Flora (CITES) regulations. It should be clearly noted that any such materials which Michael used were acquired prior to the law changes and at legitimate natural history auctions of lots consisting predominantly of surplus stock from museums, and were generally over 100 years old when purchased. No such material was purchased after 1989 and any netsuke carved from material now banned under CITES were carved before those regulations came into force.

Michael was always on the look-out for materials, the more unusual the better. He was often the beneficiary of the gift of some part of an obscure beast, sometimes an obscure part of a familiar beast. Among the materials he commonly used are:

Antler

Antlers are made of bone and should not be referred to as 'Stag horn'. Antlers can be deciduous or permanently joined to the cranial bone, depending on the species. Michael explained that they vary within the same species: male and female; juveniles and mature adults; virgin and lactating females; each can have a different growth pattern. The antler of un-castrated reindeer has a small spongy centre, which is much larger in the lactating female. Male Molokai Taxis deer antler is pale, solid and ivory-like when impregnated with waxes and oils, while that of the red deer is extremely porous.

The 'coronet' of a set of antlers, where they join the skull, have naturally uneven edges that vary with each set of antlers. Michael often used this coronet, uncarved, to represent the folds and edges of garments in representations of Dutchmen and Tanuki.

Among the species Michael used are: Elk *(Cervus canadensis)*; Chinese swamp deer; English Fallow deer; English Roe deer *(Capreolus capreolus)*; Molokai Taxis deer *(Hawaii)*; Red deer *(Cervus elaphus)*; Highland deer.

Bone

All bones are hollow, the cavity being filled with a spongy material. Cuts across some bone show a pattern of minute holes looking like dark dots. Lengthwise, such bone displays many narrow channels which appear to be dark lines of varying lengths. Polished, bone is more opaque and less shiny than ivory.

Oxen *(Bos primigenius)*: Michael used a knuckle bone to carve a portrait head of his father, who was, he said: a dignified, erudite, and most un-bullish English gentleman.

Walrus penis bone (Odobenus Divergens Phallus Baculum): Oosik is a term used by the North American Inuit people for the baculum or penis bone of walruses, seals, sea lions and polar bears. The bone exists in most mammals including primates, but not in humans. Michael was given an example of a complete walrus penis bone which measured almost twenty-two inches in length.

One material which Michael was not able to use in his netsuke was a human spinal bone (Homo Sapiens). He wrote:

In the nineteen-eighties I was sent a rather small fragment of his spinal bone by Cornelius Roosevelt that had been removed during surgery. Corny enquired if I could make use of it for carving. I could not, but there followed an interesting correspondence between us where I was eventually persuaded to promise that should he ever have a larger part of his skeleton removed, I would certainly wish to investigate its possibilities.

Eyes

Always important to create character in a carving, Michael used a number of materials as inlays for eyes. Although these include ruby cabochons, horn, antler, umimatsu, pearls, gold, onyx and amber, Michael made many of the eyes for his carvings from drawn crystal rod. In a letter to a collector he described how they were made for the Fukurokuju in oosik:

The eyes are made from fine crystal glass rods (1/2 mm) using a technique passed on to me by Kangyoku.

The end of the rod is held over a flame and pulled out to a very fine thread. The tip of the thread is then placed in the flame for a fraction of a second to form a bead (the eyeball). For your piece I used blue rod for that purpose. A fine tapered thread is then formed using a black rod. The tip of the black thread is then brought into contact with the blue thread at the edge of the flame to form the pupil.

The trick is to achieve matching eyes. It took 27 attempts before getting an acceptable result.

Horn

This is composed of keratin, a nitrogenous substance which forms the basis of horns, hair, fingernails and claws.

Rhinoceros horn *(Ceratorhinus)*: The horn is composed of compactly aligned fibres in a keratinous growth and the diffraction of light by the hair fibres can be observed if held up to the light.

It is a material that sometimes has subtle transparent blond hues and a dense black core. The material has occasionally been carved longitudinally from the dark mottled section of the horn surrounding the black pigmented core of the crown. A contrasting configuration can be achieved by cutting the horn across the grain.

Greater kudu *(Tragelaphus Strepsiceros)*: The hollow centre of this antelope's dense black corkscrew horn contains a bony substance from its base to within 4 inches of its tip. (In Japan, a few scrapings reduced to ash were thought to be a remedy for both gonorrhoea and baldness.) Michael carved a sinister looking Dutchman using the horn as his cloak and the bony core for his head and legs. See The Conspirator.

Among the other horns that Michael used were: Buffalo *(Bubalus)*, including Indian, African and Nile; Blue cow *(Bos Primigenius)*; American Cattle *(Bovidae);* Eland antelope *(Taurotragus)*; Ram *(Ovis Arries)*; Impala *(Aepyceros)*; and Springbok *(Antidorcas)*.

Baleen: The mechanism by which whales filter food from the vast quantities of water it takes in. Usually known as Whale bone, it is actually made of keratin like horn, nails and hair. It has been used by sailors for centuries as a carving material.

Inlays

Michael's studio walls were lined with boxes and trays stacked on top of each other, full of strange materials. Amongst them were those he used for eyes; for facial features; and for decorative inlays on his carvings. Tucked away in containers were sheets of gold; silver; emeralds; rubies; lapis lazuli; turquoise; jade; black onyx; glass; and pearls including those from both salt- and fresh-water mussels and oysters.

In addition, there were the remnants of a lifetime of organic material collecting. The bones of birds and small mammals found while walking in the woods; dead beetles, butterflies and moths; debris found on beaches all over the world. He saved the smallest scraps of material; lacquer; crab's claws; steel springs; computer parts; it was a veritable 'case of curiosities'.

Amber:A fossilised tree resin which is difficult to carve because of its brittleness. In some cultures it is believed to promote longevity if ingested in powder form. The rare material was used as a netsuke to provide scrapings for curative and life-enhancing purposes. Michael used a wide variety of different amber: from the Baltic, Lebanon and Indonesia; clear golden amber (Ching Peh); amber containing insect and flora inclusions; and an exceptionally rare one with a spider on a web with its victim.

Coral *(*Class *Anthozoa* of phylum *Cnidaria)*: Pink, Red & Hawaiian. True coral is a hard calcareous substance secreted by marine polyps for support and habitation. It is composed of calcium phosphate and calcium carbonate and has rarely been used for netsuke carving other than as a decorative feature or inlay.

Mother-of-pearl (Nacre) is the generic term for the iridescent area of the inside of mollusc shells; it also forms the outer coating of pearls.

Abalone shell (Family of *Haliotidae* and genus *Haliotis*). Known as Aogai, it is the blue/green iridescent area of the inside of abalone shell.

One of the most familiar, other than the abalone and the oyster, is the Nautilus shell. Michal also used other miscellaneous seashells.

Hornbill *(Bucerotidea)*: A dense, ivory-like substance found in the solid casque (helmet) growing above the upper mandible (the bird's forehead). Structurally, it is not ivory, horn, or bone, yet it has been called ivory for many centuries. It is softer than real ivory and is a creamy yellow in colour, becoming red at the top and sides. I have been unable to find an illustration of the netsuke Michael carved in this material, which was given to him by Masatoshi.

Tree fungus *(Polyporus Dryadeus)*: Known as 'monkey seat fungus'. According to Michael, he found a small dry specimen at the base of an oak tree in the garden. He consolidated the interior, lacquered it, and placed gold ants on the upper surface of this objet trouvé netsuke.

Möbius Strip

Topology is the branch of geometry that is concerned with the properties of an object that do not change when bent, stretched or shrunk. One such example is the Möbius strip. It is a three-dimensional conceptual shape, with a single surface and a single edge that is not found in nature. This complex shape was named after its discoverer, the German astronomer August Ferdinand Möbius (1780-1868).

A single Möbius can be made by taking a strip of paper or ribbon, twisting one end 180° and joining the two ends. (If cut in two lengthways, this shape remains in one piece but with a double twist, and two surfaces and two edges and is not a Möbius.

To form a double Möbius, one end must be turned through 540° before joining the ends.
For a triple Möbius, one end should be turned five times for a total of 900°.

Umimatsu

The Japanese word umimatsu means 'sea pine' and it is so named because its fronds resemble arboreal branches. It is in fact a colony of keratinous marine polyps, often seen with skeletal marine organism inclusions. Unlike coral, which lays down its own substrate and is therefore mobile, these polyps are stationary, permanently attached to a substrate such as a rock or ship's hull. Hawaiian umimatsu is dense black and has been mistaken for jet and black coral; from the Alaskan waters, the material is light in colour, with a striking marbled configuration.

ACCORDING TO RAYMOND BUSHELL:

As material, umimatsu is more acceptable to collectors than carvers. Leading carvers naturally avoided the material; it is prone to crack, crumble or chip. Carvers find that it is risky for carving details and subtle effects. Perfect pieces of black coral are difficult to obtain.

Nevertheless, Michael managed to produce a small number of netsuke using this material. The exceptionally ornamental nature of the material demanded designs of great simplicity of line. But that very simplicity showed the material at its best.

Wood

Bamboo *(Poaceae)*: The largest members of the grass families, they have a rapid growth rate, increasing by up to 60 centimetres (24 in.) in a day. Netsuke are usually carved from a section of the root, although occasionally from the stem. The polished material reveals an interesting texture and patina.

Bois D'arc *(Maclura Pomifera)*: A small fruiting tree resembling an orange which grows in the central and southern states of America. It is known as Yellow Wood to Native Americans who used it to make bows and as a dye.

Nigerian Ebony *(Diopyros Crassiflora)*: The black hardwood that is so dense that it sinks in water.

Macassar Ebony *(Diopyros Celebica)*: A striated black variety

Mexican Manzanita *(Arctostaphylos)*: A group of evergreen hardwood shrubs and small trees that grow in poor soil on the south-west coast of North America. Of most interest to carvers is the wood with burls: evidence of grain growth deformity as the result of climatic stress, injury or insect infestation. The wood can graduate in colour from cream to dark red. Michael used this material to carve: Namazu; Thoughts and Riddles and for various inlays

Pink ivory *(Berchimia Zeyheri)*: A rare tight-grained wood from Africa that graduates from light pink to deep red. One of the rarest of the commercial hardwoods. Michael used this material to carve: Daruma Meditating; Echoes in Daruma's Heart; and The Millennium Phoenix Hatchling.

Other woods include: Boxwood *(Buxus)*; Lignum Vitae (*Guaiacum)*; Olive wood *(Olea Europea)*; Rosewood *(Dalbergia)*; Jet, *(Lignnite)* a semi-petrified wood;

Glossary

Anamorphic Art The depiction of deliberately distorted images that are returned to normal by viewing the picture from a specific perspective. The earliest known example is the Leonardo da Vinci painting: *Leonardo's Eye*, c.1485. Perhaps the most famous example is the 1533 painting by Hans Holbein of *The Ambassadors* which has an anamorphic skull at the base of the painting.

Aogai The blue/green iridescent area of the inside of abalone shell.

Ashinaga Portrayed with Tenaga, the two are legendary skilful fishermen. Ashinaga wades through deep water with his long legs, while Tenaga, riding pick-a-back, gathers their customary diet of seafood with the help of his long arms. They symbolise the moral ethic of mutual help.

Baku A mythical Chinese animal that uses its elephant-like trunk to snatch bad dreams and nightmares from the air. Images and depictions are given as a wish for the recipient to have 'sweet dreams'.

Benten The only female among the seven Gods of Luck. She represents the attributes of Learning, Literature, Music and Art.

Bishamon-Ten One of the seven Gods of Luck, he is the God of Wealth and Riches, and is the defender of the Buddhist faith.

Ching Peh Clear golden amber.

Chryselephantine Sculptural works that combine gold with elephant ivory.

Corozo The nut of a South American palm tree, Phytelephas Macrocarpa, usually referred to as 'vegetable ivory'.

Daruma According to legend, an Indian missionary who spent nine years in China crouched in motionless meditation contemplating the Buddhist doctrine of Zen. During that time he was exposed to temptations by demons of both sexes, had his ears and other sensitive parts bitten by rats, and his legs became atrophied – he arrived at the profound conclusion that 'nothing has ever really existed'. He is said to have crossed the sea to Japan on a reed.

Dosojin An element in primordial pre-Shinto Japanese folk religion, Dosojin ensures fecundity and abundance in agriculture, protects against sickness and evil spirits, and serves as the guardian spirit of roads and travellers. The male/female deity is depicted in many different ways: natural phallus-shaped stones and pairs of trees at crossroads; symbolic straw effigies at village fairs; and sophisticatedly realistic stone carvings.

Fukura Suzume A sparrow in winter, with its feathers plumped to keep it warm.

Fukurokuju The Japanese God of Longevity and of Good Luck (one of the Seven Lucky Gods), and always depicted with a full beard and a tall forehead that is often longer than his body. His high forehead contains all the wisdom gained from his long life, although how much of his luck contributed to his long life, and how much was due to the wisdom gained throughout his extended years is unclear.

Futen The God of the Winds.

Hako Netsuke A box-shaped netsuke, often with much of the design or carving within the interior.

Himotoshi Two connecting holes in a carving, through which is threaded the sagemono cord. One hole is carved larger than the other to allow the single knot in the cord to be hidden.

Hozuki	The Japanese name for the decorative plant: Physalis, (also known as Cape gooseberry, and Chinese lantern plant). It has edible fruit, and leaves with a wide range of herbal medicinal uses.
Icarus	The Greek mythological figure who drowned while attempting to escape from Crete. The wax securing his feather wings melted when he flew too close to the sun and he fell into the sea.
Ikiryo	The spirit of a person separated from their living body during an effort to harm another.
Inro	A group of cases, smaller than sagemono, to hold items such as money, seals, or medicines, traditionally made of wood, ivory and bone. Lacquer pieces are highly prized.
Jo and Uba	A long-lived and loving couple who died within minutes of each other in the forest that had been their home, and where their spirits remain.
Jurojin	The God of Wisdom and Long Life. One of the Seven Lucky Gods.
Kagamibuta Netsuke	Circular shaped netsuke, usually with a metal disc serving as lid to a shallow bowl carved of wood or ivory. The metal is often highly decorated with a wide variety of metallurgical techniques.
Kakihan	An identifying signature or symbol; an artist's name, either wholly or in part.
Kappa	A mythical amphibious monster in Japanese legend. It has the carapace of a turtle and entices children into the water – finding young girls especially delectable – where it devours them. In districts supposedly inhabited by Kappa, the villagers throw cucumbers, his favourite vegetable, into the water at harvest time in order to appease the creatures.
Karamono	The historical name for toggles, literally, 'Chinese things'.
Karashishi	The stone lions found at the gates of Buddhist temples and in gardens all over China and Japan.
Katabori Netsuke	Sculptural netsuke, the most familiar style, a compact three-dimensional figure carved in the round, usually one to three inches in height.
Katachi	The word closest in the Japanese language to 'art'. It is usually interpreted to mean: form and design, sensitivity, and the art of living.
Kimono	The traditional Japanese robe.
Kirin	An ancient mythical creature of Chinese origin, described as having the single-horned head of a dragon, the body of a deer, the legs and hoofs of a horse, and the bushy tail of the Chinese Buddhist lion. Its body is covered with hair and its armpits discharge flakes of fire which denote its divine origin. It has not always been depicted by artists in strict accordance with tradition, and its name has, to some extent, become a generic term for a variety of fantastic creatures bearing some similarity to the original.
Kosode	An alternative form of traditional Japanese robe.
Lao Tsze	Considered the founder of the Chinese Tao philosophy that teaches the three ways to reach harmony: by dwelling on the beauty of nature, by being self-sufficient, and by desiring nothing.
Manju Netsuke	A flat, circular type of netsuke, named after the round rice cake or bun that it resembles in shape. The carving is usually done in relief, sometimes made of two fitted halves.

Mask Netsuke	Often imitations of full size Noh masks.
Namazu	A legendary giant catfish with the power to cause earthquakes, that carries the islands of Japan on its back. When annoyed, the monster wriggles violently from head to tail, creating the seismic disturbances from which the country suffers. Traditionally, once a year local fishermen in bays around the coasts of Japan's islands sailed out to offer the Namazu a drink of saké in the hope that it would calm the turbulent waters for the following year.
Netsuke	Functional carving used as a toggle to prevent the cord of the inro slipping from the kimono sash.
Noh	The traditional theatre art of Japan incorporating music, dance and drama.
Obi	Kimono sash.
Objet Trouvé	A natural object displayed as a work of art as found or after minimal human alteration.
Octopus beak	Octopuses have no internal or external skeleton (although some species have a vestigial remnant of a shell inside their mantle), allowing them to squeeze through tight places. The beak is the hardest part of its body.
Ojime	A small carved bead used to fasten the cord of the inro or sagemono to keep it closed.
Okame	Goddess of Mirth, often depicted with Fukurokuju.
Oosik	The word used by the North American Inuit people for the baculum or penis bone of walruses, seals, sea lions and polar bears. The bone exists in most mammals including primates, but not in humans.
Rokurokubi	Supernatural female monsters from Japan who appear to be normal human beings during the day, but have the ability to elongate their necks and change their faces at night, all the better to terrify mortals.
Ryujin	The legendary King of the Dragons.
Sagemono	Containers designed to hold small objects such as pipes and tobacco, or brush and inks.
Sashi Netsuke	An elongated form of katabori, similar in size (about six inches long) and shape to the sticks and gourds used as improvised netsuke before carved pieces were produced. It was worn thrust inside the obi.
Shibui	The Japanese notion of an artist's ability to convey the essence of what he wishes to communicate in the most simple and concise way.
Shojo	A mythical creature that lives by the sea whose favourite occupation is the consumption of intoxicating liquid. Not aggressive, both male and female are usually depicted either laughing and cheerful or fast asleep after their alcoholic exertions.
Shunga	Japanese erotic art most familiarly seen in woodblock prints. It depicts, either in a subtle manner or more explicitly, couples during the sexual act, or individual male or female genitalia.

Squid beak	See Octopus beak.
Sumi-e	Ink wash painting using varying ink densities from deep black to palest silvery gray. The ink is applied with a bamboo brush made in a wide range of sizes, and with hair from a variety of animals. Once a line is painted it cannot be altered and the technique, similar to calligraphy, requires years of practice.
Suzume	A legendary pet sparrow whose tongue was cut off by a wicked neighbour for stealing starch. The bird's owner was rewarded with silks and jewels for caring for the sparrow, while the neighbour's greed led to her death at the hands of goblins and devils. The sparrow is the emblem of gracefulness and gentleness in Oriental art, and a symbolic subject in heraldry, generally represented in stylised form squatting with outstretched wings and rounded tail.
Tagua	See Corozo.
Tanuki	The legendary raccoon-like mischievous Badger credited with supernatural magical powers is, in fact, a racoon-faced dog. According to one legend it disguises itself as a monk and, feigning sleep, squats motionless, eager to waylay and harass passing travellers. By beating its distended stomach or scrotum like a drum it frightens them away and then steals the possessions they dropped as they fled in terror.
Tenaga	See Ashinaga.
Tengu	A mythical bird-like goblin that has been depicted in many legendary disguises. A universal myth, it has also been a model for extra-terrestrial alien figures for writers and illustrators of science-fiction.
Teruko	One of the daughters of the moon, who was sent to earth as punishment for refusing to obey her mother, and adopted by an elderly woodcutter. When she grew up she set a series of challenges for any would-be suitor. The Emperor saw her and fell hopelessly in love, but after even he had failed the tasks, Princess Teruko returned to the moon. The Emperor climbed to the top of Mount Fuji and built a fire which no-one has ever been able to put out, and the undying embers have smoked to this day.
Tokata	The ivory from the tip of the tusk of an Asian cow elephant, highly prized for its pale creamy colour and its homogenous fine-grained quality.
Umimatsu	A highly decorative marine material found across the Pacific Ocean area.

Acknowledgements

While this book has been a labour of love, it would not have been possible without the advice and support of many friends, both old and new.

My heartfelt thanks go to Neil Davey, who saw the very first draft and encouraged me to continue and who has been bothered interminably ever since; to Robert O. Kinsey and Charles and Hollis Kinsey, who looked after me on my research visits to USA, answered all my questions, suggested improvements, and reassured me that I was on the right track; to Norman Sandfield who searched for missing pieces, and made so many suggestions and, with Jeffrey Moy at Paragon Books, encouraged me when it was really needed.

For assistance with the netsuke section, I have many current and past members of the International Netsuke Society to thank for information, advice, and for allowing me to quote from their correspondence. Many artists, collectors and dealers have freely given their help, guidance and valuable information, but I must mention the following David Burditt, Sharen Chappell, Richard Silverman, Renee Topper and Nicholas Westover; and Lynn Richardson who allowed me to use her drawing of a kimono with netsuke, ojime and inro ensemble.

I also acknowledge the assistance given by Arts of Asia, Aoife Burke, Dessa Goddard of Butterfield & Butterfield, Alison Huftalen of Toledo Museum of Art Library, Bernard Hurtig, Jushō Kobari, President of the Japan Ivory Sculptors' Association, Marcia Light, Emma Martin at World Museum, National Museums Liverpool; and Linda Meredith, Editor of the I.N.S. Journal.

For details of his personal history and business career, my thanks go to Michael's old friends Jimmy and Sally Dempster, Sos and Gillian Green, and Cyril Harper; and to Christopher Green and Pamela Sydenham. I am also grateful to Dr. Ian Beavis at Tunbridge Wells Museum & Art Gallery; Liz Calder of Bloomsbury Publishing; David Hibberd of The Magic Circle; and The Vintage Optical Shop.

Extra thanks go to my editor, Rosemary Wells, who made many creative suggestions, and stopped me from making too many mistakes. I am grateful to John Wayte for introducing me to Grant Bradford whose creative contribution to the design has resulted in a book which is so much better to look at than I could ever have imagined possible. The work of Grant's team – Steve Kashdan, Tony Sambrook, Derek Askem and Roger Multon is also much appreciated.

I must thank all those collectors who allowed me to borrow pieces to be photographed, or arranged for new images to be taken, without their generosity this book would be so much poorer. Additional photographers include H.I.H. Princess Takamado, Colin Beer, Michael Bernstein, the late Carol Lynn Birnbaum, Bridgeman Art Library, Joey Chait of I M Chait Gallery, Christie's of London, Stuart Gordon, Andy Jordan, Hollis Kinsey, Anthony Lee, Sydney L Moss Ltd., National Museums Liverpool, and members of Michael's family.

Friends who helped in so many ways and encouraged me to continue with the book must also be acknowledged, so my thanks go to Michael's sons, Jonathan and Patrick; and to Jennifer, Nichole, Rosemary, Rodney, and Joss. Lastly, this book would not have been completed without the support of my daughter who, apart from spending many hours checking my research notes and reading through the text, making her own creative contribution, has been of more support since Michael's death than she can possibly imagine. Clare, thank you.

Index

Page numbers for illustrations are in bold

"Thinking"

FRONT ENDPAPERS

Cracked Ice
Oil on Canvas Size 64 x 150cm
Signed Birch. Undated

Reverse - Katachi
Sumi-e ink on Paper 48 x 35.5cm
Initialled MHB. 1979

BACK ENDPAPERS

Left - Ghost Leaf Procession
Sumi-e ink on Paper 45 x 31cm
Signed & Initialled. August 95

Right - The Bulb
Sumi-e ink on Paper
Initialled. 1980